CLASSIC RE

Vanya

Blood Brothers

Streetwise

This omnibus edition first published 1997

Reprinted 1998

ISBN 0 85476 745 2

Designed and produced by Bookprint Creative Services
P.O. Box 827, BN21 3YJ, England for
KINGSWAY PUBLICATIONS
Lottbridge Drove, Eastbourne, E. Sussex BN23 6NT
Printed in Great Britain.

Reproduced from the original typesetting
of the single-volume editions.

VANYA

Myrna Grant

KINGSWAY PUBLICATIONS

EASTBOURNE

Biblical quotations are taken from
the New American Standard Bible © The Lockman Foundation
1960, 1962, 1963, 1968, 1971, 1972, 1973.

Foreword

I have talked about him to people who knew him personally. For example, to Ed, the young African who was studying in Kerch, the town where Vanya (nickname for Ivan) was doing his military service. They were together until a few days before Vanya's death; they talked and prayed together and encouraged one another.

For Ed, Vanya is the symbol of the Russian soul, which will never bow to the image that the atheists have set up so arrogantly: man and his so-called learning. He is also a proof of the power of God and the Word become flesh. Ed told me about Vanya's rock-like convictions and the power to carry them out. He never looked for compromises. He just didn't need them: truth is always victorious, everywhere and always.

Because of his contact with Vanya—and the deep insight into the spiritual battle raging in Russia which he acquired as a result— Ed was deported from the country. Vanya himself also had to be disposed of. But that could not be achieved by means of an exit visa: there was another way for him...and that's what this book is about.

I also spoke to his pastor. Few Christian leaders will have the privilege of saying about one of their church members what this man shared about Vanya. At the age of 16—he had not known the Lord for very long then—he was already speaking in church. He didn't only have a message, he *was* one! Vanya followed Jesus radically and he seized every opportunity to testify to his Lord and Saviour. He had an intensive prayer life. What could the Almighty do but answer those prayers and give him a life of continuous answers to prayer, a life full of miracles?

That, however, did not go unnoticed by the authorities. Today, Vanya still speaks to the youth of Russia. Many young people were converted through his testimony while he was still alive and maybe even more through his death. The book that you are now holding is also known in Russia. Not so well-produced and colourful as this one, but the story is the same.

The same secret printing press which has printed thousands of Bibles and hymnbooks was also used for the production of Vanya's story. That was one of the reasons for the intensive search that the KGB (Russian secret service) made to find the printing press. Result: those who manned the press were arrested. Nine young people, just as dedicated as Vanya! They were given sentences ranging from two-and-a-half to four years in labour camp.

The KGB held an exhaustive search all over the country for the forbidden publications about Vanya. Agents broke into believers' houses. In one case, they had a remarkable success. One of the KGB men came across a book, opened it and exclaimed excitedly, "Yes, here we have something about Moiseyev. Look, it says: 'First book of Moisev.'"

The man had found a Bible. And indeed one of the first pages states, "First book of Moses." Vanya's second name and the name of the writer of Genesis are almost identical in Russian!

The Bible held a central place in Vanya's life and actions. Is there any other book that could have changed him so radically and prepared him for eternity? And is there any other book than the Bible that can change the Russian people, the British people and the whole world in the same way?

God's book speaks about God's creation. And about the recreative power of God's Spirit in human beings. It also tells us what atheism is: "The fool says in his heart, 'There is no God.'" And about Jesus, who through His death and resurrection has the right to world dominion. He alone! And radical acceptance of that dominion also has consequences. This book is about those who have paid the price for following Jesus.

The martyrs. The Vanyas and those who are still in the concentration camps of Russia. They are suffering for the name of Jesus.

I've been very moved by this book. And I've asked myself, If I should be arrested on account of my faith, could sufficient evidence against me be put forward to convict me? And to make me a "witness-martyr"? In Vanya's case, the evidence was abundantly available. Hence this book. That's why he now has the reward: the martyr's crown.

With fear and trembling, and very reverently before God, I would like to sign my name at the bottom of the application form for that title. Here it is then:

BROTHER ANDREW

Harderwijk, Holland
25 September 1986

Foreword

On July 16, 1972, a young man, a soldier, died in the Crimea. He was a church member, and his death was a violent one. Details of how it happened and why are told in this moving book. Documentary evidence at the Centre for the Study of Religion and Communism confirms the facts related in this book.

Vanya's death was an event out of the ordinary, and it turned the attention of thousands, probably millions of people all over the world, to the Soviet Union and its religious policy. The murder of this young Baptist was not an everyday occurrence. The community of churches to which he belonged brackets it together with the murder of Nikolai Khmara in a Siberian prison, which took place as long ago as 1964. Young Baptists in the USSR compose poems about these two martyrs and read them in meetings to encourage the believers. But although the death of Vanya Moiseyev was untypical, it highlighted a situation which demands the concern of Christians and, indeed, all people of good will everywhere

The fact is that Soviet hostility towards religion has not changed since the Bolshevik revolution. Actual tactics have swung between violent and illegal persecution and a more subtle propaganda approach. But at no time has the Soviet leadership abandoned its declared aim of rooting out all religious survivals.

This militantly atheistic policy has affected all churches in the Soviet Union. In the early years after 1917 it was the ancient, established Orthodox church which suffered the full force of the atheist onslaught, while the Baptists and other denominations enjoyed a relative freedom—which they used to the full. But it was not long, as Stalin took the reins of power more and more firmly into his own hands, until all the churches felt the cold wind.

During the terror of the 1930s, thousands of Christians and others suffered and died in Stalin's purges. But the Second World War changed the situation abruptly. The government found itself in need of maximum support from the people as the country suffered heavier and heavier losses. Appeal was made to Russian patriotism, and the churches were encouraged to rally their members to the national cause. Concessions were made in private interviews between Stalin and certain church leaders, and these led to a relaxation of pressure and, in turn, to a religious renaissance that probably surprised the authorities.

But the new policy did not last long. As the immediate crisis passed, so old patterns of repression returned. Then came Krushchev. Despite his popular image as a "liberalizer", Khrushchev in fact unleashed a vicious campaign against religion that lasted from 1959 until his fall from power in 1964. It is reckoned that half the Orthodox churches in the country were closed. The Baptists also suffered from the new repression.

One aspect of this was the introduction of some new statutes which, although presented by the Baptist leadership to the churches, were clearly the result of state pressure. This unhappy situation caused a sharp reaction among Baptist believers throughout the country. An action group was set up to agitate for a congress to set things right. This aim was not achieved, and in 1965 the split in Baptist ranks became final.

The reforming group which split away in 1965 exists to this day in a technically illegal condition. It calls itself the Council of Churches of Evangelical Christians/Baptists, and it was to this movement that Vanya Moiseyev belonged. The leaders of this group call for an uncompromising loyalty to Christ, for continual spiritual renewal, for evangelism. They also call for justice towards Soviet believers; they appeal to the Soviet Constitution and to the original decrees of Lenin. They can thus be seen within the context of the wider Soviet human rights movement, to which they have contributed much. Indeed they may be said to have blazed the trail for much that was to follow: human rights activity in the USSR which has hit the headlines in recent years. It was the Baptists first who, in a highly organized fashion, produced unofficial documents, lists, and even regular journals telling about their life and problems. The Baptists are the only group in the Soviet Union to have produced regular lists of their members in prison, giving unbelievably detailed information, including addresses of hundreds of labour camps. These data have been of incalculable value to researchers on modern Soviet society. The Baptists are the only dissenting group in the Soviet Union to operate a clandestine printing press. Called "The Christian", it has been in operation at least since 1971 and probably earlier.

This is the background against which the murder of Vanya Moiseyev must be seen. It was a brutal act, revealing the fear and anger of a small number of men in authority. And yet at the same time it was the manifestation of a hostility that is constant and which threatens at any time to erupt in such violence. It is to be hoped that anti-religious campaigns like those under Stalin and Khrushchev will not recur. One factor to prevent their recurrence would certainly be the continuing concern and positive action of all those who read this book and who care about the fate of Soviet Christians today.

MICHAEL BOURDEAUX
Director, Centre for the Study
of Religion and Communism
Chislehurst, Kent. England

Preface

Holiday crowds were pouring out of the circus, tourists from all over the Soviet Union and eastern Europe, children with dazzled eyes, students and local families out for a treat. The fountains of the circus plaza sprayed cooling patterns in the south Russian heat. But through the crowd, a terrified man was walking quickly, his eyes searching for the American friends he had promised to meet.

The night before I had sat in the single "prayer house" serving his city of a million people, listening to him preach a radiant sermon on the power of God. He had cited David Livingstone and Dostoevsky as examples for the congregation—men who had ventured all for their faith.

Now, less than twenty-four hours later, he was being closely trailed by the KGB, and he knew it. His mind churned in a torment of anxiety for what he might bring upon his family, his church, his American friends —all because of a clandestine agreement after the church service to meet the next day and talk.

On the plaza, in those moments of fear, I was plunged with him into the suffering sub-culture of the Soviet Christian. I too felt panic. The pastor's words were frantic: "I can't talk; I'm being followed—God bless you—good-bye." Instantly he fled into the crowds. Why? Why should the secret police be immediately concerned that two American Christians and a Russian pastor should privately talk?

It was at this point that I knew Ivan's book had to be written. In a more intensified form, his is the story of all believers in the Soviet Union—gentle, humble citizens whose lives are a kaleidoscope of fear, uncertainty, caution, sacrifice, incredible courage, endurance, and triumph.

It was sometimes difficult inside Russia to ask about Ivan, because the KGB was conducting an aggressive campaign to find and destroy the documents which appear in this book and to threaten and arrest believers who passed on the story. But in spite of the danger, believers were eager to talk. Often tears sprang to the eyes of men as well as women as they said, "*Verno, Verno.*" ("It is true. It is true.") Nowhere in any city did I ever ask about Ivan and find his story not known and verified.

A young woman chemical engineer from Omsk in Siberia told me of a compulsory political meeting called in her factory to denounce the "false rumours" of Ivan's death and to provide the official statement.

In the Georgian republic I shared a park bench with a middle-aged mother whose eyes were red from weeping. I had arranged earlier to meet her, and she was keeping the appointment in spite of her great distress. The night before, while she was at the prayer house, the secret police had searched her home. They were looking for Moiseyev documents but had found none. (She had passed some along only the day before.) Instead, her few religious papers and bits of Scripture had been taken. Her voice was tightly controlled as she told her story, at the end breaking down into weeping and repeating the words, "It's terrible. It's terrible."

In western Europe more information came from Ivan's former youth pastor from Moldavia. Because of having close relatives in Germany, his family had been permitted to emigrate. Also present was a believer from Ivan's church who had attended his funeral. All of them wanted to talk about Ivan's fervent faith and to give what help they could for this book. Each one could have told his own story of personal suffering if he had wished.

The Russian author Alexander Solzhenitsyn continues to focus world attention on the suppression of basic human rights within the USSR. He is one of several famous spokesmen for the present dissident movement in the Soviet Union, an action group of intellectuals who plead eloquently for freedom of thought and expression and denounce the Soviet system of police terror. Now the Soviet government has exiled him following the Paris publication of his explosive book *The Gulag Archipelago*.

What is not well-known in the free world is that there is another heroic protest movement in the Soviet Union. It has risen from the ranks of the repressed and suffering evangelical churches all over the USSR. Some local churches protest individually. Since 1964 there has been an organization in Moscow called poignantly "The Council of Prisoners' Relatives". This group appeals for religious freedom and resolutely protests the discrimination, persecution, arrests, and sometimes killings of Christian believers in the USSR.

In contrast to Solzhenitsyn, the council has no protection in the form of international publicity. Its leaders have been consistently arrested or exiled. New leaders of the same courageous calibre step into the vacant places and its activities continue.

It was to this council that the parents of Ivan Vasilievich[1] Moiseyev appealed for help. Through its efforts his story was successfully brought out to the West. Men, women, and young people within this group risked their freedom and their lives to protest Ivan's death.

People of good will the world over are repelled by the denial of basic human rights in a totalitarian society. But that is not enough. There must be a mobilization of revulsion, a ground swell, an outcry on all levels of free society on behalf of these powerless people who are the subjects of repression.

Vanya's story I have written down, remembering the Voice that spoke to John in Patmos saying, "What thou seest, write in a book." That same Voice also said, "Be ye doers ... and not hearers only."

---

[1] For readers unfamiliar with Russian nomenclature: middle names are formed from the father's first name plus a masculine or feminine ending (-vich or -ova). Thus *Ivan Vasilievich* means *Ivan, son of Vasiliy* (which is not unlike the biblical format, e.g. David the son of Jesse).

Though it may sound awkward to us, Russians generally call each other by both the first and middle names.

I

He who weeps from the heart can provoke even the blind to tears[1]

Joanna Constantinova didn't want it to be time for the coffin to arrive. Ever since the telegram had come from the army on the seventeenth, she had dreaded this moment above all others. She slowly turned her swollen eyes to the place in the crowded parlour where her husband, Vasiliy Trofimovich, was standing. A group of brothers from the prayer house stood with him, their faces profoundly grave. Only her husband's face was hidden, his head bent sharply towards the painted floor.

But the moment was here. The pick-up truck bearing Vanya's coffin from the train station was grinding to a stop in the rutted road outside. Through the lace curtains, motionless in the July heat, Joanna could see the military escort vehicle pulling up behind the truck. Three men in the grey dress uniforms of the Soviet army stood stiffly beside their Pobeda as the coffin was carefully pushed from the truck bed and eased on to the shoulders of the sweating pallbearers. Her son, Semyon, directed them through the wooden gate and towards the house.

At the sight of the soldiers, Joanna's terrible fear of what she might do left her. There would be no crying out, no fainting at the sight of her dead son. If there were to be difficulties, she would need all the will she had. Her eyes met her husband's. He too was ready. A holy strength seemed upon him.

The two officers and a young private entered the room awkwardly, bending their heads to pass beneath the low door frame, uncomfortably aware that they were unwelcome in the suddenly charged atmosphere of the congested parlour. The village people pulled away from them, making a small path through the crowd that ended before the person of Vasiliy Trofimovich.

The coffin advanced, held aloft by four of the young people who had been Vanya's friends. Joanna was shocked at its huge size and the expensive gleam of the metal. Her husband swayed slightly as the young men lowered it on to the table she had made ready. Most of the women in the room wore their dark babushkas pulled low over their foreheads. A few now began to weep, hiding their faces behind white handkerchiefs so that their heads were completely covered with cloth.

For the first time Joanna noticed that the coffin was welded shut and sealed with several insignias of the Soviet army. The senior officer, Captain Platonov of Special Affairs, cleared his throat nervously, bowing slightly to the parents. "On behalf of our Lieutenant Colonel V: Malsin and the officers and men of Unit 61968T, I extend to the parents and relatives and comrades of Private Ivan[2] Vasilievich Moiseyev our condolences on the tragic death of this young Soviet soldier." His eyes moved uneasily from face to face about the room, each pair of eyes returning his gaze.

Under her shawl Joanna fingered the letters Ivan had sent the last few days before his death. As if to hold back part of her son from the captain, she pressed the thin letters to herself, shielding them with the flat of her hand from Platonov's lies. She had arranged them in a small packet according to the postmarks smeared in red ink over the red stamps June 15, 1972; June 30, 1972; July 9, 1972; July 14, 1972; July 15, 1972. She felt the dates crying out against her hand, protesting the hypocrisy before the casket. Condolences! Her eyes burned.

"Of course we shall require that my son's coffin be opened." Vasiliy Trofimovich's voice was steady.

"But that is not necessary!" Platonov spoke more sharply than he intended, his tone jerking up some of the bowed heads at the back of the sweltering room. "Your son's body has already been identified in Kerch by yourself and your son, Semyon Vasilievich." He pressed a folded handkerchief to his forehead before continuing in a softer voice. "Such a terrible accident has been a great shock to you and your wife. You must spare yourselves further distress." His words became almost a whisper. "Death by drowning can be ... very disfiguring."

With her free hand, Joanna pushed to her husband's side. "Comrade Officer——?"

"Platonov."

"Platonov. As Ivan's mother I insist that the coffin be opened. I wish to see my son. And we desire him to be buried in civilian clothes. That is our right."

A crowbar was passed through the crowd and handed to Vasiliy. Platonov bent in a whispered conversation with his two companions. After a moment, Vasiliy fitted the crowbar's tip into the space under the top of the coffin. The special officer, with a motion of his hand, detained him. "I regret, Comrade Moiseyev, that another duty calls us away immediately. What you are determined to do is very foolish." With a glance at Semyon standing beside the father, the three men made their way through the crowd and disappeared.

Again Vasiliy raised the crowbar to the top of the casket and pushed down. At the same instant that the coffin creaked, so many things occurred at once that Joanna stood gaping, unable to make out what was happening. Like a madman, Semyon hurled himself on to the coffin, flinging his arms over the top, his voice a strangled protest. "Papa! No! Papa! Don't open it!"

The crowbar crashed to the floor. Vasiliy tried to push his eldest son out of the way. People were crowding forward to see what was causing the disturbance. "What's going on?"—"Semyon is fighting his father."—"Not fighting. He won't let him open the coffin."—"Who's fighting? I can't see."—"What a shameful thing! His own brother."

Two of the pastors, their thin shirts wet under heavy black suits, moved quickly towards Semyon, each to pull an arm and successfully drag him away from the coffin. A few women in the back of the room began praying aloud, their frightened petitions rising and falling in a rapid torrent of emotion and tears. Semyon grappled desperately against the restraint of the pastors, lurching back towards the coffin, his voice muffled. "Papa! Papa! Momma! Please! Let Vanya be! Don't open the coffin."

Joanna stared at her son. In the midst of the confusion, a great weariness came upon her. Long ago she had been proud of Semyon's boyish ambitions, his dreams to advance beyond the backbreaking labour of the collective, to make a place for himself in one of the administrative committees of the farm. He had been a hard worker, and when one day he had come home from school wearing the red scarf of the Young Pioneers,[3] the family's disapproval could not persuade him to take it off. He had become the Moiseyev to be reckoned with, full of self-assurance, confident of his future. Now, seeing the frenzy of fear that reduced Semyon to begging like a terrified child, she looked away. All the wonderful advantages of the Komsomol had brought him to this: orders from the party to help them hide his own brother's body.

The pastors were pushing Semyon through the crowd, outside into the tiny garden of cabbages and roses that lay untended. There was a renewed scuffle at the door; then it was quietly shut. Vasiliy leaned on the crowbar, and the slight, splintering sound of pressure drew the attention of the villagers to the coffin, now lit by the early afternoon sun. Fearfully, the top was raised.

The pastors filed forward and glanced hesitantly at the body. Panic twisted wildly inside Joanna as she saw the look of horror that passed over their faces. One of the oldest, Fyodor Gorektoi, leaned his white head against the coffin, his eyes averted. Tears poured down his weathered face. In fear, Joanna clutched the hand of the sister beside her. An arm went around her and led her slowly to the coffin. Joanna heard her husband sobbing. The sound seemed far away. Her trembling body moved towards the body of her son, but everything within her seemed to flee back, out of herself, out of the room, away from the thing she could not bear to see.

She forced her eyes to look into the casket and gazed in bewilderment at the body inside. It wasn't Vanya! She continued to stare, troubled that she felt no surge of relief. It was some older soldier, heavy-jowled, his face bruised badly on both sides, as if from a desperate fight. The mouth was swollen, somehow broken, and the forehead and sides of the head were blackened and oddly lumped. His dark hair was brushed away from his face in some way like Vanya's. Her heart lurched.

Someone close by moaned terribly. Suddenly her eyes blurred with tears. It was her Vanya. She slumped and began again to weep.

---

[1] The chapter headings throughout the book are traditional Russian proverbs.

[2] The Russian pronunciation is e-*von*. Hence, the familiar nickname *Vanya*.

[3] Virtually all Russian children belong to the Young Pioneers, the Communist Party organization for ages 9–14. It provides all their camping, athletic, musical, and cultural training.

The Komsomol, for ages 15–28, continues the activities of the Young Pioneers but with intensive indoctrination; members must be atheists. The Komsomol is the introduction to the full party membership.

2

Hope in the Lord but exert yourself

Ivan was filled with praise as he strode across the blackened vineyards under the icy November sky. The hymns of the evening turned in his mind and he half-sung, half-spoke his thoughts to God.

"Thank You for the young people, for the farewell meeting, for the bread and grapes and honey. For the fresh grape juice from our own Moldavian fields, for Boris and Vladimir and Luba and Yakov and Victor and Svetlana. Praise to You, Lord for Your Word, for the preaching of Stefan and Sasha. For the birthday of Elena Kuzminichna that permitted us to have a meeting."

His mother, gazing from the tiny frosted window of her kitchen, followed his moonlit progress over the fields. "What's to become of him in the army, I wonder?" She spoke more to herself than to her husband, who was cleaning his boots by the gas heater.

He dropped a boot heavily to the floor and straightened his back. "Thus far the Lord has helped us," he quoted from the Old Testament. Vasiliy was a man who hoped to live quietly and avoid trouble when he could. "We've had our times, all right." His wife nodded without turning her head from the window. He was thinking about the Stalin years. Vasiliy had once heard a tourist in the city say twenty million Russians had been killed in those times.

It couldn't have been that many, she knew. Joanna sighed. It wasn't like her to be troubled. Vasiliy watched her thoughtfully as she moved towards the brick stove to add a piece of wood. "He's only eighteen. Only a believer two years. It's going to be hard for him." Her babushka had slipped back on her head like a young girl's. She reached for the box of tea. "He'll be wanting a hot drink."

Her voice was low but she spoke without whispering. It was a particularly Russian art, Vasiliy thought, this manner of quiet speech. Even in families but certainly in public places and at work, one spoke softly and without emphasis. Moldavians like them had had to learn it.

The curtains lifted in alarm as Ivan opened the door and slipped in, pulling gloves off his reddened fingers.

Joanna could read in his smile what a wonderful evening it had been. "Many young people?" She lifted the kettle on to the stove.

"Everybody. Stefan and Sasha spoke."

"Oh, Stefan and Sasha spoke!" Semyon ducked out of the bedroom where the younger children were sleeping on their couches and cots. He enjoyed making his parents a little uneasy. They didn't like him to hear conversations about the believers. The fact that they pretended not to care amused him.

"Hello, Vanya. Home for your secret meeting?"

"It was Elena Kuzminichna's birthday, Semyon. You ought to have come."

"And the fact that this is your last night before leaving for two years in the army had nothing to do with the meeting. I'm sure no one paid any attention."

"You're welcome to tea, Semyon." Joanna set out the glasses with some irritation. Was Semyon going to argue on Vanya's last night?

"At least Stefan spoke! That must have taken the eyes of the girls off Ivan Vasilievich for some moments!" Semyon laughed as a blush deepened on Ivan's face.

Joanna smiled. "He'll make a good-looking soldier." How could Semyon understand about the preaching of the Word?

"He made a good-looking taxi driver. I don't know what all your customers will do tomorrow when you're gone! I can just hear all the old babushkas crying on the way to the clinic. 'Where is young Vanya?'"

"They'd soon forget about me, if you would be kind to them."

Semyon choked on the word. "*Kindness!* That is not a Bolshevik word. Kindness and love! Love is a biological reaction. Everybody knows that." His eye caught his mother's flowered cardboard motto on the kitchen wall. "God is love? How can a God who is supposedly spirit have biological reactions?"

"Your love for Momma is biological?" Ivan set his empty tea glass on the table thoughtfully.

"Of course. There is a dependence tie because she is my parent. Papa too."

"And when you marry? Will you not love your wife?"

"That is more biological than ever!" Semyon smiled in a small triumph. "At first, it will be sexual attraction; then, I hope, friendship based on mutual respect."

Joanna shook the fire so vigorously that red embers fell into the smoking ash box. Her husband began cleaning his second boot.

Ivan drew his chair closer to his brother. "And Moldavia? What of the love you feel for Moldavia? What is that?"

Semyon tipped his chair back in a position of supreme thought, bringing it down upon the floor with a decisive bang. "I am trying to tell you that you won't find kindness and love in the Red army. Life there is no joke. It's nothing to me if you won't listen. You can sit there and smile if you like. But you won't smile after tomorrow."

Ivan's look of confidence included his parents. "Of course I'll smile, Semyon. It is not the government that insists I join the army for my time of service. It is the Lord who puts me there. And will He now leave me? I don't think so!"

Semyon attempted a shrug. "There's no point in discussing it. You're determined to have a hard time. So good-night!" He picked up the blanket and pillow being warmed on the chair by the gas heater and made for the small porch on which he slept. At the door he turned. "It's not only that you'll make the usual happy fool of yourself talking about God and praying all the time. I am telling you, such activities are not allowed. It is not my fault if you won't listen to me." The springs of his cot creaked repeatedly as he flung himself down and began pulling off his boots.

Vasiliy Trofimovich broke the uneasy silence. His voice was so low Joanna stopped shaking the fire to hear him. "You have to do what God tells you, son. We know that. If what Semyon says is true. . . ." His voice trailed off helplessly. He stared for a moment at the glowing embers in the ash box. "I wish there were some way I could help you." His eyes searched his son's face lovingly. "Your mother and I, all the family, all the brethren will continue in prayer for you. You know that."

Joanna had left her crouched position by the stove and, putting the ashes to one side, sat down again beside her husband, her right hand reaching for a basket of handwork. A draught from the window blew the thin drapes hanging in the entranceway into the room as if they too were trying to hear the conversation between father and son.

There was a sureness about Vanya that didn't belong to his eighteen years. She had seen it in the brothers who returned from terms in labour camps. They had faced the worst and found it to be endurable. It was as if the camp were still within them, and they moved in a way different from other men. There was a common saying that the only place to be free is in prison, because everything has already been lost. Yet Vanya had this freedom.

It was as if he had never learned to be cautious, to glance behind him before speaking, to take measure of who was nearby. Even in the registered prayer houses, believers had many fears. A police informer might observe a believer talking too long to a visitor. A pastor might make too many visits to homes. He might preach too enthusiastically or fail to report any irregularity in his congregation. Among unregistered congregations such as theirs discretion was even more a way of life. But not for Vanya.

With a glance at Semyon's room that she could not resist, Joanna leaned out of the light that fell on her sewing to hear her son's voice. Even in the shadow she could see the relaxed confidence in his face.

"Once I had a dream," he was saying softly. "I was standing watch with an angel on a large rock. A great storm came up. I was frightened and saw a ship floundering in the high seas. People were drowning and the angel told me to jump into the sea and save them. I remember I was in the water and somehow dragged many people to shore. The waves roared, and when I pulled the last person out, I fell down without strength. But the angel picked me up and put me back on the rock, and there I stood guard again."

Joanna wished she knew what her husband was thinking. What could be made of Vanya's strange stories? But Vasiliy Trofimovich sat in silence, his head towards his son as if he were still speaking. Vanya continued.

"The Lord has told me to speak for Him wherever I am and not to be silent. This confirms what our pastors say when they preach that we must witness to God's love and not be fearful about consequences. Stefan spoke of this tonight—that we are all to preach the gospel wherever we are in school, in our work, wherever, following the examples of the prophets and apostles."

Vasiliy hesitated before he spoke. At last he turned, smiling slightly to his son. He leaned towards him, and after a long embrace replied, "So you must obey God, Vanya. So we will pray."

The night was long for Vasiliy Trofimovich. While all the children slept, Ivan with his already packed suitcase beside the couch that was his bed, Vasiliy knelt near the stove in a blanket, striving in prayer for his son.

3

No threshold without God

It was almost two in the morning and Ivan's head was swimming with sleep. It was colder in Odessa than it had been in Moldavia. The snow was not yet deep, but its surface was frozen and slippery as the draftees jumped down from the oppressive warmth of the army trucks that had brought them from the train station. Now, as they half-slid, half-ran to keep up with an escort car that directed them to a cluster of buildings ahead in the darkness, Ivan tried to make sense out of the confusion of voices calling from different places in the darkness.

"Over here—quickly!" "Convoy's an hour late. We've been waiting out here one hour." "Stand at attention! What's the matter with all you stragglers? Quickly now!" "How are they going to be assigned to beds at this hour, I'd like to know? There's a regulation that all new arrivals must be here before ten P.M." "What do you want to do then? Stand them in the cold all night?" "Who's to give the welcome?" "Where's Karetko?" "Someone run for Karetko. They're here."

A dim figure in a greatcoat and scarf wrapped almost to the tip of his officer's hat clumsily mounted a few steps of the building before which the freezing group had come to a halt. He addressed them in muffled shouts. Because of the lateness of the hour, he barked, greetings would be brief and the men would be dismissed to their barracks for the night. The barracks were the large buildings facing directly on to the square in which they were standing. As they could see in the floodlights, the buildings were five storeys high. Each floor of each building consisted of six dormitories, each one accommodating thirty-two soldiers, so there would be 192 men to a floor. The men had received coupons on the train designating the number of their barrack, their floor, and their room. Officers were present who would direct new soldiers to their bunks.

The officer paused suddenly to clear his throat, pull his scarf out of the way, and spit emphatically into the snow.

They would be awakened at six A.M. by a bugle call. They would have five minutes to get up and dress and make their beds. At that time they would receive further instructions. Dismissed. The muffled figure wheeled into the open door behind him.

Immediately a frenzied kaleidoscope of activity began. Officers sprang to life—pushing, shouting, scattering small groups of men in different directions. Inside the barracks the weary draftees pushed through the rows of bunks in the glare of bare light bulbs in the ceiling. In a search hurried by the cries of officers, they looked for numbers that corresponded to the rumpled blue coupons they held in their hands, like so many late theatregoers looking for their seats after the first-act curtain.

Accents strange to Ivan filled the rooms—Lithuanians making themselves understood in broken Russian, Byelorussians, the famous Moscow accent blending with the slower, softer speech of the North—and at every turn, the blur of fatigue that churned the whole mosaic of bunks, arms, legs, laughter, and cursing into a tumble of unreality.

By morning a light snow was falling. Tiny flakes fell on his lashes and the rim of his bugle as Boris Yakovlevich Frolov raised his instrument for reveille. Grimly he pointed it at the windows on the third floors of the barracks where he knew the new recruits had been taken during the night. Never too soon to discover the rigours of army life! Taking a blast of cold air into his lungs, he blew.

Only too well he could imagine the scene in those rooms: the apprehensive rush to get dressed, not to be left behind, not to be singled out as slow or stupid. The strangeness of their new uniforms would begin now, and the mutual sizing-up, and the cold walk to the mess hall for a breakfast of fish and tea. The first day of running from drill to class to orientation to meals to gymnastics was upon them. He blew the bugle again in an opposite direction. For him, only eleven months left. That was something to be thankful for. Already the men in his own unit were hurrying out of the barracks stripped to the waist for running. They would cover their course of fifteen kilometres in the hour before breakfast.

Boris Yakovlevich lowered his bugle and marched the goose step to his barracks. Perhaps today at target practice he would save a bullet for himself. It was an idea that haunted him.

The important thing, Ivan was thinking as he made his way to the dining hall, *is to find a place to pray*. Already the crowds of soldiers, the noise in the barracks, the difficulty in being alone pressed upon him. Even the bare poplar trees he passed huddled together in thickets as if it would be suspect to grow in solitude.

The smoky smell of sturgeon hung over the vast mess hall as Ivan joined a long line for the mugs of tea that steamed invitingly in the cold. At home at this hour, he would be praying. Prayer times were easy to arrange at home, even in the busy days when he was taking his chauffeur's training at the institute. There were hours in which he could pray before his train left for the city. In the winter on a morning like this, two of the younger children would be bedded on top of the kitchen stove, hunched together for warmth. It had been pleasant to pray beside them as they slept, their regular breathing undisturbed by the soft rising and falling of his voice.

Perhaps after the meal he could look for a quiet place. The plates of fish were empty now, but every one of the thirty soldiers at the table was still hungry, passing the plates of dark bread up and down until they too were bare. An orderly moved among the rows of tables with a huge kettle of tea, slopping out extras of the tepid drink into uplifted metal cups.

A feeling of loneliness tightened Ivan's throat. It was as he expected, of course, but perhaps he had underestimated the enormity of the task ahead of him. Each person seemed caught up in a microcosm of his own: choking down the last dregs of tea, wiping up a plate with a crumpled bit of bread, climbing over the bench deftly balancing plate and cup, hurrying to the door, stopping to chat with a friend made on the train. Lines of soldiers pressed in at the entrance as others pushed through them into the icy November dawn. "Confess Me before men and I will acknowledge you before the angels of God." There was no questioning that Voice that had spoken so many times in his spirit. Ivan put his fork and spoon in the mug on his plate and lifted himself back over the bench, moving with the others towards the door. The first thing to do was to find a place to pray.

Staff Sergeant Strelkov had a long smooth face with hollow cheeks he sucked in when irritated. For two weeks he had been trying to get the new unit in shape; two weeks of the invariable questions, disorder, and interruptions he detested. A clump of icy mud clung to his boot and he kicked it off impatiently. This new lot was a poor bunch. His eyes, narrowed in the cold, shifted to the place in the shivering formation where a man was missing. Movement on the near edge of the drill grounds caught his eye. He watched impassively as the straggler approached in a desperate run. It was Moiseyev.

Gasping for breath, he took his place in the line. Not a man moved so much as a sideways glance. Strelkov was slightly gratified. Perhaps a lesson could be made of this.

"Give your reason for being late, Comrade Private Moiseyev." Strelkov's disciplined bearing was mute witness to the fact that he himself had never once been late.

Ivan's bare chest was heaving from the long run across the field. Uneasily he viewed the ramrod form of the sergeant as he steadied his breathing. A tension slowly built in the formation as Strelkov's question awaited an answer.

"I am sorry, sir. I was praying, sir."

Strelkov stared. There was no hint of the buffoon in Moiseyev's grave expression. Someone in the line coughed suddenly. Strelkov glared at the motionless men. Did they think he didn't know they were suffocating with laughter?

Strelkov had been in the army long enough to know how to handle irregularities. "You will drill with the unit, Moiseyev. When we have completed the exercises, you will report to me." He stepped back to address the formation, his order scattering the men to different sections of the field to begin their drills. In an instant the grounds were alive with bodies leaping, jogging, arms flashing in exercise formations.

Ivan longed to throw himself into performing the callisthenics, to purge himself of the shame of being late and of abusing the wonderful gift the Lord had given him. How easy it had been to rejoice at finding an unused office for a prayer room. The old babushka sweeping the floor had assured him the room was not in use until ten in the morning. She herself unlocked the door at five when she came to clean. Praise had rolled over Ivan every morning since, as the stillness of the place settled in on his soul. There was a leather chair so that he could kneel on the floor, leaning his elbows on the seat, shielded by its generous back from a cracked window.

But to forget the time! To be late for drill. With a renewed pang of embarrassment he heard Strelkov calling him again.

The sergeant's atheism was third-generation. His grandfather had been one of the earliest Bolsheviks, a midshipman on the battleship *Aurora* who had fought in the streets of Leningrad during the Revolution. During the Great Patriotic War his father had been an officer in the siege of Leningrad and had died of wounds and hunger in the last days of the siege. His Communist Party card had been in his pocket when he died. Strelkov carried his father's card next to his own in his wallet.

He was disturbed by the presence of what he called "bourgeois remnants" in the army. He rubbed his gloves together and began walking, indicating with a jerk of his head that Ivan was to follow. "What's this about praying, Moiseyev? You weren't joking?"

"No, sir."

"Then what's the matter with you?"

"Nothing, sir. I feel fine."

"Orthodox? Are you a churchman?" Strelkov tried to think if today was a religious day for the Orthodox. Every now and then there would be incidents on religious days.

"No, sir. Baptist."

That was worse. Baptists[1] were unpredictable and stubborn. In the Komsomol, Strelkov had conducted anti-religious seminars in rural communities. The Baptists attended, but they frequently gave such lengthy answers to religious questions that it was difficult to get the better of them.

"That won't do here, Moiseyev. Praying. Religion. Not in the Red army. It is unfortunate to find religious survivals anywhere in Soviet life but especially so in a young man training in the army of the Union of Soviet Socialist Republics. It is certain that you will have to change your ideas."

Ivan continued walking silently with the officer, wondering if an answer was expected of him.

"I am sure after you make some friends, begin to enjoy army life a little more, you will see the childishness of your religious ideas. It was only after Russia threw off the shackles of the czar and the church that she was able to become strong. It is the same for a man." In spite of his greatcoat, Strelkov was getting chilled. He ought to be inside at his desk. He glanced at Ivan. His skin was bright with the cold.

Strelkov stood stamping his *valenki* in the snow and watching as Ivan ran across the field to his unit. In spite of his knee-length felt boots Strelkov's feet were getting cold, and he had missed his morning tea. It had not been a satisfactory interview. The other men had heard Moiseyev say he had prayed. The polit-officer would have to be notified.

The Polit-Ruk[2] office was poorly lit. The faint winter light that struggled to enter the room was in part blocked by limp green drapes that hung dispiritedly over the grimy glass. The polit-officer was Capt. Boris Zalivako, a hammer of a man, short and powerfully built with inscrutable bushy brows. A matter of unpunctuality was of no interest to him, but Strelkov's story, if it were not a poor joke of Moiseyev's, was.

Waiting for Moiseyev to arrive, Strelkov had misgivings. Perhaps he should not have taken Moiseyev seriously. He wished he had not conversed with him. He had hoped to give him some advice, to help him along. But it might well be that Moiseyev had made a fool of him. At least the men in formation could verify that he said he had been praying; he wouldn't be able to deny it. How many had actually heard him? Strelkov tried to remember who had been standing close enough to hear.

Captain Zalivako glanced lazily at Moiseyev standing at attention on the other side of the table. His side cap was at the proper angle. He had saluted correctly and with respect. Zalivako's interest was slightly stirred by the ease with which Moiseyev met his look. The young fellow was sure of himself, but there was no hint of insolence in his expression.

Zalivako motioned for him to sit down. "You don't look like the sort that would be late for a drill. What is the problem that you cannot manage to report on time with the rest of your unit?"

"I am very sorry, comrade captain, for my tardiness. It won't happen again."

"You didn't answer my question. What explanation do you give for being late?" There was a tightening of Zalivako's voice. He disliked evasiveness.

"I was praying, sir." The answer hung in the air, almost visible in its strangeness.

Strelkov took a deep breath of relief. He had been quite right to report Moiseyev. Everyone knew religion was a menace to the Soviet way of life, in whatever harmless a form it might appear. Lenin himself had said that the goal of the Communist Party was to free the working masses from the idea of religion. Strelkov straightened himself conspicuously.

Zalivako tapped his fingers. "To whom were you praying?"

"To God, sir. The Creator of the universe, who loves all men."

"To God." Zalivako closed his eyes in a deep sigh. "It has been scientifically proven that God does not exist. Our Soviet scientists have studied this question thoroughly and they have verified the teachings of scientific communism that there is no God. The idea of God was invented by early man to explain economic conditions that could not be understood in primitive times."

"That is what atheists teach, sir."

"That is the correct view. That is the position of the Communist government, the Academy of Sciences, and every other great institution in Soviet life, including the Soviet Department of Defence. This is the position of the Soviet peoples."

"Comrade polit-officer, I know atheism is our official view. But the Bible teaches that God made man after He created the entire universe. This is the Christian belief."

Zalivako had been writing on the report sheet before him on his desk. He paused in his work. "You have a Bible?"

"No, sir."

"The Bible is not a welcome book in the Soviet Union. It is full of unscientific errors of all kinds. It promotes passivity and subservience. It is not permitted in the army. In fact, I can't understand why anyone would read such a book."

"It changes lives, sir."

"The army changes lives, Moiseyev. And opinions. Perhaps you need assistance in realizing this. It is a far more profound truth than anything your Bible declares."

"I am eager to serve in the army to the best of my ability."

Zalivako began to be angry. Religious recruits were difficult to deal with. Believers were deceptive. Outwardly they appeared to be good citizens, quiet, peace-loving, harmless people. And under the cover of virtue, they spread their false teachings.

"I am happy to hear you say that, Moiseyev. Such a statement naturally means that you have decided to throw off your subversive ideas about God and enter fully into the programme that has been planned to develop you as fully as possible into a Soviet soldier, unquestioning in your loyalty to the state. I congratulate you."

Strelkov glanced admiringly at Captain Zalivako. The Polit-Ruk knew how to handle men. But Zalivako was continuing, ignoring the distress on Moiseyev's face. "I will take special interest in your political development and in your participation in the full range of military and political activities required of you."

Zalivako rose from his chair, watching Moiseyev intently as he waited for his response. The boy would be a fool not to take the exit he had been given. But believers were fools to start with. He wished Moiseyev's Russian were better. It was tiresome to listen to his halting speech.

"I am happy as a Soviet citizen to serve in the army and to help build socialism in any way I can. But there is another place of which I am a citizen, and that is the Kingdom of God. It is a Kingdom that can never be a threat to the Soviet state because this Kingdom is within the hearts of believers, and the laws of this place are the laws of love. I cannot renounce my citizenship in this Kingdom or my loyalty to the King, who is God. He is building His Kingdom everywhere, even in the Soviet Union, a Kingdom of forgiveness and love."

Zalivako's voice began to shake as he answered. "We have done away with kingdoms in the Soviet Union, Moiseyev, and with kings! Perhaps in your zeal you have somehow forgotten that fact. We have places only for those loyal to the Soviet state, nothing else!"

Strelkov was deflated. He had hoped to see a demonstration of how smoothly these matters could be handled. And it was incredible to him that any Soviet youth could have been so thoroughly poisoned by religion.

But Zalivako was not finished. "It is evident that you resist teaching, Moiseyev, and the advice of your superiors. That is a concern to me. You are in need of a lesson. Since you are fond of praying on your knees, I shall give you an opportunity for constructive socialist labour in that position. You are to wash the barrack's drill hall and all the corridors on your knees with a bucket and brush. You will work all night. Perhaps an exercise of this nature, and before your comrades, might help to persuade you to be teachable. You will have opportunity to consider if you wish to cling to your anti-Soviet views. Dismissed."

Strelkov stood smartly to attention, saluting Captain Zalivako. The matter had been brought to a satisfactory conclusion. A good feeling passed briefly between the two men as Moiseyev saluted and left the room. Such degrading labour would teach Moiseyev what knees were for.

Before the pale December sun had climbed halfway to the top of the frozen sky the news of a believer in the unit had passed through the whole company. Smiles appeared as the story spread from man to man with heads shaking or shoulders shrugging in amusement or disinterest. Fast upon the first story came the second, that the Polit-Ruk had set Moiseyev to scrubbing the enormous barrack hall with a small hand brush and a bucket. Incredibly, he was in good humour, singing and smiling as he worked in spite of continuous interruptions by officers who called him into their offices to harass him. By lunch, soldiers were drifting into the hall on their way to the dining room, watching him work, listening to the quiet hymns he sang with such evident joy. He was a mystery.

[1] In the USSR, the word *Baptist* is a general term meaning *Protestant*, as contrasted with *churchman*, which refers to a member of the Russian Orthodox Church. There are two groups of Protestants: the government-registered All-Union Council of Evangelical Christians/Baptists (AUCECB) and the unregistered, illegal Council of Churches of Evangelical Christians/Baptists (CCECB). The Moiseyevs worship with a CCECB congregation.

[2] The shortened term for *Politicheskoye-Rukovodstvo* ("Political-Directive" department).

4

*Where is there any book of the law so clear to each
man as that written in his heart?*

Tolstoy

Kerch, the colourful Ukraine seaport in the lush strait
jutting into the Black Sea, was an exciting place to a
young soldier of limited travels. Ivan strained his eyes
as he bumped along in the back of the troop transport
truck. In the distance he could see the streaming smoke-
stacks of the iron and steel mills. Close by, the smell of
the glittering sea and the screams of seagulls quickened
his enthusiasm for new sights. This city was a very old
one, the soldiers had been told in a preliminary
briefing. It had been founded in the sixth century by
the Greeks and called Panticapaeum. The soldiers were
to observe the highest hill in the city, named Mithra-
dates. On it still stood the crumbling Greek ruins of an
acropolis.

The acropolis, the officer had informed the young
men, was the seat of the Greek "soviet". It would be
interesting to them that in Kerch the glorious Soviet
traditions of human dignity and freedom that had only
truly begun with the Revolution were now carried out
under the very shadow of the Greek acropolis itself.

That was all very well, Ivan was to reflect later. But
it was at the new base in Kerch that his testings began
in earnest.

For the first few days he was free to join the streams
of soldiers hurrying in every direction, chatting
quietly, their briefcases swollen with books and papers.
He felt refreshed and lighthearted. Often in fitness

drills, in classroom lectures, in military training sessions he prayed "Lord let me excel in this. Let me be a good soldier for Your glory."

Ivan had hoped that after leaving Odessa the interrogations would cease. He was as glad to be gone as Zalivako was to have him gone. But Zalivako had been thorough in sending an alert to the Kerch Polit-Ruk about the presence of a believer in Unit 6168T. Private Moiseyev had admitted openly that he prayed. was a Baptist believer, and would attend meetings of believers whenever he had the opportunity. He had stubbornly withstood vigorous indoctrination and refused to be silent about his beliefs.

Hardly two weeks had passed before reports of barracks discussions began to reach the Kerch Polit-Ruk office. The decree of Lenin, point 5, gave members of cults free celebration of religious rites, but not the right to propagate religion, which infringed upon the freedom of other citizens. Why couldn't Moiseyev understand? Ivan tried to explain to the polit-officers that the men in his unit often asked him about Christ. If they wanted to know about salvation. where was the law that said he could not answer their questions? How could he refuse them? All believers are to be witnesses.

And if it were not a command of Christ to share His love, how would it be possible to hide the joy that met Ivan at every turn? A leaf falling from the frozen sky was God's touch. The sudden remembrance of a forgotten Scripture was God's voice. The blasts of wind spoke of God's power, the moon His beauty, the strength of his own body was God's strength poured into him.

Junior Polit-Officer Captain Yarmak was young and restless. He itched for a challenge that would help him

to rise in the party structure. All the better if Moiseyev
were difficult. His success with him would look doubly
good on his record. Yarmak took his responsibilities
seriously. Every one of the eleven hundred soldiers at
Kerch must be totally committed to the Communist
Party and the teachings of scientific atheism. Only then
could the military be assured of the total and immediate obedience that was required of every Soviet soldier.
Decisively, he raised his eyes from the papers on his
desk as Moiseyev was brought before him. He stared for
several seconds before speaking, changing his expression to match the harshness in his voice. "Have you
ever been sick, Moiseyev?"

He was gratified to see Moiseyev's surprise.

"No, sir, I've never even seen the inside of a hospital."

Yarmak folded his arms dramatically. The brass buttons on his cuff caught the light in a way that pleased
him. Political development was so often a matter of
shock offensive.

"It is fortunate you are well. You will be needing a
strong constitution for the next few days—or a change
of mind, which seems to be so difficult for you." He
paused for the maximum effect. "You showed an un-
sound and rebellious attitude in Odessa. Attemps have
been made to persuade you to renounce your anti-
Soviet views and to increase your military and political
knowledge. But you refuse. Until you agree to submit
yourself to the authority of this base and to obey the
orders given to you, you will be confined without
meals. Dismissed."

The room to which Ivan was taken was not a cell
but a detention room used by the polit-officers for
questioning and confinement. A cot, covered with the
regulation-grey army blanket, a table, three chairs, and
some army manuals on a shelf made up the furnish-

ings. In a corner was a filthy toilet beside a tap. The large window was barred and the double doors locked twice. The room was very cold, bathed in a pale late afternoon light.

For Ivan, it was a chapel. Thankfully he sank down on the cot, his head whirling with the faces of angry officers from Odessa and Kerch fading and dissolving like scenes from a military film. What bliss to sleep and to awake to pray!

Many times before, the Lord had called Ivan to periods of fasting and supplication. Ivan smiled at the holy joke. In such times he had been greatly strengthened and refreshed. Captain Yarmak couldn't have given him a greater gift. Full of gratitude, Ivan turned his attention to the Lord, to seek Him in prayer and fasting. How long he would fast was in God's hand, not Yarmak's.

The second night he was awakened by a distant, rhythmic pounding. He lay trying to distinguish the sound when a key was turned in the lock. Yellow light splashed into the room. An officer Ivan did not know stood in the doorway. Without turning on the light he spoke to the dark room.

"You're wanted in the lecture room at the end of the hall. Come at once." The noise of his boots faded rapidly in the long corridor.

Ivan struggled to rouse himself fully as he saw the elite group of officers waiting to question him. He focused his eyes on the electric wall clock. Two-fifteen in the morning. Most of the officers were sprawled informally in the desk seats, smoking and sipping from steaming mugs of tea. Sometimes they would speak quietly, asking a question and waiting for his reply. At other times shouts would suddenly come from different officers in a rapid fire of accusations and statements.

Was he not ill? Had he changed his attitude? His ideas were imperialist, relics of czarism and capitalism. His ideas could not be tolerated in the Red army. He need not think he was suffering anything for his beliefs. He was being disciplined for avoiding his obligations to the army. How long was he going to evade his responsibilities to his comrades and to the Soviet state? Supposing God exists, could He then make a space too small for Himself? Why did he deliberately withhold food from himself? He was creating questions concerning his mental stability. Did he not understand that a rejection of Marxist–Leninist teaching was a rejection of the Soviet way of life? God was created by man to explain famine and disease and economic conditions he was too primitive to understand. The idea of God was no longer necessary. It impeded the development of the free socialist citizen. People who propagated such ideas were enemies of the Soviet state.

At all times of his fasting, Ivan was called for interrogation sessions, sometimes at night before several officers, sometimes before polit-officers, once or twice before an officer who would begin in a fatherly manner and very quickly continue in abusive shouting.

It was five days before the testing came to an end. On the last morning, in a tumult of argumentative voices and clatter of equipment, an ancient x-ray machine was wheeled into the hall to the doorway of the detention room. Ivan could hear a furious controversy ensuing as to the size of the doors and whether they would admit the machine. In the end, Ivan was thrust into the hall to have an x-ray made of his digestive tract. The technician, a Jew from Estonia named Myakaev, was sputtering with frustration. This clearly was not a medical matter. To bring him out in the cold, all the way over from the hospital, and to expect a machine to operate properly after bumping it up and down ramps and over icy broken pavements was criminal negligence of socialist property.

Later in the day Captain Yarmak entered the room, the x-ray and a report sheet in his hand. As if the question had not already been asked a hundred times, he sat quietly in one of the wooden chairs and looked closely at Ivan as he spoke. "Well, Moiseyev, have you changed your mind? Five days without food have passed."

The captain seemed smaller and farther away than the few feet his chair was distant from Ivan's cot. Ivan was tired, but he tried to concentrate on Yarmak's question and his own answer.

"One night I was praying," he began. "I was rather cold and wishing for sleep because I had been awakened twice that night. But I was awake and praying to God for my family and friends, and for you, Captain Yarmak, as well."

Yarmak stood up impatiently and gazed at the snow falling behind the bars of the window.

"It wasn't as if I was especially conscious of being hungry, but I was very tired and certainly cold. As I prayed, God suddenly touched me in a wonderful way. I was warmed and felt as full as if I had eaten a large and delicious dinner. Soon afterwards I fell asleep. When I awoke, it was morning with the sun streaming in the window. A bird was outside on the sill, singing. There is a Scripture that says, 'Call upon Me in the day of trouble; I shall rescue you, and you will honour Me.' It is because of God's rescue that I am not hungry or sick. How can I possibly 'change my mind'? You can look at me and see for yourself what God has done."

Yarmak stared at the swirling flakes of snow, his mind a turmoil of anger. As a political leader his position depended on success with men like Moiseyev. Already Colonel Malsin had sent him a memo. "Let

Moiseyev eat. I don't want to be blamed if he dies of starvation because of you." With freezing dignity, Yarmak left the room.

It was during the morning long-distance running that Ivan met Sergei. A thick fog had rolled in from the Black Sea, obscuring the barren trees that were landmarks for the drill. Until the unit reached the maximum distance of fifteen kilometres before breakfast, the course was being lengthened each day, forcing the men to the outer limits of their endurance. Across rigid fields, down gulleys, jumping ditches half-hidden in the fog, the men ran in growing agony. It was as if the landscape itself was grunting with effort, the thudding of hidden feet throbbing like a painful heartbeat beneath the crust of frozen snow.

Ivan was lagging, trying to pace himself carefully and ignore the terrible thirst that tore at his throat. Gradually he became aware of a soldier from another unit keeping pace beside him. The soldier suddenly shouted in a hoarse grasp, "He is risen!"

What had he said? Ivan tried to fit phrases into the rhythm of the words. Perhaps, "Will it blizzard?"

A light wind was blowing at the smoking fog. Ivan turned to see the soldier's face. It was grey with effort but strained in a smile. Again he shouted. "I said, 'He is risen,' brother! He—is—risen!"

It was as if the frozen earth had tipped up from behind and Ivan was suddenly running downhill in a flood of joy. With a yell that was almost a whoop he responded to the ancient Easter greeting. "He is risen indeed! Hallelujah!" The greeting of embrace would wait till later.

The place they found to meet was one of the large garages for army vehicles that flanked the front gate of the base. It was an old stone building that had once been used to stable horses. Before that, and during the war, it was said to be a barrack. Its thick walls kept out the worst of the cold, and the wide parking aisles made ideal paths for walking and praying. Occasionally another soldier or two would duck into the building to have a cigarette out of the wind, but in general Ivan and Sergei were undisturbed in the few minutes they could find to be together.

Such meetings were infrequent in the relentless pace of army life. But the knowledge of Sergei's presence on the base was encouragement enough. Meeting a brother unconsciously lulled Ivan into a feeling that all would be well, after all. It was with an unpleasant shock that he received a summons to report to Maj. Alexander Petrovich Gidenko in the Polit-Ruk.

5

A saint sleeps not on soft beds

Major Gidenko was a huge man with a leonine face and military stance that set off his height. As a youth he had excelled in athletics, and the awards and prizes he had won had made him a favourite of his teachers and classmates. Russia had been good to him, and the fact that he had been born in the same year as the Revolution gave him a sense of destiny that had inspired courage in his difficult university studies. From university, he had made the army his life. As head of Kerch's Political-Directive Committee he was determined that this problem with Moiseyev be resolved before the Polit-Ruk commissar for the Crimea would have to be brought in.

Gidenko sighed. He had been in the army thirty-two years and had seen every kind of man come and go, but he had never understood the *religiozniks*. To him they were merely half-hearted creatures creeping around the backstairs of Soviet life. Why did they not renounce their strange practices and enter fully into the life of the Soviet state, contributing fully as they should and fully reaping the benefits?

The great Patriotic War had been the climax of Gidenko's life. As a young soldier in the Battle of Stalingrad, he had stared horrified at the guns of fascist troops a hundred metres away. A conviction that he would never survive the battle had gripped him. The Nazi atrocities he had witnessed had weakened his will to live; he felt he was going blind from the snow and the glare of the sun on his comrades' white uniforms.

Under shellfire he had dashed to the party headquarters in the corner of a bombed mill and had joined
the Communist Party. He had carried his party card
into battle. That he survived only deepened his sense of
destiny. He was born and lived to serve Russia.

That people could cling to the idea of God was incom-
prehensible. Perhaps the old were too fearful to
change, but how could a young person take such folk-
lore seriously—even in its most harmless form? Moiseyev had been properly educated in socialist schools.
He had been taught the depravity of religion, the decaying influence that Christianity had had upon Russia
with its corrupt priests and churchmen landowners.

A cold wind whipped across the snow fields stretching for miles beyond the base. Gidenko sighed again.

He had dealt many times with believers. Experience
had taught him that effectiveness was often not so
much a matter of persuasion or political re-education,
although he believed in trying. It was very often a matter of discipline.

"When you think of it," he had ruefully smiled at
his wife over his plate of steaming cabbage soup the
night before, "for all our programmes on scientific
atheism, we succeed in changing the opinions of very
few believers. Severe punishment too often is the only
recourse. I could just as well close down the Polit-Ruk
if we had to depend on indoctrination alone."

Yet he would be responsible to Colonel Malsin for
this Moiseyev, one way or another.

It was a long walk to Major Gidenko's office, and as
Ivan strode along the shovelled streets of the base, he
was giving praise to God for the time to pray. A Scripture verse his small brother Ilyusha had taught him to
sing at home was in his mind, and he sang it softly,
keeping time with its music while he walked. "The joy

of the Lord is your strength. The joy of the Lord is your strength. The joy of the Lord is your strength." The tune was light-hearted and fit the brightness of the sun on the snow.

It was a clear day. Something flashed and glittered in the sky overhead. "The joy of the Lord is your strength." Joy was filling him. The trees in the small park in the central square of the base seemed dusted with a heavenly light. Ivan saluted every passing tree in Jesus' name. The light was dazzling, like sunlight on a mirror. He lifted his eyes upward at the same instant that he heard a voice. "Vanya, Vanya."

The angel was above him with a brightness and presence that caught terror in the joy and held both sensations motionless in his heart.

The voice was like a memory, unmistakable, clear, and strangely wordless. "Do not be afraid." Through the transparent form of the angel Ivan could see the large trees on the opposite side of the park. The form of the angel seemed to be moving. Staring, Ivan slowly resumed walking. The radiance of the angel lit the park far more brightly than the sun. But he was speaking again.

"Do not be afraid. Go. I am with you." There were no words in which Ivan could reply. His joy was like a fire within him. Or perhaps the warmth came from the angel's light. How he came to the door of Major Gidenko's building he was later to wonder. But as the brightness faded the sense of presence did not. He made his way to the major's office and knocked quietly on the door. Gidenko smiled at Ivan expansively. This would be easier than he thought. What was the matter with Yarmak? If he didn't know Moiseyev's age, he would have guessed sixteen. The lad hid a farm-boy face. "Sit down, son." With an open palm he gestured to the leather chair on the opposite side of his desk.

There was a gentleness about him.

"You're a long way from Moldavia, Moiseyev."

"Yes, sir."

"After a year, you'll have leave."

"Yes, sir."

"Miss your family? Mother, father?"

"I do, sir."

"I remember my first days in the army. I used to write home every day. Seems funny, now. You write home a lot?"

"Not so much as every day, sir. I don't have time."

"No? Why not?"

"The interrogations, sir. I spend a great deal of my time being questioned at the Polit-Ruk."

"And these questionings. Are you not learning the correct answers? You don't look like a poor pupil to me."

"Sometimes there is a difference between the correct answers and the true ones. Sometimes God does not permit me to give 'correct' answers."

"Indeed? And who is this God of yours?" As soon as the question was out, Gidenko regretted it. Moiseyev was leaning forward in his chair, his face alight with opportunity.

"Sir, He is the Creator of all the universe. He is a spirit and greatly loves man. . . ."

"Yes, yes. I know the Christian teaching." Gidenko shifted in his chair. "These correct answers that you cannot give: is it because they are untrue? You disagree with the teaching of the glorious Red army?"

"No, sir."

"But you do not accept the principles of scientific atheism upon which is based our entire Soviet state and the military power of the army?"

"I cannot accept what I know to be untrue. Everything else I can gladly accept."

"It is not possible to prove the existence of God. Even religious people agree to that. Priests and pastors agree to that."

Ivan could hear the warmth die out of the major's voice. He began to pray in his spirit before answering.

Gidenko pressed his point. "You see, even your own teachers do not talk as you talk—about *knowing* God."

"Sir, they speak about proving God. There is no question about knowing Him. He is with me now, in this room. Before I came here He sent an angel to encourage me."

Gidenko stared intently at Ivan. Was the boy pretending to be simple-minded? Was his behaviour a ruse to be discharged from active service? There was a simpleness about him. A deliberate simpleness!

He rose massively from his chair. "Moiseyev, we have had men in the army before like you. No doubt there will always be one or two." He averted his eyes from the sudden look of pleasure that appeared in Ivan's face. Gidenko was becoming convinced that Moiseyev was not a dangerous *religioznik* but a homesick boy desperate for a leave. He had seen games like Moiseyev's played before. And hadn't the lad gone without food five days and pretended he wasn't hungry? Gidenko had seen soldiers who pretended not to understand when food was placed before them. A visit to the psychiatrist had cured their pretended mental illness!

But there was no question as to Moiseyev's sanity. He was too simple even to lie well.

When Gidenko spoke, it was wearily. "I am sorry, Moiseyev, that you persist in your irregular behaviour. It will achieve nothing for you except discomfort. However, I feel you will come to your senses with a little discipline and be cured of your delusions of angels and talking gods. I am going to order you to stand in the street tonight after lights-out until you are willing to come to me and apologize for the nonsense you have been circulating around the base about yourself and your so-called experiences with God. Since the temperature is likely to be some twenty-five degrees below zero,[1] for your sake, I hope you quickly agree to behave sensibly. Tomorrow we shall make a plan together for your political re-education. You are dismissed."

Gidenko was unaccountably irritated by the courage with which Moiseyev seemed to take the order. He had expected a hesitation, a reconsidering, but Moiseyev's face was quiet and his shoulders squared as he walked the correct pace to the door.

"Comrade private!"

Ivan turned. Gidenko observed he was a trifle pale. He *had* understood the order, then.

"You will obey my instructions in summer uniform. That is all."

The ageing corporal in the quartermaster corps was incredulous at Ivan's requisition for the issue of a summer uniform. Was not the snow already two feet in the fields? He studied the order in bewilderment, his wrinkled hand rubbing his chin pensively. It didn't seem, somehow, that the order could be correct. He didn't want to be blamed if something was wrong. What was the use of a summer uniform in winter? What was it wanted for? Ivan's explanation brought an expression of craft to his crow-footed eyes. A joke was being played on him, and he'd end up on the short end of it, too.

A brusque telephone verification from the Polit-Ruk sped the light trousers, shirt, jacket, and side cap into Ivan's hands. The corporal was silent, handing the articles to Ivan with a grave shaking of his white head.

Ivan could almost hear the laboured thoughts behind the sympathetic eyes. It was to be a bitter night.

A wind came up as the moon rose, lifting powdery snow from the corners of the buildings and swirling it across the well-swept streets. It was already cold in the barracks as the soldiers undressed for the night, huddling in their bunks under the heavy blankets for warmth.

Igor Alexandrovich Markov leaned against the wall, swathed in his blanket, smoking a Kazbek cigarette. From Georgia, he had the luminous dark eyes and black hair of his homeland and the easy temperament. Moiseyev was a mystery to him, and he gazed wonderingly as Ivan changed into the summer uniform.

"Tell me again, Moiseyev, what you're doing." The low conversations in the bunks within hearing distance became hushed. On the bunk above Ivan's, Vladimir Yakovlevich Albu coughed suddenly, hiding a smile.

Ivan was getting tired of telling his story. The news of this new punishment had spread like wildfire through the mess hall at supper. The private assigned to ladling the soup at his table had heard the account from the quartermaster corporal, and he distributed the news with every bowl of borsch. Ivan had been questioned or admonished at least a dozen times as he made his way out of the hall after supper.

And his answer sounded absurd. "At lights-out I am to report to the duty officer and stand outside in the street." He didn't blame the men for smiling. If the Polit-Ruk wanted to make a public example of Ivan, they were succeeding. Now, the men listened to Ivan and Igor jumped into the conversation. "How long are you going to stay out in the cold?" "You will have to give in. You will die of the cold." "Why do you refuse to be quiet about religion?" "Why can you not believe and be silent?" "You will be inside after five minutes."

Igor raised his voice above the others, quieting them. "Ivan! Why? What is it that you believe, that you would do this?"

"I believe God wants men to know that He exists, and loves man, and came in the form of Jesus Christ, as a real man, to this earth. It is almost Christmas. At this time we believers celebrate the coming of Christ to Bethlehem as a baby. All over the world, believers observe this great thing that God did and give glory to God. I believe He came to die for the sins of every man who wants forgiveness. For me. For you too, Igor."

Demchenko, a Komsomol enthusiast a few bunks down, interrupted loudly. "I don't think we want to be listening to this talk, comrades. I for one am not interested. I am surprised it has appeal for anyone. Especially Comrade Markov!"

There was a snicker from Vladimir Yakovlevich as the small group broke up. "Igor's not interested! Christmas talk is all right for the Baptists, maybe. But not Igor! He's too fond of his cigarettes and vodka!"

There was perfunctory laughter from the bunks cut suddenly short. In the distance the soft notes of a bugle could be heard. The light was immediately switched off. Hurrying, Ivan made his way to the door. From the window the brilliant moon lit the aisle between the bunks as he passed. There was silence behind him as he made his way down the stairs and to the street outside.

At first the cold was a shock slamming into his face with an impact that left his head aching and his eyes full of water. He recoiled from the icy wind that burned at his ears. He knew faces at the darkened barracks windows would be peering into the street. The moon lit the road and the snowbanks against the buildings. He stiffened against the freezing blast, glancing at his watch. It was one minute after ten o'clock.

He would have a long time to pray. He began haltingly, a slow fear rising in him that he tried to push away. How long *could* he stand out here? What if he became so cold he gave in? What if he froze to death? Would they let him freeze to death? He tried to concentrate on praying, but a panic constricted his chest. How long would it take to freeze to death? Would it be quick? What if he were *almost* frozen by morning but revived? He had heard the pain of frozen limbs was terrible. What if they had to amputate? He had to get his mind off it. He began to sing. "The joy of the Lord is your strength. The joy of the Lord is your strength."

Suddenly the glory of the morning revisited him. He looked at the park in the central square, distant in the moonlight but visible. An angelic light seemed to linger upon it. "Do not be afraid. I am with you!" The angel's words! They had been for tonight! Even the warmth of those moments seemed to resettle upon him. Fervently Ivan opened his mouth and softly began to pray.

It was twelve-thirty when his attention was distracted by the crunching of steps in the snow. Bundled in their greatcoats, three officers slowly were making their way towards him from the barrack.

Their voices were gruff and almost blown away by the wind. "Well, Moiseyev, have you reconsidered? Are you ready to come in? Have you had enough of standing out here?"

Even in the moonlight Ivan could see that they were looking at him with a measure of apprehension. Was it possible that he was warm?

"Thank you, comrade officers. I would like very much to come in and go to bed. But I cannot agree to remain silent about God." "Then you're going to stand out here all night long?" Each of their faces was twinged with fear.

"I'd rather not. But I don't see how anything else is possible, and God is helping me." Ivan was rubbing his hands with his fingertips as he stood at attention. Excitement shook his voice. His hands were cold, but no colder than they had been while dressing in the barracks. He tentatively wiggled his toes. They moved easily, without discomfort. A feeling of astonishment grew in him. He looked at the officers in excitement. He could see that even in their coats they were cold. They were stamping their feet and slapping their hands, shifting their weight, impatient to return to their heater in the barracks. He would feel differently in another hour, the senior officer mumbled as they wheeled away. Ivan couldn't resist a wondering laugh.

Soon the surge of relief subsided and a feeling of brokenness took its place. He was no better than any of the young people in his congregation at home. His parents had suffered in difficult situations for years. He knew of pastors who had been questioned, arrested, even sent to prison camps. Yet he was touched again and again by God's direct power and deliverance. Something in him pulled away from such magnificent singling-out. He didn't want to be special, he didn't deserve miracles and mysteries. He *ought* to be freezing. He wasn't good enough. Hot tears rimmed his eyes.

By three o'clock in the morning he was dozing on his feet. His prayers of repentance were long over. His intercessions for all the believers he knew he had made over and over. He had sung Christmas carols. He had prayed for every officer he knew and knew of. He had cried out to God on behalf of the men in his unit. But gradually his mind seemed to be floating somewhere outside cf his head. As much as he tried to command prayer, it eluded him.

Suddenly a voice in his ear startled him fully awake. The senior officer on duty was speaking gently.

"All right, Moiseyev, you are to come inside." The moon had set and the wind died down, and in the pitch-black, Ivan strained to see his face. The officer hesitated, standing still beside Ivan, the yellow light from the barracks caught in the gold oak-leaf insignia of his hat. His voice was intense. "What kind of person are you?"

"Sir?"

"What kind of person are you that the cold does not bother you?"

Ivan also spoke softly. "Oh, comrade, I am a person just like you. But I prayed to God and was warm."

The officer turned and began walking very slowly back to the barracks, touching Ivan's arm as a signal to accompany him. "Tell me about this God," he said.

Major Gidenko was profoundly disturbed. The report to Colonel Malsin concerning Ivan Moiseyev defied reason. For twelve nights in a row he had stood in sub-zero weather in a summer uniform. It was impossible that he did not freeze and beg for mercy. Last night Gidenko himself had gone to see him. It was true that his face was blue with cold and he had been swaying with fatigue. The powdery snow, lifted by the wind, had dusted his hair and uniform so that he looked frighteningly like a statue. But he was composed and not as cold after four hours as Gidenko was in five minutes. Was it possible that a young man could endure weather like that and not feel it? Well, it was possible, of course. Moiseyev had done it for two weeks. Gidenko was more disturbed than he had been in years. He had not slept well recently. Something would have to be put in the report for Malsin and the Polit-Ruk district commissar. It was clear that the punishment was not effective. The whole base was talking about Moiseyev. He would have to order a stop to these public vigils.

[1] −25° Centigrade is equivalent to −13° Fahrenheit.

6

Fear not the law, but the judge

Although the regulation bunk beds were only two feet wide and hard, Ivan stretched out between sheets and beneath a blanket and thanked God for the luxury. For the first time in 1971 he was in bed. No hours in the cold. No interrogations in the snow, in the officer's rooms. No watching the moon set behind the tiny park in the central square. Even before lights-out were sounded, Ivan was blissfully asleep.

Although he had only heard it once before, the Voice was so familiar Ivan was instantly awake. "Vanya, arise!" In a second he was on his feet between the bunks gazing at the crystal brilliance of the angel. His mind was working rapidly. He was aware that no sleeping soldier in the rows of bunks stirred. Mechanically he began to pull on his trousers and feel for his shoes, his eyes never leaving the radiant loveliness of the being before him. The angel's gaze was so full of love he felt no fear. In an instant they began to rise, and effortlessly the ceiling opened, and then the barrack's roof, and Ivan and the angel flew through time and space to another world.

The grass was deep and lush and seemed to stretch to the very horizon of this unfamiliar planet. It was a fresh and vivid green. Dazed, Ivan followed the angel, and after what seemed a long time they came to a brook. Its waters were as clear as glass so Ivan could see to the bed of the stream, and the brightness of the water dazzled his eyes. The angel passed over the brook without effort and turned questioningly when Ivan held back.

"Why do you fear, Vanya?" The voice was unhurried and tender. Inexplicably a horror of snakes had entered Ivan's mind.

"Snakes." As he said the word his glance moved through thick grass under his feet. The strangeness of what was happening gripped him in an unreasoning fear.

Although the angel was a distance from him, Ivan heard his voice as if the shining creature were standing by his side. "Do not be afraid. You are with me. Here it is not as on the earth. Here there are no snakes."

As suddenly as it had come, the fear left him, and Ivan moved easily over the brook. In the brilliance of this world, every detail of blade of grass and petal of flower stood out as if floodlit. The patterns of the bark upon the trees were indescribably beautiful. The expanse of the branches were profoundly graceful, so luminous that the light seemed to pour from within each tree. Instinctively Ivan lifted his eyes to the sky, gazing in every direction. There was no sun.

When his eyes returned to the angel there was a form beside the being, more exalted and at the same time somehow more loving in his brilliance than even the angel. In some way the angel seemed to do him deference, and Ivan knew him to be the apostle John. Through the angel, the apostle communicated with him. Ivan stood transfixed, his mind absorbing every holy word. A series of three beings followed the apostle, recognized in some mysterious way by Ivan to be David, Moses, and Daniel. So intense was Ivan's concentration and so overwhelming his awe and joy that when the last form was gone Ivan felt he would fall into a deep sleep. But the angel, now alone in the streaming light, spoke again.

"We have travelled a long way and you are tired. Come and sit."

The tree under which Ivan sat was large and welcoming with a fragrance that reminded him in some unexplained way of the grape fields of Moldavia. If the angel had not spoken again Ivan felt he would be content to sit for ever, smelling the tree and looking at the landscape in the sparkling light.

"I wish to show you the heavenly city, the new Jerusalem. But if you see it as it is, you cannot remain in the body you now have. And there is still much work for you left on earth." There seemed a silence before the angel resumed speaking. "We will fly together to another planet and I will show you the light of this city for you to know, while you are yet alive in your earth body, that in certainty there is a new Jerusalem."

In an instant they flew to another planet where there were high mountains. Again, the glory of the light illuminated every detail of this world. Ivan's gaze rested on diamond streams coursing down the mountain slopes into mists that rose from vividly green valleys. When they had come to a very deep canyon, the angel and Ivan descended until they were at the bottom.

The angel seemed a flame of joy, the Voice more ceremonious and jubilant than Ivan had yet heard it. "Vanya, look upwards and you will see this light of the new Jerusalem."

At the first glance Ivan recoiled in dismay. The brillance was so intense that even though he had seen it only for a second, he was sure he had been blinded. The angel spoke immediately. "Nothing will happen to you. Look."

No man rescued from a desert ever drank water more thirstily than Ivan drank in the splendour of that light. So great was its power it could be felt, tasted, heard. The sight of it was not a sensation of his eyes but of his whole being. Ivan could have wept with grief and disappointment when the angel said, "The time has come to fly back to earth."

At the instant that Ivan's feet touched the floor beside his bunk, three things happened. The angel disappeared, the bugle for reveille sounded, and the lights in the room were snapped on. Staring stupidly at his neat bed and himself fully dressed, Ivan heard a gentle laugh from the bunk beside him. Grigorii Fedorovich Chernykh, his neighbour, was also a Moldavian and took a fraternal interest in his strange countryman. Now Chernykh was pulling himself expertly out of his bunk and shoving his feet into trouser legs as he whispered in a conspiratorial tone, "Vanya, where were you last night?"

With a tremendous effort Ivan pulled his thoughts together. The barrack was alive with bodies hurtling past his bunk to the door. Good-natured bantering, the groaning of exhausted soldiers, the flash of uniforms seemed unreal. He turned to look intently at Chernykh.

"You don't mean that you didn't see me getting undressed and into bed last night? We turned in at the same time."

Chernykh was buttoning his shirt rapidly. "You went to bed the same time as I did, all right, and to sleep, too. But you didn't sleep long. I woke up about three A.M. and your bunk was empty. Vanya, you were nowhere in this room." Reaching for his jacket, he gave Ivan a sly smile. "Of all people, did you actually go absent last night?"

He had not been dreaming! He *had* journeyed with the angel! Excitement tore through Ivan like electricity. They were moving hurriedly to the door.

His voice shook as he spoke. "Let's ask the duty officer if anyone left during the night."

The duty officer was indignant. "Certainly no one left the room. Get going! Are you trying to get me arrested?"

Ivan and Grigorii Chernykh moved out into the morning, both in silence. Finally Chernykh broke the spell of strangeness with a question, and Ivan began to tell him about the angel.

By that evening, Ivan's account had spread through the unit. Nobody believed it, Chernykh thought with satisfaction. In spite of Ivan's sincerity, his stories were impossible. Yet they contained a mystery that made everyone uncomfortable. How was it possible to go five days without food and not be ill? How could a man stand in below-zero frost for hours and not be cold? And if Ivan Vasilievich had not left the barracks all night, yet was not in the room, where did he go?

Chernykh stretched on his bunk. Four hours of free time a month was too precious to waste on day-dreaming. He reached for a pencil and paper. He would write home. But he remained on his back, staring at the ceiling.

Perhaps the Polit-Ruk would get to the bottom of it. For a full month they had been relentlessly questioning Ivan until Grigorii wondered how he could remain sane under the pressure. For most men, army life was a merciless ordeal as it was. They were kept in a run all day long from the six A.M. reveille to the ten P.M. lights-out. And when they all should have been sleeping, there were the night battle alarms. How they dreaded the siren in the early hours of the morning that pulled them out of bed and propelled them, half-conscious, into a simulated enemy attack in the frozen night. Chernykh had a score to settle with the army for what had happened at the last alarm. Snow had been falling so thickly he had been unable to see the way. Straining his eyes to peer through the swirling snow he had plunged into an open well. Shouting over the wind and the snow and hanging on to the sides of the well for his life, Grigorii had been dragged out by a fellow soldier. With the water freezing on his *valenki*, his trouser legs stiff as cement, he had gone through the manoeuvres shaking violently with the cold.

But they were never awakened only once in a night. Speechless with cold and exhaustion, the men would fall into their bunks only to be aroused again an hour or so later to repeat the whole pandemonium. Grigorii had lost count, but from his initial furious records (he had intended to produce them for his family on his first leave) he knew the alarms were sounded every second or third night. It was unscientific to expect men to train and study the next day on three or four hours' sleep.

How Ivan Vasilievich bore up under the constant interrogations in addition to the regular schedule Grigorii could not imagine. He had seen Ivan summoned from meals, from study periods, from sleep. Day or night, it didn't matter. Ivan's bunk was often empty these nights.

He was in trouble, all right. There had been too many incidents, too many unexplainable happenings. Perhaps Chernykh didn't agree that the Baptists were enemies of the state. But it was certain they were fanatical and foolish. One didn't argue with the Red army. It was hopeless to think one could withstand. If an officer said cabbages were sunflowers, they were sunflowers.

In a way, perhaps it came down to a question of obedience. Perhaps that was why the Polit-Ruk was dealing so decisively with Moiseyev. After all, in a manoeuvre, where would any of them be if one of them wouldn't obey orders? Chernykn stretched again in his bunk, the paper and pencil for his letter still idle on the coarse blanket. He had heard from one of the men in his unit that the commissar for the whole Crimean Polit-Ruk was visiting Colonel Malsin. There was talk that Moiseyev would be sent to the military detention centre in Sverdlovsk in the Urals. With a determination to put it out of his mind, Chernykh seized his pencil. It had nothing to do with him. It certainly was not related to *his* telling the men Ivan's story about going up to another planet with an angel. Ivan spoke openly to anyone about God or His angels. Writing furiously, Chernykh tried to forget. Last evening, walking back to the barracks from a field drill, he had been afraid to look deeply into the night sky.

The landscape had long withdrawn into winter as the train jolted from side to side along the icy tracks. Fields, woods, small lakes, ravines glided past the half-open sliding door of the special railway car used for military prisoners. Wooden benches were piled in a shelf formation along the sides and centre of the car where the prisoners sat or slept in the airless dusk, some quarrelling, some chatting, most wrapped in their own bitter thoughts.

Ivan stayed close to the partially open door, breathing in the cold air and ignoring the arguments that sprang up from time to time about the door's closing or remaining open. A sense of deep peace pervaded the sweep of the land that drifted dreamlike before his view. The guard, a private from a base outside of Moscow, leaned against the shuddering walls of the car, his gun slung loosely over his arm, his head nodding in sleep. Waves of irritability rippled over the crowd of prisoners, came to nothing, and ebbed away. Ivan felt himself to be suspended between the mixture of soldiers behind him in the car and the remote countryside.

His mind reviewed his attempts to demonstrate his determination to be a good soldier. In his political sessions, he had made a point of explaining that the Bible taught believers to love the country in which they live, to respect its authorities, and to give them all that is due.

Instead of success, his efforts had resulted in his being pulled out of his bunk in the middle of the night and driven over frozen back roads to the prison train bound for Sverdlovsk, a military prison two thousand kilometres in the direction of Siberia.

They had left the plains of central Russia as they journeyed east, and Ivan watched the dusky blue curves of snowhills rising in the twilight. Only two days before he had been brought before the area commissar, Maj. Andrei Dolotov from Simferopol. Dolotov's almond-shaped eyes had been gloomy as they viewed Ivan. He seemed a strangely passive and unhurried man for an officer in such high position, and he had had a withdrawn and secretive manner that gave his bulky body the appearance of a wall. His way of speaking was emotionless and hushed.

He had seemed mildly surprised that Ivan had been in the Red army for nearly two months and still had not adapted to army life. He had reviewed his records. Every effort had been made to rehabilitate Moiseyev, to give him opportunity to change his views, to reform politically, but he had refused to co-operate. His file contained complaints from Odessa, from the Polit-Ruk of Kerch, and from the officers and men of Moiseyev's own unit. There had been the problem of Moiseyev spreading his subversive ideas among the other men, so that they were becoming contaminated with his un-

desirable ideology. This was, of course, in direct viola-
tion of orders from the polit-officers. Dolotov was curious as to why Moiseyev would not obey.

His voice was so quiet Ivan was unsure he had finished speaking, and hesitated a moment. There was an
oppressiveness in the room that made it hard to think.
Ivan suddenly felt that he needed air. With a great
effort he prayed briefly and took a breath. His head
suddenly cleared as he addressed himself to Dolotov.

"Comrade commissar, the Bible teaches believers to
obey the authorities placed over them. It is my deep
desire to do this. But the Bible further teaches us that
our supreme Master is God. His authority demands from
us complete obedience and commitment. I beg of you to
understand that I have two sets of loyalties—loyalty to
the state and loyalty to God. If I am commanded to do
something that would cause me to disobey God, then I
am obliged to put my loyalty to Him first."

A dark flicker of change passed over the commissar's
face; then he seemed to ponder an idea before he
spoke.

"You are bound and shackled by these Baptist ideas.
Very well—perhaps it would be helpful of you to experience the seriousness of your position if you had a
taste of real prison. It is possible such a procedure will
be more effective than all the re-education programmes
in Kerch. Then we will see if you do not change your
story."

Why the commissar had chosen such a far-flung
place, Ivan could not guess. There were prisons close
by on the Black Sea. Perhaps the ordeal of a long journey in the dead of winter was part of the strategy.

Ivan inhaled deeply. The air coming in the train door
had somehow changed. It seemed heavier, with a
chemical sharpness. Behind him in the car, there was a
stirring. People began gathering their things more

closely about them. An old man produced a rope from the inside of a lumpy blanket and began deftly tying the blanket into a bundle. A burly Cossack finished off the pan of melted snow that rocked on the floor in front of the small heater. An unshaven sergeant cursed as the train lurched suddenly. Two young soldiers, their eyes hard with anger, stood together. In the far distance, almost melting into the deep twilight, Ivan could see a forest of smoke-stacks pouring black clouds into the sky. Here and there tongues of orange flame seemed to lick the heavens.

The old man hunched behind Ivan at the door, peering out ahead of the train as far as he could see. " 'Sverdlovsk, the City on the Ridge.' " His words were spoken in the lifting, questioning accent of Odessa. " 'Worker and Warrior.' Well, I'm to be both there, and so are you, comrade." The guard, now roused from his dozing, pushed the old soldier roughly from the door and stationed himself beside Ivan without comment.

The engine began to brake. Shuddering, the train rattled and bumped over switches. The men crowded as close as they dared to the open door, straining to see the city, eager for the end of the tedium of the long journey. A pale star twinkled above a row of firs along the side of the track. Ivan watched its gentle light. His mind stirred, remembering a fragment of Scripture that his father loved "And those who have insight will shine brightly like the brightness of the expanse of heaven, and those who lead the many to righteousness, like the stars for ever and ever."

7

He goes from the bear to fall in with the wolves

His cell was very small and cold and without light.
When his eyes became accustomed to the dark he
could make out a bunk along one wall and only enough
space in the cell for him to fully extend his arm and
touch the opposite side. The cell door had a small window near the top through which the guards shone
flashlights during the night. His bones ached with in-
activity. Painfully he pulled off his boots and pressed
his stockinged feet against the damp cement wall.
After the constant swaying of the train, the clatter of
the wheels, and the hum of prisoners' voices, the cell
was grave-like in its deathly stillness and silence. Ivan
lay in the cold, his exhaustion unrelieved by sleep. The
old man's words, "warrior and worker", turned in his
mind like the wheels of the train. His mind moved to
his experience on the heavenly planet with the angel.
"You still have much work to do," the angel had said.
Warrior and worker. Cold fear like a thin sheet of ice
seemed to hang over his bunk close above him in the
dark. What work was ahead? What warring? The
fear, as if suspended by ropes, seemed to slip a notch
closer to his face. "My soul waits in silence for God
only; from Him is my salvation. He only is my rock
and my salvation, my stronghold; I shall not be greatly
shaken."

The interrogation room of the prison was in a frame
building a few paces from Ivan's cellblock. It was a
spacious room, with sagging wood floors and a painted
radiator that ran the length of the room and reminded

Ivan suddenly of his kindergarten on the collective farm in Moldavia. Some ferns at the end of the room decorated a few wooden steps leading to a very small platform on which was placed a picture of Lenin. Ivan guessed that the room was used also for cultural events.

An official of the prison sat behind a conference table covered in purple cloth at the side of the room. Four other men in plain clothes sat at another table near by. But it was the prison officer who spoke. In his hands were Ivan's documents.

It was commendable that Moiseyev had taken the oath of loyalty to the Red army. This was something Baptists often refused. Moiseyev had started off well, but had quickly proved to be an agitator, refusing correction, determined to cling to his old beliefs and to reject Soviet socialist teaching, seeking to persuade others to do the same. His loyalty to the Red army was under question, and his attitude towards authority ran afoul of all military life. In spite of dedicated efforts on the part of his superiors towards his re-education, Moiseyev had spurned all such assistance and had created incident after incident in his desire to disrupt. It was an example of the clemency of the Soviet state that he was given so many opportunities to change his views. There was no question that already there was much evidence against him. Did he know that he could be brought to trial and sentenced to prison for seven years? Article 142 of the criminal code could be brought to bear since he had openly admitted he was a member of an unregistered Baptist group. There were articles 181 and 182 concerning bearing false witness. It had been established that much of his conversation was composed of utter, impossible lies, and that he had several times perjured himself. Article 190, paragraph one, was relevant. In his letter writing he had deliberately distributed literature containing false statements slandering the Soviet state and the Red army. His letters to his family had been copied and were positive proof. In the matter of article 58, paragraph 10, concerning anti-Soviet agitation, his situation was very serious indeed. Already he was inside the walls of a prison. Still, he was given yet another opportunity to avail himself of re-education here in Sverdlovsk. If he refused to co-operate, persuasive measures would be administered.

Ivan spoke slowly, concentrating on his words as he formed them. It was often difficult not to be able to speak in his native Moldavian. Russian constructions and endings would vanish from his memory when he was tired or most needed them.

"I have done nothing against the Soviet state. I have desired to quietly do my work in the army and at the same time worship and praise God. As for disturbances, it is the military who makes them, not I. As for staying here for seven years, I will, if it pleases God. If not, then tomorrow I shall be sent back to my base. Of this I am certain."

The new cell to which Ivan was sent was a tiny cubicle like a cage, four feet square. Taking up most of the floor space was a small bench similar to the ones small children use in schools. Like the first cell, it was very cold and without light. For two days Ivan painfully huddled on the stool, time wrapped around him like a dark cloth, torn only by the opening of the cell door for bread and weak coffee to be passed in and the waste bucket to be passed out.

Once or twice when awakening in a suffocating panic after a sleep, the sense of Christ's presence with Him was so tangible and quieting that Ivan wept with joy, the freezing agony in his cramped limbs dulled.

Hot pain shot through his muscles when he was finally pulled out of the cell and stood upright in the blazing light of the corridor. A guard jabbed him with the barrel of a machine gun, prodding him outside into the intense cold to the interrogation building. The same prison authority stood beside the table, his hand fingering a dog whip he had tucked into his belt.

"So you are out of your hole and breathing good socialist air! It seems you did not spend your time begging for release in the past two days; you have done some thinking, then. Perhaps you are willing now to take off the blindfold you have put over your own eyes and to enter the real Soviet world."

Ivan felt the rims of his eyes burning in the pale sunlight. He tried to control an irrational feeling that if he spoke his voice would be too faint to be heard. The official's face blazed before him. His words were slow in coming.

"There is a Scripture that says the lives of believers are hid with Christ in God. That is the real world and I am in it."

At Ivan's reply the officer stared speechless for a long minute. Grasping his whip he struck the conference table dramatically. He struck it again and again as if lashing a beast, his eyes never for a moment leaving Ivan's face.

As a child on the collective farm, Ivan had seen a drunken worker beat an ox. The animal, yoked and tied in a pen, had no escape. Blood had run down its legs and dripped in the mud from the flesh laid bare by the worker's whip. Some shift in Ivan's mind suddenly filled him with horror.

"This is the real world!" the officer was shouting, advancing to Ivan, the whip erect in his shaking hand. "You imagine that God can hide you from what is ahead for you? We will see how you feel when your

God does not save you from the reality I will choose for you."

For a moment Ivan braced himself for the cut of the whip he expected. But the officer wheeled abruptly, his steps firing like bullets across the long room. In an instant two guards appeared, shoving Ivan ahead of them towards the prison.

Ivan hesitated in fear at the small door opened for him by the guard. "Inside, inside!" The guard heaved his rifle into Ivan's back, sending him skidding into the small cell. The door was instantly slammed and bolted. Water splashed over his boots and streamed down the walls. A dim light hung in a cage from the low ceiling, partially obscured by a crisscross of ice-covered pipes. Water dripped rapidly from every pipe, trickled from the seams, spurted from the connections, and drained sluggishly into a drain coated with ice in a corner of the cell. Almost immediately Ivan discovered it was not possible to stand anywhere out of the dripping, icy water. It showered his coat and ran down the back of his neck as he hunched into his clothing. An impulse to pound on the milky ice of the door seized him. Within minutes he began to shake violently. "Be gracious unto me, O God, be gracious unto me, for my soul takes refuge in Thee; and in the shadow of Thy wings I will take refuge, until destruction passes by. I will cry to God Most High, to God who accomplishes all things for me. He will send from heaven and save me." Through the ragged curtain of water he was startled by the unmoving eyes of a guard watching him from the door peephole. "Thou hast taken account of my wanderings; put my tears in Thy bottle; are they not in Thy book? Then my enemies will turn back in the day when I call; this I know, that God is for me."

By pressing himself into a corner of the cell, his back to the downfall, Ivan found he could avoid most of the water. Over and over he repeated the words of the psalm that seemed to come from beside him, from all around the cell. At the same time, his mind, independent in some way from the Scriptures he was half-shouting, was in a torment to escape.

As time passed the frenzied shaking of his body slowed into a terrible ache that began to spread from every joint in his body and to his back and head. His feet, pressed into his soaking boots, were in an agony of pain that forced him on to the floor of the cell. Half-kneeling in the ice and water, he began to imagine he was in an Orthodox cathedral with banks of candles flickering warmly on richly framed icons. Many people were worshipping all around and a glory of music and praise filled the cathedral. The service was long, very long.

This time the interrogation room was within the prison block itself, a large stone room with a smoky fire burning near a desk. Ivan lay on a cot at the far end of the room away from the fireplace, an electric heater glowing on the floor beside him. How he had been brought to the cot or how long ago, he had no idea. He was aware of the smell of singed cloth as he began to rouse. Stiffly he raised himself. A high, barred window, dry walls, a few prison officials around the fireplace came into view and then slid away as he fell back. A guard standing behind him yanked him violently to a sitting position, cursing the dead weight of Ivan's body.

It seemed unimportant what the officer was saying, but Ivan tried to listen. He felt terribly ill. ". . . You will receive your ration of bread and coffee. It is our determination to return you to your base at Kerch conformable to the standards for a Soviet youth. Those are our orders. You have proven to be obstinate, Moiseyev, but I think we have demonstrated to you that you are not going to have your way. As soon as you indicate your willingness to reform, we will consider that sufficient progress to discharge you from here and see that you are able to resume your training period as the military intends and as is your obligation to the Soviet Union."

A mug of weak coffee was placed on the table beside Ivan's cot, a thin tin plate of bread serving as an unsteady lid. Prayerfully Ivan lifted the cup to his lips, breathing in the steam of the coffee. Never had the symbolic wine of the Lord's Supper seemed as holy as this cup. Christ's words flooded his mind. "This is My blood of the covenant, which is to be shed on behalf of many." With a surge of love, Ivan drained the mug. Reverently he broke off a chunk of bread. "Take, eat; this is My body."

"We have some papers here, Moiseyev, which you might wish to sign," the officer continued. "They indicate your willingness to co-operate fully with Colonel Malsin, commander of your base in Kerch, and to give your complete obedience to any order that comes from any officer of any department for the duration of your service in the Red army. When you finish eating, your signature is all I need to begin the procedure for your release."

In the following days Ivan was even further plunged into the prison's nightmare world. "You are being sent to the 'room of the frozen'," an old guard had whispered to him. "Give in! You won't live." How many hours *could* he live, Ivan wondered, in a refrigeration cell? Light snow covered the cells on the walls and ceiling as the thick door thudded shut. Time passed with his fear mounting. Pain began, and still the door remained sealed. The whiteness of the cell seemed luminous. Scriptures he knew, memories of home, and the knowledge of the light-filled place to which he was going finally quieted him. Gradually the fear and pain subsided and he began to doze. Profoundly thankful, he lay down on the floor of the cell.

At the beginning, he had thought the pressing and squeezing was a dream. He was a cosmonaut, drifting into freezing space. But the pressure suit was real and the shouts in his ears, "Will you give in? Will you change your beliefs?" jarred him into consciousness. He was strangling. He couldn't breathe. In space there were angels appearing and disappearing in their brilliance. "For He will give His angels charge concerning you, to guard you in all your ways." *If I explode, I shall explode into heaven.* The pressure was increased. Ivan tried to help the suit, tried himself to break through the anguish and suffocation to that lush place he had been with the angel. "Will you change your beliefs? We will stop the pressure. Change or you will be here seven years." He was not sure they could hear his voice. He gasped the words with tremendous effort. "If it is God's will, I will be here. If not . . . gone tomorrow. . . ."

The prison officer crumpled his empty Belomor package into the waste basket by his desk and fumbled through his drawer for more cigarettes. He lit one and inhaled with concentration. He had no further instructions on how to proceed. As a soldier Moiseyev ought to be charged and sentenced by a military tribunal. It was possible to keep him indefinitely at Sverdlovsk, of course, but he had no orders to that effect. Technically the prison committee had carried out its responsibility. For twelve days Moiseyev had been exposed to the most thorough of interrogations and re-education techniques. Other than shipping him to Kerch in a box, there was no more to be done. Moiseyev would have a long uncomfortable train journey back to Kerch in which to recover and think over his future. Let the commissars in Kerch or Odessa worry about what to do with him. They could not complain that Sverdlovsk techniques had not been vigorously applied. Sverdlovsk would wash its hands of Moiseyev.

The officer's eye was caught by a small bird alighting on the smudged snow of his window sill. It pecked at the frozen crumbs he placed there day by day. There were fewer birds every year since all the new industry came in. He watched the bird anxiously. The sky was dirty. The snow was dirty. Everything was dirty these days.

8

*You shared your bread with me, and in the act gave
me back all Russia*

The end of winter was unseasonably warm for Kerch.
Lace circles of slight snow still fell lazily in the early
mornings, but the rigour of training eased a little in the
milder temperatures. The Polit-Ruk had warned Ivan to
say nothing about his assignment in Sverdlovsk—an
order easy to obey since his every moment was engaged in a hectic programme of catching up to his unit
in military and political studies. In addition, he had
been assigned as chauffeur to Colonel Malsin himself,
with sudden and unpredictable calls for his services.
Once in a while, when he was seated in class with the
other soldiers, Ivan's sped-up world seemed to slow
down and blend momentarily into a peaceful whole.

The horrors of Sverdlovsk were retold but once, in
quite murmurs over a chessboard to Sergei. The bishops
and pawns and knights never moved more erratically
as Ivan and his friend sat in an obscure corner of the
common room. Verses of Scripture and phrases of encouragement floated back and forth almost impercept-
ibly under the swells of laughter and banter that rolled
over the room.

As spring came, Ivan began to notice a wonderful
thing happening. Even on days when a time of prayer
was impossible, increasingly he was experiencing an
almost overwhelming sense of the presence of God. Love
blazed like an icon candle inside him. He was astonished that no blast of injustice from outside caused it
to flicker. Even tonight, hurrying to the evening lec-

ture on scientific atheism, he felt no impatience. He was tired; his muscles ached. But praise to God welled up in his heart.

There had been no need for haste. The soldiers were clustered around a glowing heater in the front of the classroom, joking as they faced the red electric coils. Ivan sat down and rested his head on the arm of his desk. His bunkmate, Vladimir Albu, noticed him and was not surprised that he could sleep even in such clamour. The wall clock showed several minutes after the hour. The instructor was still missing from the room.

The men began diffidently to take their seats, unwilling to leave the comfort of the heater, yet uneasy at being found in the wrong place if an officer suddenly arrived after all. But the time wore on. Suddenly Vladimir had an idea. "Let's have our own lecture! Let's have a political debate."

Interest stirred slightly. That would be one way of passing the time. No one dared to leave the classroom without an order.

"Our comrade, Ivan Vasilievich, has sometimes taken a stand against the theories of this class. Yet we have not heard his position fully articulated. We shall debate the question: What is the difference between Ivan's God and our god (which he claims is the state)?"

Ivan had been praying before the class began. Now, with an inward lift he agreed to the debate. Some of the men pulled out their cigarettes and twisted towards him in their chairs. There was an intensity in the classroom.

Vladimir started it off. "All right, Ivan, who is your God?"

Ivan's pleasure at what looked like an opportunity to preach to the class was short-lived. "My God," he began, "is almighty and all-powerful——"

In the middle of the room a sergeant from Armenia

coughed on his cigarette and stamped impatiently on the floor. He groaned in exasperation. "Just a minute, Moiseyev. Your God is *all-powerful*?"

"Yes."

"He can do anything?"

"Yes."

The sudden challenge in the sergeant's eyes was unmistakable. The soldiers stared in enjoyment.

"If your God is all-powerful and can do anything, prove it!"

Murmurs of assent came from all corners of the room. Ivan's life had awakened disturbing questions in many minds. The sergeant spoke loudly. "If your God can do anything, let Him get me leave tomorrow to go home. Then I'll believe in Him!"

"Fair enough!" Vladimir exclaimed. Here would be something scientific. Black and white. Yes or no. Leaves were rare. There would be nothing inconclusive and mysterious about a contest like this.

Responses to the challenge came quickly.

"Yes, Ivan Vasilievich. I've listened to you! Up to now, everything you've said sounds like fairy tales. But if your God gives Pyotr Alexandrovich Prokhorov a leave then we'll believe there is a God in the sky."

"Right! If your God does it, we will believe that He is a living God and can do everything!"

"Most certainly. Let your God prove Himself! Then even we will believe."

Gazing at the excited men, Ivan prayed fervently in his spirit. The soldiers waited, gradually sobered by the earnest struggle they could see in Ivan's face.

Lord! Can this be from You? Will You be tempted by men? What they ask, is this right, Lord?

"Come on, Ivan Vasilievich! Let's prove your living God!" The sergeant shifted uneasily in his chair. Somehow the challenge was being taken too seriously.

Suddenly Ivan thought of the Old Testament contest between the prophets of Baal and Elijah. With a new inward quietness he asked again for direction. Unmistakably the words came into his consciousness: "Tell them I will do this."

Every eye in the room stared as Ivan answered. His voice had an assurance that astonished the men. Turning to the sergeant he spoke clearly enough for every person to easily hear his reply. "Tomorrow the Lord says you will go home on leave. Now, you must do what I tell you. Throw away your cigarette." The sergeant obeyed. "And now pull the pack out of your pocket."

With an elaborate shrug Prokhorov produced his pack of cigarettes. Pulling himself up from his desk he walked slowly to the heater and dropped the pack behind the red-hot grate. In a moment it flared up and burned brightly.

For the first time Ivan noticed that a large crowd of soldiers had gathered at the two side doors of the lecture room, spilling over into a line around the walls of the room. A stillness like an invisible mist seemed to hang in the air. Finally the spell was broken by the arrival of several breathless officers. The evening's class began.

It wasn't until after lights-out that Ivan was able to speak again with the sergeant. He found him lying sleepless on his bunk, staring at the sprinkle of stars he could see from the window near by. The assurance of Ivan's reply had unnerved him. He had been able to think of nothing else all evening. It was absurdity, but over and over he found himself in a state of excitement. He half-believed that something might happen in the morning!

"There is much to talk to you about, comrade." 's voice was a whisper. Prokhorov raised himself on one elbow, pulling his blanket over his shoulder.

"Why aren't you asleep, Moiseyev?"

Ivan smiled. "Because there is much to talk to you about. Since you will become a believer tomorrow, there are many things I must tell you."

"You're crazy, Moiseyev. Why don't you go back to bed? And you're going to get cold."

Pyotr Prokhorov squinted nervously at Ivan in the dark. The story of Moiseyev standing all night in below-zero December weather flashed into his mind. He was reassured to see that Ivan carried his blanket with him and swept it around himself as he huddled on the end of Prokhorov's bunk.

"You said you would believe if God gives you a leave tomorrow morning?"

"Of course. Many of us said we would believe."

"But it is for you, Pyotr Alexandrovich, that God is going to do this miracle. I must tell you what the Bible teaches."

In spite of a feeling of uneasiness, Prokhorov's interest was captured by the things Moiseyev said. Never before had he heard such ideas spoken with such absolute conviction. The teachings of the Bible were a world away from the strange icons he had seen in museums or the bizarre stories he had been told about the Christian Scriptures. Was it possible that the emptiness in himself he had long ago accepted as part of the human condition was a longing for God as Moiseyev said? If God exists!

"Is there a prayer house in your city?"

The sergeant was amused. "You mean for the old ladies? Anyway, I do not think so."

"It is not only old ladies who go. Many men. Many young people. They will be able to help you. I can find out for you some names of believers in your city, but it will take time. The brethren in Kerch will know."

"There are people that believe like you do, in Kerch? And in my own city?"

Ivan grinned suddenly. "Of course! And you are going to minister joy to them when you tell them what the Lord has done. What praises they will raise! How they will welcome you!"

Prokhorov felt intensely uncomfortable.

"In the meetings of believers there will be some who have Bibles. At least one of the pastors will have a Bible. Probably most. Someone sometime will lend you Scriptures to read and they will suggest where to begin. I am sorry I have no Bible to lend you. For the moment you will have to believe what I say is true. I want to tell you all I can of what the Bible says. We must discuss the world and man and sin and God's plan for man's salvation."

The night wore on as the whispered monologue became a discussion. Two hours before reveille, Prokhorov stood and stretched quietly as Ivan ended a prayer. "Moiseyev, my head is so full of ideas, I may never sleep again. But thank you, comrade. Morning comes."

At the sound of the bugle, Ivan awoke immediately with a thrill of expectation. This would be a wonderful day. For once he was eager for the morning ordeal of long-distance running. Perhaps he might find Sergei and be able to tell him about Prokhorov and what the Lord had promised to do. But unexpectedly, there was to be no morning drill for Ivan.

The night delivery of bread had not been made. Ivan would leave for Kerch and pick up the bread supply that would be needed for breakfast. Ivan climbed into the cab of the small truck, singing as he turned the key in the ignition.

When he pulled back into the base almost an hour

later, he was surprised at a small commotion near the garages where the trucks were parked. Curiously he jumped down from the truck and ran towards the crowd of soldiers milling about the gate. They were men from his own unit.

Excited shouting split the air.

"Ivan Vasilievich! Comrade Prokhorov has left on leave! Prokhorov has gone! We have been waiting to tell you!"

The soldiers were gathering around Ivan eagerly.

A general or a colonel had called their base from headquarters in Odessa with the order that Prokhorov be given immediate leave to go home. He had departed ten minutes after the phone call, running and leaping like a crazy man, jumping on the back of a mail truck that was leaving for the train.

Vladimir pushed to the front of the crowd and grabbed Ivan's arm. "The officers came out when they saw us all laughing and cheering. We told them what happened last night at the political lecture. You should have seen their faces when we said everything had turned out as you said, Vanya! Major Gidenko came out to see what was going on and when he heard the story, he sent some soldiers off to the train to bring Prokhorov back again. They left in a cloud of snow, skidding all the way to the front gates. They arrived at the train station to see the very end of the train disappearing in the distance. Prokhorov was gone!"

Major Gidenko had only a moment of impatience as he watched the scene of Moiseyev's return to the base through binoculars from his office window. Good thing he had ordered Moiseyev brought immediately to him. With satisfaction he observed Ivan being pulled away from the excited group and the soldiers dispersed to their work. Gidenko had assumed that after Sverdlovsk, Moiseyev would settle down. He had sent a communiqué to Commissar Dolotov in Simferopol with assurances that the matter was in hand. Yet here was another disruption. Moiseyev was achieving a kind of fame in his unit. He was popular and a good soldier, and the men were interested in him and in his Baptist views. It was impossible to train a unit for military and political effectiveness with continuing incidents. There was something altogether unexplained about Moiseyev. Colonel Malsin, acting for Commissar Dolotov, had suggested Gidenko get to the bottom of it or arrange a transfer for Moiseyev to another unit where he was not known.

There was more involved in this present situation than met the eye. Moiseyev must have had contacts in Odessa to have known about Prokhorov's leave. Gidenko felt depressed. These difficulties were time-consuming and involved an uncomfortable number of men. He had lost confidence that the Moiseyev problem would be easily resolved. The question of Prokhorov was another matter. He had always been politically sound. Some troublemaker had invented the story that Prokhorov had declared himself to be a believer. That could be cleared up when Prokhorov returned.

It was too bad that Colonel Malsin had decided to become involved. There were enough leaders in the Polit-Ruk to handle ten Moiseyevs. But Malsin was particularly sensitive about religious matters. Gidenko rose and saluted as Malsin's small figure came into the room. Unfortunate that Malsin wouldn't leave these matters to others.

"If it weren't for his popularity with the men, *I* could have him taken care of." Malsin's sharp voice pointed accusingly at Gidenko. "He's an excellent chauffeur—believe me, I watch him carefully. Always on time, car in perfect condition, always sober, always correct in every way. He's even earned merit points from various officers. Merit points, and he's only been in six or seven months!"

A long time, Gidenko thought, for a young man to defy the authority of the Red army. It was difficult to explain.

"I've seen how Baptists operate before this. They're stubborn and underhanded," Malsin continued, "and they're secretive. But they make sure they have good work records. They know more about the laws of our country—or think they do—more than all you political lawyers put together."

"Technically, according to the law, Moiseyev has committed no criminal act," Gidenko responded. "No doubt he is aware of that." Gidenko opened the window of his office to let in some fresh sea air. Spring was a beautiful season in Kerch—it came early and stayed late. He took a deep breath and wished Moiseyev would arrive.

"Nonsense! You'll have me questioning your competence, Gidenko. I could have Moiseyev arrested this minute as an agitator. For one thing, there are laws, I believe, against anti-Soviet activity and the propagation of religion. Moiseyev is guilty of both. And as far as that goes, there are those occasions, as you very well know, where some laws must be set aside and one is called upon to act 'administratively'."

Gidenko disliked debating with the colonel. "Unfortunately, Moiseyev cannot be dealt with quietly. He has become the centre of attention. The men in his unit must not misinterpret our actions as anti-religious, colonel. And as for his actions being anti-Soviet, that is clear to us, of course. It may not be so clear to the men. It is not altogether a simple problem."

Malsin frowned irritably at Gidenko as he lit a cigarette. The case had not been handled correctly from the beginning. Five days without food! A few hours in the snow! Time enough for him to fantasize a story about angels, that was all. And now another incident again with Moiseyev and his God in the leading role. Malsin's tense face was momentarily lit in the dim room by the flare of his match.

"There is a scientific explanation for Prokhorov's leave, if we can procure the facts. There are no mysteries in this world. There is only ignorance."

There was a brief knock as Ivan was escorted into the room. The door shut hastily.

Malsin inhaled deeply. The boy was handsome enough, with chiselled features and clear, steady eyes. His expression was attentive but set in a way Malsin did not like.

"Moiseyev, I'll come straight to the point. I am Colonel Malsin, the supreme commander of this entire base. I have reason to suspect you of subversive, anti-Soviet activity. In order to have known about the order which arrived at our base only this morning for a leave for Sgt. Pyotr Alexandrovich Prokhorov you would have had to work through accomplices in Odessa."

Gidenko turned in his chair and gazed impassively out of the window. Four storeys below and in front of his building, he could see passing soldiers glancing up from time to time. So word had been passed already that Moiseyev was being questioned once more.

"It has been established that you have been attempting to draw into your religious fantasies as many soldiers as possible who do not have a strong materialistic and socialist view of life. You have been trying in every way to tear them away from productive activities and active communist creative training and labour. As your commander I order you to desist immediately from all such activities and to fully confess your subversive activities."

The major swivelled slowly to face back into the room. Moiseyev had not flinched. He said nothing.

"First of all," Malsin continued in an even more brittle voice, "how did you learn of Prokhorov's impending leave? There was absolutely no advance notice of it at Kerch. I require a complete explanation."

Ivan's voice was steady and distinct. "Comrade colonel, I did not know that Sergeant Prokhorov would be granted a leave. God told me He would give him leave to demonstrate His existence. And God did."

Malsin flushed furiously. More distinctly, as if he had not heard, he repeated his question.

Gidenko wished he had had a drink. This was going to take a long time.

The morning dragged into the early afternoon, punctuated by fury and threats, elaborate intricate questionings on tracks familiar to Gidenko. Malsin's energy seemed enormous, yet Moiseyev answered quietly, sometimes waiting so long with his answers that Gidenko wondered if he were ill. Surely without breakfast and dinner the boy would wear down. Gidenko wished he would: the session seemed endless. And he could have handled it better himself.

Suddenly Malsin's deathly voice excused Moiseyev to his unit. As the door closed behind him Malsin spoke through clenched teeth. His face was white with anger. "And he eats Soviet bread!" he said.

9

The poor sing, the rich listen

Uncertainty had hung in the air all summer. Ivan had heard a rumour that he was to be sent away to another unit. He knew Malsin was determined to get rid of him. But the fragrant seaport spring gave way to the glories of summer and early autumn, and still he remained in Kerch, propelled through the hot days and nights by a schedule that left no time for speculation. He tried to excel in everything : political classes, target practice, callisthenics, advanced mechanics, his hours of chauffeuring, night drills, field manoeuvres. Each was an opportunity to bring glory to God.

But late this afternoon something more of the transfer had leaked out. He had been hurrying to the base post office before a class to mail a letter home when he heard his name raised in a small crowd of soldiers standing at the door of the officers' dining hall.

"What has Moiseyev *done*?" Vladimir Yakovlevich was demanding. "Is it not true that our Constitution guarantees freedom of conscience to anyone? Is it against the law to be a believer? What law does he break that he is so frequently questioned?"

Ivan could not hear the officer's reply or the curt response of the polit-officer.

A husky Ukrainian edged closer to the centre of the group. "Why is he to be sent away? What has he done to be transferred out of our Unit?" The officer began to answer again, but his reply was lost to Ivan as he pushed open the heavy door of the post office. His hand was unsteady as he sorted out the small kopecks for a stamp. Any incident was excuse enough for the political leader to initiate another series of interrogations. Colonel Malsin or Major Gidenko would be infuriated if informed that the men were defending Ivan.

Several sets of tyre tracks led down the road towards the lecture hall. They had been made earlier by the small pick-up truck that delivered wood for the kitchen ovens. Dust lay in the ruts and covered his boots as he walked. All over the world, he supposed, there were men and women who lived freely as Christians and bore witness to Jesus Christ. His eyes scanned the lush fields in the distance. They used to call this "Holy Russia", he was thinking. But no more.

A few leaves spun in the evening air, rocking to the ground in splashes of gold. As uncertain as his days were, the Lord was certain. His help would never fail. *Praise, praise, praise to God most high. Most holy, most worthy, most wonderful, mighty God. Prince of Peace.* He lifted his face in joy towards the evening sky. Flames of fire lit the heavens so brightly that the few early stars faded instantly in the glow.

Ivan leaned in terror against the trunk of a tree in a small grove on the corner of the road. The sky seemed to be pouring flame, yet the torrents of fire came no closer to the earth. Waves of warmth and sweetness melted his fear as he stared transfixed at the sky. Gradually letters appeared in the midst of the flames. So overwhelming was the spectacle that Ivan gazed uncomprehending at the scene. There was an inner urging. *Read!*

Like a child learning to spell he gazed at each individual letter. Slowly the message sank into his mind. *Ya pridu skoro* ("I will come soon"). They seemed to leap with a joy that grew in Ivan's heart. Over and over the words repeated themselves in a dance of celebration.

With a rush of despair Ivan realized that the vision was disappearing. The flames fell back into the darkness of the sky. Suddenly they were gone. Perhaps it was only a moment that he stood there before a passing classmate pulled his arm.

"Come on, Moiseyev. This is no time to day-dream. We'll be late for our lecture."

Blindly Ivan fell in beside him. A sense that his heart was breaking made it impossible for him to speak. His companion was chatting as they walked. Ivan tried to concentrate, to nod, to enter the hall normally, to take his seat composed. Like the others he took notes, trying to keep up with the instructor's rapid delivery. At the end of the lecture, like the others he snapped his briefcase shut and hurried to the next class, the evening drill, to the barracks, to bed. When the battle alarm was sounded in the middle of the sultry night, he was still awake, caught up in a joy and longing that made sleep impossible. Through the drill, through the second drill that came on the heels of the first, through the remaining hours of the night, he lay praying and wishing the angel on the planet had not told him he still had much work to do on earth.

The first light of morning that pulled Ivan out of bed still praising God, fell irritably on Colonel Malsin. He coughed wearily as he tried to sit up in bed and remember why this was an unpleasant day. In the apartment kitchen, he could hear his wife preparing breakfast and talking softly to their young son. The smell of fish hung on the air. He could hear the water being poured into the samovar for tea.

Ah! Today Unit 61968T was being assigned to the harvest detail at Zhostena. Moiseyev's unit. Malsin didn't like unfinished business. The problem with Moiseyev was that he had succeeded in winning so many friends in the unit. It wasn't hard to understand. He was personable enough, worked hard, helped anybody. Of course it was a technique to spread his teachings. But Gidenko was right. Really he had done nothing wrong. And he was clever enough to attract all the attention he could.

Malsin stirred his glass of tea. His wife, Galina, watched him pensively.

"It's bad business," he finally said, "letting Moiseyev go off with his unit to the harvesting. I should have transferred him to another unit where he isn't known. Steps could have been taken privately and quickly."

"It makes me nervous. All these strange stories about the boy. You say they have scientific explanations, but. . . ." Her voice trailed off and she turned her eyes to gaze at the brightening morning sky.

Malsin swallowed his tea so quickly he burned his tongue. "What are you saying, Lena? You of all people, a Soviet teacher, and you doubt that science can explain everything? That's very strange. I understood it is your very task to educate the young students in the spirit of Marxist–Leninism."

Impulsively his wife leaned across the table towards him. Her slightly greying hair was bleached in the modern way and a yellow strand fell across her cheek. Her wide-set blue eyes looked suddenly playful. "Volodia, don't be stuffy with me. Doesn't all this scientific materialism sometimes *bore* you? Surely it must."

Malsin threw a look over his shoulder at their son dressing in the bedroom as his wife continued.

"Don't you ever marvel that some of the best people in our country—the hardest-working, the most honest —are Moiseyev's Baptists?"

"What I wonder is how a woman of your education and position can speak this way!" Malsin became suddenly infuriated at the restless sigh his wife didn't bother to stifle. His voice quickened. "The very idea of God is a catch-all explanation for natural phenomena that is as yet not understood. Or what is worse, *God* is simply a word that has been used in our country's history for centuries to confirm injustice and support cruelty and hypocrisy. These things you know very well."

His burned tongue would be sore all day. Jamming his papers into his briefcase he ignored the plate of fish his wife placed on the table. "This cancer of religion must be cut out of our society if communism is to fully triumph. How can all citizens advance into the twenty-first century if some are still shackled to religious prejudices that have not been overcome? Where is the New Soviet Man then?"

Galina hesitated before she spoke. "But Volodia, we are told that the struggle against religion requires ideological weapons alone, since compulsory tactics increase religious fervour. You aren't thinking of compulsory tactics for young Moiseyev?" A memory troubled her face.

Malsin's voice was impatient. "When I need to answer to a schoolteacher for my military or political tactics I will join the line of ten-year-olds at your desk." It was a credit to him, he felt, that he would not slam the door.

The weeks in the harvest fields, living in tents and under the vast Ukrainian sky passed far too quickly for Ivan. Many of the others, especially soldiers from the cities, had grown tired of the drudgery of harvest and the bleakness of the bare countryside. The agricultural workers on the state farm, with their simple speech and muddy hands, were uninteresting to them, and in the evenings they yawned restlessly in the tents, reading or playing chess and hoping that the harvest would soon be in.

But for Ivan, it was home. Not that the collective on which his parents worked was as large as this one, nor was the harvest similar. But the feel of the hazy afternoon sun on his back, the smell of the earth, the sound of voices calling back and forth in the open air sometimes made him forget where he was, and he would straighten his back, expecting some of his brothers or his mother to be working near by.

It had been a good time of rest and spiritual refreshment, over too soon, Ivan thought. He sat watching the tow truck ahead of him as it pulled his own Zil-164 with its disabled driveshaft. The convoy of army trucks filled with earth and returning soldiers snaked over the rolling hills of the evening countryside towards Kerch.

Suddenly the peacefulness of Ivan's thoughts was dispelled by a loud banging under the truck. He honked for the attention of Fyodor Tarusov in the tow truck. They were approaching the top of a hill. Fyodor eased the tandem to the side of the road and jumped out, along with Alexi Kuprin.

"The universal joint?" Alexi guessed.

Ivan nodded, hopping out into the cold evening countryside. "Give me the flashlight and repair kit. I'll just disconnect it. Put the emergency brake on, will you?"

A dog howled somewhere in the distance. An owl hooted. It was a starless night. Fyodor glanced at his watch with a groan. "Ten o'clock at night. We'll never get any sleep."

Even in the poor light of the flashlight Ivan could see it was the universal joint. With a grunt of effort in the small space he finally scooted his body under it. He rummaged in his kit for a wrench, then managed to take the joint apart. The instant he felt the shift of the truck he knew Alexi had not put on the emergency brake. With a lunge he tried to roll out from under the truck as it moved forward. He let out a desperate shout "Reverse!"

The strange thing in the next few minutes of pain was that he was aware of everything. The rear wheel crushing into his shoulder and chest, the horror on Fyodor's face, the churning of the engine as Alexi tried repeatedly to get the tow truck to reverse. The smell of tyre rubber and oil filled his nostrils in the intense dark under the truck. From the corner of his eye he could see the flashlight where it had rolled on to the road. In the tiny spot of its light small insects began to fly. Pain was ripping through his chest, strangling his breath. He was perfectly aware that Alexi couldn't get the truck into reverse. Surely soon he would be with the angel. "Jesus." "Jesus."

With a slight jolt, the engine roared and the six pairs of wheels rolled back. Ivan pulled himself away from the truck and collapsed on to his mangled arm and chest in the road.

When he opened his eyes, a hot sheet of pain seemed to be burning into him. A small group of doctors beside his bed came into focus and beyond them a white wall and a narrow window curtained in sagging white cotton. He tried to speak, but his mouth was crusted with fever.

One of the doctors bent over him with interest, reading the question in his eyes. Her voice was kind. "You have been transferred to Simferopol Military Hospital, Ivan Vasilievich." Her expression remained unchanged as she pulled the thermometer from under his arm.

A nurse began bathing his face in cool water. He tried to suck the moisture from the cloth as it touched his lips. Smiling, she held a glass for him to drink. The slightest move seemed to fling open floodgates of pain. The shallowest breathing took enormous effort. His eyes followed her hand as the nurse set the glass down on a small table beside his bed. His right arm was lying outside the covers. He stared at it in astonishment. The whole hand and wrist and the part of the arm he could see not covered by a sling was a dusky grey. It seemed unattached to his body. It was impossible for him to will the smallest movement in the swollen fingers. With his left hand he reached through the pain and touched the right wrist and back of the hand; it was ice cold. The rest of his body was fiery hot.

With the nurse raising him to a half-sitting position he thirstily gulped more water. He could see he was in a large ward. Some of the patients appeared very ill with dripping bottles and tubes and whirring machines attached to them. Some slept. Others were convalescing, stooping like old men from bed to chair or cautiously sitting up reading. A few watched Ivan intently.

The nurse moved away, carrying her basin and cloth with her. Ivan closed his eyes and began to pray.

By the time of the evening meal a surgeon came to tell Ivan that surgery was scheduled in the morning. A specialist had been sent for to perform the operation. His right arm that was so frighteningly cold was to be amputated. Part of his crushed lung would be removed.

Ivan watched the doctor leave the ward, stopping at occasional bedsides as he wearily made his way to the corridor. His white coat moved from one patient to another, pausing, nodding briefly, the back of his shoulders stooped in fatigue. When he had gone, the patients sank back into their private struggles with depression or pain or loneliness. A desperate rejection of the surgeon's words swept through Ivan's mind. His heart pounded against his injured lung. He began to be horrified at the thought of his body without an arm. "Hear my prayer, O Lord! And let my cry for help come to Thee. Do not hide Thy face from me in the day of my distress; incline Thine ear to me; in the day when I call answer me quickly."

Somehow Ivan had to get out of bed. He felt himself falling into a grief from which he could neither pray nor hope. In a rush of anguish he heaved himself to the edge of the bed and threw his legs over the side. He staggered wildly for balance as pain blackened the room. Desperation gave him breath.

Every eye in the room was fixed upon him in fear and astonishment.

"I cry aloud with my voice to the Lord; I make supplication with my voice to the Lord. I pour out my complaint before Him; I declare my trouble before Him. When my spirit was overwhelmed within me, Thou didst know my path. I cried out to Thee, O Lord; I said, Thou art my refuge, my portion in the land of the living. Give heed to my cry, for I am brought very low."

A passing nurse stopped in the doorway and entered the room slowly.

"Bring my soul out of prison, so that I may give thanks to Thy name; for Thou wilt deal bountifully with me."

Guiding Ivan with her hand under his left elbow, the nurse moved him into bed.

A great joy seemed to shake his body. Ivan smiled suddenly. "Thou *wilt* deal bountifully with me."

He remembered the nurse wiping his face with a wet cloth as he sank into a blessed darkness.

It was six o'clock in the morning when he awoke. For several moments Ivan lay motionless, trying to hold on to the sweet lightness of a dream. Gradually he became aware that he was lying on his back instead of hunched on his uninjured left side. His breathing was quiet. Cautiously he took a deep breath. His arms were folded above his head and he was able to gaze at the ward still wrapped in sleep. Quietly he began to give praise to the Lord for the enormous relief of this dream. He brought his right arm down carefully from behind his head to his side. It was perfectly whole, the fingernails pink, the flesh still slightly tanned from his work in the harvest fields. With both hands he raised himself to a sitting position and got out of bed. Smiling in wonder at the reality of the dream, he lightly punched his pillow and patted the side of the bed. He waved one arm above his head playfully, then the other. With his hands on his waist, he did a few deep bends.

In a supreme happiness he knelt in prayer at the end of his bed. Softly he whispered praises. "Praise the Lord. Praise the Lord, O my soul. I will praise the Lord while I live. I will sing praises to my God while I have my being. The Lord opens the eyes of the blind; the Lord raises up those who are bowed down; the Lord loves the righteous. Praise the Lord."

Eventually the man in the bed beside him began to moan. Someone on the other side of the ward was struggling to reach a glass of water. Daylight streaked the slate-coloured sky in the window.

The lifelikeness of the dream amused Ivan. With a sleepy sigh he crawled into bed. He imagined himself floating into a delicious sleep.

The day nurse reached mechanically for the thermometer in the drawer of Ivan's table. He opened his eyes and gazed sleepily at her. The thermometer remained suspended in air as she stared fearfully at him. In an instant she was gone.

Rapid footsteps in the ward roused him a second time. The surgeon was standing beside the nurse. Some other doctors were hurrying into the room. Everyone appeared startled.

Ivan sat up defensively. What was happening? Suddenly a glory rolled over him. He had sat up! He stared at his hands in front of him. The sling lay on the top of his covers at the bottom of the bed. He began breathing deeply, entranced. He rubbed his hands together, then separated them in wonder.

The doctor was frightened. He groped for words. The nurse backed slightly away from the bed.

Finally, in a shaking voice, the doctor spoke: "Shall I take your temperature, Comrade Moiseyev?" Ivan flushed with happiness. "Of course I don't need my temperature taken, comrade doctor."

The surgeon continued to stare. Finally he put the medicine on the table. Hesitantly, his fingers probed Ivan's right hand. Gently lifting the sleeve of the hospital gown he glanced at the arm, his eyes returned again and again to the radiance of Ivan's face.

"I saw that you could not heal me." Ivan noticed that the nurse's face was white and that she had been joined by a small crowd of astonished employees. "And I turned to my heavenly Doctor, who healed me last night.

"Look!" With a grin, Ivan pulled back the blanket and stood on the floor. "Last night I was very ill. My temperature was high."

The nurse began to tremble as she nodded.

"Now I shall show you what my God can do." Ivan handed the thermometer to the doctor, who shook it down and placed it under Ivan's tongue. Some of the patients in the ward were gathering about the bottom of the bed. Others were calling softly from bed to bed, trying to discover and report what was going on.

The doctor removed the thermometer. "The temperature is normal, Moiseyev. Obviously. However, please return to your bed."

It was difficult for Ivan to comply. He wanted to jump, to shout, to fill the ward with the praises of God. When the small group of staff had finally gone, he raised himself on his elbow and began telling the electrified ward what God had done while he slept.

10

What is taken in with the milk only goes out with the soul

Lieutenant Colonel Malsin slammed his report book on his desk. Never before had he had such an infuriating telephone call. The surgeon-general at Simferopol was an incompetent idiot. Yesterday he reported that major surgery was to be done on Ivan Moiseyev. Well and good. Let them amputate if they could not save his arm. Moiseyev would be away from his unit a very long time. Of course he understood that. His condition was critical. Certainly it was critical. The matter was settled. Malsin admitted to himself he had been relieved not to have Moiseyev back in Kerch. It seemed that fate had done his work for him. Moiseyev would be handicaped, perhaps discharged from the army. At any rate he would not be Kerch's problem any longer.

And today the surgeon-general telephones a preposterous story. There will be no surgery. Several surgeons have examined Ivan Moiseyev and he is miraculously healed. A man of science sputtering about miracles! This critically ill patient of yesterday has already been discharged and is on a bus returning to his unit. A man of science! Malsin would see that he was reported. Obviously he is unstable and incapable. Certainly Malsin would recommend examination by a psychiatrist.

His voice had trembled on the telephone. Malsin tried to disregard the ring of sincerity in his words. "Colonel, for the first time in my life I see that there really is a God. He healed Moiseyev! His condition is perfect. Even with months of work, I could have done nothing like that!"

It was disgusting to try to hide incompetence. If there had been a gross error in diagnosis, far better to admit it and take the consequences. With grim satisfaction, Malsin wrote out the report of Moiseyev's medical discharge. Every word the army surgeon had said about miracles and God would be sent to Moscow. Ringing the bell on his desk, he summoned the clerk to type the report.

Malsin took a deep breath as he poured his vodka. The Polit-Ruk would be ready for Moiseyev when he returned.

Much of the journey back to Kerch, Ivan sat praying and praising God in his spirit, watching the late November countryside spin by in a haze of frosty grey. It would snow any day. Agricultural workers, deep in the fields, gave a comradely salute as the bus rolled by. Small villages like his at home seemed to huddle into the cold earth for warmth. Small children, fat in their warm clothes, stood beside frozen puddles pondering the mystery of the bus as their babushkas stooped patiently to whisper in their ears. He loved it all: the people, the vast sky, the fields as far as he could see, the workers lashing the last crates of cabbages to the trucks. For a time he forgot his struggles and sat tall against the window, proud to be part of the great stream of life that was the Soviet Union.

"I have often had it happen," he had once written to his parents, "that after a mighty manifestation of God's power over me, Satan rages and tries as best he can to do evil." Now, short hours away from Kerch, he tried to prepare his heart for what might be ahead at the base. But the suddenness and viciousness of the attacks from the moment of his return shocked him.

Commissar Dolotov, from his Crimean headquarters, had given out the order: "Moiseyev must be broken." The head of the Kerch Polit-Ruk and the head of the military would answer to him for Moiseyev. Already one year of Moiseyev's service had passed and still he was an open believer. There were to be no further incidents and no problems from the men in his unit. Mismanage this case and both Gidenko and Malsin were finished.

Ivan had no sooner unpacked than he was called first to one polit-officer, then to another. He was investigated, questioned, lectured, threatened. He was summoned out of classes, during meals, often in the middle of the night.

It was known that in civilian life he had taken part in illegal activities in an unregistered church. That he was engaged in subversive work in the army was a known fact. How many Soviet soldiers had he already drawn into the whirlpool of his fantasies, torn away from constructive activities to secret conversations and activities? He could be sentenced at any time to seven years or more in a corrective labour camp for anti-Soviet agitation according to article 58, paragraph 10, of the criminal code. He was indifferent to the demands of his army work. He frequently seemed to be absent from classes and drills. There were sheets of complaints against him from his superior officers. He was insubordinate. The KGB was making inquiries about him. It would be necessary for him to have a psychiatric examination, a medical examination, a political examination. If there is a God, why is it that no one believes in Him? Can he quote the statements of Marx, Engels, and Lenin concerning God? Is it possible that he is deaf?

The shouting could continue for hours. Ivan tried not to listen. It was unnecessary because the questions

were most often rhetorical. When answers were required they were repeated so forcibly, often with a
blow to the back or head "to wake him up", that a
long interval could pass in which Ivan could concentrate on prayer.

"What is the matter that you are withdrawn—you
do not take part in cultural activities? Why is it men
on the base, men not from your unit, sometimes come
to ask you questions? Who are these men? Do you
admit that you try to convert others to religion? Do
you understand that such activity is prohibited by
law? Your continuing disobedience is understood as a
mad desire for suicide. Even your own religion dis-
approves of suicide. . . . You are in a religious delirium
with your talk of angels and healings. Is it not true that
such things are utterly against the philosophy of
Lenin's scientific communism? Is not what you say
about the meaninglessness of life without God simply a
disintegration of the consciousness? What friends do
you have in Odessa? When have you been in Odessa?
There are inconsistencies in hundreds of your answers.
Do you not have a commandment not to lie? What
about your loyalty to the Soviet state? Have you not
broken your army oath of loyalty? Why is it that we
atheists deceive no one but you believers deceive the
state with secret meetings and illegal publications?
You are out of harmony with society. . . .

"It is only potential enemies who deny Marxist
philosophy. You cannot be considered a Soviet citizen.
You have joined yourself to corrupt people against
whom the state must struggle and fight. We are building communism in the army more than in any other
segment of Soviet life. How can you insist you are a
loyal soldier and yet by your beliefs seek to undermine
the scientific philosophical system of the army and our
socialist states?"

There were hours when Malsin himself joined Gidenko's interrogations. At such times he would conduct
the questionings, his voice tightening in frustration.
Moiseyev was insubordinate, refused instruction,
rejected counsel, continued to believe and teach an
individualized fanatic view for the purpose of under-
mining the stability and functioning of his unit and
division in the Soviet army.

Suddenly Ivan would be dismissed. Somehow,
plunged back into a classroom or the middle of a military training session or drill he would have to catch
up, take tests, answer questions. If he was unable to
perform as required, a complaint would be registered,
and Ivan would watch helplessly as an instructor once
again entered his name on a shirkers' list.

The winter weeks faded into the spring of 1972 like
a blurred, slow-motion nightmare. Exhaustion and cold
and uncertainty were wearing him down, Ivan knew.
There would be short periods of respite in which days
could be passed normally in the army routine before
the meeting and interviews and interrogations would
begin afresh. Daily Ivan poured out his heart to God.

He had discovered that the door to the storage room
for his dormitory was a fire exit and remained unlocked all night. A window on the far wall of the narrow
room opened out on to a fire exit running down the
side of the building to the street below. With the window open to the breezes from the Black Sea and a chair
on which to prop his elbows as he knelt to pray, Ivan
passed hours of the mild nights. There was a deep healing in the profound silence of the room. Racks of
ghostly uniforms muffled the murmurings of his
prayers and tears and whispered hymns from the sleeping soldiers in the dormitory.

Sometimes a homesickness filled him as the fields
around the base greened into spring. There were nights

that Ivan felt too discouraged to pray. Often of late it seemed his answers to the political leaders and lawyers became confused. He would see by their faces that they had caught him in some statement that pleased them. His mind wandered greatly in the questionings, returning to Moldavia and his parents' small village on the collective farm.

Tonight, the moon from the storage room window sailed across the sky in a stream of clouds. That same moon would have risen over the vineyards of Volontirovka. Ivan was discouraged. Tomorrow he was to appear before breakfast at Malsin's office. "Lord Jesus! Jesus!" The stillness of the room deepened. "Jesus! I don't know how long I can endure!" He had laid his head on his arms on the wooden chair. Sometimes he dozed, waiting for the Lord's hand. A gentle melody hummed in his head, and he let it lull him in the slight warm breeze from the open window. His folded arm muffled his ear and he turned his head slightly to the song. A glint of light caught the lashes of his closed eyes. The music became sweeter.

A familiar shock pulled him to his feet and to the window. The black western sky was bright with an angelic host. Their translucent robes seemed fashioned from glowing lights of different colours and lit their faces with a fierce beauty. They seemed to be moving, but their position in the sky never changed as their song grew and swelled in the night.

> To all the ends of this unhappy earth
> Wherever men be found
> In torrents of pure and mighty faith
> Flows the gospel truth

After a long time their light faded. The sky became less black and slowly grew a pearly grey. It was close to morning. In tears of repentance and happiness Ivan

knelt in praise and wonder. A profound stillness hung
over the room. Not a bird yet sung. Into his memory
an unmistakable Voice spoke. "This is for the comfort
of your soul. Tomorrow you will not be questioned.
You will soon leave from here."

Malsin was furious that Moiseyev had left the base on
a chauffering assignment. He had signalled an order to
stop him. Malsin could not tolerate a blunder in which
an order could be lost like a schoolboy's homework!
The order would be found and whoever responsible
would be punished. His outer office was the scene of an
uproar, with clerks turning piles of paper out of
drawers and pulling military typists away from their
typewriters so wastebaskets could be searched.
  "Have you seen the order?"—"Wasn't it late yesterday afternoon that it was sent to the unit sergeant?"—
"I haven't got it, as you can see. It has nothing to do
with me!" A wire box full of papers was tipped on to
the floor, scattering its papers like an aspen tree in a
windstorm. More bumping about and exclaiming. A
door on the outer office banged. The order was plainly
lost.

It was good to be out on the open road, Ivan was
thinking, the vast expanses of fields spread out around
them. The truck rolled easily over the asphalt road, its
load of bread snug in the back and twice padlocked. A
thick hedge of blackthorn bordered this section of the
highway, and Ivan glanced at it frequently, enjoying
the small birds that darted in and out of the depths of
the greenery. The junior officer beside Ivan in the cab
was a professional soldier, an agreeable Ukrainian who
had managed to buy a melon from a lush kitchen garden as they passed through a tiny village. He was eating it noisily, cutting away the fruit from the rind with

the edge of a small pocket knife. From time to time they would pass wooden carts pulled by plodding yoked horses.

Without warning, Ivan heard an inner voice, or thought he did. "Vanya, slow down." He glanced quickly at the speedometer. The needle held steady at sixty kilometres an hour. The Ukrainian continued to eat the melon, its juice running off the edge of his chin and falling between his knees.

Impossible that God could be telling him to slow down! They were travelling at a very moderate speed. The hedge was gone now and cool-looking alder thickets followed a long path that led inexplicably into the middle of a field and then disappeared. "Vanya, slow down!"

His eyes lifted to the rear-view mirror. Behind him, as in front, the straight road was empty. Vadim Harmansky tossed his melon rind out the window and wiped his mouth on the back of his sleeve. He closed his knife and placed it in his pocket, raising up slightly in his seat to manage it.

Something bumping along the road caught Ivan's eye. Harmansky exclaimed in astonishment. "Comrade, that's a loaf of our bread!" Another brown object rolled by.

God is stopping us. With a flash of understanding Ivan immediately pulled over and stopped the truck. The officer leaped down from the cab and raced to the back of the vehicle. "Look at this, comrade—the latches are still shut and padlocked!" He looked over his shoulder at the loaves of bread dotting the road as far back as they could see. Rapidly unlocking the truck, the two soldiers stared. Half of their load was gone, strewn over the highway.

Harmansky rubbed the back of his neck in perplexity. "Vanya, tell me. You and I locked these doors together." He shook his head as if clearing out illusions. "All the latches are in place, but the bread is on the road. I have been working on this truck for six years and have never had anything like this happen. It is impossible for these doors to open by themselves. And we closed them together, I remember."

Ivan, too, was perplexed. "And I remember." He stooped to retrieve a loaf of bread. "As we were driving, God told me to slow down, but there seemed to be no reason and I did not obey. He spoke again to my spirit but again I did not obey. Now He has made us stop."

"There are such fables as this in the Scriptures I heard from my babushka as a child." The officer lifted his cap and scratched his head as Ivan eased the truck back on the road and turned it around to go back for the bread. An Ikarus bus full of Black Sea vacationers whizzed past. "My father was a religious Jew. Every Friday night he went to the synagogue in Kiev, and when he was gone, my grandmother would tell me stories by the light of the Sabbath candles. Once she told me of a dream in the Scriptures where a huge loaf of barley bread came tumbling into a camp of the Midian army. It knocked down a whole tent! She said it meant there would be a victory for the Hebrew general." He smiled as he jumped out of the truck to gather up some loaves on the road. As he slammed the cab door and the truck slowly retraced its route, he continued calling, "But what does it mean when God sends a half a load of bread through the back door of a truck?" He laughed sheepishly, but his eyes on Ivan were sombre.

"For some reason, God wanted us to slow down. Of that I am sure. When I disregarded Him, He caused the bread to escape to make us stop. I don't know why."

It was a time-consuming job picking up the bread,

loaf by loaf, on the quiet road. "Perhaps He did it to
punish you!" Harmansky called across the highway to
Ivan. He grinned. "Next time, I'm going to request a
different driver.

"You Baptists are a strange lot, Vanya," the sergeant
offered as they resumed their route, the dusty bread
once again locked safely in the back of the truck. "You
don't seem to care what happens to you. Perhaps I believe in God sometimes. I suppose many people do, a
little. But what is the purpose of making life miserable
by going about broadcasting it to the authorities?"

Ivan answered slowly. "We have freedom of conscience in our country. The Constitution says people
may be free to believe or not believe as they like, and
to practise religion, or not. There should be no necessity to hide the fact that one believes, comrade."

The officer lit a cigarette impatiently. "You are talking about laws! Don't you realize that the Committee
of State Security[1] doesn't give a damn about laws?"

Out of habit he lowered his voice. "These are not
things I would say to anyone, Vanya, but you are well-
liked. Many know you and have heard all you say
about God. It is no secret among the common soldiers
that some have changed their minds about atheism because of you and what they have seen in your life.
They too are now under suspicion." He raised his hand
in warning as he saw Ivan about to answer. "For myself I want to be able to say, if I am questioned, that
you never spoke to me about religion. Please—do not
spoil that "

The officer shifted restlessly, leaning his back against
the door of the cab. "But I am telling you. The KGB
have been with Malsin and the Polit-Ruk asking questions about you. You are a good lad. I'm not saying I
can explain the things that have happened to you. I try
not to know about them or think about what I know.

But everyone realizes you are a good person. Can you not choose a way to live in which you can stay out of trouble? What use are you to anyone, shut up for hours and days with the authorities, dragged out of bed, called to interrogations all the time? Eventually you will be destroyed and any good your life could have done will be lost. Surely you have considered that you may be arrested. It's your affair, of course, if you want to throw away your life."

His voice trailed off in horror at the scene approaching them on the road. The Ikarus bus that had passed them as they were gathering bread lay twisted in the roadside ditch. Bodies were strewn in every direction, some caught horribly in an overturned crane into which the bus had apparently collided. Several passenger cars were also crumpled together in what had clearly been a chain reaction. The body of an old man hung grotesquely from a shattered windshield. Police cars and ambulances were beginning to arrive. There was running back and forth through showers of broken glass, slippery with blood. Terrible moaning was coming from all directions.

Ivan and Harmansky sat sickened in the cab of the truck. Harmansky's voice was hollow. "If we had not stopped for the bread, we would have been in this accident. We could have perished. God saved your life." Tears stood in his eyes. His shaking hands were steadied against the instrument panel of the truck.

Ivan spoke with difficulty. "God saved *our* lives." His voice was full of emotion. "It is not only me He loves. It is everybody. It is you, comrade."

Harmansky suddenly bowed his head on his hands and began to weep.

---

[1] KGB (Komitet Gosudarstvennoi Bezopasnosti).

II

Every cricket knows its own hearth

Malsin spit out the piece of fingernail he had just torn with his teeth and sucked the raw edge of cuticle. His hands were sore, he was sick from excessive smoking and before him on his desk was once again the open file of Ivan Moiseyev. Yet another report would have to be made, this time on the disturbance caused by Moiseyev and Comrade Officer Harmansky on their return to the base in the bread truck. Already there were far too many incidents, recorded, unexplained, uncorrected.

Clearly there was to be no end to the incidents. What was he to write? "Normal routine on the base was disrupted last week by reports by Ivan Moiseyev and Vadim Harmansky that God had propelled army bread from their locked vehicle to the road in order to detain them and thus prevent their involvement in a serious accident." Malsin himself had investigated the crowd of soldiers forming around the bread delivery truck. Harmansky had been weeping as he told the story. Obviously he had suffered a nervous collapse. A new thought disturbed Malsin. Perhaps he should have had Harmansky arrested for negligence. It was quite obviously a case of irresponsibility that he had not locked the back of the truck. He shrugged. Now that he was with psychiatrists, better to leave it at that.

But why did it have to happen with Moiseyev? Always Moiseyev.

The Office of Special Affairs had verified the bus accident and this added to the excitement on the base. Moiseyev was a genius at being able to exploit a situation in order to claim yet another miracle for his God.

In spite of every re-education procedure, Moiseyev continued to propagate his views. Malsin had been gratified to discover that at least Moiseyev had attended an unregistered congregation in Moldavia. A criminal case could probably be made of that but it was now far in the past. It was Moiseyev's deliberate programme of disobedience that ate at Malsin day and night. Repeatedly he had been ordered to be silent about his religious beliefs. The military and polit-officers had worked with him in every legal way. And in other ways as well.

A May breeze from the open window scattered cigarette ashes over the papers on the desk. Malsin continued to stare at the pile of Moiseyev reports, not bothering to brush off the ashes.

The situation was becoming embarrassingly difficult to manage. The report from the military hospital in Simferopol with its official seal was under his hand. Two hundred men in the harvest convoy last autumn claimed to believe some sort of supernatural healing of Moiseyev's injuries. No doubt they were influenced by stories filtering down from the surgeon-general's office. The memory of the surgeon's shaken voice on the telephone still rankled Malsin. "For the first time in my life I see that there really is a God!" What kind of doctors did they have in Simferopol? Not people of science. Malsin wouldn't take an animal there! He lit another cigarette. It had been good fortune that the men in that convoy had been from many units in differing cities. What if the convoy had been entirely from Kerch? Two hundred men returning to the base with wild-eyed stories of miracles!

All happenings had natural causes. In the matter of Moiseyev standing in the snow perhaps he had some innate ability to withstand cold. In the war it had been

window to get a glimpse of Ivan as he·sat in a place of honour at the front of the room with the pastors. He was dressed in the same clothes he had always worn to the meetings, but he looked years older. Svetlana wondered if she had changed so much. They were singing the Moldavian hymns everyone loved, one after another. It was a way of celebrating Ivan's return and encouraging him. Svetlana joined in with all her heart. She had heard Ivan had been having a difficult time.

Several of the pastors would speak, but before the meeting was over Svetlana knew that Ivan would be asked to preach. She leaned her chin on the sill and gazed at all the Moiseyevs sitting together near the pastors. Every one of their faces shone with excitement and joy. Even some unbelieving neighbours became curious and were pressing against the young people at the windows, trying to see inside. A woman Svetlana knew to be a foreman at the silk factory pulled her back from the window. "What's special today?" she demanded. "What's going on in there?"

Some other village people pushed past the young people and jostled at the windows to watch. Nina Kopnik, a cousin of Svetlana's, sighed in exasperation. All the young people had given up their positions by the window. "But unbelievers will hear the gospel," Svetlana whispered. "Be glad."

After the singing, Ivan was invited by the pastors to speak first. He began to read Old Testament verses from a borrowed Bible.

" 'Then the Lord opened the eyes of Balaam and he saw the angel of the Lord standing in the way with his sword drawn in his hand; and he bowed all the way to the ground.' " Ivan raised his eyes from the small book with a radiant smile. "Even so today God can reveal His angels to His followers and demonstrate His power." The silk factory foreman by the window

shifted her weight, her eyes upon Ivan in fascination.
Svetlana caught a glimpse of his expression of loving
earnestness. "I should also like to quote Mark 14:35,
which says, 'And He went a little beyond them and
fell to the ground and began praying that, if it were
possible, the hour might pass Him by.' So, dear
brothers and sisters, such hours of trouble that come to
us do represent times of great difficulty, and many of us
have these experiences. In such an hour the Lord re-
sorted to prayer. He was aware of all that awaited
Him, but we have no such awareness. Instead of a sermon, I should like to invite you to pray. As the Lord
Jesus prayed, so let us engage in prayer."

Something in his voice made Svetlana's eyes smart
with tears. The foreman and some others moved away
with a shrug. It was nothing exceptional after all. The
Baptists were always praying. Svetlana moved forward
with the other young people, back to their places at
the windows. So Ivan was not going to preach. Instead
he had asked that they pray.

It was after the long service that the adults made
way for the young to find places around Ivan, filling
the already cramped living room to overflowing. There
was shyness in the welcome of the young people. No
one wanted to ask embarrassing questions, yet everyone wanted to know the details of his difficulties.
Someone softly closed the open windows and the front
door. An old grandmother sitting next to Ivan holding
his arm suddenly jogged him. "Vanya, Vanya," her old
voice cracked with loving emotion. "Tell us how it has
been."

It was an afternoon Svetlana would never forget.
What wonderful things the Lord had done! The miracle of the healing! Of the bread! Of the sergeant's
leave! Often hymns of praise began in response to
Ivan's stories. Sometimes a brother or sister would pray

for Ivan's officers, for the new brothers in the army Ivan told about, for the other soldiers who had heard the gospel. At times their voices would fall silent, and Ivan, his face lit with the happiness of being home, would speak again of the wonderful works of God.

Dusk was falling as the Moiseyevs made their way along the rolling dirt road from the prayer house in Slabodzeya to their own village of Volontirovka. The younger boys were drowsy, stumbling beside their mother, oblivious to the beauty of the gentle light gilding the curve of the hills and the young green of the treetops. His sister and two of the older boys were softly singing hymns, every once in a while glancing over their shoulders with a smile for Ivan as they sang. Each tree and path and fence that they passed was achingly familiar to Ivan. As they walked he could see in the distance the house of his married brother near the small thicket where he had hunted for mushrooms in the summer.

His father, keeping pace with him, walked silently, unwilling to disturb the memories that were almost visible on his son's face. An oriole making its three-note call pierced the air with sweetness. "It's so beautiful." Ivan's voice was low, as if he feared to break the hush of the twilight. Vasiliy Trofimovich smiled indulgently. Far off in the fields he could see the heavy equipment of the collective farm waiting to begin the morning's cultivation. Abruptly Ivan stopped walking and grasped his father's arms, his eyes wet. "It's hard, Papa. I want you to know. I'll never see Moldavia again."

Such things as tape recorders and microphones were as foreign to the tiny Moiseyev cottage as they would have been in the court at Saint Petersburg in the days of the czars. But Brother Zheluak from Slabodzeya had appeared with his machine on Ivan's last evening home, enthused about a plan. For years Zheluak had taped the Christian radio broadcasts he received on his shortwave radio, replaying them for his family and for the believers after the services. It would be a simple matter to record Ivan telling of his experiences in the army. Why should the few believers in the Suvorovskiy region be the only ones to hear the wonderful things the Lord had done for Ivan in the army? A tape could be made and carried by the pastors all over Moldavia and played in congregation after congregation. What glory to God and what encouragement to the brethren!

For some reason, when Ivan began the taping, Joanna Constantinova began to weep. The months had been difficult for her as she had read and re-read between the lines of Ivan's letters home. Vasiliy had hoped that seeing Ivan would have quieted her fears, but since Ivan's return his wife had hardly slept, staring at her son with a face so full of concern that even Ivan had laughed. "Momma, I think you will battle the whole Red army for me," he had teased, adding, "These things are in the hands of God. You must pray, yes, but we may not choose for ourselves what is to be. What God wills shall be. Our concern is only to be worthy of Him." Joanna had tried to smile when she met Ivan's glance, but there was a detachment about him that filled her nights with fear and her days with dread. Nothing must happen to him. He was her son.

12

In the land of the naked, people are ashamed of clothes

Malsin paced his small apartment restlessly, walking from window to window, glancing down at the busy Kerch street watching for the quick figure of his wife making her way through the crowds. His ten-year-old son was already bent over his homework spread out on the table in the living room. He worked quietly, occasionally raising his head to observe his father's impatience.

"Momma will be home soon." He had his mother's way of soothing. "I expect she stopped for some vegetables at the market."

Malsin nodded, throwing himself into a chair.

It was going better with the Moiseyev affair. He was pleased. But Galina should be here. He wanted to tell her what a good thing it had been after all that Moiseyev had gone home on leave. The interval had given him time to think, to plan a stratagem, to confer with the district Polit-Ruk, to see the issues with clarity. The boy looked up again from his books, his pale blue eyes full of light. "Momma's home!"

Galina Ivanova kicked the apartment door shut with her foot, swinging the string bag full of beetroot on to the kitchen table and dumping an armful of small parcels alongside. She eyed her husband apprehensively, recovered herself, and smiled warmly at the boy in the next room.

"Would you like some tea?" Automatically she moved to the sink with the kettle, her bare arms already slightly tanned from the hot spring sun.

Malsin reached in his pocket for a cigarette. "Yes, tea would be welcome." He inhaled deeply. "You'll be happy to know I'm feeling very pleased about the Moiseyev business."

Galina placed the kettle on the gas flame with elaborate carefulness. In an effort to be calm, she sat down in the chair opposite her husband. The beetroot and parcels on the table made a wall between them. "We had agreed not to discuss the matter."

"But the difficulty lay in the fact that I was uncertain as to how to proceed. It is no ordinary case. His uncanny ability to resist discipline, to create bizarre incidents, to publicize his fanaticism have been most unusual. It came to me that what was essential was to work out to the last detail all questions concerning the progression of his case. It was a very good thing, after all, that he was sent home on leave. His absence gave me a needed respite. I have planned a stratagem with the utmost of precision."

"A stratagem." Galina moved towards the steaming kettle, mechanically pouring the boiling water into the small samovar that had been a wedding present years ago. How much they both had changed.

Malsin pushed the packages aside to put down the cup of tea his wife handed to him. "Of course this has been on your mind, Galina, making you nervous. It has been hanging over our head for months. How do you think I know you haven't slept well? I haven't slept. It is a miracle that I haven't had to give an explanation to the *Spetz-Otdel*[1] before this for the irregularities up to now. There seems to be no end of the tricks this Rasputin with the innocent face can pull out of his bag."

His wife's cup remained invisible behind the groceries. "A miracle," she repeated. Malsin became irritated at the disagreeable way she was staring at him, repeating his words.

"I understood that the Communist Party does not believe in miracles. You have a strange vocabulary."

"I am trying to remember that you too have been under a strain because of this. I came home to tell you that the difficulties with Moiseyev will soon be resolved. I have taken decisive action. This morning he returned to Kerch. Already he has been arrested. I assumed that it might put your mind at rest to know that together with the security agents a procedure has been established, and he has been formally arrested."

"I don't want to know the procedure. I don't want to know about Moiseyev. I've told you many times not to talk about him to me."

It was difficult not to despise the incredible weakness in women. Even today there were very few women who had achieved the socialist ideal of objectivity necessary for full liberation. Malsin had once hoped Galina was such a woman.

"The problem has been that Moiseyev is quite willing to go openly to prison. He is so lost in the labyrinth of his imagination that it is of no concern to him where he is. One place will do as well as another for his anti-Soviet activities, his Baptist preaching, his 'miracles' to flourish. What a victory! For the Red army to provide such a preacher for the prison camps!" Malsin inhaled deeply. "Every man has his breaking point. Moiseyev has his. That is the point we have determined to reach."

Fury choked Galina Ivanova's voice to a whisper. "I have told you not to tell me these things. I have told you I will not stand them." In a flash she was in front of the sink with her tea. Deliberately she raised the cup and smashed it against the side. The saucer followed with redoubled violence.

In a reflex of rage Malsin struck his wife in a swing
of his hand that spun her against the kitchen wall.
With the return of his arm he grabbed his briefcase and
was in the hall of the apartment, staring at her redden-
ing face and defiant eyes. Deliberately he reached into
the room for the side of the door, slamming it at her
violently. In a freezing calm, he walked slowly into the
gentle sunshine. Galina be damned.

In spite of the clement time of the year, the cell was
cold. High in the wall, near the ceiling the small window was outlined in a brilliant blue. Outside, the sky
stretched above the prison, over the city of Simferopol,
and further, a vast canopy for fields and hills bursting
with early summer for dazzling rivers and at last the
fragrant vineyards of Moldavia.

Ivan had been staring for hours at the window. He
finally pulled his eyes away from the blue and tried to
pray. A feeling of weightlessness, disembodiment
plagued him. It was as if real life had stopped and he
was suspended in the cell, unable to feel that the events
taking place around him were genuine. Was it a melo-
drama of his imagination that he might die? Had
Malsin actually meant that he was neither to be
sentenced to prison nor discharged from the army if he
refused to change his convictions? Surely he had
misunderstood. The Russian language was difficult.
Possibly sometimes he did not understand.

All along it had not been death he had feared, but
the possibility of denying Christ, denying the angelic
visions, the healing of his body, the love of God that
had many times literally filled his body with life-giving
heat. He was unsure what might be done to a man behind the closed doors of special cells to make him re-
cant, blaspheme, embrace all that he abhorred. It was
his own weakness that he feared.

But something like the lingering of a shadow seemed to pervade his cell. It was impossible to be rid of the one tormenting thought that was recurring in a thousand different forms: In the end, his dying would accomplish nothing. In renewed anguish Ivan paced his cell. If it came to dying, if he withstood, if it were possible by God's power he were able to withstand, then he would be gone. No more than that. A torment of loss wrenched his mind. Once his future had stretched before him with the promise of goodness and mercy all the days of his life. Images of his family, his home, his friends, his country pushed upon him. He began to think of the bride he would never have. Small faces of children floated in the air of his cell.

"I am going mad!" It was said that religion caused madness. Desperately Ivan fixed his mind upon Scripture. "Save me, O God. For the waters have come up to my soul. I have sunk in deep mire and there is no foothold; I have come into deep waters, and a flood overflows me. I am weary with my crying; my throat is parched; my eyes fail while I wait for my God. Those who hate me are more than the hairs of my head; those who would destroy me are powerful.

"O God, it is Thou who dost know my folly, and my wrongs are not hidden from Thee. May those who wait for Thee not be ashamed through me, O Lord God of hosts. May those who seek Thee not be dishonoured through me, O Lord God of Israel."

The face of Prokhorov, the Armenian sergeant, flashed into his mind. He saw again the wonderful smile with which he had greeted Ivan after his return from the harvest fields. Over and over he had embraced Ivan, kissing him on both cheeks, embracing him again, calling him "my brother". He had joyously kept his promise to believe. The memory of Prokhorov eased Ivan's pain. He sat quietly on the metal cot in his cell.

Many had believed. His flesh shrank back from the ordeal ahead, but would not God prove faithful? "Steadfast, steadfast!" Ivan said aloud. "You go forward on Christ's orders."

The military prosecutor in Simferopol had assembled the same bewildering and familiar charges that Ivan had heard so many times before from officers of the Kerch Polit-Ruk. Under article 142 he was charged with violating the codex in being a member of an unregistered Baptist congregation in Moldavia. In Kerch itself he had attended unregistered meetings in hours the army had provided for his rest and relaxation. According to article 190, paragraph 1, of the criminal code he was further charged with the distribution of literature containing deliberately false statements slandering the Soviet state. A letter to his parents was produced which included the reference that he was suffering for Christ. "Freedom of conscience is guaranteed to every citizen of the USSR. You have deliberately besmirched the Soviet Union and the Red army." The tribunal officer had picked up a small paper and began to read a few lines. "The Decree of Lenin, Point Five: 'Free celebration of religious rites is guaranteed insofar as they do not disturb public order and do not infringe the rights of citizens of the Soviet republic.'" He gave Ivan a measured look before continuing. "Repeatedly, Comrade Moiseyev, you have infringed upon the rights of your fellow soldiers in your unit and company and in other units with which you have had contact. Your continuous observance of prayer and preaching are intolerable to others around you. You have been repeatedly ordered to desist from this harassment of others, but have refused. Your religious observations on state property have violated the regulations on the separation of church and state. You are condemned, not by this tribunal, but by your own actions. Still, an opportunity is being given to you today to accept the judgment of this court, to confess your anti-Soviet activity and publicly change your views. You will be given three days to think it over."

From Simferopol he had been returned to Kerch for the three-day waiting period, then taken to the military prison there. Again the interrogations began, with Major Gidenko and Captain Yarmak reading the lists of accusations, shouting that it would be at Kerch that he would spend his seven years in prison. Ivan shifted uneasily in the prisoner's dock. Gidenko was giving him another three-day ultimatum. Why was it that the courts were unwilling to sentence him? He had told everyone repeatedly that he was ready to accept prison.

Malsin yawned. It had been a long session with Gidenko and he had stayed throughout. He had not been to his apartment since the argument with Galina. He entertained the idea of going home, then rejected it. The Moiseyev matter required his full attention. The strategy that had been planned needed to be carried out with absolute precision and without the incredible blundering that had plagued this case from the beginning. By staying on the job he had seen the matter through this far. He wasn't going to rest now.

With a feeling of satisfaction Malsin checked off the progress this far. Moiseyev had already seen Commissar Dolotov in Simferopol and been charged. Since he had not pleaded guilty, he was returned to the Polit-Ruk at Kerch where he had a hearing and was examined by his own polit-officers. Again, a deadline was given to him. If he failed to comply (and Malsin was certain he would), he would be sent for examination to the district Polit-Ruk in Odessa before being returned to Simferopol for what Malsin called "the final outcome". It was of little importance that the interrogations and threats had not proved successful this far. Malsin shrugged. It was of little importance to him at what stage Moiseyev broke. Break he would. In a short time he would be entering the special session phase at Simferopol.

It was becoming difficult for Ivan to remember what day it was. There had been so much shunting back and forth between prisons and hearings and the base at Kerch that he was losing track of time. He stood unsteadily once again in the Simferopol prisoner's dock, his face pale. Already the tan with which he had returned from Moldavia had receded into a prisoner's pallor. He was hungry. He had been abused by the guards. He had had little sleep in the past two weeks. The officers gazed impassively at him, waiting his testimony. His voice was hoarse from weariness, but he tried to speak distinctly in the still unfamiliar Russian.

"I plead not guilty to the charges against me and I ask again to speak to the tribunal."

Commissar Dolotov's mournful face nodded in assent.

"When I was drafted into the army, I took the oath of loyalty and I have tried never to break my promise to give full allegiance and obedience to the military of the USSR. There have been orders I have received that it was impossible for me to obey, orders I believe that are improper and violate the Constitution's guarantee of freedom of conscience. I did not obey these orders, not because I am disloyal to the Red army, but because they were improper, and most of all because I have one higher allegiance, and that is to Jesus Christ. He has given me certain orders, and these I cannot disobey."

Dolotov spoke with quiet interest. "You have received particularized orders from Jesus Christ?"

"No more than any Christian in that we are told to

tell what great things the Lord has done for us, to be witnesses to His glory where we are. Comrade commissar, I have never harassed others with the preaching of the gospel. Where there has been interest, I have spoken of the love of God and His care of me and all those who love Him. I don't consider it a crime to give bread to the hungry. Many of the things that have happened to me and to others are miracles. In our day many say there is no God, yet He is doing miracles because he loves all men and wants all men to be saved. The only religious observances in which I have engaged on the base is prayer, and what law forbids Soviet citizens to pray? You tell me not to talk about my faith, but the love of God cannot be hidden. It is written, 'If I say, "I will not remember Him or speak any more in His name", then in my heart it becomes like a burning fire shut up in my bones; and I am weary of holding it in.' I do not ask this tribunal for mercy, because mercy comes from God. I am ready to accept prison with joy. I have been told my sentence is to be seven years. Then let me receive it. Another period for me to reconsider is useless. I cannot deny God who has given me so much happiness. I can only praise Him."

Without a word, Dolotov nodded brusquely to the guard. Malsin controlled the irritation that scalded his stomach. He must be patient. All was going according to plan, even though Moiseyev's composure could be infuriating. Signalling to the security agents of the Spetz-Otdel, who had been observing from a small table at the back of the room, Malsin carried a chair to their table and sat down. His smile was thin, but he made an effort at sociability. "It is simply a matter of time, comrades. At this moment he is on his way to the prison security units for as long as it takes."

---

[1] *Spetzialnij-Otdel* ("Special Department", or KGB).

13

Death does not take the old, but the ripe

With growing certainty, Ivan was becoming aware of what was ahead. The tribunals had repeatedly threatened him with imprisonment if he did not change his views, only to extend his deadline when he refused. As clearly as possible Ivan had said, "Jesus Christ has given me the order to proclaim His word in whatever city I am in, in my military unit, and to officers and soldiers. I must follow His order." Still his sentence was withheld.

At first Ivan had thought the authorities were considering the reactions of the men in his unit if he were sent to prison. Many soldiers had believed. And many more declared that God exists and that they had seen miracles. Even Sergei had become a centre of attention in his own unit. Soldiers sought him out to ask questions, to pray with him, to read his Scripture portions. Ivan sighed. A longing to see Sergei haunted him. Repeatedly he had asked that Sergei be permitted to visit him, but his guards and cells were changed so frequently that he was unsure that the request had been delivered to the officials. Sergei and many of the soldiers would be praying for him, Ivan knew. But the authorities would not be afraid of their reactions. Multiple arrests were common after a sentence had been passed.

Repeatedly the Lord had spoken to him. "Jesus Christ is going into battle." Yes, he knew that. Had not the days since his return from leave been a battle? Water lay in pools on the floor of his new cell. The air was foul. For breakfast he had had no bread. Was this not a struggle? Was he not fighting down his fears, his longings for a natural life, his dread of the unknown? Was he not enduring the strain of repeated threats, hearings, interrogations, deadlines, movings from prison to prison, from cell to cell? Was he not witnessing to the guards, to the interrogators? But something assured him the battle was not to be prison.

This cell was wet, and had no bed. It reminded him painfully of the cell in Sverdlovsk where he had hunched over a year ago. He shuddered, remembering the nightmare progression of cells: the cubicle with icy water pouring from the ceiling, and after that, the refrigerated cell, and then the agony of the pressure suit. "Jesus Christ is going into battle." As the words turned over and over in his mind an overwhelming sense of Presence jarred him alert. Joy spread gently through him, warming, burning, bringing him to his knees in the water. "For Me you are to do battle. But be of good cheer. I am with you. I have overcome the world." "Jesus Christ is going into battle." He had overcome the world. Ivan, too, *would* overcome. His questions fled. There would be no prison sentence and no discharge. Tears soaked Ivan's face. He bowed as low as he could in the cramped space, and wept and worshipped.

A guard making his rounds glanced into the cell with interest. This was something he could report to the tribunal. With the stub of a pencil he wrote in his book, "Moiseyev lying in the water, weeping." The guard hoped this was a good sign. Perhaps the young soldier would break before long.

It was bad business drawing it out. They called it a fancy name, but it was torture, all the same.

For ten days Ivan endured agony, at the end deliriously praying for death and the release the Lord had promised him. Finally the tribunal refused to continue. Malsin had been beside himself with fury at their report. "It is our judgment that persuasive efforts are futile. This prisoner can be quickly sentenced and sent away. Continuance of security efforts will produce unpredictable results." In other words, if the procedures were to continue, let the "results" be the responsibility of the KGB and not the Simferopol tribunal. But it was not according to plan! Malsin had an intense headache. He had made his plans with precision. It had not been his intention to return to the base with Moiseyev unbroken.

The coffee shop in the prison was a filthy place, the few tables smeared and sticky with a bitter smell of rotting cloth about them. Malsin longed for vodka as he stirred his thick coffee with a tin spoon. The KGB were planning to continue the programme by working Moiseyev over in their branch headquarters in Kerch. Perhaps turning it over to them was for the best after all. A military tribunal had to have legal scruples which were unnecessary in the security force. The KGB had sanction to act administratively, to overrule courts of law and close legal loopholes when necessary for the security of the working people. Malsin pulled himself heavily to his feet. His headache was killing him.

It was a few days before Moiseyev was recovered enough to return to Kerch, where he was placed in special quarters. Malsin was anxious for everything to appear as normal as possible. No incidents must occur with the enlisted men. Malsin adapted his plan with elaborate care, concentrating in spite of the headache that would not go away.

It was in the middle of the night when he remembered when the headache had begun. The interrogator in Simferopol had placed Ivan's foot in a freezer unit. It had been a superfluous idea. Malsin disapproved of such warning procedures. Moiseyev should have been placed immediately in the cell freezer unit itself. The shock alone would have been as effective as the below-zero temperatures, especially for an already weakened constitution. But the foot incident had served to indicate that his speculations about Moiseyev's unusual cold endurance had been correct. Where any normal man would be screaming with pain, Moiseyev continued his maddening praying and claimed to feel only some pain. It was obvious his foot was frozen. Malsin reached for the vodka on his bedside table and corrected himself. It was obvious that any normal person's foot would be frozen. The interrogator insisted it was frozen, that the equipment was in perfect order. In spite of his deteriorated condition, Moiseyev had turned the incident into another one of his miracles. God, of course, had healed his foot in answer to prayer. It was the look of fear on the interrogator's face that had given Malsin this infernal headache. He drank quickly for the maximum effect of the alcohol. It didn't matter.

Well, he had given Moiseyev a last deadline. And tomorrow it was up. He poured another drink in the dark. Soon, he would go home to Galina and young Sasha. All the unpleasantness would be over. Galina would be happy. He fell into a restless sleep, dimly aware of the dull, throbbing pain that drummed in the back of his consciousness.

All the morning of July 16, he was detained by a delegation of party officials from Yugoslavia. He had expected them to be handled by any one of the other senior officers, but the instructions from Odessa had specified that Lt. Col. V. I. Malsin was to extend the courtesies of Kerch and conduct the delegation on a tour of the base. It was madness to be describing military training methods, political science curriculums, and programmes of leaves while the morning hours wore away with Moiseyev at liberty.

Today was the last deadline. Today pressure would be applied until Moiseyev broke. Malsin had great difficulty keeping his mind on the Yugoslavs. He could hardly restrain the rush of triumph that filled him when he thought of Moiseyev standing in the packed auditorium of the base's Palace of Culture, humbly repudiating his religious views, confessing his slanders against the Soviet state. Let the soldiers who had sunk into belief see their leader then! Perhaps Moiseyev should appeal for clemency and the opportunity to correct the views of the men he had led into error. That would make an impressive report for Dolotov.

Around noon he was able to excuse himself from the farewell amenities with the Yugoslav delegates because of "pressing business". The officers of the KGB had been waiting most of the morning in Malsin's office. He was astonished at their calmness. Now that there was the pressure of time, he was gratified that he had worked out a precise plan. Every detail had been thought of. The secrecy that had been possible in Simferopol would be maintained in Kerch. There would be no rumours or speculations among the soldiers of Moiseyev's unit.

Moiseyev would drive himself to the KGB headquarters in the city as if he were on an ordinary assignment. Malsin and the civilian security officers would leave the base in a Pobeda. A sense of exultation stirred Malsin. It was unfortunate, of course, that severe measures had to be taken. But keeping the end in view —the cleansing of men's minds, the building of pure socialism—there were times when these procedures were required. And the KGB were .experts. With a glance at his watch, Malsin picked up the telephone to order the cars. In a matter of minutes they would have Moiseyev in the special soundproof office of the security police. Today he would break!

Somehow it had never seriously occurred to Malsin that Moiseyev would prefer to die. The eventuality had not been in his plans. His death was of no concern to the KGB, of course. They had anticipated it as a probability. But for Malsin, the brutal end of the work swept away his dream of victory.

He had been sweating heavily during the frenzied afternoon. Now he was shaking with cold in spite of the July heat, his mouth dry with fear. His head was exploding. He stared unbelieving at Moiseyev's motionless body on the floor of the soundproof room. There would be explanations to provide, reports to make out, the boy's parents to notify, and the soldiers in his unit to satisfy. The believer, Sergei, could be detained. But how could Moiseyev's death be explained to the soldiers?

The KGB men were silently cleaning up the room. Malsin stood erect, controlling his trembling with folded arms across his chest. He wanted to sit down, to lie down. If only there were time to go over what had gone wrong, to listen again to what Moiseyev had said before his moans and prayers were silenced. "Christ . . . loves all sinners." Was that what he had said?

Small trickles of blood continued to ooze from the puncture wounds around his heart. The KGB were confident that he was not yet dead and that his death could be made to appear an accident. They were treating Malsin like some kind of fool, moving him out of the way, deftly wrapping Moiseyev in a blanket. Surely there was a doctor for a headache like this. Malsin sat down, holding his head. Let them drown Moiseyev if they liked. The Black Sea was close enough. Malsin felt there was something he had to remember. If only the pounding would stop. It was something Moiseyev had said.

The straight can't become straighter

From the moment she had held the terrible telegram in her hand Joanna Constantinova determined not to cry. It was as if a cannonball had torn through her, leaving so little of herself behind that giving in to tears would for ever waste what ebbing strength she had. White-faced, she sent a child speeding to the fields for her husband. Another son, as frightened as his brother, ran to the collective director to tell that his mother would not be at work. Joanna tried to think. There were things to be done, arrangements to be made if they were to claim Ivan's body.

Her eyes had been dry during the long hot journey to Kerch. The fields on both sides of the creaking train lay basking in the blinding yellow glare of the torrid sun. She wondered that Semyon could stare so long at the shimmering landscape.

It was right that Semyon, the oldest, should come with them to help with the arrangements, but Joanna wished he had stayed at home. It was oppressive not to be able to speak freely to her husband when her heart was bursting with pain. Semyon believed too heartily in the telegram, imagining aspects of the drowning, sometimes repeating anguished questions as he gazed at the moving countryside. "How could he have drowned with comrades present? Why could he not have been revived? Why did such a senseless accident have to happen?"

At such moments Joanna glared at her husband in hopeless anger. What opportunity did a village boy from Volontirovka have to learn to swim? The whole family knew Ivan couldn't swim. If there had never been any letters, if he had never come home on leave with his stories of what was really happening, every one of them still would have heard the drowning accident strike a false note.

Joanna was surprised at the size of Kerch, its seaport streets crowded with sailors as well as soldiers, the smell of fish and the screams of gulls mixing with the sounds of traffic and filling the city air. Her thin face was flushed from the hotness of her black dress and black kerchief in the July heat. Her husband and son moved more easily through the crowded streets, directed by an ice cream seller to the bus stop that would take them to the military base.

She had not expected to meet Colonel Malsin himself. She clung tightly to her husband's arm, her mind a torment as he spoke. Surely the Moiseyevs would have some tea. There were some official procedures to take care of, but their son Semyon could prove helpful in the situation. The army wished to burden the grieving parents as little as possible. It had been a terrible shock.

It seemed to have been a terrible shock to the colonel also. Joanna watched his trembling hands and drawn face with astonishment. He was shaking Semyon's hand, making what appeared to be an enormous effort at civility. Semyon was a member of the Komsomol in his Suvorovskiy region of Moldavia. Excellent. A fine son. He could assist in the military arrangements and permit his parents rest after their long journey. Malsin walked a few steps with Semyon towards his office. Coming back, he stood hesitantly before the parents. A strange moment passed before he nodded towards a cluster of chairs in his outer office. Apprehensively, Joanna sat down beside her husband. Malsin's voice was husky with smoke and fatigue.

Joanna had difficulty hearing him and understanding his Russian. A burning cigarette smouldered in his hand. "Comrades Vasiliy and Joanna Moiseyev, there's something for you to know." He lowered his voice even further and spoke haltingly. "I was present when your son died. He fought with death. He died hard, but he died a Christian." The word hung in the stuffy outer office. Joanna gazed in stupefaction at the colonel. Had she understood? What an incredibly strange thing for an officer in the Red army to say. Her husband's steady voice broke the silence. "Thank you for telling us. We had no question in our minds about that. The Lord is faithful unto death."

Malsin turned and strode uneasily into his office. What was the matter with him? Why did he feel impelled to talk about Moiseyev? He had drowned. That was the important thing to remember. He must concentrate on that fact. He would discuss everything with Galina when he went home. Telling her would get it out of his system. He closed his office door and gazed at Semyon. As a member of the Young Communist League there could be no question as to where his loyalties lay. He must be made to fully understand his responsibilities. Malsin took a deep breath and lit another cigarette.

A hot night breeze was blowing in the slightly open window of the train as they had travelled back to Volontirovka. Joanna had not been surprised that Semyon had said not a word to them about his long interview with Malsin. The lights inside the car made mirrors of the train windows and Joanna stared at the reflection of her son in the window. The small crescent of the summer moon in the black sky outside over his head appeared like a sickle. The car was crowded with tired holidaymakers, some nodding in sleep, others

sharing sausage slices or bits of cheese from bundles
they carried with them. But Semyon sat erect, staring
at the screen of night that had dropped over the window. His hair fell over his face like stone. Not a part of
him moved.

Once during the night he had turned from the window with a long look at his parents. His eyes rested on
his father, bent forward in his seat in prayer. Without
speaking, he glanced at his mother and turned silently
back to his window. Something in the brief tableau was
so like the shutting of a door that Joanna turned her
head impulsively to the door of the passenger car. Had
it suddenly closed? It was her imagination. The closing
had been in Semyon. At that moment, she finally began
to weep. In some way she didn't understand, Semyon
too was gone.

They would carry his body through the village in an
open coffin as was the custom. Joanna Constantinova's
weeping continued from the other side of the crowded
room as the men prepared Ivan for the funeral. The
unfamiliar smell of flash bulbs hung in the hot air as
the pastors worked in silence, lifting and straining
against the unyielding weight of the corpse as they
dressed it in village clothes. What was the use of taking a picture of what the army had done to him?
Joanna tried to sip from the glass of water that the
sister beside her on the couch urged upon her, but then
pushed it away. Someone wiped her face.

Joanna closed her aching eyes. In the room, the
brothers were gathering up Ivan's uniform and motioning the sisters to bring the flowers for the inside of the
coffin. Involuntarily her eyes opened again at the
sound of shuffling. A paper was brought forward.
Faintly Joanna remembered that Vasiliy had been preparing a statement for people to sign. He was deter-

mined to have it shown and witnessed that his son's corpse did not correspond with the death certificate of "mechanical asphyxiation" that Officer Platonov had delivered. The burns, the stab wounds, the marks of beatings would be verified before burial. But who would dare to believe it, even if it were signed by all Moldavia? Vasiliy was bending over, tenderly speaking her name. Under his name, she added her own. Dully she watched Vasiliy moving about with the document. There was so much one didn't need to explain. Wisely, he was giving the pen not only to the believers present, but also to the other neighbours and villagers in the room.

Seemingly without direction the believers began to sing. Joanna rose awkwardly, helped by the sisters who sat with her on the small couch. The hymn, "I Am a Pilgrim", streamed out the open windows to the streets and fragrant summer fields beyond. Many from the village were already inside the tiny house. More stood outside, listening at the open shutters and against the side of the cottage. There would be one or two gospel messages, she knew. Perhaps even in his death, Ivan could bring people to the Lord. Certainly most of the people in the village had never heard a Christian sermon or seen a Christian funeral. The believers continued to sing until Brother Chapkiy made his way to the front of the coffin, his Bible opened. The last strains of the hymn died out in the still air before he spoke. Quietly, he began. "Blessed in the sight of God is the death of His saints." Several women began to weep softly. Joanna sat down neither speaking or thinking.

Time seemed to have stopped. She knew that several of the brothers would have preached, especially with so many unbelievers present. And the young people would have read poems. Oddly it seemed that nothing had happened at all, yet they were in the street, mak-

ing the funeral procession to the cemetery. The glare of
the sun almost blinded her as she walked with her husband behind the coffin. Let the world see what had
been done to her son! She was glad that the Scripture
banners were held high, weaving on their poles in the
waves of heat that seemed to rise from the rutted road.
Most of the believers had begun a hymn, but Joanna
had no heart for singing. The texts had been printed in
Moldavian and Russian, and Joanna fixed her gaze on
the Moldavian words. "For to me, to live is Christ, and
to die is gain." "Do not fear those who kill the body,
but are unable to kill the soul." Let there be a witness
to the village and the country and to anyone that hears
of it that we are not so ignorant that we do not know
what has been done! "Seeing on the altar those slain
for the Word of God." Let the texts cry out what we
cannot speak!

The procession wound slowly along the village road
to the cemetery, pulling crowds of workers from the
fields and old people from the small farm cottages as it
passed. Their son Volodia preceded the coffin, carrying
against his chest the large photograph of Ivan that had
been taken on his leave. The young face seemed to
gaze eloquently at the onlookers as if communicating
some profound wisdom. Many from the fields curiously joined the march because the deceased had been
after all a young soldier, and this was an unusual funeral. The pastors marched together, singing, the two
worn Bibles they had among them carried reverently
by Fyodor Gorektoi, the oldest of the pastors, and his
cousin, Pyotr. Their white heads and beards glistened
in the brilliant summer light.

There was a grove of birch in the corner of the
cemetery where the grave had been dug. The long procession formed into a group under the trees, the onlookers squinting curiously in the hot sun. The believ-

ers sang "One Sweetly Solemn Thought", and Pastor Chelorskii opened his Bible and preached once more, his eyes returning again and again to the large number of farm workers and old people with small children who listened to his words.

There was something inexorable about the progress of events. Joanna reached suddenly for her husband's arm as the lid with its broken army seals was placed on the coffin and lowered into the earth. The believers were singing "To Our Home Above". Joanna looked painfully over the bent heads of her younger sobbing children to the faces of the young people who had been Vanya's friends. They had carried flowers through the streets and held them in their arms throughout the long service. Now, as shovels of earth thudded on to the coffin top, they slowly moved forward, placing the flowers in heaps around the grave's edge. Stefan Alexandrovich had been carrying the garland-text, "For to me, to live is Christ, and to die is gain". With a thrust he anchored the pole in the grassy earth. The young people moved towards it, kneeling quietly under the banner. A stillness fell upon the crowd. Even the sightseers who had been straining to watch the lowering of the coffin became silent. Under the open sky, on socialist earth, the young people began to pray.

Epilogue

Twelve days after the funeral, the Moiseyevs began telling their story to the world. In a formal protest to Moscow (see following documents), they called for a prompt investigation and an autopsy by a team to include two local Christian doctors.

There was no immediate response. Meanwhile, Ivan's Unit 61968T in Kerch was broken up. The men were re-assigned to all parts of the Soviet Union. No two soldiers were left together.

Colonel Malsin's young son fell off a wagon and died as the result of injuries.

Galina Malsin was commited to a psychiatric institution.

Malsin himself was dismissed from his post. He is reportedly distraught and obsessed with the idea that God is punishing him.

The CCECB Council of Prisoners' Relatives immediately gave wide publicity to the martyrdom through its underground bulletins. Letters of condolence from Leningrad to Siberia began to pour into the Moiseyev home. The story soon reached Western news agencies and was published in both secular and religious media in thirty countries, triggering bitter Soviet denials.

Believers passing the story along have been charged and arrested. Two pastors in Sverdlovsk were put on trial, one for simply showing the photo of Ivan's corpse in a church meeting, although he had made no comment about it. Believers report that twenty-two were arrested as far away as Poland.

Russian homes and prayer houses are subject to repeated searches for documents, letters, and tape re-

cordings about Ivan. In parts of Moldavia, overzealous agents ripped the Pentateuch out of believers' Bibles after spotting Moiseyev (the Russian word for "Moses") in many places throughout the text.

An inquiry commission finally came to Volontirovka in mid-September, 1972, fifty-two days after the burial. They began by cross-examining each villager who had signed the funeral document. Each non-Christian, frightened, denied having ever seen the corpse or having said anything about it.

The following day Ivan's body was exhumed. Only his parents and one brother were allowed to observe. The commission, which did not include Christian doctors as requested, excised the heart and surrounding tissue from the body before reburying it.

No commission report has ever been made public.

The last news of Sergei, Ivan's Christian friend, was that he too was undergoing persecution in the closing days of his tour of duty and had been given deadlines to reform.

Another believing Moiseyev son is now in the Red army.

Акт   19-20 VII ·72

Мы нижеподписавшиеся являемся
свидетелями в том, что привезённый
труп Майсеева Ивана Васильевича
1942 г. рождения с военной службы
в г. Керчь в/ч 61968 "В" не подтверждается
свидетельством о смерти №286064 1-АБ
диагнозом "Механическая асфиксия
от утопления," но утверждаем, что
смерть постигла в результате
умышленного насилия. Подтверждаем
снимками и фактами: сердце проколото шесть
раз, ноги и голова сильно побиты, на груди ожог.

Свидетели тела Волошировки подписались:

1. Майсеев В. П.   Моисеев
2. Майсеева И. К.   Маисеева
3. Моисеев В. В.   Моисеев
4. Майсеев С. В.
5. Майсеева Н. В.   Моисеева
6. Ченкши К. М.   Ченкши
7. Алба С. И.
8. Прокопович Н. И.   Прокопович
9. Нмопу П. С.
10. Слюсаренко А. С.   Слюсаренко
11. Трубецку В. А.   Ант
12. Каскара Р. И.   Гаскар
13. Алба М. Ф.   Алба
14. Ефремов В. И.   Ефремов
15. Менкош Е. Е.   Минкши
16. Ефремов М. С.   Ефремова
17. Ефремова А. С.   Ефремова
18. Кышелник А. Ф.   Кышелник
19. Шоров И. И.   Шоров
20. Тэлмишся А. М.   Тэлоча
21. Колисниченко Г. И.

22. Тэлм. М. А.   Тэлма
23. Тэлм В. С.   Тэлма

STATEMENT

July 19–20, 1972

We, the undersigned, are witnesses to the fact that the corpse of Moiseyev, Ivan Vasilievich, born 1952, brought home from military service in the city of Kerch, military unit 61968T, did not correspond to the Death Certificate No. 2860641-AT giving the diagnosis of "Mechanical asphyxiation due to drowning", but we state that death occurred as a result of premeditated violence. We confirm this with photographs and facts: the heart was punctured six times, the legs and the head were severely beaten, and there were burns on the chest.

Witnesses—residents of Volontirovka village

1. Moiseyev, V. T.   /signature/
2. Moiseyeva, J. C.   „
3. Moiseyev, V. V.   „
4. Moiseyev, S. V.   „
5. Moiseyeva, I. V.   „
6. Chapkiy, S. P.   „
7. Albu, S. I.   „
8. Prokopovich, M. M.   „
9. Romonu, D. Ye.   „
10. Slyusarenko, A. S.   „
11. Butesku, V. G.   „
12. Paskar, T. M.   „
13. Albu, M. F.   „
14. Yefremova, A. I.   „
15. Mankosh, Ye. Ye.   „
16. Yefremov, Ya. V.   „
17. Yefremova, A. S.   „
18. Kotelnik, A. F.   „
19. Blomitskaya, A. M.   „
20. Shorova, I. I.   „
21. Kolisniczenko, Ye. I.   „

22. Toma, T. A.   „
23. Toma, Ye. S.   „

Excerpts from Vanya's last letters to his parents

Date unknown
Peace to you, my beloved parents. Brothers in Christ from Zaprozhiye spent some time with me. I rejoice, even though someone from a union meeting (AUCECB) betrayed me last week for preaching Christ.

Even though I am a soldier, I work for the Lord, though there are difficulties and testings. Jesus Christ gave the order to proclaim His word in this city, in any meeting, in a military unit, to officers and soldiers. I have been in a division head-quarters and in a special section. Though it was not easy, the Lord worked so that it turned out well there. I had an opportunity to proclaim His word to the most senior personnel, but I was reviled and thrown out of the meeting.

Those will be saved who will live not by human will, but by God's will. Observe the commandments of Jesus. You will hear later that I have had many miracles and revelations.

In the Lord,
Your Vanya

June 15, 1972
Christian greetings to my beloved parents. I received your letter and it made me happy. I want to say that by the grace of the love of our gracious Father I am healthy. I wrote you when the Lord revealed to me which is the most correct way and how all Christians must live. In the second letter you will learn about this work, because the Lord has revealed everything.

My dear parents, when I was home, Ilyusha taught me a psalm. I asked you to write it out. Here we see Ilyusha already learning psalms and teaching them to his elders in order for them to sing because they do not know how. Yesterday I was in the Kerch assembly and met there with brethren from another assembly, since we are not associated with the union [AUCECB]. There was a brother from Sochi. And they knew about me. The visit was very good. And everyone here and from Sochi sends greetings in the Lord to all brethren in Moldavia.

My dear parents, the Lord has showed the way to me and I must follow it. And I have decided to follow it. But I do not know if I will return, because the battle is harder than at first. I will now have more severe and bigger battles than I have had till now. But I do not fear them. He goes before me. Do not grieve for me, my dear parents. It is because I love Jesus more than myself. I listen to Him, though my body does fear somewhat or does not wish to go through everything. I do this because I do not value my life as much as I value Him. And I will not await my own will, but I will follow as the Lord leads. He says, "Go", and I go.

Do not become grieved if this is your son's last letter. Because I myself, when I see and hear visions, hear how angels speak and see, I am even amazed and cannot believe that Vanya, your son, talks with angels. He, Vanya, has also had sins and failings, but through sufferings the Lord has wiped them away. And he does not live as he wishes himself, but as the Lord wishes.

Now I want to say a few words to those who do not believe in our Lord Jesus Christ. You call yourselves anti-Christians because you know, though you do not believe, that there is a Lord who has given me life because this body was dead. You, Semyon, my dear brother, know that the heavenly Father can give you life. Even I have grown very weary with you. Much has passed since then, and I am far from you. But I want you, Semya, to know that there is a God. Know and believe that I have spoken with angels and have flown with them even to another planet where life eternal awaits us. Believe, believe, if you can, all of you who do not yet know Him. I am writing to you because I have seen it all and I know it exists.

June 30, 1972

We greet you all with the great love of Jesus Christ. Your least among the brethren, Vanya, writes you.

I can still write you this letter freely, and you can find out that after my joyous meeting with Sergei, there was not only another storm, but many more. I was glad for everything; when there were no storms, not even adverse winds, then it can become a little tedious. But I am now becoming accustomed to these storms.

Oh, how wonderful and marvellous it is that far from our earth, there is joy! Oh, brethren, keep advancing bravely. Don't be afraid if you have to pass through fire on your way to the heavenly goal.

If your heart will love anything more than Christ, then you are not worthy to follow Him.

Now I want to write to you what kinds of wonderful bodies

angels and we will have if we are faithful unto death. I greatly
wished to see angels, and I saw them; I saw how they were
dressed and told you about them. But their bodies are not like
ours; their bodies do not interfere with anyone seeing past
them. You can look and see things right through them, as
through a glass, and within and without they are pure, pure as
crystal, as glass. And everything within can be seen. They have
not a single sin, not a single defect. These spiritual bodies we
will obtain sometime. With such bodies we can see Jesus Christ
and angels, and the heavenly Father; then we will know what
one or another is thinking. Oh, what joy, what purity, and
what love exists there. How pure everyone is, pure, and even if
you polish the best glass, it still remains duller than those
bodies awaiting us.

I anxiously await your reply. I wish all of you dear brethren
to go forward to this heavenly land.

July 9, 1972

The greetings of your son will soon come to an end. I am
weak, but I am still greeting you with the love of Jesus Christ
and with the peace of God. They have forbidden me to preach
Jesus and I am going through tortures and testings, but I told
them that I will not stop bearing the news of Jesus. And the
Lord shamed them before the entire unit, when they were
torturing me. A soldier stood up who had miraculously gone on
leave and had told everyone, and he asked, "Whose power was
this?" The authorities did not wish to let me go, and they were
put to shame. They then asked me why this tree is green, and
the other dry, since the two trees were side by side, one green,
the other dry. I asked them what the difference was. They
answered, "The difference is great because one is alive and the
other is dead." And I told them this is the difference between a
believer and an anti-Christian. They still remained nonplussed
and greatly embarrassed.

July 11, 1972

I greet you all with the love of Jesus Christ. Vanya writes
you this letter. I am very glad for you, and perhaps we can still
meet one another. You may have found out that a discharge
for me is strictly forbidden. But I am working at full steam for
Christ, and I do not want to boast, but I want you to know it,
and I hope that you do not forget me in your prayers.

On the tenth of this month, in the evening, I preached Jesus

Christ, and after a lengthy discussion one soldier became a believer. I was very glad, and even more strength filled me. There has not yet been a meeting with Sergei.[1] Glory to the Lord for everything. If I meet with you I will tell you about things in detail, but I cannot write about them in a letter.

When he sees how the sea rages
For those returning from the fray,
   "Fearsome waves over us roll,
   Joy and courage fills our soul."

For those who from the fearsome, pressing waves
Returned with victory to the shore.
   "We move onward towards the shore,
   We move to victory evermore.

   For you will be days without dawn again,
   As a soldier, the anguish of separation's pain
   Nor easy months in depths most troubling,
   Hearing, it seems, the groans of brothers doubling."

But no! Might abundant sends the Lord
In their example hope upon him is poured
Whatever sternness his lot affords.

He does fulfil heaven's most difficult order
His last strength he shares with another
Oft struggling with the sea's raging weather.

What he does he is ordered to do
Though it is hard for him to go through
He obeys Christ's sacred command!

I feel that you will not see me any longer, ... and if you think about coming to me, it is useless. I will not forget you in prayer. I very earnestly wish to meet with Sergei. Perhaps, my last work has already been done. Receive my heartfelt Christian greetings from the least of the brethren. I do not await your answer and I ask you not to write.

Till we see one another, God be with you, dear friends. I have become sad thinking about you, but one thing I remember: I go fulfilling Christ's orders....

                      Greetings from Vanya

---

[1] Evidently this is in addition to the 'joyous meeting' with Sergei mentioned in the June 30 letter.

July 14, 1972

The work is great, and I follow Jesus' command. The testings are great and the sufferings are not light. I have much to write that I cannot write in letters. I am awaiting the visit from Sergei as the Lord promised. Oh, that we may not now be ashamed of speaking about the Lord. All have seen the miracles and say that in truth God exists. I will plant seed and will move ahead, as the Lord teaches me through the Holy Spirit and the angels.

Don't be offended but I am striving in this work. Also know that it is not easy for the body. Now I go to meetings, though they have forbidden it. The brothers send greetings to all. And I send greetings to all: Slabodzeya and Yernokley [village ECB churches].

I wish that Semya and Galya could believe in and see the power of the Lord to see that He exists, just as all do here: officers and soldiers say that there is a God and fear Him, for they see miracles and His might. I also wish that grandmother could believe and that she would know that the path she is following leads to hell. Jesus Christ is still calling you and He would give you life eternal, but I cannot give life. Believe in the gospel. If you hear that I am not at liberty, then know that here in the city of Kerch I have left a notebook where I have described the miracles, and maybe you can come, or they can bring it to you; the Lord knows all. Be true Christians. He will fortify you and send you His strength.

Ask, for He is rich in all, and all that you wish He gives free.

I do not forget you in my prayers.

In the Lord, Vanya

July 15, 1972 (to his brother, Vladimir)

Dear brother, I received your letter and am late in answering you because there was a great storm. When Sergei came, even he got it, and his literature and even post cards were confiscated.

Don't tell our parents everything. Just tell them, "Vanya wrote me a letter and writes that Jesus Christ is going into battle. This is a Christian battle, and he doesn't know whether he will be back."

I desire that all of you, dear friends, young and old, remember this one verse. Revelation 2: 10—"Be faithful unto death, and I will give you the crown of life."

Receive this, the last letter on this earth, from the least of the brethren.

Vanya

The Moiseyevs' formal protest to the world

To:

A. A. Grechko, Minister of the Armed Forces of the USSR

L. I. Brezhnev, General Secretary of the Central Committee of the CPSU

K. Waldheim, General Secretary of the UN

International Committee for the Defence of Human Rights at the United Nations

Professor M. V. Keldysh, President of the USSR Academy of Sciences

Chairman of the Union of Writers of the USSR

Editors of the Newspapers:
Sovetskaya Rossiya
Pravda
Izvestiya

Council of Churches of ECB in the USSR

Council of ECB Prisoners' Relatives in the USSR (CPR)[1]

To all Christians

From:

The Parents of Moiseyev, Ivan Vasilievich Killed during torture for his faith in God in the ranks of the Soviet Army, a resident of Volontirovka Village, Suvorovskiy Region, Moldavian SSR

"And it came about that all who saw it said, 'Nothing like this has ever happened . . . to this day.'"   Judges 19 : 30

---

[1] The Council of Evangelical Christian/Baptist Prisoners' Relatives in the USSR (CPR) was formed by members of the CCECB in 1961 for the defence of men and women imprisoned because of their Christian beliefs.

EXTRAORDINARY REPORT

On July 16, 1972, our son and brother Moiseyev, Ivan Vasilievich, born 1952, died for the convictions of his faith in God from terrible martyr's torments in the city of Kerch while in service in the Soviet Army (Military Unit 61968 "T").

Covered with wounds, haggard from torture, but still alive, in the presence of Lieutenant Colonel Malsin, V. I., he was forcibly drowned in the Black Sea at a depth of 156 cm. while his height was 185 cm.

The death certificate cited "Mechanical asphyxiation from drowning". The autopsy analysis read: "Death followed as the result of violence."

On July 17, 1972, at eight A.M., we received a telegram: "Your son has died tragically. Please inform us of your arrival." On arriving in the city of Kerch, we decided to inter him in his native village. We were shown the face of our son in the coffin, after which the same coffin was soldered shut. With us was our son Semyon, a Komsomol member, whom the military unit commander summoned individually into his office and talked to him about something for a long time about which our Semyon told us not a word.

For participation in the funeral ceremony and delivery of the coffin to Volontirovka village, from the military unit were sent Captain Platonov, V. V., also an extended-service sergeant, and a private, who brought the coffin to the village on July 20, 1972. On receiving the coffin bearing the body of our son, we decided to inspect the body and to photograph it. To do this, we began to break the welds of the coffin lid.

Platonov, V. V., and the sergeant seated nearby us, became alarmed on seeing this and immediately announced, "We have to go, we're in a hurry", and quickly got into the vehicle and disappeared. On opening the coffin, we began to remove clothing to inspect the body, but Semyon, using physical force, did not allow us to inspect the body and to photograph it, declaring to all his relatives, "Photograph him dressed." Those present saw the following marks on the body: in the area of the heart six deep punctures with a round object, on the head abrasion wounds to the left and to the right, the legs and back were severely beaten, large burns on the chest so that rapping with a finger along the skin was audible, and bruises around the mouth. All this was confirmed by twenty-three witnesses, residents of Volontirovka village, by a statement dated July 20,

1972 (we attach the statement).

From the testimony of the unit commander Malsin, V. V., in a conversation with us, Vanya's parents, the following must be noted: "On the morning of the sixteenth I was occupied and had a conversation in the unit with a group of governmental guests. In the afternoon I drove with Moiseyev to the beach in a GAZ-69 truck." In the words of soldier eyewitnesses, Malsin drove in a Pobeda car together with unknown civilians, and Moiseyev followed after them alone in the GAZ-69 truck in an unknown direction.

On July 19, 1972, in handing over Moiseyev's body, Malsin stated: "Moiseyev died hard, he fought with death, but he died a Christian. Today I am smoking my seventh pack of cigarettes." On August 1 of this year he said, "My wife lost nine pounds in a week from the experiences of Moiseyev's death," declaring that "She no longer will ride in the vehicle he drove."

(Next follows excerpts from Ivan's tape recording and letters to document his persecution while in the army.)

We wish again to repeat the words of Lieutenant Colonel Malsin, V. I.: "Moiseyev died hard; he fought with death, but he died a Christian."

WE, THE PARENTS, ASK THAT:

1. A medical experts' commission be sent at once to autopsy and establish the cause of death of the tormented body of our son.

2. An investigation be made to find and convict the criminals who tortured him.

3. We Christian parents have four other sons younger than Ivan who face service in the army, but until the murderers are found and charged and a necessary guarantee of the safety of our believing children in the army is given, we will not hand over our four sons to serve in the same.

4. Considering that believers in our country have been subjected to undeserved insults and slander, and many incidents of the victims have been deliberately distorted, we believe that the experts' commission will be incompetent without the participation of a doctor from among Christians. Therefore we

will give our agreement to autopsy the body of our son Ivan only in the presence of our relatives and two doctors from among believers, whom we will present on the day that this commission arrives. We request that its arrival be announced to us four days in advance.

We attach to this report the following:

1. Statement of witnesses.
2. Copy of the death certificate.
3. We will present the photographs of the body areas to the commission of experts at the time the body is autopsied.

Respectfully: (signatures) Moiseyev, V. T.
Moiseyeva, J. C.
Moiseyev, V. V.
Moiseyev, R. V.
Moiseyeva, M. V.

Please reply to: Moldavian SSR
Suvorovskiy Region
Volontirovka Village

August 1, 1972

January 5, 1973

Wire service release
which appeared in many Russian newspapers

On a hot July day in 1972 a soldier named Ivan Moiseyev drowned approximately a hundred metres from shore at Cape Borzovka near the city of Kerch. Many were in the water with him, so the chap was quickly dragged to the shore. Everything was done to save him. At first artificial respiration was administered. Later, after the indirect massage of the heart, Dr. E. Novikovo injected adrenalin into the heart and ofedrin into a vein. However, the struggle for life was in vain, and the following autopsy showed that he was drowned, with paralysis of the heart following immediately.

The death of the young man was taken very hard by his comrades in the service, but it would never enter their minds that this unfortunate accident would be used by base people who counted Ivan as their "brother". Among his relatives there turned out to be Evangelical Christians/Baptists. The leaders of the Council of Churches of Evangelical Christian/Baptists decided to use the death of their "brother" to achieve a provocation. They told those who gathered at Moiseyev's funeral in the village of Volontirovka [Moldavia] that Ivan was "tortured". The marks on his body were from the attempts to save his life and from the autopsy, but they were falsely interpreted as evidences of horrible tortures. At the funeral the provokers obtained a collection of signatures under a slanderous "document".

I CANNOT BE SILENT

My brother is dead. It is hard to believe it. For he was only twenty years old when the senseless death cut off his life. To me he has always been and still is very dear.

We grew up under the same shelter; we were both caressed by the gentle hands of our mother. We went to the same school in the village of Volontirovka, Suvorovskiy district. I regret one thing. I broke the chains with which the Baptists bound our hands and feet, but Ivan did not.

He is gone. The so-called brothers in Christ set up a wail nearly through the entire world, maintaining that Ivan suffered for the cause of his belief, that he was drowned by force. I cannot be silent, when some people talk all kind of nonsense, threaten our Soviet rules, and throw shadows on the Soviet people. You tell lies, you malign the remembrance about my brother, you malign my mother and my father. He and I had different opinions about the world. He remained a believer, and I not. However, the difference in opinion did not make us enemies. We argued at times. I thought that it would not be long and my brother would break up with the Baptists. I was grieved when I learned that Ivan had a misfortune. The family and I went to Kerch to get his body and bury him in the homeland.

Ten or fifteen days later, the so-called Council of Churches of Evangelical Christians/Baptists composed a fake document about my brother's death. I read that bulletin. It contained sheer nonsense. Just listen to it. "It has been affirmed that Ivan was persecuted for his faith, he was punished, he was deprived of free time to go to the town, he was tortured, etc." All that is a slander.

I was honoured to be where my brother served in the army.

I conversed with his commanders and with the soldiers. They had nothing against him. He carried out his duties faithfully, he was the chauffeur of the commander of the military unit where he served in the military service. Within one year of military service he had seven merit points from his commander. He was twice offered short-term leave home. The Baptists try to persuade that Ivan was oppressed in the army. It is not true. I have been in military service myself, and I know that the soldiers are not persecuted, even those who profess religious faith. Ivan had an opportunity to exercise religious ceremonies. For he, like the other soldiers, received passes. On his free time he could go, and he attended prayer meetings.

The Baptists try to contend that my brother was martyred and later drowned. It is an outrageous lie! I talked to those who were present at the accident. He drowned by accident. It can happen to anybody. Indeed there were marks on his body, but not from torture or scorching iron as the Baptists assure it was. Those marks were signs from the massages and shots, when people applied all means to save Ivan.

We brought my brother's body home in a coffin made of zinc. Here I understood that the Baptists' leaders were plotting something. They decided to take pictures. They pushed me aside from the coffin; there were many of them in the house. At the funeral, the Baptists pushed a blank sheet of paper to the fool countrymen to sign their names on it. People agreed to do it. They did so without thinking that later, above their names, the Baptists' leaders would compose an "act" in which they maintain that Ivan's death was caused as a result of premeditated murder. What a dishonest counterfeit!

Who did it? So-called Baptists and, above all, their leaders. Ivan knew about those illegal brothers; he met with them; however, he did not tell them the truth. On his second leave, he told to all of us, including Uncle Verebtchany, that he was content with the military service. He had taken the military oath, he met with the illegal servants of God in Tiraspole; he refuse to take the military oath.) A day later, after he took the oath, he met with the illegal servants of God in Tiraspole; he did not tell them that he had taken the oath. He misled them.

The leaders of the Evangelical Christian/Baptist church composed the letter on behalf of my parents, which accused honest people. Why did you do that? Yes, my parents are Christian, but they will never get involved in dirty business; they will never slander our people or our governmental system. They know that the Soviet regime opened up a door for them and their children to a happier life. And if in our family misfortune took place, then do not try to take advantage of it. It will not work! We swept aside your slander! Do not erase, with your dirty hands, the respectful memory of a son and brother Ivan.

Your bulletin is a fraud. It is needed by the leaders of the Christian/Baptists who gave you orders from abroad. I know, for example, that the slanderous information about Ivan Moiseyev's death was translated into many languages, multiplied, and spread into fifteen countries.

Thus it was found out why you were so quick. Remember, however, you cannot fool Soviet people.

Semyon Moiseyev,
truck driver

Moldavian SSR

I KNOW THE TRUTH

Due to the circumstances I personally witnessed how Ivan Moiseyev perished. I know the whole truth about his death.

Believe me, for us who know the tragic story, it is hard to talk about it. In the full bloom of life, a young man unexpectedly perished; he would have still lived a full life. Whose heart will not wring from grief! However, the necessity to refute the slanderers and to tell the whole truth to those who were deceived by the slanderers forces me to come back to the event which took place in July of last year.

We decided to spend a few days with my cousin, Larisa. Early in the morning Vladimir, her husband, a Soviet military officer, wanted to show us the sights of the Crimea. Our automobile broke down, and while it was being repaired, Vladimir made arrangements for us to get a military car. We drove to Kerch. The driver was a young soldier. Later I found out that the young soldier was Ivan Moiseyev.

It became very hot and we decided to go to swim, so we drove to the cape of Borzovka. Vladimir told the children and the driver, "Do not rush into the water. First cool off, then go to swim." Later he added to Ivan, "And you go dive into the water and come right back to the automobile. We will be going on soon."

They went to swim and I stayed behind. While I was conversing with the people, suddenly Larisa came running and shouting, "Our driver perished!" "How did he perish?" I asked. "Look!" she said. As I looked I saw Vladimir was still swimming, looking for Ivan, and from the shore people were shouting and showing him where Ivan plunged into the water. Later those who were at the seashore were telling that Moiseyev came to the surface, shouted something, and went down again.

Ten minutes went by. Vladimir was still looking for Moiseyev. Then suddenly a wave brought his body up to the surface. His body was immediately picked up by the people and given artificial respiration. They sent me to get an ambulance. Not far away was either a boarding school or a holiday house. I called the ambulance. In the meantime a doctor from that place came to the seashore.

The doctor began to give him artificial respiration. Then he said, "Get me some alcohol." Where can one get alcohol? We went to the tents at the seashore; tourists lived in the tents. They had some alcohol.

Somebody was shouting at the doctor, "Whatever you need, tell us and we will find it. If we only could save the young man's life." But the massage with alcohol did not help. The doctor said, "We need to apply mustard plaster." Mustard was found in the tents.

The ambulance arrived. They gave an injection to Moiseyev. Shortly after another ambulance arrived. They gave another injection and gave him artificial respiration.

For three hours they worked on Ivan, trying to bring him back to life; unfortunately, all efforts seemed to be in vain. About fifty people gathered around Ivan's body, and they all were weeping bitterly at the death of the young soldier.

Now, all of a sudden I find out that there are some slanderers who took advantage of such deep grief for their provoking purposes. The marks which were left in efforts to save Moiseyev's life were used as a proof of torture. One must be unscrupulously cynical to do such a thing! I know where the slander came from. I was still there when the relatives came to take Ivan's body. One of them just looked at the deceased, and without even giving tribute of grief began to affirm, "I know they killed him, they tortured him to death." It seemed to me that he already came with a prepared version and was looking for every possible way to confirm it. How can the leaders of the Evangelical Christian/Baptist church talk about sanctity and love towards your neighbour when they themselves lack the simple human conscience! To what kind of high ideals of faith can they call their co-religionists?

There were fifty of us who witnessed Ian Moiseyev's death. And if people who declare Ivan their brother speculate on his death, if they sell conscience for thirty imported silver coins, then we will not permit them to take advantage of the misfortune of others; we will not permit them to hide their black souls behind the filthy slander.

L. A. Martinenko,
inhabitant of the city of Stavropola.

Among other documents available to the author was the transcript of Vanya's tape-recorded account, made in May 1972, of his experiences in the army up to the time he was sent back from Simferopol to Kerch.

BLOOD BROTHERS

Elias Chacour is ordained in the Melkite Church, an ancient body of believers that has existed in the Middle East from the earliest centuries of Christianity. Educated in Paris at the *Seminaire du Saint Sulpice,* Chacour was the first Palestinian to earn a degree from the Hebrew University where he studied Bible and Talmud. Currently he is building schools, libraries, community centres and youth clubs throughout Israel's Galilee region.

BLOOD BROTHERS

ELIAS CHACOUR

with David Hazard

KINGSWAY PUBLICATIONS

EASTBOURNE

Contents

Dedication

To my father who will not be mentioned in the world history books, though he is written in the heart of God as His beloved child: Michael Moussa Chacour from Biram in Galilee, refugee in his own country and one who speaks the language of patience, forgiveness and love.

And to my brothers and sisters, the Jews who died in Dachau; and their brothers and sisters, the Palestinians who died in Tel-azzaatar, Sabra and Shatila refugee camps.

An Urgent Word Before

Before I had set my hands to the typewriter keys I was aware that this could be "a controversial book." The reason is that *Blood Brothers* breaks new ground in what has been written about the Middle East turmoil and goes beyond the usual political wrestlings over "who owns the land?" It will disturb certain people and please others, and for the same reason: it probes those ever-murky areas of conscience and heart. Above all, this is a story about people, not politics.

Before I had heard of Elias Chacour (pronounced shah-*koor*), I was not aware that I held certain prejudices regarding Middle East issues. Leafing through the *Sojourners Magazine* one afternoon, I was stopped by an article entitled, "Children of Ishmael in the Promised Land,"* by Jim Forest, and pored through an arresting interview with Chacour, a Palestinian Christian leader. I was amazed at my mixed response.

What moved me was his soul-felt cry for reconciliation between Palestinians and Jews and his obvious love for both. I was stirred by reading about a side of the Arab-Israeli

_____
* *Sojourner's Magazine*, September 1980.

vii

conflict that is little known. Yet something was interfering with my sympathies.

Had I not heard countless news reports about Arab terrorism and the Palestinian Liberation Organization? I had never considered that there were also Palestinian Christians who were living the challenging, non-violent alternative taught by Jesus Christ in the midst of the world's most bitter conflict. Why had I never heard of Chacour and his people before?

Forest's interview stuck with me a long time, like a nail in my conscience. Finally, in the spring of 1983, it spurred a trip to Galilee where I was to meet Chacour in his small village of Ibillin. Perched on the green hills northeast of Nazareth, overlooking the citrus groves along the Mediterranean, Ibillin has a mixed population of Christians and Moslems. There, my Western mentality towards Palestinians was exposed blatantly, and I felt chagrined.

Somehow I was expecting Chacour, the pastor of Ibillin's Melkite Church, to be naive and unsophisticated. Instead, I was captivated by this man of medium stature, barrel-chested, with a black, prophet-like beard that is streaked by a lightning slash of gray—an intense and intensely warm human being.

I discovered that Chacour is Paris-educated, holds a doctorate, speaks eleven languages including Ugaritic, the ancient mother tongue of both Hebrew and Arabic, and has a degree from the Hebrew University in Jerusalem. Moreover, his frequent travels carry him to several continents, to churches and synagogues, before queens and prime ministers. With each person he meets—Irish Catholic or Protestant, Indian or Pakistani, Gentile or Jew—he shares the secrets of lasting peace.

Neither was Ibillin what I expected in a Palestinian village.

True, the cinder-block houses, cramped against the road, are poor by Western standards; goats and donkeys wander about, and cats are anything but domesticated; in 1983 the village was just constructing its first high school building. But beneath the surface poverty, the life of the spirit is rich. Dramas and public poetry readings abound, teenagers dance and sing in honor of their mothers on a special day of celebration and the church is alive with young singing voices.

Nevertheless, I was challenged by Chacour's strong statements. Among them, that Palestinians have a God-given right to live in Israel as equals, though many Israelis claim the land is theirs exclusively and by scriptural mandate. And Chacour has a gentle impatience with those who come to Israel to venerate shrines of the past while ignoring human beings; who come to see only "holy stones and holy sand." With a spreading smile he directed his challenge at me: "Did you come for the shrines—or do you want to learn about the *living* stones?"

Preeminently, he was concerned that I was one more writer from the West who would present a cut-and-dried view of the Middle East. "Can you help me to say that the persecution and stereotyping of Jews is as much an insult to God as the persecution of Palestinians?" he begged. "I wish to disarm my Jewish brother so he can read in my eyes the words, 'I love you.' I have beautiful dreams for Palestinian and Jewish children together."

Our encounter sent me on a search for some truth amid the muddle of violence and recriminations, politics and spiritual claims. The fact that I was writing the story of one man's life did not make my work any easier. My strong desire to set Elias Chacour's personal story in perspective made writing painfully slow. And all the while my political opinions and my long-held beliefs about Bible prophecy were stretched further than I imagined possible.

What drove me to completing *Blood Brothers* was the human drama—the compassion and the rare treasure of peace within Elias Chacour that I wanted to discover for myself. His is a true account that moved me as few before—an account of faith in the midst of indignity, hatred and violence in the furnace that is the Middle East.

In that furnace, Elias' story begins.

David Hazard

1

News In the Wind

Surely my older brother was confused. I could hardly believe what he was telling me. I leaned dangerously far out on a branch, my bare feet braced against the tree trunk, and accidentally knocked a scattering of figs down onto the head of poor Atallah who had just delivered the curious news.

"A celebration?" I shouted from my tilting perch. "Why are we having a celebration? Who told you?"

"I heard Mother say—" he called back, dodging the falling figs, "that something *very big* is happening in the village. And," he paused, his voice sinking to a conspiratorial hush, "Father is going to buy a lamb."

A lamb! Then it *must* be a special occasion. But why? It was still a few weeks until the Easter season, I puzzled, sitting upright on the branch. At Easter-time our family celebrated with a rare treat of roasted lamb—and for that matter it was one of the few times during the year that we ate meat at all. We knew—because Father always reminded us—that the lamb represented Jesus, the Lamb of God. And, of course, I realized that Father was not going to *buy* a lamb. We rarely bought anything. We bartered for items that we could

11

not grow in the earth or make or raise ourselves, the same as everyone else in our village of Biram.

I'm sure Atallah knew that if he waited around, he was risking another barrage of figs and questions. He was already trotting away toward the garden plot beyond our small stone house where I should have been helping Mother and the rest to clear away rocks. It was an endless job even then, in 1947, since no one in our village of Biram owned farm machinery to make work easier. When school had ended an hour before, I had hidden up in this fig tree—my tree, as I called it—to escape the labor. Now, watching Atallah disappear, I wondered what exciting event was rippling the too-regular course of our lives.

I must find Father and ask him myself, I decided.

Instead of dropping down into the deep orchard grass to trail after Atallah, I shinnied higher up the fig tree—up to the very top, where the branches bent at dangerous angles under my weight. This was my special place. Besides being a good lookout post, it bore not one, but *six* different kinds of figs. My father, who was something of a wizard with fruit-bearing trees, had performed a natural magic called grafting and combined the boughs of five other fig trees onto the trunk of a sixth. A thick, curling vine trellised up the trunk and spread through the branches, too, draping the tree with clusters of mouth-puckering grapes. Many afternoons, I monkeyed my way up onto a high branch, sampling the juicy fruit until my stomach cramped. Then I would ease down into Mother's cradling arms and she would comfort me, her littlest boy— her dark-haired, spoiled one.

"Elias," she would coo over me, shaking her head. "You'll never learn, will you? And I would bury my face in her thick hair, groaning as my four older brothers and my sister rolled their eyes in disgust.

Now, with one arm crooked around the topmost branch, I

pushed aside the curled leaves, thrusting my head out into the spring sun which was slanting toward late afternoon. Perhaps Father was in his orchard. Row after row of fig trees spread for several acres, stretching down the hill away from our house, covering the slope with rustling greenery. The broadening leaves concealed a fresh-water spring and a dark, mossy grotto where our goats and cattle sheltered themselves in summer. Beyond our orchards rose the lush majestic highlands of the upper Galilee. They looked purple in the distance—"the most beautiful land in all of Palestine," Father said so often. A dreamy look would mist into his pale blue eyes then, as it did whenever he spoke about his beloved land.

Search as I might, I could not find Father ambling among those trees just now. Most days he worked there with my brothers, teaching them the secrets of husbandry. At seven years old, I was considered too young—and too impish—to learn about the fig trees. With or without me, my father and brothers had busheled up three tons of golden-brown figs in the last harvest.

With a recklessness that would have paled my mother, I swung down from the treetop and flung myself to the ground. Then I was off, running toward the center of the village. Surely someone had seen Father.

I darted through the narrow streets—hardly streets at all, but foot-worn, dirt corridors that threaded the homes of the village together beneath the shade of cedar and silver-green olive trees—dodging a goat and some chickens in my path. Biram seemed like one huge house to me. Our family, the Chacours, had led their flocks to these, the highest hills of Galilee, many hundreds of years ago. My grandparents had always lived here, nearly next door to us. And there were so many aunts, uncles, cousins and distant relatives clustered here, it was as if each stone dwelling was merely another

room where another bit of my family lived. All the homes fit
snugly together right up to our own, the last house at the far
edge of the village. Biram had grown here, quietly rearing its
children, reaping its harvests, dozing beneath the Mediterranean stars for so many generations that all households were
as one family.

And today this whole family seemed to be keeping a secret
from me. I ran from house to house where small knots of
kerchiefed women in long, dark skirts were talking with
hushed excitement. Eagerly, I burst in on a group of older
women, some of my many "grandmothers." They stopped
clucking at each other only long enough to *shush* me and
shoo me out the door again.

My feelings bruised, I trotted toward our church which
was the living heart of Biram. Here the entire village
crowded in on Sundays, shoulder to shoulder beneath its
embracing stone arches. The parish house, a small stone
building huddled next to the church, doubled as a school-
house during the week, its ancient foundations quaking from
our noisy activities. This year was my first in school, and I
loved it. Now, in the church's moss-carpeted courtyard, a
group of men were talking loudly. Father was not among
them, so I bounded off toward the open square just beyond.

Normally I hesitated before entering the square. This was
the realm of men—especially the village elders—and it held a
certain awe for me. Children were tolerated here only because we were plentiful as raindrops and just as unstoppable.
However, we knew enough to keep a respectful margin between our foolish games and the clusters of men who came in
the evening to hear news that the traveling merchants carried
in from far-off villages along with their shiney pots, metal
knives, shoes and what-not. Tottering at the edge of the
square were the stoney, skeletal remains of an ancient synagogue. On this spot, Father had told us, the Roman Legions

had built a pagan temple many centuries ago. The Jews later destroyed the temple and raised on its foundations a place of worship for the one, true God. Now the synagogue stood ruined and ghost-like, too. It was forbidden to play among the fallen pillars and any child brazen enough to do so suffered swift and severe punishment, for it was considered consecrated ground.

That day I shot out into the sun-bright square—and nearly toppled to a halt. The square, it startled me to see, was not abandoned to the clots of older men who usually nodded there in the afternoon warmth. Men young and old were huddled everywhere, talking about . . . *what?* Surely everyone had heard the news but me!

Impatiently, my dark eyes scanned the groups of men for Father's slender form. It was no use. Nearly all the men wore *kafiyehs,* the white, sheet-like headcoverings that shaded their heads from the Galilean sun and braced them from the wind. At a glance, almost any of them might be Father!

On tip-toe I carefully laced my way between these huddles, peering around elbows in search of that one lean, gentle face. The faces I saw looked pinched and serious. Whatever they were discussing was most urgent. Otherwise they would not be gathered here on a spring afternoon when fields wanted ploughing and trees awaited the clean slice of the pruning hook.

Not that I was eavesdropping, of course, but amid the murmur of discussion I picked up the fact that Biram was expecting a special visit. But *who* was coming? Visits by the Bishop were quite an event, but regular enough that they did not cause this kind of stir.

My sneaking was not altogether unnoticed, however. Poking my face into one circle of men, I stared up into a pair of black deepset eyes, belonging to one of the two *mukhtars* of Biram—a chief elder in the village. I tried to duck, but—

"What do you want here, Elias?" the *mukhtar's* voice was
gravelly with an edge of sternness.

My face reddened. Would I ever learn not to barge into
things?

"I . . . uh . . . have you seen my father? I have to find
him—it's important." I hoped that I sounded convincing, and
it was true enough since I was about to die with curiosity.

The sternness of his look eased a bit. "No Elias, I haven't
seen him. He's probably—"

"I spoke with him earlier," another man interrupted. "He
went trading today—I don't know where. Maybe over in the
Jewish village." Then he stepped in front of me, closing the
circle again. Thankfully, I was forgotten.

The Jewish village? Perhaps. As I fled from the square, I
remembered that Father often went there to barter. Many of
these Jewish neighbors came to Biram to trade as well. When
they stopped by our house for figs, Father welcomed them
with the customary hospitality and a cup of tar-like, bit-
tersweet coffee—the cup of friendship. One man was a perfect marvel to me, roaring into our yard almost weekly in a
sleek, black automobile—the first one I had ever seen.

At the far edge of town I stopped, craning my neck to look
far down the road. It was empty. If Father was on his way to
the Jewish village, he was long-gone.

My eagerness fizzled. And still I could not take my eyes off
the road, hoping for some glimpse of him. Beyond the next
hill, the road wound southward to Gish, our nearest neighboring village. And further down the valleys, not many kilometers, the Mount of Beatitudes rose up from the Sea of
Galilee's northern shore. I could not see the Mount from
where I stood and had never seen it for that matter, for even a
few kilometers seemed a long journey from our mountain
fastness.

Past the Sea of Galilee I knew almost nothing. I could not

imagine the unreal world beyond—a world that Father said had just warred against itself. I could not fathom such a thing. Mine was a peaceful world of fig and olive groves, countless cousins, aunts and uncles. Time passed almost seamlessly from one harvest to another, marked only births, deaths and holidays. I felt safe and sheltered here, as if the very arms of God embraced our hills like the strong, over-arching stones of our church.

Certainly, this was a child-like vision. Only vaguely was I aware of distant disturbances.

There had been trouble in the mid-1930s, before my birth. Father told us there had been opposition to the British who had driven out the Turks and now protected us under a temporary Mandate. Strikes and riots had shaken Jerusalem, Haifa and all of Palestine, but these were quickly quelled. It was just one more incident in the long history of armies that traversed or occupied our land. Then things had settled, so it appeared, into a lull. Soon, it was hoped, the British would establish a free Palestinian government, as they had promised. Without a single radio or newspaper in all Biram—even then, in the late 1940s—we had no inkling that a master plan was already afoot, or that powerful forces in Jerusalem, in continental Europe, in Britain and America were sealing the fate of our small village and all Palestinian people.

Standing dejectedly on the road from Biram, with the sun settling low and red on the hills, my only thoughts were of Father. And Mother . . . *oh no!* I had forgotten about Mother! Surely she would be home from the fields, upset to find that I'd wandered off again. My feet were flying before I'd finished the thought.

At the edge of our orchard, the sweet scent of woodsmoke from Mother's outdoor fire met me, and the steamy sweet-

ness of baking bread. Mother was stooping over her metal
oven which stood on a low grate next to the house. My sister,
Wardi, fed sticks to the licking flames, and on the grate, a pot
of tangy stuffed grape leaves boiled. My brothers were haul-
ing wood and water. If only I could slip in quietly among
them, Mother might not realize I'd been away . . . But
Atallah spotted me first. Nearest to me in age, he was my
best ally—and sometimes my dearest opponent.

A tell-all sort of smirk lit his face, and he announced in a
clarion voice, "Mother, here's Elias now."

Mother looked up at me, the firelight playing about her
pleasant, full face. A brightly colored kerchief drew her hair
up in a bun. I cringed, expecting a sound scolding. At that
moment, however, she seemed unusually distracted, her gentle eyes clouded in thought. "Go and help Musah carry the
water," she murmured, waving me away.

Musah, who was the next oldest after Atallah, was beside
me in an instant. He thrust an empty bucket at me. "Get
busy," he ordered with a triumphant grin.

I had to know before I exploded. "Mother, what's happening in Biram? Is Father buying a lamb? Is it a celebration?"

"Take the bucket," Musah demanded, his grin fading.

"Mother, tell me. Everyone knows but me and—"

"A celebration? Well, yes. Perhaps. Father wants to tell
you himself. I said go help your brother."

"Take the bucket," said Musah, thumping me with it.

"*Mother,*" I stomped impatiently. At that moment, a familiar voice called to me through the trees.

"Hello, Elias. I'm glad to see such a happy helper." From
the shadowy green darkness beneath the fig boughs, a lean
figure stepped out into the circle of firelight. Behind him, led
by a short cord of rope, was a yearling lamb.

Father was home!

When Father returned home at the end of each day he

brought with him a certain, almost mystical calm. His eyes lit up in the flicker of firelight and a placid smile always turned up the corners of his thick mustache. At his appearance, disputes between children ceased instantly. For one thing, Father was stern with his discipline. Play was one matter, but rude behavior did not befit the children of Michael Chacour. More than that, I believe we all felt the calm that seemed to lift Father above the squabbles of home or village. Above all, Father was a man of peace.

I raced to catch his hand, absolutely dying to ask a million questions. The weary slump of his shoulders made me think better of it. Father was no longer a young man, in fact, he was almost fifty. His light brown hair and mustache were tinged with silver-gray. For once I held my tongue, and instead, quietly stroked the lamb's dusty-white face.

Turning to Mother he smiled. "Katoub, has the Lord sent us anything to feed these hungry children?"

Mother knew, without Father's gentle hints, that he too was hungry and footsore. "Come children—quickly," she said, sparking into action. She waved Musah off to the stable on the far side of the house to pen the lamb. Then she mustered the rest of us into a circle around the fire. It was our daily drill: children were organized and quieted, for evenings belonged to Father.

If some important news was in the wind, Father did not seem ruffled by it in the least. No matter that I was about to split in half with curiosity! He accepted a steaming plate of food from Mother, settling with a regal quietness beside the sputtering fire.

Just when I was certain I would explode, Father set aside his plate. "Come here, children. I have something special to tell you." he said, motioning for us to sit by him. It had grown fully dark and chilly, and I pressed in close at his side.

"In Europe," he began, and I noticed a sadness in his eyes,

"there was a man called Hitler. A Satan. For a long time he was killing Jewish people. Men and women, grandparents—even boys and girls like you. He killed them just because they were Jews. For no other reason."

I was not prepared for such horrifying words. *Someone killing Jews?* The thought chilled me, made my stomach uneasy.

"Now this Hitler is dead," Father continued. "But our Jewish brothers have been badly hurt and frightened. They can't go back to their homes in Europe, and they have not been welcomed by the rest of the world. So they are coming here to look for a home.

"In a few days, children," he said, watching our faces, "Jewish soldiers will be traveling through Biram. They are called *Zionists*. A few will stay in each home, and some will stay right here with us for a few days—maybe a week. Then they will move on. They have machine guns, but they don't kill. You have no reason to be afraid. We must be especially kind and make them feel at home."

I glanced at the others. What were they thinking? Wardi's face seemed a mixture of emotions. On the verge of womanhood, she was graceful and lithe as an olive branch, favoring Father's slenderness. I could not guess her thoughts. Next to her sat Rudah, my oldest brother. In the leaping firelight, he looked like an artist's study of Father in his younger days with fair skin, lighter hair, a narrow face and an aquiline nose. At his side was Chacour who, because of an old custom, had been given the improbable name of Chacour Chacour. Like Rudah, he sported the first faint shadow of a mustache. Though Chacour looked a little uneasy, Rudah's frown told me he was more deeply troubled. Musah and Atallah both sat stiffly quiet. In a few years, it seemed that they, too, would inherit Father's lean, wind-carved looks. Only I was dark, with black hair, olive skin and Mother's rounded face. And I did not know what to make of such news.

Father saw the somber look on all of our faces. With a sudden change of tone, he announced festively, "That's why I bought the lamb. We're going to prepare a feast. This year we'll celebrate the Resurrection early—for our Jewish brothers who were threatened with death, and are alive."

Then Atallah was right. We were celebrating. The strange chill mood was broken.

"And the best news of all," Father continued, a child-like spark of fun in his eyes, "the best news is that you will get to sleep up on the roof."

Sleep on the roof! Wonderful! Our house roof was flat, as were most of the roofs in Biram. On summer nights when it was too hot in the loft where we children slept, we were allowed to sleep up there under the stars. On these cold spring nights we would have to bundle up, but the skies would be brilliantly clear and star-strewn.

Before the excitement bubbled over entirely, Father quieted our cheering. As usual, we would finish our mealtime with family prayers. I crept onto Mother's lap, though I was really too big by then, and listened as Father bowed his head.

"Father in heaven," he began softly, "help us to show love to our Jewish brothers. Help us to show them peace to quiet their troubled hearts." As he continued, I imagined his words rising into the night sky like the smokey tendrils of incense that was burned at church. He finished with a soft "amen."

Mother was strangely quiet, and slipped inside where she lit a small fire on the hearth to warm the house. Later, the six of us children climbed the ladder to our sleeping loft, where a toastiness had gathered beneath the rafters. As we curled up beneath our blankets, we could hear Mother and Father beneath us, stirring the fire and talking in low voices.

In the coming days, Father would kill and prepare our lamb, and Mother would prepare vegetables and cakes, accepting, at least with surface calmness, the coming of the soldiers.

How could they have understood the new force that was invading our land? It was a force that our Jewish neighbors did not yet fully understand.

And as for me, a way was opening—a way of peace through bitter conflict. And I did not know.

For now, I edged up against Atallah. My breathing slipped into a slow rhythm with his. And I slept for one of the very last nights in my own house.

2

Treasures of the Heart

After the news about the coming soldiers had rippled through Biram, the village never quite calmed itself again. Among the adults, I noticed, conversations took on a slightly uneasy edge.

However, the insistent rituals of daily life beckoned. Men went back to their fields and herds, leaving the village square to the dozing grandfathers. Father went to his orchard. Mother and the other women busied themselves with cooking and baking, stopping in at a doorway here or there to ask for a recipe that might help stretch their family's store of flour, grain, sugar and vegetables to feed the extra mouths. The mothers of Biram were miracle workers when it came to multiplying a little food to feed a multitude. They had to be, for few of them had less than seven children and some had fifteen or more.

As for us children, our main job was to go to school and study. Since few of the adults in Biram could read or write, our education was of great importance.

In the week that followed Father's announcement, I bounded off to school with an eagerness that never ceased to surprise my parents. I had loved school from the first day.

But I never slipped out in the morning without a ritual inspection by Mother.

Stepping into the doorway with an earthen bowl cradled in the crook of one arm, she barred my hasty exit. With the heel of her hand—the only part that wasn't already coated with flour—she smoothed my thick dark hair. She had been up since daybreak, mixing together something delicious. One day it was a confection called "circles," rounded sugarcakes flavored with anisette. Another morning it was bread dough. Lifting my chin between a floury thumb and forefinger, she would smile. "Elias, you're a good student. I'm very, very proud of your schoolwork. Be good in class today, won't you?"

Then Atallah, or one of the others who had been impatiently waiting for me in the yard, would poke his head inside urgently. "The bell is going to ring."

"Better hurry," Mother would say, "or Abu 'Eed will be upset."

We hurried through the streets, meeting up with cousins and other bands of children on the way, until we burst like the hordes of Asia into the churchyard just as the huge bronze bell began to ring. The first four grades, which included my class, met in the parish house. The men of Biram had built it with their bare hands out of the ever-plentiful supply of fieldstones and clay. The walls were thick and squat, meeting at odd angles, with huge open windows that peered out on the valleys and let in every stray wind. We were all proud of our school, just as we were proud of the lofting church across the small courtyard, which the people of Biram had also built stone by stone. Pride overruling modesty, they had named the church Notre Dame.

With every child in Biram cramped into one small space, quietness, order and obedience were crucial. We were lined up quickly according to grade. Then we marched into the schoolroom under the all-seeing eye of our teacher, Abu 'Eed.

A kind and small man, Abu 'Eed, had a thick beard that bristled out by his ears like a lion's mane. He was the only priest in our village, a bustling occupation, and he also taught us squirming, younger children math, spelling, reading, geography and the Bible. Since priests were allowed to marry according to our custom, Abu 'Eed had a rather large family, and his gentle fatherliness made him a favorite of mine. If, however, a student foolishly upset the delicate order that held rein on potential chaos, his eyes flashed fiery above the black beard.

It was Abu 'Eed who made school a place of new and wonderful ideas that challenged my imagination. The talk about far away lands needled my sense of adventure. The sound of letters rolling off my tongue as I spelled out a new word—all of it excited me.

Yet I was happier to go home at the end of each day—though not, I'm sure, as happy as Abu 'Eed was to see us go—to my *real* teachers. Mother and Father had always taken our education as their responsibility, not leaving it all up to the school or the church. They were convinced that no one could teach us better than they in such important matters as our heritage, culture and faith.

Every afternoon—on those days when I, myself, was not helping in the fields—I would listen for Mother's return. Then I would hear it—the merry, tell-tale signal that gave out her approach. For Mother jingled. As a wedding gift, Father had given her a necklace, a simple chain of tiny brass links, decorated with fish and doves. The fish, which represented Peter's fish in the nearby Sea of Galilee, were cleverly jointed so they swayed back and forth like real fish—jingling, jingling. And the doves, I knew, represented the Holy Spirit as it had lighted upon Jesus at His baptism in the Jordan River. Mother loved that necklace and wore it always.

When she saw me, Mother would say, "Elias, come here. I found something for you today under one of the stones in the field." Those stones! Our lives were so rooted to this land that the stones even found their way into our play. It took someone as gifted as Mother to transform the backbreaking work of clearing stones into a game, a way of teaching.

"I found a story," she would say with a tired smile. "Would you like to hear it?" No answer was necessary—I was already in her lap. Mother's stories were always rich and beautiful, spinning out of her uncanny memory.

Though Mother could not read or write, she had only to hear a story or poem once or twice and it belonged to her. She knew by heart many of the long epics of Arabic literature. Stanza after stanza, she would weave the tale of some prince or sultan, holding me on her lap as some tragedy or romance or comedy poured out.

The stories she loved best and told with the most vividness, were those from the Bible. Her words set my imagination soaring. I heard the *snap-and-whizz* of David's slingshot as he toppled the giant Goliath; felt the roaring Red Sea split and heave aside in towering waves, letting Moses and the people escape the Egyptian chariots; and I envisioned the dark, lovely, perfumed Queen of Sheba bearing exotic gifts to the foot of Solomon's gold and ivory throne. Mother had chosen to name me Elias—a variation of Elijah—after the fiery prophet who was fed by ravens. Each story formed a familiar footpath of sounds and images in my head. Yet, only one man in the Bible fully captured my awe and love.

The stories about Jesus were, to me, the most wonderful and alive. Jesus, in my young mind, was a flesh-and-blood hero who may have walked the dusty roads into our own village. Mother said He had come to Galilee first, to our hills and our people, after His temptation in the wilderness. It was from His lips that we first heard the good news: God and man were reconciled. Perhaps some forefather Chacour had eaten bread and fish miraculously multiplied by Jesus' hand. Maybe a Chacour boy or girl felt the brush of His fingertips when He blessed the little children, or watched as He healed the sick and the blind. These wonders were real to me, for they had occurred on streets and in homes like those I saw every day.

For instance, I could picture vividly the New Testament story of the men who could not squeeze their paralyzed friend inside a crowded house to meet Jesus. The Lord, as I pictured Him, was seated inside a simple Galilean home just like ours with two rooms and a loft where children slept. In the cold months meals were cooked and eaten in the largest room where children played and guests were welcomed. There were two doors. One led out to a stable where cows, donkeys, goats and chickens were kept in winter. The other led to a small room behind the house used to store hay for the animals' winter feed. Its wooden tiles were easily removed so the hay could be pitched in from the outside.

Jesus, as an honored guest, would have been seated against the rear wall of the house next to the storage room. So the men were not rude, but clever, when they removed the roof tiles and lowered their paralyzed friend right down to the Master's feet. Jesus, of course, had honored their faith and healed the man's stiff, useless limbs. In my imagination, the miracle could have happened on the very spot where Father often rested in the evening, his back against the cool stone.

In this way Jesus became the hero of my whole, real world of stones, sparrows, mustard plants and vineyards. I could easily imagine Him stopping at our house or walking with his disciples through the cool shade of Father's fig orchard.

What Mother treasured most dearly were the words Jesus

spoke to a crowd of Galileans on a hill very near to our house—the hill that Mother loved—the Mount of Beatitudes. The Beatitudes were, to Mother, the very essence of all Jesus' teachings, like the rare extract of a perfume. I would sit on her lap, quietly fingering the doves and fishes of her necklace, listening to the strangely beautiful words:

> "Blessed are the poor in spirit,
>   for theirs is the kingdom of heaven.
> Blessed are those who mourn,
>   for they will be comforted.
> Blessed are the meek,
>   for they will inherit the earth.
> Blessed are those who hunger and thirst for
>   righteousness,
>   for they will be filled . . .
> Blessed are the merciful,
>   for they will be shown mercy.
> Blessed are the pure in heart,
>   for they will see God.
> Blessed are the peacemakers,
>   for they will be called sons of God.
> Blessed are those who are persecuted because of
>   righteousness,
>   for theirs is the kingdom of heaven.
> Blessed are you when people insult you, persecute
>   you and falsely say all kinds of evil against you
>   because of me. Rejoice, be very glad, because your
>   reward in heaven is great, for in the same way they
>   persecuted the prophets who came before you."

What did He mean? I puzzled. *How can you be blessed— or happy—if you are poor or in mourning—if someone insults or persecutes you? How can you be hungry and thirsty for righteousness? What is a peacemaker?*

These things were a mystery to me. What I understood about Jesus, what attracted me, was His strong, sometimes fiery nature: the way He erupted into the temple courts, driving out the greedy merchants and scattering the coins of the moneychangers; His habit of helping the crippled and blind, even if He broke the laws and offended the overly-pious religious leaders. Sometimes I thought He was the only one who could understand a small boy who also threw himself into situations—somewhat blindly—a boy whose tongue sometimes got him into trouble, too, like the time I committed a capital crime in Abu 'Eed's classroom.

The older students were struggling with a difficult mathematical equation one morning while Abu 'Eed turned to us, his first-graders, for simple addition. He spewed out several numbers and asked for a quick sum. Most of the heads were still bowed, pencils scratching and erasing, when my cousin Charles shot up his hand. Mine shot up a split second later.

Abu 'Eed nodded to Charles who announced his answer proudly: "Eight."

"No, Charles," Abu 'Eed replied, shaking his head. "Check your work more carefully."

I waved my hand desperately, bursting with the right answer. When Abu 'Eed called on me, I blurted, with a smug look at Charles, "*Nine*. The *right* answer is nine."

Abu 'Eed smiled at me and was about to give another set of numbers. But I could not bear the temptation. Charles was usually a faster, better student, and now it was my turn to gloat. Foolishly, in a stage whisper that ricocheted off the old stone walls, I hissed, "See that, Charles? You're a donkey!"

The quiet, contained classroom split open with laughter. Abu 'Eed strode toward me, like a storm blown up from the

Mediterranean, thundering for silence in the room. His stinging chastisement left me teary-eyed and embarrassed in front of everyone. Even worse, I was afraid that a wagging tongue—in the mouth of who knew which brother, cousin or aunt—would report the incident to Mother and Father.

When school was out, I fled from the mossy courtyard and ran all the way to Father's orchard. The quiet orchard was my special hideaway, my sanctuary where I often went to pour out my small, troubled heart. And who else could I pour it out to but my Champion, Jesus? If Mother's stories taught me anything, it was that He cared for us and He was always eager to listen.

I waded in the cool grass beneath the fig boughs, telling Jesus with all sincerity, "I didn't mean to upset Abu 'Eed. And I didn't mean anything bad when I called Charles a donkey. It just came out . . ." Was He listening? Did He care?

A peculiar stillness seemed to engulf the orchard, although a breeze was rustling the leaves. A sudden sense of awe swelled inside, a feeling of majesty and holiness and—what was it? Friendship. My heart skipped. The sense could hardly have been more real if Jesus Himself had physically fallen in pace beside me.

I simply went jabbering on, imagining the understanding smile. The sense of His presence, the possibility that He had time to listen to my troubles, did not seem at all unusual. So many times before, I had sought Him in my orchard retreat, or in the hills, and there poured out my childish dilemmas, that it seemed most ordinary. Imagined or real, I cherished these times. For then, unknowingly, I first discovered the slim, strong thread of inner peace.

I was thankful that my classroom blunder was not reported to Mother and Father—not that time, at least. Deeply repentant, I hoped I might learn how to harness my tongue.

While Mother captivated me with her Bible stories, Father was the one who forged an unbroken chain of history that led from Jesus and His followers to our own family. Like Abraham or Noah in the Old Testament, Father wanted to be sure his children knew their rare and treasured heritage. After all, our family were Melkite Christians. We were not like some weed newly sprung up after rain, but our spiritual heritage was firmly rooted in the first century.

Night after night, Father would gather all of us under the open stars or around a low fire as the winter wind beat at our door. For the thousandth time he would carry us back through the dim ages with his brilliant histories. I loved every delightful word.

After Jesus' crucifixion, we learned, the flame of His Spirit continued to burn brightly in our villages—though our ancestors were forced to meet in secret for fear of the religious leaders. James, the brother of our Lord, became the spiritual overseer of the believers in Jerusalem.

Not very long after James and the other apostles died, the Church was split, nearly destroyed by a creeping, cultic darkness. A certain group, the Gnostics, claimed that Jesus was a mystical being, and not a man at all. Just when it seemed that these false teachers would scatter the flock like wolves, the King of Byzantium, newly a Christian, took a strong stand on the side of the early apostles, asserting that Jesus was the God-Man; He had bridged the chasm between God and mankind, bringing peace when He took on our frail, human nature. My family, among many others, sided with the king. Their angry detractors dubbed them with the derogatory name, "Melkites"—or "king's men"—"melech" being the Arabic word for "king." It was these early Melkites who united the splintered churches.

Our Melkite family belonged to a spunky group, it seemed. Many centuries later, after the Crusaders fought bloody wars to implant the influence of Rome in our soil, the Melkites stood firmly against such foreign authority. They remained a separate group of believers, holding to the simple, orthodox teachings of the early church, which angered several popes. Several centuries later, the Melkites built bridges of reconciliation with Rome. This ability to reconcile opposing powers seemed to be an historic hallmark of our Church fathers.

Should Father stray from the familiar trail, all of us would clamor for the *whole* story. One part we loved, with that strange, gruesome tendency of children, was about the horrifying fate of a certain Chacour generations back.

In the 1700s, a cruel Turkish sultan named Jezzar Pasha spread his rule over our land all the way to the Mediterranean. When he took the city of Akko on the seacoast, he decided to raise a fortified wall against foreign warships. Its design called for secret labyrinthine escape routes through the enormous stones. One Chacour was among those forced to work on these sea-walls. While the last bit of mortar was still drying, Jezzar Pasha rewarded them for their backbreaking labors: every one of the builders was buried alive beneath the wall. And so the sultan's defense secrets were guarded forever.

This was Father's most effective way of teaching us two things. First, we should love and respect our Galilean soil, for our people had long struggled to survive here. We were rooted like the poppies and wild, blue irises that thrust up among the rocks. Our family had tilled this land, had worshiped here longer than anyone could remember. And second, our lives were bound together with the other people who inhabited Palestine—the Jews. We had suffered together under the Romans, Persians, Crusaders and Turks, and had learned to share the simple elements of human existence—faith, reverence for life, hospitality. These, Father said, were the things that caused people to live happily together.

Father told his story unvaryingly. At seven, I did not understand much of it, to be sure, but it fascinated me.

And Father taught us something even more valuable than our colorful history. He taught us, in a quiet, subtle way about character. Whether I knew it or not, many of the attributes I imagined in Jesus, my unseen Champion, most likely came from this other hero in my life.

Whenever Father was wronged, for instance, he handled it in a way that amazed me—and caused me to chuckle. One time, he had traded away a huge number of figs and got a very bad piece of merchandise in exchange. The swindler was long-gone when Father realized he had been cheated. But Father never cursed. With a placid tone, and a wry smile on his face, he said, "May God bless that man—and take him to heaven!"

Father's gentle spirit had an influence far beyond our immediate family. One man that father influenced was a certain Father Maximus, who often visited in our home. Over the usual cup of steaming, thick coffee, he would politely inquire about our family, then probe Father for a solution to some touchy, upcoming debate among the Church heirarchy. He continued his visits after he became *Bishop* Maximus. Later, he would become *Patriarch* Maximus IV, a famous reformer in the Vatican Councils. This great man recognized that Father's opinion was not subject to changes of emotion, or the pressure of other men.

Even news about soldiers coming to Biram with guns could not unsettle Father. Since the announcement of their coming, the soldiers had sent word to the village *mukhtars* that they would stay for only a few days and they would take nothing. They were just looking over the land. Father accepted their word as a gentleman. If need be, these Jews from

Europe could settle in our village and farm the land that lay open beside our own fields.

But my brother Rudah was alarmed at the talk of machine guns. A few days after Father first told us the news, Rudah shocked us all by bringing home a rifle—one of the two or three guns in all of Biram, a rusted antique used for shooting at wolves that came to prey on the village flocks. The wolves were in little danger of being hit.

When Father saw the rifle he erupted in a rare show of anger. "Get it out of here! I won't have it in my house." Mother and the rest of us stood frozen and mute.

Poor Rudah was wide-eyed, stunned. "I—I thought we might need a gun to protect ourselves in case—"

"No!" Father would not hear more. "We do not use violence *ever*. Even if someone hurts us." He had calmed a bit, and he took the gun.

"But Father," Rudah persisted, anxiously, "Why do the soldiers carry guns?"

Slipping his arm around Rudah's shoulders, Father replied, "For centuries our Jewish brothers have been exiles in foreign lands. They were hunted and tormented—even by Christians. They have lived in poverty and sadness. They have been made to fear, and sometimes when people are afraid, they feel they have to carry guns. Their souls are weak because they have lost peace within."

"But how do we know the soldiers won't harm us?" Rudah pressed him.

Father smiled, and all the tension seemed to relax. "Because," he said, "the Jews and Palestinians are brothers—blood brothers. We share the same father, Abraham, and the same God. We must never forget that. Now we get rid of the gun."

It is extraordinary how a voice from our childhood, even one word spoken at a crucial moment, can bury itself inside only to reveal its simple wisdom in a crisis our adult minds cannot begin to fathom. Then our whole life is re-fashioned.

I listened to the exchange between Father and Rudah, and watched as they went out to dispose of the gun. Then the incident passed, was locked somewhere inside me with the other jewels of heritage and faith that Mother and Father had carefully hidden there.

The time was soon coming when I would have little else to hold onto but these treasures of the heart.

3

Swept Away

Early one morning, nearly two weeks after the first word about the soldiers, Biram was still resting, quiet in the mists and growing light of dawn. And then the hillside was flooded with the unfamiliar rumbling of trucks and jeeps. Men in drab-colored uniforms with packs slung across their shoulders filled the narrow streets. My brothers and I watched from a corner of our yard, whispering among ourselves as four or five soldiers strode up to our door. They spoke with Father, who welcomed them, and they lugged their gear inside. For the next week, we were told, the soldiers would sleep in the large room beneath the loft where Mother and Father usually slept. My parents would join us on the roof.

Two details I recall most vividly.

Father had prepared us for house guests—but these Zionist soldiers were not at all like our Jewish neighbors who chatted in the yard with Father over coffee. Not that they were unkind or rude. When Father killed and roasted the lamb, blessing the feast and the men, they politely bowed their heads. Mother served them heaping plates of lamb and vegetables and bread which they ate heartily. But they remained aloof, almost brusque. To my disappointment, the feast turned out to be much less of a happy celebration than I had expected. I sidled up to Mother, feeling shy and uneasy in their presence.

And the second thing I recall was the guns. All the while, my eyes were drawn by their cold glint. They were always present, even when we ate. I noticed the small, carved trigger where the finger would rest, squeezing . . . squeezing . . . the long, sleek barrel . . . the tiny, death-spitting mouth . . . an explosion shook my imagination. I shuddered and looked away.

The guns set us apart entirely, no matter how polite the atmosphere. I understood even then that the guns were might—power—and that my family and the villagers of Biram had no might. In the coming days the guns were everywhere while our life went on as usual. We went off to school and the barrels glinted at every corner. At night we lay down on the roof under the cold, clear-shining spring stars, and the guns were propped beneath us.

After a week, word passed through Biram that the military commander had some urgent business with the men of the village. Father went along to the square, expecting to hear that the troops would soon be moving on. Instead, the commander, a short, bull of a man, had delivered some alarming "confidential news."

"Our intelligence sources say that Biram is in serious danger," he announced tersely. "Fortunately, my men can protect you. But it would risk your safety to stay in your homes. You're going to have to move out into the hills for a few days. Lock everything. Leave the keys with us. I promise nothing will be disturbed."

When Father told us about the order, he reported that most of the village men were disturbed. They remembered the turmoil of the 1930s with the occupying British forces. And there had been word of new bombings in Jerusalem, of trouble between the British and the Zionists. If there was to be any confrontation between these forces, the men of Biram decided it would be best to keep their families safely out of the way. The commander urged them on, saying, "Travel light. Take nothing with you. You must leave today—as soon as possible."

To any other people, sudden evacuation—leaving home and all the conveniences to live outdoors with a large family—would be threatening if not entirely miserable. For us, it did not seem so difficult. We were accustomed to spending entire days outside, and we often slept on the ground when travel or work among the flocks and fields took us away from shelter. Then we would simply huddle together beneath a tree or beside some rocks and be content. Often, as in times of mourning for a deceased relative when no one cooked, we relied solely on our land,·eating nothing but figs and olives for several days at a time. Since we children had already been sleeping on the roof, we accepted it as another part of the adventure.

Quickly, Mother and Father set the house in order, urging us to hurry and leave behind everything but the heavy clothes we were wearing. I was the only one permitted to carry a blanket with me. Having just been in a scrap with my cousin Asad, I was allowed to wrap this covering over my face to hide a black eye which was somewhat painful and embarrassing. Then we were hurried outside.

·Father locked the door behind us. Then he handed the key to one of our soldier-guests who was leaning against the front wall, his gun hanging casually from a strap over his shoulder.

"I know that God will protect our house," Father said sincerely. "And you'll be safe, too."

"Yes," the soldier replied with a smile. That was all.

When we left our yard, I was amazed to see dozens of people moving through the streets, joining other families and

streaming out of Biram. Father led us down the steep hill-
sides, toward a grove of olive trees, with Rudah and Chacour
walking manfully beside him. Mother held my hand as I
stumbled along, the blanket held protectively over my
bruised eye. A woman who had been struggling along ahead
of us with a child balanced on each hip had to stop and rest.
Now I saw that she was an aunt, one of Father's sisters. At the
edge of the grove, I caught a glimpse of my cousin Asad and
his family. Our eyes met, and he ducked his head with a
guilty look. Then he disappeared amid the hundreds of other
villagers who were trekking out of Biram.

Every family seemed to have the same idea: The olive
grove would be the perfect place of refuge during our vigil.
The crowd spread out beneath the old and twisted boughs
that spread for acres and acres down toward the valley. It was
said that the trees had grown here since the time of Christ or
before. Perhaps He and the disciples had eaten olives from
these very branches. Now the trunks were cratered and dark
with age, but the fruit was still plentiful and delicious. The
silver-shading leaves would protect us from sun and rain.
And from here, the men could best watch the comings and
goings in Biram on the hilltop far above us.

Living as a nomad would be a great adventure—at least I
thought so.

In a day or two, when the pain and swelling left my eye and
I was ready for fun, the novelty of camping had worn off for
everyone else. My brothers were simply sullen. The men, I
could tell, were beginning to feel nervous that they had left
their homes and lands under the protection of strangers. The
older people were starting to suffer from sleeping on the
damp, stoney ground. Though the days were sunny, the
temperature dropped rapidly at sunset, plunging us from a
hot afternoon into a shivering night. Everyone was thankful
that I had brought my blanket. All six of us children would

try to squeeze under it while Mother and Father huddled together uncomfortably on the ground.

The cold was somehow bearable. The rain was not. A heavy, gray bank of clouds covered the hills on the fourth day. A chilling drizzle spattered through the olive leaves, soaking the grass, mixing the gravel and dirt into mud beneath our feet.

Father led us through the trees to the grotto at the edge of our land. The inside walls were layered with gray and green moss, and a faint smell of damp humus and of goats hung in the air. It was small, but all of us could fit inside, protected from the night drafts and sudden rains.

For nearly two weeks, the men kept up their vigil, watching for threatening activity in the village. Occasionally, a fleet of trucks would arrive in a cloud of dust, and shortly they would drive out again. Mostly, things remained quiet. The people of Biram continued to camp under the olive trees, foraging for food, drinking from artesian springs and getting stiffer each night from sleeping on the ground. Still there was no word from the soldiers.

At last the elders decided not to wait for the military commander's signal to return. A delegation of men collected in the olive grove and climbed the hill to Biram.

Before long, they came running back, their faces a confusion of anguish and fear. The horror of their report spread through the grove.

Upon entering Biram and passing the first house, they had seen that the door was broken in. Most of the furniture and belongings were gone. What was left lay smashed and scattered on the floor. At the next house, it was the same, and at the house across the street. Chairs were smashed, curtains shredded, dishes shattered against the walls.

Then they were stopped by armed soldiers. The one who

appeared to be in charge waved his gun menacingly and barked, "What are you doing here? Get out!"

Angry, and certain that these impudent soldiers needed a reprimand from their superior, the men stood their ground.

"Where is your commanding officer? We are the people of Biram, and we want to bring our wives and children home!"

The one in charge approached them, his gun held squarely across his chest. "The commander is gone," he said coolly. "He left us to protect the village. You have no business here anymore."

At once, all the men raised their voices.

"Protect our village? You're destroying it!"

"Intruders!"

"Get out—leave us in peace!"

The soldiers leveled their guns at them, flicking off the safety switches. Angrily, one of them growled, "The land is ours. Get out now. *Move!*"

The betrayal cut like a knife. A few of the men were bitterly angry, seething with the thought that we had been tricked out of our village by these European men we had trusted. Others were simply bewildered. Pain etched every face.

Father and Mother seemed as bewildered as children by such a callous betrayal. I think it was simply beyond their understanding.

The poor *mukhtars* were mobbed with questions: "How can we get Biram back?" "What's going to happen to our homes?" "Can't you make the soldiers leave?" Of course they could do nothing—two aging, unarmed and bewildered men against the guns of these soldiers.

More immediate was the need for shelter and protection from the weather. Obviously, we could not continue to live exposed to rain and the cold nights.

After a brief discussion, it was proposed that we climb the next hill to Gish, our nearest neighboring village. Surely the people there, who were also Christians, could made some provision for us temporarily while we sorted out this mistake by the rude, young soldiers.

Cresting the hill that rose between our village and Gish, we felt a strange somberness. No shepherds greeted us as we crossed the open fields. The lot where young boys played soccer was vacant. A frightening pall of silence hung in the streets between the empty houses where young women and grandmothers should have been chattering among sleeping babies and old men.

After a long search through the empty village, we discovered ten elderly people who told us they had been left behind. From them we learned that these unarmed people had suffered a fate similar to our own.

Soldiers had arrived in trucks, they told us. But for some reason, they did not use the ruse with these people that they had used in Biram. With machine guns leveled, they abruptly ordered the people to get out, not bothering to drive off these few old men and women who were apparently too feeble to abandon their homes. One old man was certain that the soldiers were impatient to get the evacuation over, because he had heard gunfire just outside the village, "Just to warn the people to move along faster." Most of them suspected that the villagers had fled into Lebanon, which was only a few kilometers distant.

"We do not know when they will return," said one old man, next to tears.

"Or *if* they will return," added another grimly.

Even with this weight of sadness, they offered us a sort of ruined hospitality: "You are welcome to stay in our village" they told us, "though little is left here."

He was right. The soldiers had rampaged through most of

the homes, smashing or carrying off the furnishings in their trucks. At least it was shelter.

Unfortunately, there were fewer dwellings in Gish than families from Biram. In some homes, two families were cramped into a single room with old sheets or worn carpets hung for dividers. For families with ten or more children, conditions were utterly miserable. Abu 'Eed visited, offering comfort and encouragement.

Father was fortunate enough to find a tiny, one-room house for us. He was also able to find a small room nearby for his aged parents who had suffered terribly during the nights outdoors, as had all the elderly of Biram. Our room was dilapidated, barely larger than the grotto on Father's land, and empty but for a few broken chairs. In one corner I found a smashed toy—a doll with its head crushed in. Fingering it, I thought of the child who must have dropped it in fear and confusion and a ghostly feeling came over me. I drew my hand away suddenly and never touched the doll again.

Straggling groups that had been driven from other villages carried more distressing news as we settled uncomfortably in Gish. The soldiers were moving systematically through the hill country, routing the quiet, unprotected villagers. Many were fleeing on foot for Lebanon or Syria. And there was talk of violence in the south. A certain, unnamable eeriness clung to the air with each fragment of information that came.

We wondered, as we tried to piece our lives together, when the soldiers would return and what they would do if they found us in our neighbors' village. And though Mother and Father repeatedly assured us that we were safe, one thought remained fearfully unspoken: What had happened to the men, women and children of Gish?

I would be the first to learn the answer.

A week or more after our arrival, Charles and I were

shuffling glumly through the streets together when we found a soccer ball. It was slightly soft from the cold, but still had enough life to respond to a good kick. Immediately, Charles broke into a trot, footing the ball ahead of him. "Come on, Elias," he called. "Let's have a game!" From side streets and open doorways, ten other boys joined as we passed.

Dodging through the streets, we reached a sandy, open lot at the edge of Gish. With the innocent abandon of small boys, the fate of Biram was momentarily forgotten. We raced up and down the lot, loosing our pent-up energies in a swift-footed competition.

Charles' team scored two points almost at once. One boy was lining up for another attempt, eyes riveted on the goal, when I charged him, roaring, laughing, waving my arms. He kicked hard, and the ball breezed by my head, high and wild, out of bounds. I pivoted and tore after it. The other team dropped back to defend their goal, and my teammates took their field positions awaiting my return.

I reached the ball where it had thumped and settled in a stretch of loose sand. Oddly, the ground seemed to have been churned up. I stooped and picked up the ball, noticing a peculiar odor. An odd shape caught my eye—something like a thick twig poking up through the sand. And the strange color. . . .

I bent down and pulled on the thing. It came up stiffly, the sand falling back from a swollen finger, a blue-black hand and arm. The odor gripped my throat. . . .

"Elias, what's wrong?" Someone was hollering in the reeling distance.

Numbness dulled all feeling. The stiff arm lay in the sand at my feet—a boy's arm. I imagined the face—sand in the sealed eyes—gagging the slack mouth. I thought I was yelling. No sound could escape my throat. Vaguely, I could hear Charles beside me calling. . . .

Later, the shallow graves were uncovered. Buried beneath a thin layer of sand were two dozen bodies. The gunfire that the old man had heard had done its bitter work.

The victims were hastily re-buried in honorable graves. There was seething anger and talk of retribution. But how could there be any retribution when we had no power against this madness? Most of the men, Father especially, would have no part of such ugly talk.

As for me, the innocence and durability of youth were on my side. No one mentioned the incident to me at all. Mother, Father and my grandparents were overly kind, ignoring my outbursts of impatience or tears. My brothers and cousins eventually distracted me with more games, though we avoided the sandlot for quite some time.

In the coming months, as summer crept into Galilee, I was little aware of events outside our secluded hills. But major decisions were being made by nations far more powerful than ours--decisions that would soon leave us without a homeland or an identity. Father and the village elders honed their disbelieving ears to news about the drama that was unfolding across Palestine and in the world's supreme court of justice—the United Nations.

The elders learned, as news and rumors traveled like wildfire through Galilee, that the "question of Palestine" had come before the U.N. It seemed that the Zionists no longer wanted the British to control Palestine, and they wanted to establish their national homeland in place of ours. The British, whose military and financial ability to govern Palestine were bankrupted by the long war in Europe, could not stop the Zionists from taking over the land. The Zionist forces, known as the *Haganah,* had taken over the munitions factories in the south and were using the mortars, bombs, machine guns and heavy equipment against British and Palestinian alike. Each time a Palestinian village was raided, a few of its men would gather in the hills with their donkeys and antiquated carbines in a pathetic attempt to protect their land. These ill-prepared bands were subsequently crushed by the *Haganah* in further reprisals. It was hardly a contest. And now the United Nations had been called upon to arbitrate a peaceful solution to the bloodshed.

Certainly, the men of Biram reasoned hopefully, the powerful nations of the world who controlled the U.N. would reach a just solution. The summer of 1947 passed, the rains of autumn soaked the earth, and still we waited as refugees. Month after month in our cramped quarters, we prayed for the news that we could return to our homes in Biram.

In November, refugees fleeing from larger towns brought more devastating news.

Palestine was to be partitioned in what the U.N. called a "compromise." Our elders and hundreds of thousands of Palestinians throughout the land were shocked beyond words, for the terms of the "compromise" were brutal.

The Zionists were to possess the *majority* of Palestine—fifty-four percent—even though they owned only seven percent of the land! In five major areas that were being handed over, well over half the people—up to seventy and eighty, even ninety-nine percent—were Palestinians. The "compromise" gave the Zionists almost all the fertile land, including the huge, main citrus groves that accounted for most of our peoples' export income. It gave away the vast Negev region where the Bedouins produced most of the barley and wheat grown in Palestine. There was three times more cultivated land in this one area than the incoming, European settlers had cultivated in all Palestine in the previous thirty years. [1]

Such concessions, in the eyes of the Palestinian people, could hardly be called a "compromise." Our people were being told to hand over more than half of our well-cultivated lands that produced our only livelihood.

How had such a sweeping and one-sided decision been reached? Among the nations of the world, the U.N. vote was accepted without question or protest.

As an eight-year-old boy, the elders' talk was just words to me. It would be years before I discovered the truth about international intrigues and clandestine agreements that had led to this Middle East tragedy. For now, the eyes of all were blind to these political machinations. And I was only aware that my peaceful homeland of Palestine, known as the Holy Land, had become a land of war.

Shortly after the U.N. vote, the British announced that they would be withdrawing all forces from the Middle East the following spring—by May 15, 1948.

Throughout the winter months and into spring 1948, we heard of more terror, of villages blown up by barrel-bombs while others narrowly escaped the flaming ruins of their homes. Thousands were now uprooted, living in the hills and arid wastelands.

Most especially, we came to fear one name—the highly-trained and single-minded Zionist organization called the *Irgun*. One of its leaders had been among the ten terrorists most wanted by the British for his part in bombing the luxurious King David Hotel in Jerusalem. His name was Menachem Begin and his proclaimed goal was to "purify" the land of Palestinian people.

In April of that year one of these acts of purification was the destruction of a village on the outskirts of modern Jerusalem. The scene at Deir Yassin was later recorded by an eyewitness, Jacques de Reynier, the head of the International Red Cross emergency delegation.

On April 10, Reynier was stopped on the Jerusalem road by members of the *Irgun*, who refused him entry to the village. He bravely pushed through their lines and into homes where he found "bodies cold. Here the 'cleaning up' had been done with machine-guns, then hand grenades. It had been finished off with knives, anyone could see that. . . . As I was about to leave, I heard something like a sigh. . . . It was a little girl of ten, mutilated by a hand grenade, but still alive. . . . There had been 400 people in this village; about 50 of them escaped and were still alive. . . ."[2]

The native Jewish people were shocked and disgusted. In tears, they protested that such things violated their ancient beliefs. Upon hearing the news about Deir Yassin, the Chief Rabbi of Jerusalem flew into a fury.

Unfortunately, religious censure was not powerful enough to stop the military machine.

As May approached, more trucks rumbled into peasant villages. And daily, refugees swarmed through Galilee bringing word of more towns sacked. Others drowned in the Mediterranean as they tried to swim for overcrowded refugee ships leaving from Haifa and Lidda.

Early on May 14, while the last British were scrambling to get out of Palestine, a young man named David Ben Gurion assembled more than two hundred journalists and photographers to proclaim the establishment of the State of Israel. Within hours, the government that the new Prime Minister Ben Gurion and his comrades had been carefully planning for months was in place. Within sixty minutes, the United States officially recognized the new nation of Israel under Zionist rule.

The same journalists and photographers who attended Ben Gurion's proclamation soon recorded for the world our summer of tears. Through May, June and July, almost one million Palestinians were driven out of the newly-proclaimed democracy. Soldiers from surrounding Arab nations of Egypt, Iraq, Syria, Jordan and Lebanon fought to stop the takeover, but were driven back. In the confusion and terror, husbands and wives were forever parted, parents lost small children never to see them again and many elderly died.

The Jews who had been our neighbors, our friends who lived with us and shared our customs, ached for us. They could not understand or accept such violence, but they were powerless to help. And the nations were silent.

By autumn of 1948, the Zionists had swept north and were close to us again. The forces were "cleansing" the towns around the Sea of Galilee, almost at our doorstep. As winter set in—our second winter in Gish—the Zionist advance stopped short of the upper Galilee. Thin blankets of snow fell, and only one question was discussed in low voices around guttering fires: Would the soldiers find us here in our hill-country refuge—or would they think we had fled to Lebanon or Syria or Jordan as had so many others?

Although we had been refugees from our own home for almost two years, Father never prayed for us, for our protection or provision. He continued in his simple belief that his children were like "the birds of the air" that God had promised to feed and he refused to worry over us—though I think Mother had a more difficult time when food was scarce. We had barely survived our first year, eating animals from the abandoned flocks, making bread from the stores of grain and working small gardens.

I was increasingly aware of Father's unbelievably forgiving attitude toward the soldiers. He faithfully continued our times of family prayer and never failed to pray for those who had made themselves our enemies. Night after night I would lean my head against Mother, fingering the fish and doves on her necklace, and hear Father pray: "Forgive them, oh God. Heal their pain. Remove their bitterness. Let us show them your peace."

As spring 1949 pounced upon us, tiger-like with its ferocious heat, I could see little peace anywhere but in our own home. An uneasy lull moved in with the blistering days and cool nights. We rose each morning with the fear that we might not lie down on our mats that evening: At any moment we, too, might be swept away.

On a sultry morning, our lull was shattered.

I was playing in some trees near the road to Gish with a few cousins and some other boys when we heard the ominous, rumbling of trucks. In the distance, rounding the side of the next hill, came the first of the army vehicles. For a split second we looked at each other in wordless terror, then scattered.

When I reached home, Father was in the doorway with Mother and the other children. The trucks had reached the edge of the village, and a harsh metallic voice rang from a loudspeaker: "All men must show themselves at once. Young men and old men. Come outside with your hands on your heads. Do not resist."

I looked at my brothers. Rudah and Chacour were now young men. Musah was a teenager. They, too, would have to go. What about Atallah and me? And what would the soldiers do to the men who surrendered themselves? My face tingled with a burning fear.

Father looked grim, but as he turned to my three oldest brothers he spoke with a perfect calm. "Come, boys. It will be all right."

Wardi clung to Mother, and Atallah and I stood numbly at her side. The four of us watched Father march bravely, with Rudah, Chacour and Musah striding uncertainly beside him, out to a large open lot where the soldiers stood with leveled guns. Atallah and I crept outside to watch. I was shaking, nearly choked with tears.

Crouched in a shadow outside the door, we stared as all the houses of Gish gave up their men and older sons. Among the somber throng we saw all of our uncles, their faces riddled with tension. Young men filled the streets, their eyes a confusion of fear and defiance. Behind them shambled the old men, not willing in their fierce pride to sit at home while their sons and grandsons faced the danger alone. As they came, they were ordered into one large circle that stretched around the entire open lot.

Immediately the soldiers began to accuse. "You are rebels. Tell us where your guns are hidden. We know you are fighters—Palestinian terrorists."

These words scorched me. Father, my uncles, cousins and the *mukhtars*—"terrorists"?

On and on went the interrogation as the heat of the day built to a searing brightness. The men began to squirm, drenched in their own sweat as the sun poured down. There was no water. Neither could they relieve themselves. Without ceasing, the soldiers demanded that they surrender their weapons. There was nothing to give up; there were no guns anywhere in our village. Still the soldiers harassed them through the long afternoon. Men weakened and some dropped as the heat and accusations pounded at them.

We could see Father at the far side of the lot. Sweat dripped from his chin. His eyes were shut and occasionally his lips would move. I knew that he was praying for the soldiers.

And suddenly, as the afternoon sun waned, it was over. The commanding officer barked abruptly: "Go back to your homes. But don't try to escape."

Father nearly collapsed inside our door. He and my brothers rested in the quiet coolness of the house while Mother and Wardi rushed to bring them water and a little food.

As the darkness settled over us, no one dared to light fires or to cook a meal. The soldiers remained in Gish, gathered around their trucks or patrolling the streets. We waited in a misery of silence, hoping they would leave.

Father seemed to have some inner warning of what would happen next. He drew close to each of us in turn, with a gentle touch and an inscrutable look. I suspected that he was praying for us one by one. His eyes looked weary, and yet some reservoir of calm lay behind them. When he smiled at me and touched my shoulder I could almost believe that the soldiers would leave soon and let us live in peace.

And suddenly there was noise and bustling in the dark streets. I shuddered to the sounds of loud angry voices, gun-butts thudding at doors and the growl of truck motors start-ing.

The loudspeaker was blaring again. "Come out of your houses. We want all men to come out and give themselves up. You are leaving here at once. . . ."

Mother seized Father's arm, sheer anguish carving her gentle face. "Michael, what are they doing? Where—?"

"Katoub," he stopped her, drawing her close. "God is watching us. You have to be strong—" he paused, his voice dropping, "for the little ones."

For a moment they held each other as the terrible blaring continued. The wailing outside cinched the knot in my stom-ach. Tears streamed down Wardi's face. Then Father turned to my brothers and said quietly, "We'll go now."

Mother trailed after them, kissing Rudah, Chacour and Musah, wiping her tears with the back of her hand. I stood frozen beside her on the doorstep, Atallah and Wardi peering mutely over my shoulder. In the glare of headlights and flares, we stared into the darkness and chaos.

Soldiers were hurrying the men and older boys at gunpoint onto the open-backed trucks. More guards stood at the tail-gates barking orders. In the doorways, women stood weep-ing, their babies and smaller children wailing loudly in their arms. Father and my brothers had already been jammed onto one of the trucks with several dozen other men, and we could no longer see them.

As the last tailgate slammed shut, the loudspeaker called out to the women. "We are taking your terrorists away. This is what happens to all terrorists. You will not see them again."

And then the trucks were rolling, rumbling away into the night. In the blackness, women flooded into the streets, sinking to their knees and weeping, calling the names of their husbands and sons.

Mother was too desolate to try to offer comfort to any of my aunts who came and hung on her shoulder. She walked numbly inside, and sat holding Wardi, Atallah and me long into the night. I clutched her skirt, shutting my eyes against the wails and screams. For a long time—I could not tell how long—I sat this way. I must have fallen asleep.

When I opened my eyes again, it seemed to me much later. All was silent but for the barking of a dog far off. Silent, but for the inner voices that begged inside us: *Where have they taken my father—my sons—my husband? Will I see them again—or never again?*

I shifted a little and looked up at Mother. In the dark I could not see her face, but heard her slight whispers.

In these, the darkest hours of her life, Mother would turn again and again to her only source of strength and inner peace. She stroked my hair, and continued softly praying.

4

Singled Out

Gish was a world in a dark dream for weeks after the men and older boys were taken from us.

Women moved through the streets and in the garden plots like solemn apparitions. Beneath the longing and sadness, their eyes stared with a frightening hollowness. If the men had been slain before our eyes, I think it would have been easier to go on with living. Women who have lost men at sea, or whose sons have simply vanished in foreign wars understand this feeling. Not knowing is a horror. In the back of each woman's mind, no doubt, during the aching, endless nights, were the shallow graves in the sand lot outside Gish.

Another unknown was disturbing. A few well-armed soldiers were still guarding Biram, yet they did not bother us. Why? Were they just waiting to return any day or while we lay sleeping, and haul us off to—what fate? Along with the emptiness of loss, there burned a certain fear.

Had there been no younger children demanding attention, had it not been for the comforts of Abu 'Eed whom the soldiers had left behind, some of the women might have opened their jaws in one unending scream, stepping into the blackness of the mind from which there is no return. Instead, they were forced into a rhythm of simple duties: childcare, work in the fields, preparing meals.

In all this, an unusual thing was happening to Mother. One by one, other women would come to her. The moment they looked into her eyes, they would fall on her shoulder weeping, broken inside. Instead of dissolving along with them, Mother would offer a listening ear, a few words, and the women would leave comforted. I had seen Mother's own tears, could sense her continuing hurt at the absence of Father, Rudah, Chacour and Musah. But somehow she never seemed alone—never abandoned. She took on a gentle strength, and to anyone around her it gave the solidness of hope.

Mother's greatest comfort was in prayer. As the weeks wore into months, and evenings lengthened with the coming of summer, she continued to gather us around her outside under the deepening skies. To Wardi, Atallah and me, it gave a certain peace to carry on Father's custom. To Mother, peace came not from habit or ritual words, but from talking to a dearly respected Friend—One who cared for us. Like Father, Mother spoke to this divine Friend in simple words, never doubting for an instant that a loving ear attended her voice.

With a solemn innocence, she prayed one evening, "We know that you watch the sparrows, Lord. And only you know where Michael and the boys are this night. Will you watch them for us? Guide their steps? We give them into your hands."

In my mind's eye, I could picture Jesus. He was looking at Mother with tears in His own eyes, drawing from her the hurt behind her brave words, leaving a solidity of spirit in its place.

"Allow us to be your servants here in Gish," she continued. "Let our hands be your hands to comfort the suffering. Let our lips bring the peace of your Spirit."

Something was happening to me during these months, too. More and more, I came to enjoy solitude. In the middle of a game I would stop, very often staring up into the hills. Then I would quit the group and wander off alone, followed by the questioning glances of my playmates. The last wild irises and poppies, anemones in yellow, pink and scarlet were pushing up between the stones. In a week or two, the hot breath of summer would burn the slopes a brittle brown.

The morning after Mother's special prayer, I climbed alone to the top of a hill and sat beneath an olive tree. To the south, somewhere beyond the hills, rocked the Sea of Galilee. I imagined my Champion striding toward me over the storm-churned waves, calming the waters with a word: "Peace." I thought of Him climbing the Mount of Beatitudes. There, as Mother taught me, He said, "Blessed are those who mourn, for they will be comforted."

What did these words really mean? For the first time, I turned them over and over in my mind like a smooth stone. Almost without thinking, I began innocently pouring out my heart. "Mother has your comfort. I can see that. But can't you just speak a word and make all this trouble go away? Do you want *us* to be your lips and hands and feet—as Mother prays—to bring peace again? If that's true, you can use my hands and feet. Even my tongue," I added, thinking of my usually fiery words.

I didn't know it then, but this was to be one of the most important prayers of my life. And a first, small step committing me to a long journey.

At the moment, I was thinking about Father and my brothers, slipping in one special request just for me. "Please bring them home," I whispered. Then I wondered if Father would have called that a selfish prayer. I should leave such matters in God's hands, Father would say.

Three months passed, and still we had no word about the men. The matter of our own safety loomed over us as the summer of 1949 stretched on. In nearby Biram, the soldiers were strangely quiet.

One evening, after prayers, Mother allowed Wardi, Atallah and me to play outside as usual until bedtime. But at dark, she hurried us inside, for few remained outdoors then. After she settled us in bed, Mother moved about quietly in the dim light of a candle or two finishing her chores for the day. The very last sound I heard each night before drifting into sleep was the metal *click* of the heavy door-bolt, our only earthly protection from unwelcome visits in the dark.

A sharp elbow woke me. Atallah was plumping his pillow and fidgeting beside me. He was having a hard time settling down. I could hear Mother preparing for bed. Still groggy, I was about to push Atallah's knee out of my back when a noise disturbed the quiet. Atallah and I both sat up, suddenly awake, listening. Mother and Wardi sat listening, too.

The sound came again and drew my eyes to the door. The bolt rattled in its lock. Someone was trying to open it. A muffled voice from out in the night hissed, "Let us in. Quickly. Open up."

I shrank back against Atallah, wide-eyed. Fear ran a cold fire up my spine. Mother had risen to her feet and stood frozen, one hand over her heart.

"Who is it?" she called bravely, but her voice shook.

"Let us in. Hurry . . ." the voice hissed again and was drowned out by others as the rattling continued.

"Go away," Mother called. Now she was next to tears.

"I say it's Michael. Let us in. We're home."

"Michael?" Mother almost shrieked.

Atallah and Wardi and I were at her heels as she hurried to

the door, slamming back the bolt. With our wits gathered, there was no mistaking that voice. Mother threw open the heavy door.

Four men pushed inside with the dark draft. I startled for a moment, as if we had been tricked and these were strangers crowding in before us in the flickering candlelight. They were very thin—almost emaciated—their cheeks sunken behind unkempt beards. Their clothes were dirty and ragged, and the worn shoes were nearly falling off their feet. In the eyes of my three brothers was a wary, hunted look. Only Father seemed as calm as if he had just spent a pleasant day in his fig orchard, though he was obviously exhausted.

Mother threw herself on them, hugging, holding, kissing them, laughing and weeping with inexpressible joy. Rudah, Musah and Chacour, who at any other time might have shown the reserve of young men, began to weep and hug everyone—even Atallah and me.

I threw my arms around Father's waist. "Hello, Elias," he smiled, gently stroking my tousled hair. "I see you've taken care of everyone while I was away."

Mother was hurrying about getting food and water. She was wringing with questions. "How did you get back here? Did anyone see you? Where did the soldiers take you? Are the other men with you?"

We sat long into the night, Father's arm around my shoulders as he answered her questions. They had come on foot, of course. No, they were not seen since they had traveled mostly at night. I watched his serene face, and it seemed a miracle to me that he and my brothers were alive and sitting close beside us as the candles burned low. Most amazing was the story of their survival.

On the night they were taken from Gish, the men were driven through the dark for hours. It was cramped and cold and windy in the trucks. They had passed Tiberias on the Sea of Galilee, so Father knew they were headed south. But where? Toward daybreak, he saw that they were nearing the hill country that rose up to Jerusalem. The trucks pulled off the road north of the city near the town of Nablus on the border between the new State of Israel and the kingdom of Jordan. Hopefully, it was the soldiers' intent to drop them across the border—and nothing worse.

As the men staggered from the trucks in the bleak light of dawn, the soldiers opened fire, aiming just above their heads. The men of Biram scattered in terror, running like wild men in every direction. Some fell and were almost trampled. Father and my brothers tore through the open fields, stumbling through bushes and over stones. At last they distanced the shouting soldiers and the rifle fire, which was meant to drive them from their homeland for good. But Father and my brothers had only one plan in mind from the first moment: They would find their way home again, or die in the attempt.

Gradually, they made their way to a road that seemed to angle in a northeasterly direction—first toward Amman, then toward Damascus in Syria. They had no idea where any of my uncles had gone, and only occasionally did they find other men from our village on the road. Many of them were too frightened to consider returning to Gish. Most frightening was the treatment they received at the hands of other Arab brothers in Jordan and Syria where Father hoped to find help and the customary hospitality. At the first town they came to, Father and my brothers were turned away as vagabonds. Our "brothers" it seemed had no compassion for "dirty Palestinians." At the next town it was the same, and the next. They were driven out like lepers. For days they walked with little or nothing to eat, forced out of every town. At times they were so desperately hungry that they grovelled in the dirt for insects to eat. Nights they spent in abandoned

animal shelters in the hills or sleeping in the dirt and grass to
wake soaked with dew and shivering. Had it not been summer, they would surely have died.

For days and weeks they traveled until they were close to
Damascus. Then Father struck a southwesterly route that
would carry them through a corner of Lebanon and into
northern Israel. Once he spotted Mount Meron, the highest
mountain in all Galilee, Father knew he was home. When
they reached the fields outside Gish, they waited until dark in
the event that soldiers were stationed in the village. Then,
furtively, they crept through the streets until they found the
right door, unsure that they would find us here after all their
hardship.

Mother almost blushed when Father teased her about her
stalwart refusal to open the door to her own husband. And he
held her close. Three months of torment were over at last.

As Father prayed with us that night, I leaned against him,
basking in the richness of his deep voice—I had missed it so
much—and I was almost too overjoyed to comprehend his
words.

"Father," he prayed, "they are treating us badly because
we are the children of Ishmael. But we are true sons of
Abraham—and your children. You saved Ishmael from death
in the wilderness, and you have saved us. You brought justice
for him and blessed him with a great nation. We thank you
now, for we know that you will bring justice for us. . . ."

In the coming months a few more men would return. One
day, a certain village house would be somber, with a mother
and her babies facing the uncertainly of life on their own—
and overnight, joy would dawn in that home again. Yet for
every family that was reunited, many more never saw their
husbands, sons, fathers, uncles and cousins again. Mother
and Father had both lost several brothers, and some of my
older cousins had simply vanished as well. Only rarely did

we hear some word—and no one could judge its reliability—that this uncle or that one was living in a refugee camp in Lebanon or Syria.

For the rest of that year I lived with a lingering shadow of fear that the soldiers would surprise us one day, roaring in with trucks to drag away the men once more. This time, perhaps, they would finish off their job more forcefully.

The soldiers never did raid Gish again. In fact, as 1949 came to a close, the new government seemed to undergo a strange, confusing reversal in its push to drive out the Palestinian people entirely. The elders began to hear that the agricultural settlements were actually hiring Palestinian men and boys—a few at a time and "unofficially"—to work at menial jobs. Later we learned why. A cheap work force was crucial to the survival of their newest *kibbutzim*, since many of the incoming settlers had lived their lives in European cities and did not know how to farm. Now we understood why the soldiers never came back to drive out the men who had returned, for they were skilled in agriculture and desperate to work, even for low pay, to support their large families.

Something else was happening behind the scenes in the new government of Israel, though the village elders had no way of knowing it yet. Soon they would see strong evidence of internal struggles within the government, clues that this new nation—which the whole world was proclaiming a "modern miracle"—was actually rife with factions vying for power.

Early in 1950, as the cold spring rains swept the hills, flooding the wild wells and driving our meagre flocks of sheep and goats into sheltering grottoes, more heart-stopping news reached us.

Plans were underway for a new *kibbutz*, an experimental, agricultural community set up by the new government for settlers from Europe and America. It was to be located just across the fields from our still-empty homes, and strangely, it would be called Biram also. More startling was the news that some of the fertile land surrounding Biram had been sold to new landlords who had emigrated from foreign countries and were living in nearby Jewish towns. Now we understood why the soldiers had stayed on in Biram to "protect" it from our return.

Most painful was the word that Father's fig orchard had been purchased from the government by a well-to-do settler as some sort of investment.

At this news, Father's face furrowed with grief. I was terrified that he would weep. He was still, his eyes shut, his mustache drooping above a faintly trembling lip. He had planted those fig trees himself one by one, straining with heavy clay jars of water up the steep slopes, caring for each sapling until it was strong enough to survive on its own. They were almost like children to him.

And in the same moment, I wished that Father would rage. Perhaps fear had numbed my anger before this time. Now as I watched Father's pain-lined face, I shook with a horrible feeling. Wardi and my brothers squirmed. None of us could bear to see Father—dear, gentle, Father—in such agony of spirit.

When he spoke in a few minutes, his voice was barely above a whisper.

"Children," he said softly, turning those sad eyes upon us, "if someone hurts you, you can curse him. But this would be useless. Instead, you have to ask the Lord to bless the man who makes himself your enemy. And do you know what will happen? The Lord will bless you with inner peace—and perhaps your enemy will turn from his wickedness. If not, the Lord will deal with him."

I could scarcely believe it! His life's work had just been torn from his hands. His land and trees—the only earthly possessions he had to pass on to his children—were sold to a stranger. And still Father would not curse or allow himself to be angry. I puzzled at his words to us.

Inner peace. Maybe Father could find this strength in such circumstances. I doubted that I could.

I am certain that Father had a strong voice in what happened next. Immediately after the distressing news, the remnant of our village elders convened and decided to submit a petition to the new Israeli Supreme Court of Justice. In short, the petition welcomed the settlers to the new Biram. What had been taken could be considered as a gift from our people. However, they asked, could we return to our homes in the old Biram to live peacefully beside our new neighbors and farm the remaining land?

Father's other response to the sale of his land was more of a wonder to me.

In a few weeks we heard that the new owner of our property wanted to hire several men to come each day and dress the fig trees, tending them right through till harvest. Immediately, Father went to apply for the job, taking my three oldest brothers with him. They were hired and granted special work passes, the only way they could enter our own property.

When she heard what Father had done, Mother stared at him incredulously. "How can you do this, Michael? It's so awful. So wrong."

Father replied simply, "If we go to care for the trees, we'll do the best job. Someone else won't know what they are doing. They'll break the branches and spoil the new growth." This was something Father could not bear to think.

And so, three years after our expulsion from Biram, Father and my brothers were hiring themselves out as laborers—just for the chance to touch and care for Father's beloved trees. I did not know the word *irony* then, but I could understand pain.

For months the elders of Biram continued in the hope that

the new government would allow them to return to their homes. However, among the younger men, this hope was not so strong. A few began to speak of moving to the coastal cities of Haifa and Akko where, they had heard, Palestinian families were clustering in hopes that their men could find factory jobs. The new Israel was struggling to westernize, and that meant rapid industrial development. Again, lower-paying jobs were opening to Palestinians a few at a time. Of course there was deep resentment. But living would be better there, the young men argued—at least they could feed and clothe their children. Here and there, a family moved out of Gish, shrugging off the elders' assurances that justice and our return to Biram were imminent.

Daily, as summer ripened, Father and my brothers hopefully climbed the long hill that separated Biram and Gish to tend our own trees for the new landlord. And each day they would report on the progress of the new Biram *kibbutz—a* dwelling going up here or there, poles being uprighted for the telephone and electrical wires, the constant surveillance by police from the nearby towns and the arrival of the first foreign tenants. Father bore, with characteristic patience, the indignity of having his special worker's pass scrutinized by the soldiers several times each week before he could set foot on what had been his own land.

In this lull, terror would single me out.

For us boys, one of the few diversions from this chancey and unpredictable adult world was still a game of soccer. It was almost a daily ritual. Though I was spending more and more time walking alone in the hills, I still loved to rough-house with other boys. At eleven, I had become quite fast, though my kicking aim was not always so accurate as the older boys who mostly made up the teams. Atallah and Asad stuck up for me if there was ever a question of leaving me out, and I was a wiry and eager player.

We were lost in a fierce competition on a hot afternoon toward the end of summer. I watched the ball being footed up the field, passed from one teammate to another, when a sound caught us by the ears. Heads spun around. Everyone stopped dead in their tracks, the ball trailing off forgotten. It was a sound we feared by instinct.

Cars were speeding into Gish. My heart, pounding from the playful activity, nearly stopped. Were they again coming for Father and the other men?

Several dark automobiles and jeeps raced into view, billowing clouds of dust in their wake. At the edge of our playing field, close to where a few of us were standing, they braked to a sudden, unexpected stop. Most of the other boys were running for home, Atallah and Asad with them. They must have thought I was right behind. In confusion, three or four of us stood transfixed, as if freezing in place would keep us from being seen. As the vehicles halted, a dozen men burst onto our playing field.

"You! Come here!" A huge man yelled, striding toward me. I could see by his uniform that he was a military policeman and, like the others, he had a gun at his belt. Roughly, he grabbed me by the shoulder, his fingers digging painfully. The other boys had been seized also.

"What shall we do with them?" shouted my captor.

I tried to twist out of his excruciating grasp, not that my shaking legs could have run if I'd wanted to, but the iron grip of his fingers dug into my neck.

"First you tell us what you did with the wire," my captor demanded, shoving me against the other boys. A wall of men surrounded us, firing questions and accusations.

"Who put you up to it? Tell us that."

"You don't want us to go after your families, do you?"

"Maybe you'd care to tell us where the terrorists are hiding in your village."

"I think they want a beating."

I struggled to hold back hot tears. The others stared, mute with fear. None of us had any idea what they were talking about. Somehow I choked out a few words.

"We don't know what you are saying. What wire? We don't know about any wire. We've been playing soccer. . . ."

"*Lies,*" one of the men barked. "All you know how to do is lie."

For what seemed an endless time, they continued to threaten and badger us. First one, then the other would scream at us, always coming back to the charge that we had cut some kind of wire. Over and over, we protested that we had no idea what they were talking about.

By this time, our teammates had sped through Gish breathlessly spilling the story that we were being held. People were flocking to see what had happened. In the crowd of men, women and children that were clustering some distance from us and the knot of angry men, I could see Mother. Father was striding toward us, his face a mask of fear. His coming, I hoped, would mean our rescue.

"What are you doing with these boys?" he challenged them as boldly as he dared. "What have they done that you're treating them like criminals?"

"They cut the telephone wire that was being run up to the new *kibbutz,*" one man declared. "It was strung along the ground, waiting to be mounted on the poles. A section has been cut. It's missing. These boys were seen cutting it, and we want to know who put them up to it."

It was obvious that they had simply grabbed us, the first children they saw, and we were to be the "culprits." I suppose they thought that by threatening us, our parents would surrender the true villain. Unfortunately, there was no one to surrender.

"You think you can get away with terrorist actions?" One of the men glared at the crowd, picking up a stick. The others searched the ground for sticks, too. "I think your boys will have some information for us if we coax them."

The men closed in on us, their bodies forming an impenetrable wall. I huddled against another boy, looking desperately for a way of escape. The huge man who had first grabbed me raised the stick over his head.

A stinging *crack* seared my shoulder. I drew a sharp breath and tried to shield myself from his next blows. The boy beside me screamed as he was struck across the back. We tried to fend off the slashing sticks with our arms, which only infuriated our captors. Another whipping blow stung my bare legs just below the short pants I was wearing. Then another. Two across my back—lashes like hot brands. Above our own cries, I could hear women begging the men to stop the beating.

As they struck us, the men shouted at our horrified families: "You are worth nothing—and your children are worth nothing. You are doing underground work. Your children are thieves and you're the ones who teach them to steal!"

I thought the whipping would never end. And then, suddenly, the huge man grabbed me by the shirt.

"Now bring that piece of wire to me," he growled in my face. Then he shoved me away.

I stumbled toward Father on shaking legs, still stinging and choking on sobs. In confusion, I blurted, "Father, where do I go?"

The man, thinking, perhaps, that Father had cut the wire, turned on him with a face distorted by anger.

"Is this what you teach your son?" he erupted. All the men were shouting and cursing. They swore at Father, calling him, among other disgusting things, that degrading name with which we were to be branded—"dirty Palestinians." I was shocked, pained more deeply than by any physical bruises, that my gentle father could be so abused in front of our whole village by these crude men.

Yet Father bore their insults silently.

The huge man doubled his fist in Father's face. "Tomorrow we'll come back" he promised, "and you give us the wire or you and your son will come with us."

Still glaring at us, the policemen stalked back to their cars and jeeps and drove off.

The very next morning they did return, shoving Father and me into an automobile. As we rocked and jolted down the rough roads to their station in a nearby town, a chilling thought tempted me to tears: *I will never see Mother again. They will throw me in jail and forget me.* And at the same time, another voice spoke from deep within my thoughts, soothing me with the words, *Peace, be still.*

For many hours, the police interrogated us, hinting that I was in for a terrible time if Father did not help them find their wire. He remained calm, a study in politeness and respect despite their angry questions, firm in his assertion that I was innocent. In disgust, the police finally gave up and drove us back to Gish. When they left us, there were no more threats, but I feared that the incident was not to be dropped.

That evening, Mother called me to sit beside her when everyone else was outside and we were alone. Now that my arms and legs had begun to stretch long and slender, I could no longer sit on her lap. I leaned against her, her bright kerchief soft against my cheek. Gently she took my hand.

"Elias, I want to give you a treat," she said softly. "I have saved an egg, and I'm going to cook it for you." For us, struggling to get by on the barest amount of food, a cooked egg was indeed a treat. This was Mother's special way, I supposed, to help me feel a little better.

She hesitated for a moment, then continued. "But first,

Elias, please tell me . . ." she faltered, "tell me where the wire is. Bring it to us, and then this trouble will be over."

I sat up stiffly and stared at her. She was no longer young, the struggle of caring for a large family under such poor conditions had lined her face. A wisp of hair—graying hair—had escaped her kerchief. A certain weariness showed through her sweet smile. Poor Mother, after all the terror she had faced—the disappearance of Father and my brothers, many members of her own family driven into exile—I could not be angry with her. She simply feared the loss of her youngest. But I was angry—and hurt that such terror tactics could cause her to doubt her own son.

"Mother, I didn't do it." That was all I could reply to her.

For the next few days I drew away from my family and my playmates, retreating into the sun-parched hills to be alone. But not completely alone. The sheep on the hillside, the twisted, ancient olive trees, the far-off blue hills of the Golan Heights that towered around the Sea of Galilee—all these things reminded me of my constant Champion. My pace quickened up the brown-burnt slopes as if He were walking right beside me at that moment. I could almost see His understanding look, and in my head I heard Him, repeating the words Mother had quoted to me hundreds of times: *Blessed are you when people falsely say all kinds of evil against you . . . for in the same way they persecuted the prophets who were before you.*

I shook my head as if arguing with a playmate. I did not want to hear these words. I was no prophet. I only wanted to know why I was being singled out for such horrible treatment.

I had forgotten my prayer of months before when I had asked Him to use my hands and feet and tongue to bring peace back to our peoples' hearts. Had I remembered, I would not have understood then that such a commitment, when spoken from the heart, means being called out, singled from the crowd. It may mean drinking from the bitter cup of rejection and humiliation—standing in the face of the lie in order for the truth to win out ultimately.

I only knew that, despite my anger, I wanted things to be put right so that I would never again hear the wail of village women grieving for their lost—never again see the hurt in Mother's eyes, or hear Father cursed. I wanted so much for us to live in peace with our Jewish neighbors as we had before the soldiers came. The thought of living the rest of our lives in fear was stifling, and as I trudged through the cedars and the scattered olive trees, I wondered what Jesus would do.

Unknown to me, someone had an eye on my daily wanderings.

One afternoon I returned home to find Father working in his small garden plot, hoeing up the dry, spent vegetable plants. He saw me coming, stopped and leaned on the long, wooden handle. Thinking I might disturb his work, I was going to pass by. He stopped me with a question.

"What do you do in the hills, Elias?"

I paused, wondering if he would think it odd if I answered, "Talk with a Friend." After a moment's thought, that was my reply.

Father nodded, his eyes scanning the hills, a faint, mysterious smile on his lips. "I thought as much," was all he said. Then he went back to work.

I walked away, and the moment passed. It would be some time before I realized the importance of that brief encounter. For Father was a man of deep insight and wisdom, and a plan for my future was already turning over in his mind as he churned the stiff soil.

By the end of the week, the question of my guilt or innocence was resolved. We learned that a wagondriver, returning to the new Biram *kibbutz* with supplies, produced the missing length of telephone wire. It fit exactly in place between the cut ends. He had run over it with his loaded wagon and the wire had sheered off between the metal-rimmed wheels and the rock-hard ground. He had carried the section away with him, planning to return it on his next trip.

We never received any apology from the police, and I was only too happy to let the entire episode be forgotten. And shortly, in the closing months of 1950, we received joyous news from the Supreme Court of Israel that temporarily wiped the incident entirely from our minds.

An official letter arrived in Gish, postmarked in Jerusalem. The elder's hands fairly shook with excitement as he read it aloud. The letter said we could return to Biram immediately by order of the Supreme Court! Hurriedly, with great rejoicing, plans were made for the move home.

While the women were gathering up the few things they had acquired in our three years of exile, some of the elders crossed the hill to Biram and there displayed our letter to the soldiers.

The commanding officer shook his head. "This letter means nothing to us. Nothing at all. The village is ours. You have no right here."

Though the elders argued with him, he would not honor the order. They were turned away.

For the first time our elders realized that something was seriously wrong within the new government. They already had ample evidence that these Zionists were not at all like our peaceful Jewish neighbors. The new Israel seemed to be a nation where the military ruled, ignoring the will of the country's judges and lawmakers, powerful enough to do whatever it wanted. The elders were devastated by this revelation.

Upon hearing the soldiers' refusal, I saw the pain in Mother's eyes, felt the ache in Father's heart for his lost land and fig trees. As Christians, they would accept their lot. Yet I could see the joy draining from their lives. And still rumors of violence whispered through the hills, bloodshed and terrorism everywhere in the land.

Were there only two choices left to us—surrender to abuse or turn to violence?

As for me, the beating had forced me to stare into the face of this frightening question. What choice was I to make? And as my twelfth year approached, I was soon to take the next step on the journey that would lead me to a third choice—one that my Champion made so long ago in these same beautiful, fought-over hills.

5

The Bread of Orphans

Early in 1951, the elders agreed to petition the Supreme Court a second time. In their letter of appeal, they explained the Zionist soldiers' defiance of the court order. Again we would wait in hope for many months, innocently believing that the Court could somehow make the military obey its legal decisions.

Though we would receive a surprising answer, I would be far from Gish when it finally came.

On a hazy, humid morning, our Bishop arrived in Gish. He had been tirelessly visiting all the outlying villages arranging for deliveries of food, clothing and medical supplies. Along with the list of urgent needs, he was accumulating a lengthy accounting of complaints.

He walked the streets of Gish, escorted by crowds of men who pointed out the overcrowded houses, the children playing in worn and too-small clothing. Gradually, their complaints turned to the loss of property—twelve acres, twenty, thirty, forty—each man topping the next as they bemoaned their confiscated land. Though they tried to contain their anger in respect for the Bishop, they were soon tirading loudly about the losses sustained. Again and again, the men tried to pin him moth-like with one pointed question: What power did he have to get their land back?

Father was walking along quietly at the edge of the crowd. In a lull between the complaints, he spoke up.

"Bishop, excuse me. I have a request also."

The Bishop knew Father well from occasional visits to Biram in the past. Possibly he expected another listing of wrongs and injuries. He nodded politely, with a hint of weariness in his smile. "What is it, Michael?"

"I have a son—my youngest. His name is Elias," Father explained. He's a good student, and I want to send him to a good school. Please, can you help me?"

The other men were jolted by the abrupt shift in conversation. Impatiently, without thinking, they interrupted. "What are you talking about? We're trying to get our homes and our land back. And you're bothering the Bishop with something like this?" As soon as the heated words were out, they flushed with embarrassment.

The Bishop's smile broadened. "Let me think on this for a little while, Michael. Come and see me before I leave the village." And then the crowd swept him along again.

Father kept the promised appointment with the Bishop. Though he did not have a proper school to send me to, the Bishop explained that there was an orphanage near his own home. I would be welcome there, and the bishop promised to see to my education personally.

Father accepted the offer at once with deep gratitude. Eagerly, he discussed his plans with Mother and found her less eager to send her youngest child—her favored son—so far from home. In the end, of course, she submitted.

Then Father took me aside. There was a slight catch in his voice as he explained, "In a few days, we will take you to the bus. You are going to Haifa on the coast to study with the

Bishop. This is a wonderful opportunity for you, Elias. You will never have such a chance here in Gish.

"And there is another thing," he said, pausing. Now Father searched my eyes with his steady, serious gaze. "You are not being sent away to be spoiled by privilege. Learn all you can from the Bishop. If you become a true man of God—you will know how to reconcile enemies—how to turn hatred into peace. Only a true servant of God can do that."

I could scarcely fathom such an enormous-sounding task. I only knew that the prospect of life in Haifa sounded thrilling. At twelve years old, I had never been beyond our hills.

On the morning of my departure, I was awake with the earliest light. Even so, Mother had awakened before me, had finished her silent prayers, and was packing a small bag with my few belongings. Rising from my straw mat, I felt uneasy. In the stillness of dawn, I heard the faint jingle of the doves and fish on Mother's necklace—and suddenly I did not feel at all adventurous. An emptiness opened in the space below my ribs. I could only pick at the special egg Mother had so lovingly saved for my farewell breakfast.

The whole family trudged together to the bus stop—at a crossing of roads not far from Gish where the bus occasionally found its way. Mother and Father were to accompany me to Haifa. Wardi and my brothers followed glumly, barely looking at me all the way to the bus stop.

And then the ancient bus lumbered up, its bitter-smelling exhaust tingling my nostrils. My bag was loaded, we climbed on board, and Father carefully counted out the coins for our fare from what he had earned by working in our orchard. Without ceremony, the bus jolted forward, rumbling down the hills. We rounded a bend—and my brothers and Wardi disappeared. With a sick feeling, I realized suddenly that I did not know when I would see them again.

"Seventy-five kilometers to Haifa," the driver shouted over the roar of the bus. The few other passengers merely nodded. To me that was an unimaginable distance—impossibly far! I sat between Mother and Father, picking at the torn seatcover, miserably jouncing with each bump. An empty, rootless feeling—one I'd never felt before—widened inside me with each passing kilometer. Mountains and towns and orchards sped by our window, and only one thought filled my head: *How can I ever find my way back home again? Where is my home?*

Unknown to any of us, I was about to face the most crucial turning points, confronted at such a tender age by events and choices that would shape my entire life.

When we stepped off the bus in Haifa I was completely bewildered. The huge station was a mass of busses, autos and travelers. The men and women standing in the ticket line wore the nicest suits and dresses I had ever seen. Their clothes seemed stunning compared to the scuffed shoes, baggy shorts and shirt I had gotten through the Bishop's relief efforts. And I could not stop craning my neck, scanning the buildings and clustered homes that covered the low, rolling hillside down to the shore of the Mediterranean Sea.

Somehow, Father guided us through the busy streets— paved streets!—to the correct address. With each corner we turned, the buildings got older and more decrepit until we reached the Bishop's orphanage—a squat, gray-looking building jammed between the others.

On the doorstep we were greeted by a young, plain-looking woman with a lilting European accent and a welcoming smile. Inside, the Bishop received us, chatting with Father, and I knew this was a great honor. Mother judiciously eyed the accommodations, nodding politely as she met the other Belgian and French ladies who, in service to the church, lived here with the orphans.

Before I knew it, Mother and Father were out on the doorstep again. A quick hug from Mother—and she turned her face away. A wave from Father whose smile seemed a little fixed.

Then they were gone.

The young woman gently laid an arm across my slumping shoulder as I stared dejectedly for a time into the empty street. "Come, Elias," she said tenderly—if unthinking. "I want you to meet our other orphans."

The European ladies immediately swooped me under their collective wing, fussing over me like so many mothers. Though they were tender and caring, the deep homesickness left an empty gap in my stomach. I was a country boy, uprooted from quiet and replanted in a noisy city, my roots pinched beneath concrete. My move to Haifa had caused me to miss home—our real home in Biram—more than I had during our exile in Gish. How deeply I missed walking alone in the hills, drinking from the clear-water springs of Galilee. Amid the busses and grimy buildings of the city, I had to force my mind from those faraway hills. During each long, grueling lesson, they beckoned to me with a wild freshness that was suddenly missing.

And in the Bishop's rigorous schedule for me, I began to lose something else. Studying the Bible as if it were a textbook was very unsatisfying. The sense of Jesus' presence, whether real or imagined, had always been so vivid. In Haifa it seemed like memory of a bygone childhood. I clutched at the New Testament promise Mother had so often quoted: "I will never leave you nor forsake you." Despite those words, I was lonely. I longed for the days when I had felt His presence in the wild places. I longed for solitude.

For several months this yearning ached in me, deep as a prayer that coursed through my whole being. And then I was surprised by an unexpected "gift."

It was bedtime. I was curled up in an over-stuffed chair in a corner of the common room which we used both for study and play. Spread across my lap was one of the huge, gloriously colorful picture books the housemothers had brought from Europe. The other children were busy with games as I leafed through the pages, escaping into a fantastic world of adventure. One of the housemothers, a French woman who was preeminently observant of the rules, came in and announced the end of playtime.

"Come, Elias," she said crisply, taking the book from my lap. "Into bed."

Another housemother—one whose gentleness and delicately scented lavender cologne made her a favorite of us all—had also come into the room. She noticed the look of discouragement on my face. Perhaps she sensed something beyond a typical, youthful unwillingness to go to bed. As the last boy filed out of the room, she came to my defense. "Don't you think we could let him stay up a little longer than the others? After all, he's a good student. And see how he loves the books. I'm sure he'll be quiet and not disturb anyone." She finished with a conspiratorial glance at me.

So it happened that I was allowed to stay up longer than the other children—all by myself in the common room! It was a small measure of solitude, not the wilderness peace of Galilee, but it would do.

Once I'd been given this glorious gift, I did not waste a moment on storybooks. I found an empty journal and began to fill it with letters to Jesus. I was too self-conscious perhaps to speak to Him right out loud in a house full of people as I had in the deserted hills of home. So night after night I spilled my heart across the blank pages with childlike innocence and dawning maturity.

"Mother says you have a purpose in everything," I wrote. *"But I don't understand what you want from us. Is it your*

plan that Mother and Father suffer as you suffered? Father
will not fight to get his land back as others are willing to do.
Is this the kind of 'peace' you want us to show the world? Will
anyone hear our cry and help us."

Many nights, during the fall of 1951, I scrawled out my
dearest hope that the Court would order the military to allow
my family and the other villagers to return to Biram. That
ancient village with its moss-covered walls and sheltering
trees seemed to me a cradle of all that was good and simple
and innocent. It was a home that had protected us. The
church that was its living heart had nurtured our spirits. If
only we could have it back. It was all I wanted.

And so, with my nightly writings, I firmly established a
lifelong practice of private communion that proved as vital as
the blood in my veins or the breath in my lungs. It was a
practice established in irony, for at the very moment I tightly
grasped my thread of inner peace again, the seeds of bitterness were about to be sown in my heart.

Christmas passed. In the orphanage our observance was
joyful. If I was still homesick, the simple European touches
added by our housemothers helped to cheer me. More mar-
velous was the sense of holiness, the solemnity and wonder I
felt at the Bishop's Nativity celebration in the huge, cathe-
dral-like church. The bells, the happy carols, the stone arches all warmed me with thoughts of home. In fact, being in
church had come to feel like being at home to me, somehow. I
loved it.

One cold Sunday morning early in January 1952, I was
huddled with the other children in the chilliness of the old
church. We stood to sing a hymn and I turned to whisper
something to the boy next to me. From the corner of my eye,
I spotted him—and my head jerked around. In the back, in a
baggy, worn coat, sat my oldest brother, Rudah. But it could

not be! Why would he come so far? It must be good news about Biram.

In response, he nodded faintly. My mouth must have dropped open in amazement, for one of the housemothers nudged me and gave a stern look. I could do nothing but fidget through the rest of the service, sneaking secret glances over my shoulder to be sure Rudah would not disappear.

When it was over, I broke from the group and ran down the long crowded aisle to him, the housemother calling after me.

"Rudah!" I threw my arms around him. I had grown some, and now we were nearly the same height. "I've missed you. Why are you here? How are Mother and Father? Can you stay to lunch?"

"Come outside, Elias," he said quietly. "I have something to tell you."

On the church steps we paused. I drew my thin coat close to my chin to block the bitter wind. Rudah faced me now with a look of deep anguish.

"Mother and Father sent me to tell you the news. They didn't want you to hear it and worry about us. Elias," he said, fighting back tears, "it was horrible. The soldiers. The bombs—"

"What are you saying?" I pressed him anxiously. Suddenly I was shaking with cold and nerves. Numbly, I listened as the story spilled out.

Some time in early December the Court had again granted the people of Biram approval to return to their homes. For the second time, the village elders marched across the hill and presented the order to the Zionist soldiers. This time, the elders were pleasantly surprised.

Without question or dispute, the commanding officer read the order. He shrugged. "This is fine." And as the elders stood in stunned silence he added, "We need some time to pull out. You can return on the twenty-fifth."

On Christmas! What an incredible Christmas gift for the village. The elders fairly ran across the hill to Gish to spread the news. At long last, they would all be going home. The Christmas Eve vigil became a celebration of thanksgiving and joyful praise.

On Christmas morning, broken gray clouds rolled across the upper Galilee, and the still air was crisp and cold. Bundled in sweaters and old coats supplied by the Bishop's relief workers, the villagers gathered in the first light of day for the march to Biram. Though they were ragged looking, their spirits were high. Mother, Father, Wardi and my brothers all joined in singing a jubilant Christmas hymn as they mounted the hill. It was the first time in nearly six years that such joy had flooded those ancient slopes.

At the top of the hill, their hymn trailed into silence. The marchers halted uncertainly. Far below them, Biram was surrounded by Zionists tanks, bulldozers and other military vehicles. But this was December 25, the morning they were supposed to return home. Why were the soldiers still there? In the distance, a soldier shouted, and they realized they had been seen.

A cannon blast sheared the silence. Then another—a third. The soldiers had opened fire—not on the villagers, but on Biram! Tank shells shrieked into the village, exploding in fiery destruction. Houses blew apart like paper. Stones and dust flew amid the red flames and billowing black smoke. One shell slammed into the side of the church, caving in a thick stone wall and blowing off half the roof. The bell tower teetered, the bronze bell knelling, and somehow held amid the dust clouds and cannon-fire. For nearly five minutes, the explosions rocked Biram, home collapsing against home, fire spreading through the fallen timbers.

Then all was silent—except for the weeping of women and the terrified screams of babies and children.

Mother and Father stood shaking, huddled together with Wardi and my brothers. In a numbness of horror, they watched as bulldozers plowed through the ruins, knocking down much of what had not already blown apart or tumbled. At last, Father said—to my brothers or to God, they were never sure—"Forgive them." Then he led them back to Gish.

I could not absorb Rudah's words. He told me that another village, Ikrit, had also been bombed at about the same time. I was simply cold.

Cold as we parted, hugging on the doorstep of the orphanage. Cold as I picked at my supper in silence. The housemothers did not press me to do my schoolwork that evening, for they had heard the news from Rudah, too.

Alone that night, I was frightened by my own thoughts. I did not know how to handle the anger. More than anger. Rage. The bombing was worse than any physical beating I could have suffered. I could not face my journal, ashamed to pour out my dark feelings there. I lectured myself, wishing that I could be just like Father, who was my indelible example of spirituality. But I was me—a young man with a growing awareness that the world seemed bent on my destruction.

So it was that I buried my feelings, denying the anger that was too ugly to admit. And in that moment a small gap began to widen inside me, an internal battle that I would one day have to reconcile.

In another week, I lost myself again in the journal, posing questions to which I had not the vaguest answer.

"*How can we ever find again the peace we used to share with our Jewish neighbors?*" I wrote. "*How can I help my parents—my Palestinian people?*"

Though I wanted to leave Haifa—to share in the hard life of exile with my family—I would remain for two more years. I was being prepared for the next step on my journey, a step that would carry me farther from home than I could have imagined. It was Father's wish that I study, and I would obey. The Bishop's house of charity would shelter and instruct me.

As with all the people of Biram, I would continue to eat the bread of the homeless and the orphaned.

6

The Narrowing Way

The bombing of our homes was a sharp blow that knocked the wind and spirit out of the people of Biram.

In the scant news I heard from Mother and Father came reports that a few more families were leaving Gish each month for the cities. Perhaps they would be better off hidden among the poor masses in a large city than perched on the open hilltops of Galilee. Understandably, they no longer wanted to stand by the elders in their continuing appeals for the return of our land. With the bombing, they had despaired.

Unbelievably, Father and my brothers continued caring for the fig trees in our confiscated orchard, which had escaped bombing. I pictured Father walking stoically past the ruins of our house. Rudah had said it was nothing but a tumble of stones and charred beams. Father, I knew, would keep his eyes and his heart set on one thing: tending the fig trees—at least for a little while longer. Silently he would plod on, hoping that his sons would follow him in bearing the cross of persecution. It was all he knew to do. Even as I admired his courage, I detected in Father a growing twinge of hopelessness. For the first time, I think, I realized that my father was human, a man with weaknesses and a limited understanding of this bewildering conflict in which we were embroiled.

As for me, I entered my second year of studies in Haifa with great listlessness. I had been away from home more than a year, and that nagging, rootless feeling left me empty. Because I was not an orphan, I was never fully accepted by the other boys. This, my early adolescence, was a bad time to be hit with so many crushing blows to my self-worth. A sense of loss—a deep mourning—threatened to cripple my spirit.

Once again, it seemed that I was not to be forsaken. In my loneliest moment, I was given the gift of a special friendship.

During the first week of classes that fall, two new boys came to study at the Bishop's school. They were Faraj and Khalil Nakhleh, and they came from a fairly well-to-do family in Ramah, another village in Galilee where there was no longer any school.

From the first moment I met Faraj, the older of the two, I sensed a special quality about him. He had a certain politeness, a joy, something quite rare that I could not touch, and yet it felt familiar. He was thirteen also, and the first thin wisps of mustache shadowed our upper lips. Though he was about my height, he was thinner, and I tended toward broad shoulders, a barrel chest and angular bones. He had a quick, easy laugh and the ability to draw me out of my grayness of spirit. Even under the heavy load of lessons, there remained a flicker of fun in his eyes. Such an immediate bond sealed between us that I, rather than Khalil, might have been taken for his brother.

What most amazed me was Faraj's unusual sensitivity.

Once, when we were taken as a group to swim in the nearby Mediterranean, I drew apart from the splashing playfulness. The other children were used to my occasional solitary habits. But Faraj appeared at my side, sticking close as I trailed along the hot sand. He listened quietly, nodding and studying my face as I rambled over my confused thoughts about the plight of our families and our own future under the new government.

"What do you think will happen to us?" I pondered aloud.

"I don't know, Elias," he replied. "We can't go to university, that's for sure. They aren't accepting—" he stumbled over the words—"aren't accepting *our kind*."

I knew he meant Palestinians. "So what do you plan to do when we're through here? Work in a factory?"

He stopped. A sweep of white foam raced up the beach and splashed warmly over our bare feet. "I'm not sure," he said in a moment. "But I believe that someone will take care of us. That much I know."

Who did he mean? The Bishop? I wasn't sure what his vague answer meant, but did not pursue it.

At the moment, I needed to be alone to think. Faraj had somehow developed, in a few short weeks, the uncanny ability to read my moods. If he was boisterous and fun-loving, he was also sensitive. He left me to wander and trotted back down the beach to where the others were playing in the crashing waves. I found a quiet spot and sat watching the restless surf, imagining that the great swells were the hills rising around Biram.

Biram that lay in ruins.

The home and church—those two "cradles" that had taught me about the Man of Peace—now in ruins. Destroyed by the violent.

In that silence of spirit, sitting before an eternity of blue sea, a vivid image flashed before me. An image of Biram resurrected beneath the ancient olive trees, of all the ransacked homes restored and the women safe within. Palestinian and Jew—sipping coffee together again in tranquil conversation. The church was rebuilt. Each man, woman and child was like a stone—a living stone—in the rebuilt village.

For a split second, it all seemed so real—so *possible*—that my heart leaped.

Then the image was gone.

Shouting at the far end of the beach shook me from my thoughts. Three or four boys had plunged into the surf. With arms flailing, they raced while those on shore cheered. Now I could see that the one about to take the lead was Faraj. All the girls were cheering him on, which made me smile. Our interest in girls was just dawning, but Faraj was the one whose charm was already landing him in one brief romance after another. I felt a sudden surge of brotherly admiration for him.

I got up and shuffled through the sand to rejoin the group. Faraj had waded up onto the beach again where the others clapped him on the back. His chest heaved as he caught his breath, and his lips were parted in that handsome smile the girls loved. The victor.

Faraj would be a success at whatever he chose to do—at school, in business. He was that sort of boy. And his family had a bit of money. Maybe they would send him to America when he was old enough. And me? What would I do?

Throughout that year and into 1953, Faraj and I grew closer together, sharing late-night secrets when we ought to have been asleep, and studying in the same classes. My grades, in fact, were quite high which pleased the Bishop. Occasionally, he would mention to me a minor seminary he was planning to open in Nazareth, a school for young men who were seriously considering service to the Church. It would be ready to receive students the following year, in 1954. Since I would then be fifteen, he thought I was old enough to be considered.

In the fall of 1953, on one of my very rare visits to my family in Gish, I mentioned the Bishop's offer to Mother and Father. They were subdued when they met me at the bus, still

grieving over the recent deaths of both my grandparents.
Father, now in his fifties, had finally stopped tending the fig
orchard. It had become too emotionally draining, and this
heaviness showed through his usual, easy smile. But at the
suggestion of seminary they both brightened a little.

"And what do *you* want to do?" Father asked.

I was about to reply, but stopped in mid-breath. It suddenly occurred to me that the decision was up to me. Three
years before, it had been Father's decision that sent me to
Haifa. Suddenly, I felt that I was stepping through the opening door to manhood, free and trusted and mature in the eyes
of my father. I could not answer him just then, but my way
was slowly becoming more clear.

Shortly after my return to Haifa, I was summoned to the
Bishop's office. I knew what his question would be—and yet
I was in for a surprise.

When I reached his office door I paused, and he beckoned
me with a wave of his hand. "Hello, Elias," he said, seated
behind his desk. "Sit beside your friend."

I entered and was amazed to see Faraj sitting in one of two
straight, wooden chairs in front of the Bishop's desk. We
exchanged surprised looks as the Bishop began to address
us.

"You've both had some time to reflect since I last spoke
with you," he said, his kind penetrating eyes moving from
Faraj to me. "Now I want to hear your decision. Are you
willing to study in Nazareth, and further consider a life of
service to the Church? Elias," his eyes riveted on me, "what
is your decision?"

I opened my mouth and heard myself answer: "Yes. I want
to study in Nazareth."

Without waiting to be asked, Faraj spoke up. "Yes. It's
what I want, too."   •

I could not believe it! Faraj, who was so popular, so charming and such a leader—I'd had no idea that he was considering a contemplative life within the Church. I would have thought it of his brother Khalil—he was sometimes quiet and meditative. And yet I felt at once that Faraj's choice was right. He was so kind toward others, so keenly sensitive. Somehow I had mistakenly thought that his light, good humor excluded him from interest in spiritual things, as if anyone who wanted to serve God had to be an unhappy drudge. I certainly didn't think of myself in those terms.

The Bishop was still speaking, though now he was staring down at his hands which lay folded on the desk. "I will be honest with you boys. It is not an easy life. It requires obedience to God and to your superiors. In Nazareth you can see what it will be like. It's a challenge I extend to you."

He continued talking to us for a few minutes, telling us about our soon-coming transfer to Nazareth. I was hardly listening. Faraj shot me a quick wink, and inside I was about to burst. If the minor seminary would be a challenge at least Faraj and I would face it together.

Our transfer to Nazareth, early in 1954, marked another sharp turning point for me. Distinctly, I began to feel that my path was carrying me into the service of the Church. Strangely, this was both comforting and disturbing.

On the afternoon of our arrival at the new school, St. Joseph's Minor Seminary, Faraj and I were shepherded into a still-unfinished dormitory by a gray-robed brother. As we marched behind him, I noticed that our accommodations would be far less homey than the orphanage in Haifa. The unglazed windows were not even protected by curtains, and a brisk wind blew steadily through the room. It gave us a sharp view of Nazareth, sprawling over the valley below us— the presumed site of Mary's well and Joseph's carpentry shop. But the room was like ice. I might have known then that our days of warm nurturing by the housemothers were really over. Though life in the orphanage had been regimented out of necessity, for order and convenience, the priests and brothers at St. Joseph's would soon impress us that the rule here was regiment at all cost.

As the brother left us to stow our few belongings beside our newly assigned beds, he said brusquely, "You are expected at prayers soon. Be sure you are not late."

We settled our things, bantering and joking with the few other boys who had arrived before us. There would be just thirty-four students in all that first year. When it was time for prayers we bounded to the church that stood beside our dormitory. Noisily we burst through the entryway and were halted immediately by a stern frown from one of the brothers. Tiptoeing, we slid noiselessly onto a bench near the back.

Up at the front of the sanctuary, a brother was reading the Bible aloud in a rich, sonorous voice that echoed through the dim vastness. The last light of day edged through the windows, warming the stone-gray interior with a certain, faint glow. I glanced up at the high-vaulted ceiling, and drank in the exotic scent of incense that hung in the air. A deep silence seemed to engulf even the voice of the brother—the wonder-filled silence of eternity.

I felt a familiar thrill. To me it was like the comfortable silence between friends, a moment of quiet when nothing needs to be said—when you simply dwell in the warmth and joy of each other's presence. Yes, that's what I felt—that familiar *presence*. The hushed and worshipful atmosphere was drawing from the wells of memory in me. I was bathed again in the wilderness peace that had steeped the hills of Biram. I was reliving, in a split second, those endless days when it seemed that I was actually walking alongside my childhood Champion, Jesus. Unmistakably, I felt a rush of joy stirring in my spirit.

I sat in this inner silence, swaddled in the feeling that in this place—this church, this very bench—I was *home*. Here, in this *presence*. I had dignity again. I thought of the words of Jesus which Mother had loved to repeat time and again: *"Peace I leave you. My peace I give you. Not as the world gives. . . ."*

Now I thought I understood the longing for solitude that had become so clear in Haifa. It was not a call to abandon humanity—but a heartcry to stand alone before God. And alone with Him I could find perfect serenity. It was so comforting. Surely this was what Father had intended when he first sent me off to be trained by the Bishop. For me, the service was over too soon. I wanted to bask in the stillness forever.

As we started into our rigid school schedule, I searched for spare moments when I might slip away into the engulfing quietude of the church. There I felt close to the Father-heart of God. Many times Faraj would join me, which I did not mind at all. I enjoyed his company, for, even when we were in the middle of a hectic day or studying for a test, he seemed to carry inside him a rare tranquility. And when we sat together in the rich quiet of the church's interior he was perfectly still. Sometimes I would open one eye and watch him. Without so much as a fluttering eyelash, he sat as if sculpted in deep contemplation.

Once while we were alone in the church, he opened his eyes and caught me watching him. He grinned at me, with that charming smile that lit up his dark eyes, and he said, "You feel Him, too—don't you?"

I was surprised. I had thought that the overshadowing presence was mostly a product of my own childhood. I did not expect the feeling to be shared by anyone else.

Apart from our visits to the church together, I began to experience a most unusual phenomenon on my own.

Many nights I would curl under the covers on my bed,

listening to the rhythmic, slow breathing of the other students until I dropped off to sleep, too. Then, some time around midnight, I would wake up as if I had been shaken by someone. I would blink into the darkness, and my first thought while swimming up from the ocean of sleep was always the same: *Come to the church.* It could not have been more distinct if Faraj or one of the others were whispering in my ear.

One such night, several months after our arrival in Nazareth, I rose and dressed quietly. Then I slipped out into the mysterious and cool-moving airs of midnight. A bright moon had risen, nearly full. I entered the still sanctuary where a silver radiance glanced off the stone pillars. The glow seemed to mirror and gather high above me near the vaulted ceiling, drawing my gaze upward. I slipped quietly onto a bench, still shaking myself awake, absorbed in the beauty of the chill and echoing sanctuary. I expected to find the joyful solemnity that so often met there.

That night I felt uncomfortably on edge.

While the moon cast shadows about me, my thoughts turned to memories of Mother and Father. Of course I thought of my family often, but this night I felt something stronger than mere sentiment. In the quiet spaces of my heart, I seemed to hear a voice repeating familiar passages from the New Testament. It had been nearly eight years since I last sat on Mother's lap listening to these beautiful phrases pour from the treasure-store of her memory. Now they were not just memories, but burning words. I found myself stuck on one passage: the Beatitudes.

As a boy I had sometimes thought them enigmatic, though they had comforted me. Suddenly they were terribly disturbing. Why did they sound so embarrassingly contradictory?

How could you be meek and inherit anything in this power-hungry world? And if you tried to live in happiness and peace, wouldn't someone just kick you out of your home, bomb it and sell off your land? What did it mean to hunger and thirst for righteousness? Were the Beatitudes impossibly beyond reconciliation—uttered by Jesus merely to exercise pious young scholars?

I was amazed as these questions—gentle but provoking—barraged me. They almost seemed to be coming from outside my own thoughts.

My eyes traced the curve of an arch until it disappeared in the blackness above me, and the irony of my situation struck me: I had just found, in my midnight ventures to the church, a haven of tranquility—only to have it disturbed by this growing inner restlessness. Why was this thread of inner peace always being stretched to the breaking point?

I had stayed in the sanctuary too long, wrestling with my thoughts when I should have been back in bed asleep. All at once, I felt greatly exhausted. Instead of getting up immediately, however, I sprawled across the bench, pulling my jacket tightly about me, and tried to shut off my turbulent mind which had gone somewhat hazy with fatigue. Maybe if I laid still for a few minutes the disturbing thoughts would go away. Then I would slip back to the dormitory. I closed my eyes to rest them, just for a minute. . . .

Someone was shaking me by the shoulder. Not the gentle shaking that had seemed to wake me at midnight, but a rough, insistent hand. I blinked. The rose glow of early sunlight colored the stone walls. I looked up into the frowning face of one of the brothers.

"What are you doing here?" he demanded.

I sat up stiffly, a little dazed, hardly knowing what to reply. "I came to be alone. To pray. And I guess I fell asleep."

He seemed not to hear. "You are supposed to be in the dormitory—not out wandering in the night. There is no excuse for this."

I was stunned. Didn't he believe me? I tried to protest: I was not wandering. Nor was I making up an excuse.

In response, he lifted me by the collar. As an adolescent I was almost the same size and height as he, but I never thought to resist. "Come. We're going to the principal," he said, shoving me ahead of him.

The principal, Father Basilios Laham, was normally a kind, if somewhat strict man. This morning he peered at me questioningly from across his desk. Quickly my story tumbled out. I had gone to pray, that was all. Surely I had done no harm. Somehow I failed to impress him as a saintly, young visionary.

"I'm sorry, Elias," he replied gravely. "You have broken the rules. What would happen if we allowed every student to do just as he wished? As I am bound by the laws of the Church, so you are bound by the rules of the school. You must be punished."

For the first time, I stood face-to-face with the unbending rules of the Church as an institution. I could not understand why strict obedience to a rule was more important than a heart seeking God. Unhappy though I was, I could not fault the principal. He was just a man carrying out his job to the best of his ability. In the end I submitted, more or less quietly, to my punishment: forty days of restriction.

Unfortunately, this would not be my last exposure to the side of the Church that seemed to have forgotten the humanity it was intended to serve. Unfortunately, too, my quick tongue, which had so often gotten me in trouble as a small boy, had only gotten quicker with adolescence. On one occasion, I was sentenced to forty days of silence for disagreeing with the brothers. I wanted more Bible study and less sports activities. I was judged insubordinate and unsubmissive.

My timing was especially bad at the most obvious moments.

One day late in 1954, we were informed that the Archbishop was coming to inspect our school. Accompanying him on this visit was a very distinguished foreign dignitary, the new Ambassador from the United States to Israel. The Bishop would be coming from Haifa to be with them, eager, of course, that the very best impression be made. Our dormitory was to be spotless, and we were warned again and again to be impeccably polite.

About a week later, in the middle of a morning lecture, there was a loud knock at the classroom door. Father Laham swept into the room along with the Bishop, the Archbishop and the Ambassador. The brother who was lecturing paled slightly, looking almost as gray as his robe. Nervously he brushed chalk dust off his fingers and extended a trembling hand to greet the dapperly dressed Ambassador. The Archbishop, who took special pride in knowing each of prospective seminarians by name and by village of origin, began introducing us one by one. As his name was called, each student would hop to his feet, bowing his head respectfully.

After several introductions, the Archbishop turned to me and smiled warmly. I was on my feet at once. "This is Elias Chacour," he announced broadly. "He is from Gish."

"Sorry, Archbishop," I spouted without thinking. "I'm not from Gish. I'm from Biram."

Suddenly everyone was staring at me. Even Faraj, who was used to my outspokenness, gulped. The brother, the principal and the Bishop colored in unison—though the Ambassador smiled and did not seem to notice my indiscretion. One never corrects an Archbishop.

"Biram does not exist," the Archbishop snapped piquantly. All his warmth was gone.

Bristling, I announced loudly, "But I have hopes it will exist again one day." I could not allow the suffering of my people to be erased so blithely, even in respect for an Archbishop.

"Sit down!" he ordered, gritting his teeth.

After a brief, somewhat stiff chat with the poor, fidgeting brother, the visitors swept out of the room and on to tour the rest of the school. I hoped my comment would be forgotten—but no. Later I was treated to a prolonged tongue-lashing for "insolent remarks."

Alone in the dormitory, I chastised myself for not keeping a closer guard on my tongue. Why did this stubbornness persist about Biram? After all, the Archbishop was right in one sense—it *was* destroyed and our land confiscated. What was it that refused to let me forget—to brush it aside as the Archbishop did? He was a man of God after all. I wished I could be more like him—or more like Faraj who was so agreeable. I vowed that I would try to be more quiet, more respectful and obedient to my superiors.

On one hand I felt this growing desire to serve my Church; on the other hand a certain voice was calling me to—what? Something more? I didn't know.

During the four years of our study at St. Joseph's, the tension would slowly strain within me. I continued in my resolve to learn obedience, absorbing the teachings and rules of the Church, trying hard to mold myself into a pliable, acquiescent seminarian.

An influx of new students swelled our ranks and crowded the dormitory, so that a few of us were asked if we would like to sleep inside the church. I quickly volunteered, as did Faraj. Ironically, I was then able to carry on all the late-night meditations I wanted with impunity.

In 1955, the Zionist forces invaded Gaza, and a year later the Sinai, that huge, wedge-like peninsula between the new state and Egypt. With the Sinai takeover, the United States intervened, insisting that Israel withdraw to the 1948 armistice lines. Though Prime Minister Ben Gurion and his defense ministry conceded, they insisted that the invasion was necessary because Israel needed a buffer zone between itself and Egypt, whose new President Nasser was talking of uniting the Arab nations to "liberate" Palestine. The Israeli press was flooded with outcries against Arab aggression which reverberated around the world. The question of Palestinian refugees—both in and out of Israel—was obscured by sympathy for the "beleaguered" young nation.

At St. Joseph's, we watched the conflict escalate and subside, discussing the political implications with the intensity of opinionated young men. When the fighting ceased with Israeli withdrawal, some of the students expressed a relief that it was done with, and moreover, that the war had been fought in the south. Though we had experienced some tightening of the "emergency laws," the trouble had not touched us or our families this time. To a few of them, personal safety was all that mattered.

Such thinking bothered me greatly.

Were we really safe just because we were gathered under the protecting wings of the institutional Church? Or were we being lulled to sleep by our own personal security? Why were we not angry—or at least pained—at the suffering of our people in the hills and refugee camps?

All of this added to my continued inner conflicts. I wished I could remain serene—aloof and undisturbed by worldly conflicts as was Father, as were Faraj and the brothers of St. Joseph's. It did not occur to me then that my unquiet heart was not a bad thing. It was like a delicate balance that had been forcefully tipped and wanted righting. It produced in me a drive—like a hunger—that would carry me to the fiery heart of our land's vast conflict.

As my final two years in Nazareth passed, one conviction flickered dimly and grew: being a servant of God meant more than drifting above earth's struggles in an other-worldly realm like some pale figure in an icon. In this, I found encouragement from an unexpected source.

Father Ghazal was a stricter teacher than most at St.

Joseph's. His voice could sharpen to a metal edge when you gave the wrong answer, making him sound more like a career man in the military than a priest. Most of the students feared him. Somehow, beneath his bristly exterior, I thought I could detect a wonderfully sensitive heart, a true concern for our spiritual and intellectual progress.

I was seated in his lecture one day toward the end of 1957, when another student posed a question: How could one be a good Christian if, well—if certain people bothered you? If, he stammered hastily, you often got angry or impatient?

For a moment Father Ghazal was absolutely frozen, staring off into space in search of the right words.

Then he replied simply, "It's not enough to try to be good—to try to be some sort of 'saint.' You must let God occupy your body. You must be tamed by Him. He may put you through many hard things—and it is these struggles that will tame you. Then you will be ready to do His good pleasure."

How, I do not know, but I suddenly recalled the prayer I had uttered years before, just after we were exiled to Gish. Then I had asked God to use my hands and feet as His own. And now Father Ghazal was saying that a servant of God is never asked to do more than that—or less.

I smiled, wondering if it were really possible that God had taken me up on my childlike prayer, guiding me first into the care of the Bishop and then here to St. Joseph's. And more than that, I wondered if God had allowed me to feel His own heart's concern for the Palestinian people. But whenever I thought about the war, the bombing or my beating, some awful twisting thing burned inside of me—something that had yet to be tamed.

Despite the feeling, I had a flicker of conviction: I was to study, not just for ordination in the Church, but as a messenger to my people. Even so, I was amused at the thought.

What was my message? That everyone should leave their villages and become contemplatives in cloisters?

I glanced across the room at Faraj. His brows were knit in intense thought. I wished I could read his expression and know his response to Father Ghazal's comments. Since we were nearing the end of our schooling in Nazareth, we would both be expected to declare our intentions formally. Would he feel as I did?

Our entire last year was one in which I pondered my direction. A tingle of indignation burned inside me each time I heard of another tightening of the "emergency laws" that governed Palestinians in Israel—each time another village had its farm land confiscated for a *kibbutz*. At the edge of my thoughts, I wondered how I could deliver a message of heavenly peace to people—Jew or Palestinian—when they lived daily with war.

One evening in the spring of 1958, as we moved into our final semester at St. Joseph's, Faraj and I were alone in our church quarters, studying for a test. I sensed him watching me and looked up from my page.

Faraj shut his book abruptly and a sheaf of paper fluttered to the floor. He sat up and braced his long, willowy arms across his chest. We were both nearly nineteen, and while I had continued to thicken at the chest and shoulders, he had stayed slender as he grew. He stretched out his lean legs, and I retrieved his paper from the floor. Curious, I asked, "What is it? What are you thinking?"

"Elias," he began, "we've grown up just like brothers. Do you know we've been together for almost six years? And it won't be long until St. Joseph's is through with us."

"That's true. And . . . ?" I smiled, wondering what my alter-ego was getting at. He lay back on his mattress, hands braced behind his head. Suddenly he unfolded a vision of the future—our future.

"You know the Bishop is making inquiries at the seminary in Jerusalem. If things work out, we can go there together. Won't that be great? We can go together as brothers, Elias. We are brothers, aren't we?"

My heart leaped at his words: "seminary . . . together. . . ."

He went on. "And after seminary—after we're ordained— we can have a church together maybe. I've been thinking of the things Father Ghazal said about letting God occupy your body. That's what we can do. We can live simply, sharing all things in common, fifty-fifty, just like the early Christians. We can live peacefully among the poor. We can give our lives to serving them. . . ."

He talked on for some time, building a bright dream. It touched my deepest wound—the need for a home, a sense of *place*. It sounded so comforting, so easy. When he finished, I found myself agreeing to his plan, eagerly trying to fill my emptiness with someone else's dream. And in that moment, I shoved aside the unsettling thoughts and the challenging voice that beckoned me.

Daily we talked with increasing excitement about the vows we would take to live lives of charity, humility, obedience, extending God's hand of love through the villages of Galilee. We would live, I thought, as Father did, in poorness of spirit, holding everything we had in open hands before God.

However, our dream flickered once, chilled by a harsh breath of reality.

During our last weeks at St. Joseph's, while we struggled under the pressure of final examinations, the Bishop delivered one more bit of hard-hitting news. Holding back tears of pain and anger, his eyes welled as he told us evenly, "You cannot go to Jerusalem. The authorities will not allow you to cross the border to the seminary."

The seminary, a very old, Melkite school, lay outside the

borders of Israel in the part of Jerusalem apportioned by the United Nations to the kingdom of Jordan. The Jordanians, the Bishop explained, did not want "contaminated Palestinians from occupied territories" coming to study in their sector of the city. Although it was the closest seminary, and though our expressed intent was to serve the Church, the Bishop had no power to sway the authorities. We were barred from entering Jordan's territory. And once again our people had been maligned with a variation of that hideous phrase, "dirty Palestinians." How I hated that!

The Bishop, in his resourcefulness, was not about to let this snag tear his net, allowing two live seminarians to get away. He quickly made inquiries through his connections in the Church hierarchy, and in a week he announced, "Elias. Faraj. You will go to study at Saint Sulpice. A good school, a very good school—in Paris. I've made all the arrangements."

In Paris? We were stunned. Neither of us had been outside of Galilee, except for our sheltered schooling in Haifa, let alone to far-off hinterlands such as Europe. But the Bishop had decided. That was that.

When I returned to Gish after graduation, the reaction of my family was as mixed as my own. Mother and Father were delighted that one of their sons would study for ordination. But in Paris? In their thinking, no one ever went to Europe and returned. As all my remaining relatives gathered to see me off, I saw the sadness behind their smiles.

When it was time to leave, Wardi and my brothers hugged me one by one. Mother and Father clutched me close to them one last time, and then released me—as parents have always set their children free in the world—with a mixture of happiness and heartache. And now I had a sense—comforting and challenging at the same time—that my way was narrowing before me.

A week later, Faraj and I tried to get our sealegs on the rolling deck of the ship that carried us away from the port at Haifa. We stood side by side like two brothers, tall, eager and still quite sheltered about things of the world. The Bishop had given us a little money—the equivalent of ten dollars—to get us from our European port of entry in Naples, Italy, to Rome. There, he had assured us, one of his contacts would be waiting to help us. Holding onto the rail for balance, we stared in silence as the green shoreline of our land faded and was gone.

"More than six years, Elias," Faraj's voice broke the concentration. "That's a long time to be away."

I felt a tightening in my throat and could not answer. Once again the raging conflict that was Israel had driven my family apart.

I could not guess the pressures that would slowly grind and pulverize our already crippled villages. In my heart was the shining plan to return and live simply, quietly among my people, dispensing the charities of the Church. I had no thought that my life was about to take another sharp turn— that my dream of a peaceful life in service with Faraj would never be. An astonishing awakening lay ahead of me.

When we left the deck, our mood lightened a bit. And then our conversation turned to Paris.

7

The Outcasts

No doubt Faraj and I looked like two wide-eyed boys roaming through Paris. The Seminary of St. Sulpice, a time-honored whetstone for sharpening the Church's young men, lay in one of the oldest sections of the city. Nearby was the vast Louvre Museum, the River Seine, Notre Dame, the acclaimed Sorbonne University and the opulent Luxembourg Gardens. Art galleries and expensive boutiques abounded. Even our quarters in the Italianate buildings of the seminary—perhaps humble by other standards—made us feel like kings. It was a breath-taking world of glamour, art, intellectualism, romance and prosperity beyond anything we had imagined.

One of our biggest problems was apparent at once: we spoke little French. The smatterings we had learned from the housemothers in the orphanage in Haifa was hardly enough to help when, on our first day of classes, we were sent to the Sorbonne for a lecture on the existential philosophies of Sartre. As the tweedy, chain-smoking professor embarked on a gamboling survey of Sartre, the other students looked intent, nodding their heads at appropriate moments—and

Faraj and I were bewildered. All that we could determine of the lecture was that it was not given in our language.

We faced an immediate struggle with learning to speak French. And yet, as we learned the language, we gradually detected another, more serious problem.

Among the members of the Church of St. Sulpice we found several warm friendships. A kind professor named Father Longère quickly became a confidant and a mentor for us as we tried to learn western ways. And a Miss Deville, a saintly, single woman in her middle years, often invited us for home-cooked meals. A devout Christian, she always opened her heart whenever our homesickness became unbearable. From the outset, however, we detected a certain wall between us. If ever we spoke about the troubles of our people, she would quickly turn the conversation to more genteel, less troubling matters.

Likewise, many of the other students in the seminary were friendly and often curious about our life in the "Holy Land." Of course, we never passed up a chance to talk about our home and the questions inevitably led to the 1948 war. Then a strange silence fell as we told about the displacement of nearly one million Palestinians, the deaths, the destruction of Biram and the terror that had come upon our families. Furtive glances passed from student to student, and they nodded faintly as if they were merely humoring us.

Their awkward silence was finally broken during a conversation some months after our arrival. Our French was improving rapidly, and talk had led me to recount the forced removal of the men of Biram. Faraj commented that the same fate had befallen many other villages.

"Well I suppose," said one student, nervously clearing his throat, "that the Zionists had to do something to protect themselves from terrorists."

"But we just wanted to live in peace with them," I blurted,

"to farm our land and be left alone." I could feel my cheeks coloring.

"Let's be completely honest," he plunged ahead with the air of an inquisitor. "We've heard all the news reports about Arab terrorism. The Zionists knew they had to clean out those villages or there would be no peace."

It was true that by that time, in the late 1950s, some crudely armed groups of men called the *fedayeen,* had begun to gather in the countries surrounding Israel, plotting reprisals. They were not even wanted by the countries they inhabited. But at the time our villages were sacked, no such organized groups had existed.

"Is that your idea of 'peace'?" I demanded. "That a group of foreigners should forcefully crush a whole country full of powerless people and take over their land?" I was alarmed at the force of the words that suddenly boiled out of me, as if from some long-capped well of angry frustration.

"Elias—" Faraj gripped my arm and gave a cautioning look, hoping to ease the tension. I took a deep breath, knowing it was useless to argue. Still, I could not let it go.

"Look," I said more calmly, "all Palestinians are not fighters. Nor are we the terrorists. We have been the *terrorized.* In French history your people rebelled against oppression. They became known as heroes just because they won. Had they lost, they would have been called rebels and traitors.

"Besides, you've known us for a few months," I pursued, indicating Faraj and myself. "We're not terrorists. Neither are our families. We don't want to hurt anyone. The Jews are welcome in our country, but we don't want their military to take over our farmland and our homes. Would you? We just want to bring peace back to our people. To reconcile Palestinians and Jews."

Our friend replied, "That is because you are *good* Palestinians."

We were deeply dismayed. Faraj and I were good Palestinians. Implied was the converse: most of the other Palestinian people were bad. I could not help recalling the villagers of Biram crowded into the church each Sunday, thankful for their simple life. Where had such an attitude come from? Did others feel the same way about Palestinian people?

Unfortunately, we were to learn that Palestinians, indeed, had been branded as ignorant, hostile and violent. And now, with no flag, no honor and no voice to shout our defense to the opinion-fashioning world press, the reputation of our ancient people had degenerated to the status of non-persons. We were the outcasts.

Never was this painful position more sharply apparent to me than during our first Christmas in France.

A wealthy and influential man in the church invited me to celebrate Christmas with his family and a few other guests in their country home outside Paris. Faraj had been invited by another family and so I accepted, not wanting to sit alone in the dormitory.

On Christmas Eve I was picked up outside my room and driven through the lightly falling snow to the outskirts of the city. As we drove, I fended off memories of Mother and Father, so far away. I would try to enjoy this Christmas with a substitute family.

Their manor-like home was decorated simply with elegant tapers in wall sconces warming the gloom of the winter night. I watched my hostess light the last taper when the door chimes sounded. As she whisked off to answer it, my host turned to me with an inscrutable look and said, "I plan to introduce you as our special guest. I—I hope you won't mind."

I felt flattered. I couldn't imagine why I should mind and merely nodded.

The children were passing a tray of steaming cider with

cinnamon, and our hostess had disappeared with the coats. As a newly-arrived couple entered the room, my host introduced me, "This is Elias Chacour."

I extended my hand. "Pleased to meet you. I am from the village of Bi—"

"From *Bethlehem!*" my host interrupted, clapping me on the back. "Elias is a Jewish student at our seminary. Can you imagine? I thought it would be a lovely surprise to have a Jewish believer from the holy land to celebrate Christmas with us," he finished with a jaunty smile.

The visitors were delighted. I stared at him in disbelief. Why was he lying about me? At my first opportunity, before any more guests arrived, I pulled him aside to ask if he had made some mistake.

"Tonight you are *Jewish—from Bethlehem,*" he said with a cool smile. "That's not such a big favor to ask, is it? You'll get along much better if you stop announcing to the world that you are Palestinian."

I was crushed. His main reason for inviting me to his home had not been kindness, but to display me as a Christmas Eve attraction. For the rest of the evening, he continued to introduce me as a young Jewish man from Bethlehem. I was too embarrassed to contradict him—and I felt miserable.

After this incident, Faraj and I became increasingly aware that, in western eyes, being Palestinian was a disgraceful thing—a stigma like leprosy. And as we entered the decade of the 1960s, that wounded reputation would be dealt a vicious blow. More bands of the *fedayeen* gathered at Israel's borders like a tightening noose.

During those first few years at seminary, I felt another tension between the simple spirituality I had inherited through generations and the modern Church philosophies. In my second and third years in Paris, I was increasingly

concerned that all of our instruction was in subjects like
Church dogma, rituals, rites and rules. Though my grades
were high and I had a quick facility for learning both ancient
and modern languages, I was ever uneasy. Where was the
deep spiritual wisdom, the strength I had hoped to find?
When it came to theology classes, I always seemed to upset
the professors who were infected by the newly-popular philosophies of the day.

One professor in logics particularly delighted in taking
blade-like slashes at my work. During his class, we were
assigned to write a paper on the "proper view of God in the
atomic age." The topic amused me a little: to think that God
needed to be "properly viewed" by seminarians as if He were
a minute germ under a microscope. I wondered if, in preparing to serve God, we ought not to consider how He might be
viewing us.

Nevertheless, I carefully fashioned my argument, starting
with the point that God had not changed from one age to
another, He was "the same yesterday, today and forever" as
the New Testament proclaimed. He was ever-present with
us, not "dead" as modern philosophy declared. I finished
with the strong assertion that we were the ones who removed
ourselves from God's love by our hateful, violent actions
toward each other.

A week later the paper was returned with a failing grade
emblazoned across the top in red ink. Beneath it, the professor had scrawled angry comments that began, "This is not
logic, but *illogic*." In his scathing denunciation, he said that
reasoning from a scriptural viewpoint was not acceptable. I
should have begun with the problem of man, the primate, lost
in an endless search for the "God idea." To this poor professor God was absent and men were hopelessly alienated.
Unfortunately, he was not the only one of this persuasion
who was teaching us seminarians.

That afternoon, Faraj and I strolled along the Seine. I had to get away from the seminary after such a blasting. First, we visited the Cathedral of Notre Dame, seeking a quiet place. But today the very splendor of the structure, which usually comforted me, was disturbing. I stared at the glorious rose window, afire with sunlight, and all I could think of was the simple church in Biram that we had also called Notre Dame. It had nourished my spirit. Now it was half rubble.

Leaving the cathedral, we sauntered past a sidewalk artist dabbing at bright, blue-green tempera impressions of the river, and Faraj brought me back to my troubles in logics class. "I thought your paper was excellent, Elias," he said trying to cheer me. "He was too brutal. I don't understand it."

"There is something *else* I don't understand. People have so much here—nice homes, cars, clothes—and so little faith. Both Catholic and Protestant churches are almost empty. What's happened here?"

Faraj nodded. "People in the West seem so taken with material things. It's as if they have nothing in their spirits, so they need to surround themselves with nice comforts." He paused and leaned against a rail at the river's edge. "I hate to say it, but that sort of thinking seems to have invaded the Church, too.

"The real problem," he said after a moment's silence, "is that Western theology starts with man as the center of all things and tries to force God into some scheme that we can understand. Then He can be regulated. Elias, we've grown up believing that God is the beginning and end of all things. He is central, not an afterthought. He's alive and has His own ways. Here, they want to tame God with their philosophy."

"Worse than that," I countered. "I'm afraid the Western philosophies have *killed* God. If there's no respect for Him, what value do men have? Without God there is no compassion, no humanity."

As we crossed a bridge heading for the Boulevard St. Germain and the seminary, I voiced the doubts that had been nagging me for weeks: "Why are we studying here? What is seminary really preparing us for?"

Swiftly, Faraj corrected me. "We've come to be trained to serve our Church. Don't forget that."

We walked on quietly together. And though we hardly noticed then, his words had fallen like a faint shadow between us, a first small parting. Even as we continued to train for ordination, I was being prepared for a riskier calling than he or I knew.

To me, it is an eternal irony that two young men whose dream was to shun the world, to live in peace and simplicity, should land themselves in Europe in the 1960s. Vast upheavals were overturning the Western culture. Life seemed a confusion of questions.

Politically it was the fear-filled era of the Cold War. Nations that were supposedly Christian and moral could justify violence by pointing to the end result. In the name of establishing democracy, any horror might be employed at the expense of humanity itself. As the world moved through the Cold War and beyond, how many rulers would be deposed or killed with the secret help of Western democracies? How many innocents would be tortured or seared with napalm by the "peacekeeping" forces of the powerful nations? Had contact with the West infected the Zionists, deadening the ancient voices of their prophets? And from the Church, no voice was heard. Those who wanted to catapult it out of its medieval slumber and into the twentieth century, were resisted by conservatives, fearful of losing long-held power and position.

Little wonder that my head was befogged: My self-worth was at its lowest ebb, the entire world was being threatened by the "Bomb" and the Church to which I was giving my life was in upheaval. How deeply I understood the spring-loaded tension of those Palestinian *fedayeen* as the world went blind to our plight in the Middle East.

Then in 1962, a strange event took place that would leave its mark on me forever after.

I was traveling by train to visit some new-found friends in West Germany. The train glided through the rolling green hills of eastern France, skirting some luscious and very old vineyards which sent my thoughts across the miles to the land that had once been ours in Israel.

A conductor sauntered down the swaying aisle. "West German border in five minutes," he announced. "Have your passports ready, please."

I fished in my travel bag for my identification papers, but my mind was on the jumble of events in the recent past and the tragic news.

A letter from Israel had arrived several months before and I had torn into it with my usual eagerness. It was not a light, newsy letter, but one that deeply cut my heart. My brother, Chacour, was dead.

Chacour, who had married during my years in Haifa, had been laboring hard at a construction job in the Carmel mountain range when he suffered something like a stroke. For almost forty days he had struggled for his life in a hospital before his heart gave out in the exertion. Now his young wife was left with eight small children.

As tragic as the news was, I felt even worse that I had no money with which to travel home to console his wife. However, I was granted some time off from my studies to seek some quiet at a Christian retreat. I was sitting alone on a bench in a gloom of private thought, when a beautiful, small, blond child with eyes the color of the sky toddled by and smiled up into my face. We struck up an immediate friendship, perhaps because the rudimentary German I had learned recently was as infant-like as his. Wolfgang was his name, and before I knew it, he had scrambled onto my lap, giggling. Soon I, too, was chuckling.

When his parents found him, we also became instant friends. Franz and Lony Gruber were an amazingly tenderhearted couple who shared my grief at once when I told them about Chacour's death. Almost unbelievably, it was as if we were true family to each other. Generously, they insisted I visit them at their home in West Germany. It was to be the first of many, many visits that would bind us together.

The hiss and squeal of the train's brakes brought me back to the present. We had pulled up to a railway siding in a border town that was picture-postcard lovely. A white-sided town hall, with its precisely regulated clock, rose against blue, snowpeaked mountains. On the platform I could see the dark-suited officials walking toward the cars to inspect our passports which the attendant had taken from us.

Then the phenomenal thing happened.

It was as if I were flung back through time twenty-five years. With uncanny clarity, I felt as if I were crossing into Germany in 1937, and in my imagination the scene had changed vividly. Men in dark green helmets and high black boots stood with their machine guns slung over their shoulders. On their woolen uniforms glowered the red and black swastikas of the Third Reich. They were demanding our papers, looking for—what? Here and there they pulled a passport from the pile, ordering its Jewish owner to step off the train. And I with an Israeli passport! Would they call for me? Men and women were stepping fearfully from their coaches, hugging small children, huddling together miserably. They would be taken to other destinations—never to be seen again.

A trickle of sweat slipped down my temple, rousing me from the mental image. My heart beat rapidly. I was handed my passport and we continued our trip into West Germany. But the impression was burned into me as if by a brand.

Lony and Franz met me at the station, smiling brightly, over-joyed to see me. And I them. We were, indeed, to become as family before I left Europe. But throughout that visit, the strange image would haunt me.

For the first time that twisting dark feeling inside me was matched—if not totally overruled—by another feeling: the ache of compassion. It was as if some calming hand was beginning to tame a wild creature within me. I hurt for the Jewish people. Why had the civilized world allowed them to be persecuted?

Other questions were just as troubling. Why did the world allow my people to be driven into diaspora only a few years after the Holocaust? Surely the Jews knew the horror of militarism—why had they used such violence against my people? How had the minds of the nations been poisoned to think of Palestinians as an idle, worthless people capable of nothing but violence?

These questions drove me, and soon I would be startled as I discovered the treachery that brought disaster to my people—the political power plays that set the Middle East ablaze with turmoil.

8

Seeds of Hope

Upon my return to Paris I was haunted by the mystery that had opened itself to me on the train into West Germany: What was the true story of Palestine? I was aware as never before that people in the West held a view that went something like this. The Jewish people, having suffered tremendous persecution, needed a haven—a national homeland. Their Zionist leaders had chosen the "uninhabited" land of Palestine. Supposedly, the surrounding Arab nations were naturally antagonistic and jealous that the Jewish settlers had turned a wasteland into a paradise. They had risen unprovoked against the Jews, forcing them to fight a valiant War of Independence in 1948.

But I had grown up in Palestine in those years and that was not the full story, nor was it especially correct. I had witnessed a terribly ironic twist of history in which the persecuted became the persecutor. As one of its victims, I had seen the cruel face of Zionism.

Now I determined to find out how a peaceful movement that had begun with a seemingly good purpose—to end the persecution of the Jewish people—had become such a destructive, oppressive force.

Along with that determination, I was driven by a respect for history that Father had planted in me. Did the seeds of our future hope lie buried in our past, as he had so often said?

Aside from my seminary studies I began to spend hours in the libraries of Paris, hunting down books and news reports on the true history of the Zionists and the Palestine disaster. Whole books and reports unifying these accounts would not be published until years later. Yet my study pieced together a startling, documented story.

In 1897, I learned, a conference had convened in Basle, Switzerland, to "lay the foundation stone of the house which was to shelter the Jewish nation." The director of the gathering was a prominent writer named Theodor Herzl. He had fathered in Europe a new political movement called Zionism—an inspiring movement that hoped to rescue the downtrodden, impoverished and humiliated Jews in the big city ghettoes. By the end of the conference the delegates had agreed on two points—a flag and an anthem, the symbols of their unity and purpose. Beyond the pomp and emotional fervor the delegates were split on the location of this homeland that was being pushed by the leadership: Palestine.

Immediately, many disputed Herzl's statement that Palestine was a "land without a people, waiting for a people without a land." Though Herzl had been willing to contemplate settlement in Argentina or Uganda as alternatives, his sights were clearly set on the Middle East. It was to this proposal that many delegates primarily and strenuously objected. By what right could Zionists expect to create a state in Palestine? It was a land with established borders and, more importantly, it had long been *inhabited* by people of an ancient, respectable culture. A homeland in Palestine, they declared with the overtones of a heinous prophecy, would have to be forgotten—or else established by force.

Devout Jews within and without the movement—particu-

larly the Orthodox—fervently argued that Zionism was a
blasphemy, because the elite, non-religious Jews felt that
Zionism was the only Messiah Israel would ever have. Such
talk incensed the religious, as did the hints of militarism that
already colored the fringes of the movement. Others, less
religious and more pragmatic, believed that Zionism would
feed anti-Semitism since it underscored the long-criticized,
"exclusiveness" of the Jewish people. They saw clearly that
no land could be simply, peacefully "resettled" without violence.

Therefore, to appease the religious consciences the Zionist leaders adopted the principles of non-violence embodied
in the Jewish *Havlaga*. This helped to rally the support of the
masses, the multiple millions who desperately hoped for an
escape from the growing pogroms against them in Europe.
Yet the leaders continued to formulate designs on Palestine.
Though Herzl would not live much beyond the turn of the
century, others would push his plans forward.

In Palestine, my own people were under too tight a thumb
to take much notice of a conference in Basle, even if they had
known of it. In the early 1900s, ours was also a downtrodden
people, struggling and praying for freedom from our own
oppressors. For hundreds of years we had suffered under the
iron heel of the Turkish Ottoman Empire. When World War I
engulfed the Middle East, the empire had already begun to
totter.

After the war, as the empire crumbled, the Palestinian
people felt the first winds of freedom. The League of Nations
bore their hopes aloft further by proposing a plan that would
help "subject peoples." Larger, powerful nations would assist weaker nations in establishing their own independent
governments. This was known as the Mandate system.

The British, who desired a foothold of power in the Middle
East, saw in the Mandate system a great opportunity. Se-

cretly, they made a proposal to Palestinian leaders: The British would help oust the Turks; in return, they would set up a temporary Mandate government in Palestine with the promise that they would slowly withdraw, leaving an established, independent country governed by the Palestinians themselves. In desperation, the Palestinian leaders agreed to this strategy. Freedom was in sight—or so they supposed—and little notice was given to the tiny Jewish agricultural communities that were sprouting in a seemingly scattered fashion across the landscape.

What I learned next in my readings truly saddened me. Once the British rule was established, the story became convoluted with political intrigues and double-dealings.

Immediately, the British met in secret with the French and Russians to divide the Middle East into "spheres of influence" with Palestine to be governed, not by the people of Palestine as promised, but by an international administration. The secret agreement was uncovered several years later, in 1917, when the Bolsheviks overthrew the czarist regime and could not resist making public such "imperialist" duplicity. Palestinian leaders were dismayed at this news and at once sent delegates to the British to protest. They chose the diplomatic route while an elite group, whose sights were set on Palestine, had already begun influencing British bureaucrats.

The year 1917 will forever be scarred with the brand of infamy for the Palestinian people. The Zionists had aligned themselves with Great Britain's Christian Restorationists, a group that believed they might bring to pass—by manipulating world events and reestablishing the nation of Israel—the Second Coming of Christ. The Zionists ignored this view, but the benefits of such a plan for them were obvious. They saw in Britain's new hold on Palestine their secret inroad to the Middle East, and so began a strange marriage between Zionist and Restorationist. It was in 1917 that the British Lord Arthur Balfour made his famous declaration—not in public at first, but privately in a letter to the powerful Lord Rothschild.

Lord Balfour wrote that the Cabinet "viewed with favor the establishment of a national home for the Jewish people" in Palestine. And in the same letter, with a stroke of the pen, he reclassified the people of Palestine—ninety-two percent of the population—as "non-Jewish communities."[3] Not only did this renege on the promise of independence, but it effectively handed over Palestine to the Zionists. The prime mover behind the British decision was the Zionist leader, Chaim Weizmann.

If Lord Balfour was acting out of his own religious conviction or a love for the Jewish people, as some historians declared, I was unconvinced. In 1906, he had played a major part in passing the Aliens Act which expressly sought to exclude Jews from Great Britain. Nor was Lord Balfour oblivious of the political treachery in which he was enwebbed. In 1919, in a memorandum to the British Cabinet, he declared:

> In Palestine we do not propose even to go through the form of consulting the wishes of the present inhabitants of the country. So far as Palestine is concerned, (we) have made no statement of fact which is not admittedly wrong, and no declaration of policy which at least in the letter (we) have not always intended to violate. [4]

To me, it seemed that the Zionists had entered into an unholy marriage, an alliance motivated by power and convenience, consummated in treachery.

At once, Palestinian leaders were dismayed. For the next sixteen years they continually presented their fears to the

British through diplomatic channels, appealing continually to royal commissions while unrest grew throughout Palestine. And the Zionists, funded by international money collected by the Jewish Agency, rapidly settled *kibbutzim* in a clearer and clearer pattern throughout Palestine, slowly forming the skeletal outlines of the land they meant to declare as their own homeland.

Through the 1920s, European immigration to Palestine rose dramatically and the Zionist leaders became less and less guarded about their plan. Weizmann told an American secretary of state that he hoped "Palestine would ultimately become as Jewish as England is English." [5] And thereafter, another Zionist leader told British officials, "There can only be one National Home in Palestine, and that a Jewish one, and no equality in the partnership between Jews and Arabs, but a Jewish predominance as soon as the numbers of that race are sufficiently increased." [6]

Increasingly, many Zionists themselves were ill at ease with those who insisted on Jewish "predominance" in Palestine. Yitzhak Epstein, an agriculturist, had warned an international congress of the Zionist Party that they had wrongly consulted every political power that held sway over Palestine without consulting the Palestinians themselves. He feared the fact that Palestinian peasants had already lost so much land as a result of Zionist purchases from absentee landlords, and that this loss was sure to breed resentment. He argued that since the incoming Jews were bringing with them a higher standard of living, they ought to help the Palestinians to find their own identity, to open to them the new Jewish hospitals, schools and reading rooms that were already in existence or in planning stages. And when institutions for higher education were established, the Jews could strengthen their old fraternal bonds with surrounding Arab nations by opening these schools to their students as well.

Unfortunately, Epstein was staunchly opposed. His detractors shouted, "To give—always to give, to the one our body, to the other, our soul, and to yet another the remnant of the hope ever to live as a free people in its historical homeland!"[7]

And though Epstein's vision of unity between Arab and Jew was overlooked by the Zionist main body, others would take up his cause until Zionism itself was riddled with factions. At the end of the 1920s, a group calling themselves *Brit Shalom* split from the Party, because they could no longer go along with the tactic of disenfranchising the Palestinians from their land in order to set up a Jewish homeland. Sadly, this group was also largely ignored. I mentally underscored these crucial details, important clues from history that could not be overlooked. All Jews did not hate Palestinians. In fact, many recognized our brotherhood and had come to Palestine with hands extended in friendship. Were there any in the 1960s who wanted reconciliation and not war? Was this fact, somehow, one of the seeds of hope?

By the 1930s, with the influx of European settlers rising like a floodtide, with no intervention by the British, and with the plan to displace the Palestinian people in motion, what were their leaders to do? Diplomatically, they might as well have been mute. No one was listening. In 1935, in port cities like Jaffa, anti-immigration demonstrations erupted into violence and bloodshed in which both Jewish immigrants and Palestinian peasants died.

As I read about these demonstrations in the context of history, I was moved anew by the frustration the leaders of Palestine must have suffered. As a Christian I could not condone the bloodshed—but it was suddenly, sharply clear that their tension had built for almost twenty years before it reached the point of explosion. The demonstrations were an extreme measure born out of a desperation to be heard.

The following year, 1936, Palestinian leaders again tried a

peaceful means of protest, calling for a general strike. Throughout Palestine, office and factory workers, taxi and truck drivers disappeared from their jobs for a full six months, crippling commerce. But violence, which had already crept into the conflict, increased. The powerful *Histraduth* trade union, established by the Zionists and led by David Ben Gurion, terrorized Jewish shop and factory owners who dared to employ Palestinians. Here and there, Jewish women were attacked in the market places for buying from Palestinian merchants. Palestinian fields and vineyards were vandalized. Orchards were guarded to keep out all but Jewish workers. At the end of 1938, the protests were finally crushed.

By that time the Zionists had behind them an overwhelming swell of world sympathy. This was true for two main reasons: First, Western nations were little concerned with events in the Middle East because they were fixated on the horror that was spreading from Nazi Germany; second, they were appalled at the insane hatred for the Jewish people propagated by Adolph Hitler. Rightly, the Jews needed somewhere to escape from this madman.

But if Western consciences were troubled, it did not translate into action. Throughout the 1930s, while Hitler's pogroms thrived, no major western nation increased its quota of Jewish immigrants. Was the tiny land of Palestine really expected to absorb millions of European Jews, its inhabitants giving up land and jobs while the large western nations were comfortably silent?

To me, these terrified masses of Jewish immigrants were never to blame for our tragedy. They were dazed by fear, pathetically desperate to escape the heinous death camps. In this, they were to become the pawns of the Zionist leaders. Upon their arrival in Palestine they were quickly indoctrinated against their so-called new enemy—the Palestinians.

Here was the second bastion of Zionist power: propaganda. Increasingly, they controlled all news emanating from Palestine. With the tongues of our leaders effectively "cut out," it was easy to mold Western opinion through the press, obscuring the real issues. The protests of 1936-38 were renamed "The Arab Rebellion." Palestinians, who in any other country being overtaken by a foreign force would have been called freedom fighters, were "terrorists" and "guerillas." Hence, the widely used term, "Palestinian terrorist" was ingrained in the Western mind.

Proof of the Zionist power hold in Palestine came in 1939. Suffering some belated pangs of conscience, Britain issued its "White Paper," instructing its Mandate government to bar further land purchases and immigration. Immediately, the Zionists decried this move as a betrayal. Unfortunately for the British, they had effectively trained a strong Zionist underground—the *Haganah*—in special brands of violence that were now turned against British soldiers and government workers in Palestine. British General Wingate had trained the *Haganah* in the use of large, destructive barrel-bombs and how to force Palestinian men to "confess" by shoving fistfuls of sand down their throats. Should it have surprised the British when the *Irgun,* bombed the King David Hotel killing almost one hundred people?

World War II forced a lull in the struggle for Palestine. But for Zionist leaders, the outcome was never in question.

Following the war the Zionists shifted their power push from Downing Street to the White House. Primarily, the British, who had now shown themselves reluctant to impose a Jewish state on Palestine, had been severely weakened. It was unwieldy and expensive to continue governing Palestine, and the Zionists had gained all but total control of munitions factories and industries there. More importantly, the U.S. had emerged as the new leader in determining the future of the free world. And in America a strong lobby of new Zionist supporters had emerged. What happened then, in the closed conference rooms of the White House, was no less scandalous than the British betrayal.

While President Roosevelt was in office he had resisted the pressure of Zionists, unwilling to see the Palestinians displaced from their homeland. He felt tremendous compassion for the half-million survivors who were expected to emerge from the Holocaust, but he had in mind a wonderfully humanitarian plan. He intended to open the free world to these pitiable victims, offering them passage to any free nation that rallied to his relief effort. However, when his emissary Morris Ernst was sent to sound out international opinion, Ernst was shocked to hear himself "decried, sneered at and attacked" as a traitor by Zionists who by then had raised $46 million to lobby for their own plan.[8]

When Truman took office after Roosevelt's untimely death, the lobbyists had a fresh opportunity, pressuring the new president. They argued vehemently that admission to Palestine was "the only hope of survival" for the Jewish people. Could this have been true when millions of Jewish people had been sheltered and protected by free nations during the war? When in fact, Jewish people throughout the free world moved easily in their societies, enjoying high standards of living in Western countries without discrimination? Nevertheless, when Truman was confronted by Arab leaders, the Zionist lobby had already done its job effectively. Truman's response: "I am sorry, gentlemen, but I have to answer to hundreds of thousands of those who are anxious for the success of Zionism; I do not have hundreds of thousands of Arabs among my constituents."[9]

Thus the vast majority of the Holocaust victims were never given a choice as to where they would live; only twenty thousand were admitted to large, free countries like the U.S.

in the three years following the war. Thus the exhausted British found themselves pressured by the most powerful office in the world, the White House, even as they watched their Mandate government in Palestine be blitzed by a campaign of terror. Guns, grenades, bombs and tanks—all manufactured in factories the British themselves had built—were now used against them.

In April 1947, war-weary and unwilling to lose more young men to defend Palestine from the Zionist underground, the British announced the plan to surrender their Mandate in one year. They were beaten and humiliated. Relinquishing Palestine was their only solution to the double-dealings they had begun thirty years before.

And as the British washed their hands of the Palestinian people they had promised to protect, violence spread unchecked. To the world, the Zionists proclaimed that they were fighting a "War of Independence." And the world, now penitent about the Holocaust, applauded. So the terror found its way into every village, even into the far hills of Galilee—and into my own home in Biram.

Sadly, the violence did not stop there.

In the years following the declaration of the State of Israel, its government needed desperately to flood the new land with settlers. Despite their claim that Israel was the one hope for Jewish survival, Jewish people in America were comfortable in their homes and businesses. Likewise, large Jewish communities in other countries showed no compulsion to uproot *en masse* and rush to the "promised land." Something had to be done. While the offerings of romance and adventure had some drawing effect on pioneering minds in America, another more sinister technique was used elsewhere. I learned much later that the Jewish community in Iraq, for instance, became the victim of "anti-Semitic" violence of suspicious origin.

On the last evening of Passover in April 1950, some fifty thousand Jewish people, celebrating an ancient tradition, were enjoying a stroll along the Tigris River in Baghdad. More than 130,000 Jewish people lived in Iraq, forming the oldest Jewish community in the world. Few of them had emigrated to Israel, though the way was freely open to them. Out of the darkness a car sped along the river esplanade and a small bomb was hurled, exploding on the pavement.

Though no one was hurt, shock-waves of fear rocked the Jewish community. Rumors of uncertain origin spread: A new, fanatic Arab group was planning a Jewish pogrom. It seemed unreasonable to many, since Jews had lived undisturbed in Iraq for a long time. But leaflets appeared mysteriously the very next day urging Jews to flee to Israel—and ten thousand signed up for emigration immediately. Where had the leaflets come from? How had they appeared so instantly?

The mystery was forgotten when a second bomb exploded—then a third, killing several people outside a synagogue. The rumors flew. By early 1951, Jews fled Iraq in panic, abandoning homes, property and an ancient heritage until only five thousand remained in the country.

Some fifteen people were arrested in connection with the bombing—and the remnant of the Jewish community was outraged. The *Haganah,* it was discovered, had smuggled arms caches into Iraq and it was *they* who had thrown the bombs at their own Jewish people. Their plan to touch off a panic emigration to Israel had worked. The Israeli Prime Minister David Ben Gurion and Yigal Allon, later to become Foreign Minister, knew of the plot. It was their way of helping along the prophesied "ingathering" of the Jews—even if the method was anti-biblical. If the world press was given to believe that hateful Arabs were responsible, it simply bolstered public sympathy for the "struggling" nation.

Years later, no less a reputable leader than the Chief Rabbi of Iraq, Sassoon Khedurri, pleaded with an inquiring journalist to tell the world the truth about Zionism. Not only had Jews in Iraq felt sympathy for the plight of the Palestinian people, but they too had suffered at the hands of the Zionist. Khedduri stated:

> By mid-1949 the big propaganda guns were already going off in the United States. American dollars were going to save Iraqi Jews—whether Iraqi Jews needed saving or not. There were daily "pogroms" in the *New York Times* and under datelines which few noticed were from Tel Aviv. Why didn't someone come to see *us* instead of negotiating with Israel to take in Iraqi Jews? Why didn't someone point out that the solid, responsible leadership of Iraqi Jews believed this [Iraq] to be their country? . . . The Iraqi government was being accused of holding the Jews against their will . . . campaigning among Jews was increased. . . . The government was whip-sawed . . . accused of pogroms and violent actions against Jews. . . . But if the government attempted to suppress Zionist agitation attempting to stampede the Iraqi Jews, it was again accused of discrimination.[10]

Amid the troubling facts, I thought I glimpsed more answers. I could not help but view the Zionists as victims, too—victims of something far worse than death camps. Beyond the hurling of bombs, the murder of innocents and bearing to the world false witness against their neighbor, the Zionists were stricken with a disease of the spirit. It was as if some demon of violence had been loosed and it whispered cunningly, *Might is right. Achieve your own ends by what-*

ever means necessary—all in the name of God. While the Church was sadly stumbling over its modern philosophies, this demon blinded the nations to the laws of the universe: Peace can never be achieved by violence; violence begets more violence. For the first time I saw clearly the face of my true enemy and the enemy of all who are friends of God and of peace. It was not the Zionists, but the demon of Militarism.

At the same time, something seethed beneath my ribs. The thought of such betrayal raised in me a feeling I had squelched so long I could hardly admit to it—much less name it. I gritted my teeth and shook off the feeling as if it were a spider that had crept onto my hand.

A more pressing question helped to obscure my feelings—the stark question of my own future. It was spring 1965, the end of my years in seminary was fast approaching, and I was just about to reach the shining ideal for which Faraj and I had come to Paris. I had set out to serve God and man in quietness and simplicity, dispensing the routine graces of the Church. For a time I had even tried to quell that outspoken nature of mine. Though I had done my best to feed my contemplative side, something like wildfire still burned through my sinews. It was as if I'd been driven to uncover this historical perspective—although Faraj had sometimes cautioned me not to be side-tracked. Had I angled onto another path—or was I slowly, truly finding the dead-center direction of my life's calling? I was a little unnerved to realize that I could not now live as that parochial priest I had once dreamed of becoming.

When, one evening, I opened my thoughts fully to Faraj, I hoped he would immediately agree with me. Late April was upon us and we were sauntering along the elegant Rue De Rivoli where trees were in full bud and the boutiques were just lighting their neon signs against the dusk. We had been

as close as brothers for more than fourteen years, and Faraj's
youthful charm had continued to mature into a quiet spirituality that I still admired. I hoped that he would help to sort
out my conflicting thoughts.

"If I were merely railing against a political system, that
would be one thing," I explained as we walked through the
thinning crowds of shoppers. "Then I'd become a politician,
too. But I believe it's more than that. It's a spiritual sickness.
There are unholy alliances between nations that talk about
God while their true motives are purely military."

"You can hardly expect to change what's happened," Faraj
replied.

"But I do."

"How? You don't throw bombs," he retorted.

"Of course not," I said quickly.

"Then what? I'll tell you. You must wait patiently, Elias.
God will move in His time. We must accept all things as from
His hand. It's no good to try to upset a whole government.
Even a repressive one."

I stared at Faraj. For an instant I saw the face of Father—
the faces of the village elders of Biram. Here was that old
question that had troubled me so long: As a Christian do you
speak out against the actions of your enemies—or do you
allow them to crush the life out of you? So many seemed to
think that submitting to humiliation was the only Christian
alternative. Should you not, sometimes, be stinging and preserving like salt?

Faraj was silent for a time. We had reached the Place de la
Concorde where thousands of French people, including clergy, were guillotined for speaking against France's revolution-
ary "freedom fighters." Then he spoke firmly, "We must
serve the Church quietly."

In that moment, I understood a crucial lesson: *Not all are
called to the same task.* Both Faraj and I were to be or-

dained—but each to a special calling. He had come to feel very strongly about the wealth and extravagance of the Church amid poor and hungry people. It was for them that he hoped to help reform the Church itself. And I—I would have to find my own calling on a lonelier path that would lead away from my closest friend. In more than six years in Paris, our paths, if not our spirits, had grown apart.

For me, a door seemed to stand wide open—to *what* end I was not sure—and unmistakably I was being beckoned to step through it.

It was during our final spring days at St. Sulpice, that my kindly mentor, Father Longère, touched a deeply resonant note, like a voice out of eternity. I had come to value his wisdom, his remarkable way of challenging us, spurring us to deeper thought on any subject in which we were certain of our opinion. During one of his final lectures, I found myself riveted to his words.

"If there is a problem somewhere," he said with his dry chuckle, "this is what happens. Three people will try to do something concrete to settle the issue. Ten people will give a lecture analyzing what the three are doing. One hundred people will commend or condemn the ten for their lecture. One thousand people will argue about the problem. And *one person*—only one—will involve himself so deeply in the true solution that he is too busy to listen to any of it."

"Now," he asked gently, his penetrating eyes meeting each of ours in turn, "which person are you?"

Faraj and I were soon caught up in plans for our return trip home. I barely had time for one more trip to see Lony, Franz and Wolfgang. A letter had arrived from them in which they were insistent—politely demanding—that I not leave Europe without a final visit.

When I got to Germany, they surprised me with a "going away" gift: a brand new white Volkswagen. I was fairly speechless at their tremendous generosity. Truly our love for each other, and my love for their beautiful blond son, had grown deep. But I had never expected such kindness.

Scarcely had I learned how to handle the Volkswagen, when it was time to drive to Genoa, Italy, where a ship would carry me and my car to Haifa. As I drove to the Italian coast, I had no idea how many nights I was to think of Lony, Franz and Wolfgang, nor how unusually thankful I would be for this vehicle.

As the ship slipped from its moorings, I watched the waving crowds on the dock alone. Faraj had made other travel plans, and we would meet again in Nazareth for our ordination ceremony in July.

Now, my thoughts dwelt on seeing my family again, holding each one of them. I was bursting with eagerness.

For a brief moment, I was surprised by another feeling: I would miss Europe—miss the luxuries of the easy life. I admit the thought of remaining in Paris or Germany had tempted me at times. Having lived in a free land where I had studied, traveled and eaten in cafes without harassment, I was hardly ready to become a person without an identity again nor to face the creeping disease that sucked the spirit and hope out of my people.

9

Grafted In

A thin wisp of smoke curled toward the high-vaulted ceiling of St. Joseph's Church—the white, sweet smoke of frankincense. Our ordination ceremony had begun. I glanced at Faraj who sat beside me at the front of the church. Was he as jittery as I? He looked as calm as ever, though I noticed that perspiration dampened his forehead.

From where we sat, I could see that the church was filled. Outside, the Mediterranean sun was white-hot. We had been back for a month and spring had turned to scorching summer. But it was the faces—the rows and rows of faces—that seemed to make us warm and moist beneath the collar, for the expansive stone church was quite cool. Almost every relative and friend I could name—those who were still in the country—had come to Nazareth for the ceremony. There were Mother and Father, seated near the front. The brothers and students of St. Joseph's school had packed the church to the doors. Though the Melkite ordination is quite unelaborate, it was a grand moment for us, culminating more than ten years of preparation. Father Longère had even traveled from Paris to celebrate with us.

Though I trembled nervously, I felt something else. What

was it? Certainly I had worked hard for this moment, had earned top grades, and along the way, learned to speak eight languages. Now the rigorous training was over. And instead of the settled feeling you find upon reaching a goal, a nagging inner voice told me that I had not yet found my true life's work.

What was more distracting were the images that kept flashing through my head while I was supposed to be concentrating on the ceremony. Two experiences since my return played through my head. . . .

I was standing at the customs line at the port in Haifa. I had just arrived from Europe, anxious to see my family. The doors to the outer waiting area opened for just a moment and in the throng I caught a glimpse of Mother and Father looking, though they were now in their early sixties, much grayer than I expected. In that moment, they smiled and pointed to the accompanying mob of family members, including Wardi, my brothers and the families that had grown around them. Then the door slammed shut.

When my turn came, I slid my passport across the counter to the customs agent. He glanced at it, then looked at me without expression. "You must go to that room over there," he said, pointing to a windowless door.

"Excuse me," I fumbled, "but why? My passport is current—"

"You are Palestinian?"

"Yes. But my family is waiting. Can't you—"

"You must go to that room. I can't stamp your passport for entry."

In the small room, I sat nervously as a brusque young man questioned me at length. For half an hour he demanded to know the names of all the places I'd been to in Europe and the names of all my "contacts." He was obviously not satisfied that I was a returning seminary student. I grew impatient with the questioning—and more than a little fearful—but I dared not become testy with him.

Finally he said in a commanding voice: "Strip."

"Excuse me?"

"*Strip*," he said more angrily. "Take off all your clothes. You must be searched."

That was my limit. "No," I said firmly. "I do not strip."

"You *will* strip or you will not get back into the country."

Moistness soaked my shirt. It was entirely likely that he could carry out his threat and not admit me. With all the calmness I could muster, I dug through my bag.

He looked at me warily. "What are you doing?"

"You are not going to admit me. And I am not going to strip for you," I replied. "And so I am going to sit here and read a book." With that I took out a book I had bought for the voyage and opened it to the first page.

Our stalemate ended after eight nerve-wracking hours. I did not strip, and was finally admitted to my home country. Outside the customs building my family swarmed around—concerned, relieved, thankful. From them I learned that travel anywhere, even by taxi, was frighteningly uncertain for all Palestinians. At any moment, you were subject to search and interrogation. . . .

The Bishop was still intoning, but another memory played in my mind.

. . . It was dusk. I had driven to a small village to visit a cousin from Biram. I was about to park in the street when he rushed out to stop me.

"Park in the yard—up near the house," he said anxiously. "It's not good to leave your car in the street here."

I was curious. Why should I be afraid to leave my car on the street in so pleasant a village?

Once inside his home I learned the reason. Most Palestinian young people were flat-handedly excluded from the universities. The reason given was that they did not have adequate education—but then, most of the village schools were poor and inferior. So even the brightest students faced lives as factory workers. And for a Palestinian girl there was little hope. As a result of such frustration, drug and alcohol abuse had slowly gone rampant and vandalism grew into an epidemic. Hence, my cousin had urged me to park my car close to the house. Our young people, the treasure of our society, could not cope with a futureless existence.

I also learned that small bands of *fedayeen* had grown and that they were striking across the borders into Israel from Lebanon, Syria and Jordan, attacking Jewish settlements. Understandably, they could never be satisfied in the ghetto-like refugee camps in which they were wasting their lives. And now, the military was cracking down on Palestinian villages with severe measures, leveling strict curfews without warning. It was no longer safe to be found in the streets after dark. . . .

I was startled by the Bishop's voice booming my name through the echoing sanctuary. Faraj and I were presented in turn to the audience, then we greeted the Bishop. He laid his hands upon us according to the ancient custom, praying for the life of God's Spirit to flood us. Then he turned each of us to the audience again, proclaiming, "He is worthy. . . . He is worthy. . . ."

In the next few weeks, as I waited to receive my first church assignment, that word would haunt me. *Worthy.* At night I would wake and see images of aimless young men— capable, bright young men—their lives wasting. Grenades would explode and I would see children—both Palestinian and Jewish—ripped apart. Angrily, I would toss in bed, seeing my own seminary-fresh face, and I would hear the voice say, *Worthy.*

Then, I would murmur into the darkness: "How? How can I ever be worthy?" I sensed the painful gap inside me that needed to be closed, opposing feelings that needed to be reconciled in me before I could ever be a real servant of God or men.

In the days following our ordination, I felt the pull—as a compass needle is drawn irresistibly—to visit the upper Galilee. Biram, I had learned, had long been abandoned by the soldiers. I had never been back since that day in 1947, but now no one would prohibit my entering the village—my true home.

Rising early one morning I left Nazareth before daybreak. The Volkswagen hummed along the highway that threaded flatly through the orchard lands of the north, then angled onto the rising dirt and gravel roads that curved up into the shadow-green, morning hills. I reached Biram just at sun-up, parking at the edge of the open area that had once been the village square. As I stepped from the car into the cool air of dawn, a sign caught my attention. In English and Hebrew it said that these "antiquities" were "preserved and protected" by the government.

The irony jarred me. Later, I learned that these "antiquities" had become a popular site visited by tourists on guided coach trips.

I passed through the square near tumbled pillars of the Roman temple and the synagogue. The light grew and filtered warmly through the olive branches. Only the chirping birds and the crunch of my steps on gravel stirred the silence. All about me the ruined stone houses were solemn, ghost-like. I climbed a crumbled wall into the dimly lit shell of the church. In the parish house, swallows sheltered in the remaining rafters. I stood frozen, dumb-struck, nearly overcome by the sense of desolation.

And yet, at the same moment I was caught unawares by a deep sense of life. From the wrecked homes, I imagined that I heard laughter, the voices of women, men deep in conversation over cups of coffee and the scent of woodsmoke. In the church, beneath the empty and teetering stone tower from which our bell had been taken, "Alleluia" was sung by children's voices again. It occurred to me then, that even bombs could never fully destroy such reverence for God and life and the land as we had felt here.

I found that I was moving swiftly down the overgrown streets to the far edge of the village, eager for the one site I had longed to see, and with each step the years peeled back. I was once again a small boy rushing home through the fig trees with some news or nonsense to share with my brothers.

Stepping from the orchard into the yard any illusion of the past was broken. The orchard itself was a ruin. For some reason it had been deserted and now grew unpruned except by the straying winds of God. The house, too, was a shambles. The roof and loft were blown away and one entire wall. Grass and weeds sprang up from the dirt floor. I could not look upon our house for very long, and I turned away with a knot in my throat.

Something in the yard stopped me. There, firmly rooted and still green with life, grew my special fig tree. I went to it and ran my hand over the rough bark and the grapevine that still trellised up its branches, thick and coarse as rope. This had always been my special hiding place—the spot where Atallah found me on the day Father announced the soldiers were coming.

Amid these vivid memories, Father's face appeared clearly—a younger face, loving yet stern, as it had been when he had lectured Rudah for bringing a gun home to protect us.

The Jews and Palestinians are blood brothers, he had said.
We must never forget that.

Now, looking at Father's specially-grafted fig tree, I knew
what those words meant. As a child, I had known that we got
on well with the Jewish people from other villages, that we
bartered with them and that the men occasionally enjoyed a
rousing religious discussion. But with my seminary training,
I was suddenly and keenly aware of St. Paul's declaration to
the young churches: God had broken a dividing wall, and
there was no longer "Jew nor Greek, slave nor free, male nor
female;" in fact, all had become "Abraham's seed, and heirs
according to God's promise" (Galatians 3:28-29). Further,
Paul said, "not all who are descended from Israel are Israel
. . . nor are they all Abraham's children . . . It is not only the
natural children who are God's children, but also the children of the promise who are regarded as Abraham's offspring" (Romans 9:6-8). We Gentiles had been "grafted in"
among God's chosen people of faith, just as Father had
grafted six different kinds of fig trees together to make a
delightful new tree. Beneath the rough bark where my hand
rested, I knew that the living wood had fused together so
perfectly that, should I cut the tree down, I could never see
where one variety stopped and the other began.

How terribly sad that men could ignore God's plan for
peace between divided brothers, even supporting one group
as it wielded its might to force out the other. Such wrong
thinking had divided the early Church, driving Hebrew and
Gentile believers apart. I had been surprised at fellow seminarians and professors. They had often become furious in
discussions when I had stated that Palestinians also had a
God-given right to live in Israel, to sow and reap from the
land, and to live as equals, not second-class citizens. Were
we not "children of the promise, regarded as Abraham's
offspring"?

Immediately, our discussions would swing in the direction of Old Testament prophecy. Again and again I was asked: "Did God not promise to regather the nation of Israel in their own homeland?"

The answer to that question was yes, of course. But that was not the only question, nor was it the main concern of the prophets. To address the full issue correctly, I had to start by asking another question: "To whom does God say the land really belongs?" And at once my friends would raise their eyebrows, wary that I was angling off the subject into some tricky, political double-talk. Not so, I was simply referring to the Old Testament Law wherein God says to the Jews:

. . . the land is mine and you are but aliens and tenants (Leviticus 25:23).

Quickly my friends would object, saying, "But God promised the land to Abraham, then to his son Isaac and also to Isaac's son Jacob who was renamed, Israel."

That was true, too. However, it is crucial to understand Abraham's response to so gracious a gift, of which he and his descendants were to be caretakers. He did not plow through the land, driving out its inhabitants, wielding power to establish his ownership by "right." Though he was to become the father of the faith for both Jews and Christians, he knew he was not the first inhabitant of Canaan to worship the one true God by any means. Melchizedek, the priest-king of Salem, once greeted Abraham with gifts of bread and wine and a message of welcome from God. Obviously, Melchizedek and his people had inhabited the land for some time before Abraham, honoring and worshiping God according to the old customs passed down from Noah and his fathers. Never did Abraham try to wrest Melchizedek's throne from him, nor did he take over anyone's land. He lived as a nomad. In fact, when his wife Sarah died, he very meekly *purchased* a cave in Hebron for her tomb.

Then I would ask a very crucial question: "What did God expect from the descendants of Abraham as caretakers dwelling in His land?"

It was to the Old Testament prophets that I turned for answers. In my own studies, I had become vibrantly aware that God had a special calling for his "caretaker people." In fact it was so high and hard a calling that I trembled to think of it: God demanded that they demonstrate His own character to the whole world, that they show forth the face of God in every action from the way they conducted their government down to the use of fair weights and measures in the marketplace. Often they failed miserably and, under God's judgment, they were broken apart by foreign powers such as the Babylonians. At last, God used the Romans to strike Israel and scatter the people throughout the nations.

Nonetheless, God would rescue them one last time after centuries of tremendous suffering. "Why?" I would ask my Christian friends. "Why would He continue to rescue a people He continually referred to as 'stiff-necked'?"

In answer, I would read from the ancient prophet Ezekiel. Speaking of this final rescue, with the powerful voice of the Lord, Ezekiel had delivered these blunt words to Israel:

It is not for your sake, O house of Israel, that I am going to (gather you from all nations), but for the sake of my holy name, which you have profaned among the nations where you have gone. I will show the holiness of my great name, which has been profaned among the nations, the name you have profaned among them" (Ezekiel 36:22-23).

Here I would pause. Clearly God was acting in faithfulness to His own promises to the Jews; it was a reflection of His own eternally faithful nature, not a reward for human goodness. I always hastened to point out to my Christian friends that God had sent "a light to the gentiles," we who had lived in "great darkness," making us His sons though we, too, were undeserving of such honor.

And still there was a more vital reason why God would rescue the Jewish people once again—and presumably this rescue was taking place now in the twentieth century. I would continue reading, for Ezekiel had revealed God's true intent:

> "Then the nations will know that I am the Lord," declares the Sovereign Lord, "when I show myself holy through you before their eyes" (Ezekiel 36:23b).

Yes, there was something much more important at stake than a piece of land. God's true purpose in regathering Israel was to demonstrate to the world that He is holy and He leads a holy nation.

Likewise, the entire book of Isaiah rings with the same two-edged prophecy: God would comfort Israelites by delivering them from their persecutors among the nations *and* require them to live up to a high calling. They were not to exhibit a form of outward religiosity and then behave like any other nation. Even while promising to rescue them once again, God Himself denounced their old ways, saying that He had—

> "Looked for justice, but saw bloodshed; for righteousness, but heard cries of distress" (Isaiah 5:7).

Therefore Isaiah prophesied, God would not merely bring the Jews together again in a typical, secular state, He would:

> raise *a banner for the nations* and gather the
> exiles of Israel; he will assemble the scattered peo-
> ple of Judah from the four quarters of the earth
> (Isaiah 11:12, italics added).

There would be some in the coming years who would
popularize the interpretation of prophecy, writing books and
claiming that since Israel was now in its rightful place, all was
in readiness for the Second Coming of Christ. But to me, that
was an incomplete view of prophecy. For Isaiah, in his long
testimony, made it amply clear that God was requiring a true
change of heart in the Jewish people, a change in their
traditional exclusiveness which caused them to believe that
they alone were God's favored ones. All the prophets had
made it clear that such thinking led to pride and error and
wrong-doing. The new regathered Israel was to be different.
Isaiah records this command:

> This is what the Lord says, "Maintain justice and
> do what is right, for my salvation is close at hand
> and my righteousness will soon be revealed.
> Blessed is the man who does this. . . . Let no for-
> eigner who has joined himself to the Lord say, 'The
> Lord will surely exclude me from his people' . . .
> for to them I will give within my temple and its walls
> a memorial and a name *better than sons and
> daughters;* I will give them an everlasting name that
> will not be cut off. And foreigners who bind them-
> selves to the Lord, to serve him, to love the name of
> the Lord, and to worship him . . . these I will bring
> to my holy mountain and give them joy in my house
> of prayer' . . . . The Sovereign Lord declares—he
> who gathers the exiles of Israel: "I will gather still

others to them besides those already gathered" (Isaiah 56:1-8).

I had sat down beneath the fig tree resting the back of my head against its knobby trunk as these prophecies flooded my thoughts again. Isaiah had always threaded justice and righteousness together throughout his prophecy. And clearly God intended to hold up His new Israel as a banner of justice before all the nations of the world. God's Israel included "foreigners," those who were not of the fleshly tribes of Israel, but who had been grafted into his family—just as the branches had been grafted into this fig tree. *And how sad*, I thought, *that we have been cut off like unwanted branches.*

Rising, I walked back to the car. I had another destination that morning. Weaving my way down the hills, past running springs and deep-green groves, I neared that other special place that I had been longing to visit—the Mount of Beatitudes.

As I drove, the voices of the ancient prophets still sounded. I found myself in hot debate, almost firing questions back at them. To me, as a Palestinian, Israel had returned to the land not in righteousness, but as my oppressor. As a Christian, I knew that I was grafted spiritually into the true family of Israel—though it certainly had not kept me or my people from suffering injustice. And how was I to respond? As a Christian, I had just as difficult a calling as a blood son of Israel. I could not join with the violent bands who were now attacking the country, even though I could feel their frustration. But neither could I live by the passive ways of Father and the other elders. Was my refusal to lay down and be trampled, to see our young people denied education, good jobs and decent homes, just my typical stubbornness? Many times I had felt guilty for my feelings, but I could no longer deny them.

At the Mount of Beatitudes, I parked in the visitors' lot. The Franciscans had built a replica of a Byzantine church on the mount, and nearby they provided a retreat house. At the moment, I was not eager to see tourists or any of the brothers, some of whom I knew. I followed the gravel pathways away from the buildings, out from the trees onto the open hillside overlooking the Sea of Galilee. As I ambled down a long flight of steps cut into the hill, I stopped, taken by the long vista of blue sea rimmed by hills on the east and west. The scene was unchanged since the days when Jesus toured Galilee on foot. Followed by a huge crowd of local people and others from Jerusalem, Judea and beyond the Jordan River, He had climbed up here to present His very first teaching to such a crowd. I could almost see them before me now.

A large group of women and children would have lingered in the background, as was the custom. In the forefront, spread across the grassy slope were the men. No doubt there were Jewish Zealots, those political activists who plotted the violent overthrow of the Roman occupation forces. Perhaps they hoped that Jesus would deliver a scorching message of destruction against the emperor. No doubt there were members of the Pharisee party, their long-tassled robes gathered about them, waiting to judge the orthodoxy of Jesus—waiting to stone him if he stepped outside their rigid tenets. To the side were the peasants, the common tradesmen and some shepherds. Respectful, humble, they quietly listened for some uplifting word from this teacher—a message that would ease the burdens heaved on their backs by both the political fanatics and the grim-faced religious. Maybe there was among them a Samaritan, a despised outcast. As Jesus looked them over, he was already blending together the teachings of the Law and the Prophets with fresh vitalizing wisdom.

> And He began to teach them, saying: "Blessed
> are the poor in spirit, for theirs is the kingdom of
> heaven. . . ."

I was drawn in afresh by His words. Through the years
they had become as part of my flesh. Perhaps their very
familiarity had obscured their true meaning from me. For
now, suddenly, with the voices of the ancient prophets still
echoing in my head, Jesus' words seared through me for the
first time with deep meaning.

The Beatitudes were prophecies! Not mere platitudes.
Jesus' prophetic ministry had begun right there on the hill
where I was standing. He had already set out to fulfill his
purpose of grafting the Jews and Gentiles together into one
family and one Kingdom by His death. Not the proud, but
the "poor in spirit" would enter this coming kingdom where
God's will would be done "on earth as it is in heaven."

Not all would welcome His idea of a Jewish and Gentile
kingdom. Yet He knew so well the pain of oppression and
loss. There would be suffering besides His own, and He told
them—

> "Blessed are those who mourn, *for they will be
> comforted. . . .*"

The next prophecy amazed me.

> "Blessed are the meek, *for they will inherit the
> earth. . . .*"

Immediately, I thought of Moses who was called "the
meekest man on earth." Yet he opposed Pharaoh and all
Egypt, insisting upon freedom for God's people. Meekness,

then, was not weakness but relying fully upon God's power as Moses had.

And I was intrigued by Jesus' use of the word, "earth." From my seminary training in ancient languages, I knew that the Greek word was *ge,* and its counterpart in Hebrew was the word *'aretz.* It was the same word used by modern Jews in referring to Israel. They called it *Ha'aretz*: The Land. And it was the same term King David, whom Jesus was quoting, had used in a psalm of comfort:

> "Do not fret because of evil men or be envious of those who do wrong. . . . Trust in the Lord and do good. . . . A little while and the wicked will be no more. . . . But the meek will inherit *the land* and enjoy great peace" (Psalm 37:1,3,10,11).

Was Jesus really saying that the true sons of Israel, whether of Jewish or Gentile origin, had the God-given right to inhabit the land of Israel? According to God's promise through Isaiah—that He would give to the "foreigner . . . a name better than sons and daughters," and that He would "gather still others besides those already gathered"—it was true.

All these thoughts had rushed upon me so quickly, I stood silent and awed. If all this were true, what could I do about it? My imagination played over the faces of that long-ago crowd that had listened to Jesus. How could these nice-sounding words make any difference when an unjust military government held sway, sending dissidents to their death? When they lived in fear of a strict, unforgiving religious code?

The next words of Jesus struck me like lightning:

> "Blessed are those who hunger and thirst for righteousness, *for they will be satisfied.*"

Isaiah had bound *justice* and *righteousness* together. And Jesus, who often quoted Isaiah, surely knew that. In fact, it was for justice and righteousness that He had come. Over and over He demonstrated that the stiff laws of the Old Testament were only a shadow of the higher law of God's love that He had come to fulfill. The woman taken in adultery, when repentant, was not stoned, but forgiven for her weakness. The blind and the crippled were healed on the sabbath, "for the sabbath was made for man." The Samaritan outcast became a person worthy of honor and concern. For one of the first things Jesus did when He reconciled man to God was to restore human dignity.

The reason Jesus' words had struck me was this: Suddenly I knew that the first step toward reconciling Jew and Palestinian was the restoration of human dignity. Justice and righteousness were what I had been hungering and thirsting for: This was the third choice that ran like a straight path between violent opposition and calcified, passive non-resistance. If I were really committing my life to carry God's message to my people, I would have to lift up, as Jesus had, the men and women who had been degraded and beaten down. Only by regaining their shattered human dignity could they begin to be reconciled to the Israeli people, whom they saw as their enemies. This, I knew at once, went beyond all claims of land and rightful ownership; it was the true beginning.

As the passage ran through my head, another phrase sounded like the thunderclap after the lightning:

> "Blessed are the peacemakers, *for they will be called sons of God.*"

If I was to go out as a true servant of God and man, my first calling was to be a *peacemaker.* With these words, it seemed that I had finally found my way. I was oblivious that a deeper work was still needed in my heart.

At that moment, a busload of camera-laden tourists swarmed over the hillside, breaking into my reverie. No matter, for the direction now lay clear before me. Besides, the heat of the day was growing. As I hurried back to the car, I felt that the elusive thread of inner peace had once again been handed to me with the words of my Champion. As a boy, the things He had spoken on this mount had comforted me when I was accused of cutting the telephone wire to the nearby *kibbutz*. Now, as a young man on the verge of my life's work, these same powerfully simple words were guiding me again, giving me the peace of purpose and direction.

Slipping into the Volkswagen another image flickered in my head. Again there were crowds of people, this time in modern dress, and it was I who was delivering to them a message of love and hope and reconciliation. With each phrase their drooping shoulders raised a bit and on their despondent faces smiles broadened. God had not abandoned them to be second-class citizens, I said. He loved them. They had a right to live in this land and now it was time to be about the business of reconciliation with our Jewish brothers.

The Volkswagen fairly flew over the roads back to Nazareth. And in my heart—now bursting with plans and hope and ideals—I was flying, too.

A few weeks after my trip to the upper Galilee, I was summoned by the Bishop. I was nervous and excited and happy all at once, because I knew I was going to receive my first assignment. I had heard that Faraj had already received his assignment—a church in Nazareth.

"Elias," the Bishop announced to me brightly, "you are being sent to Ibillin in Galilee, a village of several thousand."

"Thank you, Bishop," I replied. "But—excuse me—I've never heard of Ibillin. Where is it located?"

"Oh, you'll have no trouble finding it," he hurried on. "We'll give you a map and some directions."

Then he paused. "Ehm . . . it is a rather small village. Modest. Maybe a little poor. The situation is—not easy. We thought that maybe you could try it for a month. No harm in that, is there? If it doesn't seem to work out, we'll have another look at your assignment."

Before I could comment, he continued. "I have already sent a letter to the Responsible of the church. They have been without a pastor there for some time. He is expecting you on August 15."

Abruptly the interview was over. I was ushered into the hall with a dozen or more unanswered questions on my mind.

It hardly mattered. The message of dignity for all and of reconciliation with our foes was still clarion-clear in my spirit. I would carry this message to my people. Throughout the first part of the summer, I prepared for the move to Ibillin, imagining how I would be welcomed by my first small "flock."

On the morning of August 15, even the blistering heat could not take the spring out of my step as I loaded the car and headed off to find Ibillin. There were so many small villages tucked in among the hills, if I got side-tracked or took a wrong turn. . . .

. . . I had been searching for hours when I finally turned onto a road that was little more than a dirt track, thinly paved with broken-up tar and gravel. On the highway north of Nazareth I had picked up a hitchhiking soldier who had assured me confidently that he knew just where Ibillin was. When I finally dropped him off outside his base, he had waved me on vaguely, saying, "This way. Just a little further." I had found myself in Tiberias, at the western edge of the country where a gas station attendant smiled sadly and shook his head, pointing me back toward Nazareth. I had driven out of my way for an hour and a half. Finally I was on the road to Ibillin—at the most, thirty minutes from Nazareth.

I pressed the accelerator and lurched up the steep road to the village, winding through groves of olive trees. Like most villages, Ibillin was perched on a hill. Poor-looking homes made of cinder block stood close to the road. Three or four children strayed in the path of my car, making me brake— beautiful boys and girls with dark hair and wide, wondering eyes. They were dressed in very poor clothes with no shoes, and they ignored my greeting. Several older men, their heads swathed with protective *kafiyehs,* stared at me sullenly when I waved at them. Suddenly I was aware of how little I knew about this village.

Near the top of the hill I drove into the churchyard. Wilted from the heat and the over-long trip, I was still eager to see the church. I had stepped out of the car in front of a decrepit-looking building, wondering where the parish house might be.

It was exciting: Here would begin my life's work.

A loud, angry voice distracted me.

Lunging toward me from the open door of the church came a middle-aged man, shouting and waving his arms. In that instant, too, I noticed that the church door was hanging almost off its hinges.

"Get out of here! Turn your car around and get out!" he bellowed, rushing at me menacingly.

Bewildered, I stumbled back against the car and blurted, "Excuse me. I'm Elias Chacour, the new—"

"I know exactly who you are," he interrupted. He was right in front of me now, shouting in my face. "I received the Bishop's letter saying that you were coming today."

I could hardly believe it. This volatile man was the Responsible of the church, the man who cared for the grounds and building and looked after financial matters—the man who was supposed to welcome me.

"We don't want you here," he ranted. "Do you understand? Go away!"

10

Tough Miracles

Only a miracle of quick thinking—and some brashness—kept me from being pitched bodily out of Ibillin.

While the Responsible was still roaring in my face, I grabbed his hand reflexively. He must have thought I was going to shove him away, for his breath caught in mid-sentence and his jaw went slack. Where I got the nerve I hardly knew, but I blurted, "Let's pray together."

And there, leaning against the Volkswagen with the Responsible staring in disbelief, I opened my mouth, unsure of what would come out. "God, draw us together as Christian brothers. Help us work out our differences." What those differences were I could not fathom.

He was taken off guard only momentarily by my prayer. When I finished, he lunged ahead—though I noticed that his voice was less biting.

"If you think you're going to stay here you'd better go and bring back everything you priests have stolen from us."

The accusation staggered me. "What things? I was only ordained a few weeks ago. I didn't have time to steal anything."

"What things?" he mimicked me. "I'll show you 'what

151

things.'" And grabbing my sleeve, he jerked me toward the church.

The interior was dimly lit and cool. I was grateful—even if I was being dragged—to escape the mercilessly beating sun. But as my eyes adjusted, I was saddened at what I saw. The church was a sorry mess. The sagging door I had noticed was indeed hanging by one hinge. The interior was bare except for a few warped wooden benches. Left open to the elements, the walls were webbed with cracks and the paint was peeled and scaley. The fine frescoes that had decorated the walls were reduced to flakes of colored plaster. And at the front, once-fine draperies hung faded, dusty and limp.

As I took in this shambles, speechless, the Responsible rambled on with his accusations against the previous pastor: He had virtually disappeared one night several years before, taking with him the cup and plate used in Communion, most of the benches and even the outdoor toilet.

Then, grabbing my sleeve again, he pulled me back out into the blazing afternoon sun to show me the "parish house." As I feared, it was the small, decrepit-looking building in front of which I had parked.

"*If* you stay," he remarked with noticeable emphasis, "this is where you'll live."

A quick inspection of the building's two small rooms revealed the presence of a greasy stove, the absence of a bed—and no bathroom facilities at all, since the outdoor privy had gone off with my predecessor. A battered kerosene lamp, the only source of light, sat at the edge of a three-legged table. The only water for washing, drinking or cooking was cold and came from a leaky outdoor spigot. When the Bishop advised me that Ibillin would be "a challenge," he certainly had not wasted his breath on details. I kept trying to comfort myself, thinking, *One month—it's only for a month*.

Turning to the Responsible, who was watching me slyly, I

smiled and said, "This is suitable. Just fine. I'll be staying."
He lingered only long enough to watch me haul my suitcases
from the car, then he left in disgust. I tried to settle in, moving
benches from the church for my bed. Fleetingly, the thought
came to me that Ibillin might be the perfect place for me, my
first small experiment in becoming à peacemaker. I shoved
that idea away. I would make the best of it—just for four
weeks.

What I learned about Ibillin in the next few days was
pathetic. For, like the church, the village itself was in a
decline. Ibillin, I discovered, was an old, old settlement, one
of whose citizens was a Church father who played a master-
ful role in the Counsel of Nicea in 325 A.D. In the ensuing
centuries, the village was a battlefield for Crusader and
Islamic armies. The renowned Salah-al-din, or "Saladin,"
had constructed a stone fortress nearby, and his scimitar-
wielding forces had poured blood over these hills. Though
the light of Christianity flickered, it could not be quenched
and the Church remained strong until the twentieth century.

It was only in the upheavals of the 1940s, when families
were scattered and resettled, that Ibillin's ancient social
fabric tore apart. In the confusion of war, Moslems, Greek
Orthodox and Melkite Christians were slammed together. A
mosque, an Orthodox sanctuary and our own church now
clutched at the top of the same hill—each group vying for
power and influence in Ibillin. The divisions were disastrous.
Among the problems—such as delinquency and alco-
holism—the village counsels could never agree on a solution
to the village's antiquated, inadequate water supply. So nothing was accomplished and hatred spread.

Even families were hotly divided over issues. One of the
most tragic cases was the family where four brothers—one of
whom was the village policeman—detested each other so
vehemently that people rushed off the streets when they saw

two of them walking toward each other. It hurt me deeply to learn that these brothers were believers, once active in the church.

The most distressing thing was the vicious hatred of the Christians I had come to serve. The church was so blasted apart by hostility that only a handful of believers ever came to prayer. Primarily, there was disappointment that the church leadership avoided issues of justice and equality and seemed to court the new government that fought against us. Rather than face the Zionists, the bishops and archbishops seemed more interested in preserving their shrines—the "holy stones"—and did not speak out. The final blow had come from the previous pastor, who, when confronted with a divided, poverty-cursed situation, simply disappeared. Little wonder that the Responsible detested me for all that I represented. Little wonder that hopelessness had dulled faith.

Whatever wounds the Church heirarchy and the previous pastor had inflicted, the Responsible only aggravated matters. By visiting with a few neighbors—reluctant as they were to see me—I discovered, too, that the Responsible ruled with an iron will. He had assumed power, declaring who was welcome in the church and who was not. Most people were *not*. He was forceful and no one dared oppose him.

Perhaps that was the challenge that nudged me. The Responsible wanted to see me leave after only one month. I would stay longer—maybe a few months, maybe even a year.

At once I determined to visit every family in Ibillin, whether they were Christian or not. To me, it was an unmistakable opportunity to bear the love of the cross into this shattered place that was perched between the star of David and the crescent of Mohammed. Enthusiastically, I began knocking on doors every afternoon, telling families that they were welcome at the church again. Since hospitality is a quality so deeply ingrained by our culture I was never turned away, but was always treated to coffee and fruits and some of their carefully hoarded sweets. A few men even volunteered to make new benches and fix the broken church doors. Still, most were reluctant to come back to the church, strangely reluctant even to talk about it. And with the size of the village, I could see that it was going to be a time-consuming task to reach every family. I needed help.

One afternoon some, weeks after my one-month trial period had ended, I left off my visits long enough to drive to Nazareth. I hoped to see an old friend, a deeply spiritual woman known as Mother Josephate who headed a community of Christian women. These sisters lived simply, dedicating themselves to prayer—but would any of them be willing to leave their community and work amid the poor conditions of Ibillin with me?

Mother Josephate greeted me warmly, her lovely, aged face radiating a compassion that seemed to me more than mere human love. Graciously, she listened to my story about the problems in Ibillin and to my plea for two women from her community to come and help—even if only for a day at a time—by visiting the women of the village.

When I had finished she replied, "I believe that this request comes not from you, but from the heart of God. I'm sure some will want to go with you. Nevertheless, before I can promise you the help of two sisters, I must get the approval of our superior."

I knew that was true, since hers was a Roman community and tightly governed by their heirarchy. We agreed that I would return to Nazareth in several weeks—though Mother Josephate assured me in her kind way that there would be no problem. It was just a formality, a matter of submission and obedience on her part.

Before I saw Mother Josephate again, I found out why the people of Ibillin had been so reluctant even to talk about coming to church again. The Responsible learned that I was visiting in homes—and he became infuriated. The previous pastor had rarely bothered with home visits. Now the Responsible was jealous and suspicious of me, whom he considered a brash, obnoxious young man unfit for my calling. He began to dog me constantly, opposed my visiting certain people that he, for whatever obtuse reason, disliked.

There was one man for whom the Responsible had an absolutely irrational hatred. That was Habib, a gentle man who lived right next to the parish house. Habib often spoke out against the annexation of remaining Palestinian farmland by the Israeli government, a practice that was increasing at an alarming rate. The Responsible slandered him, calling him a dirty communist, and did not allow him even to set foot on church property.

Without question, the Responsible had a killing chokehold on the church. It had to be broken. On the other hand, the people were distrustful of anyone representing the Church. I could not simply shove the Responsible aside—in that way, I would look like one more power-grasping tyrant. I could not start an ugly argument. Yet a confrontation was coming and it would either split the believers of Ibillin irreparably or it would unite them.

Nightly, as the wooden benches stiffened my neck and bruised my hips, I imagined Jesus faced with the warring factions of His day. I thought of the Pharisees, raising their eyebrows judgmentally as He approached a prostitute, or a publican. What would He do?

One afternoon, on one of the last warm days of summer, I knew what *I* had to do. The Responsible was still dogging me on my rounds, still treating me as if I were his puppet and expecting me to dance with every twitch of the strings. Something had to break.

We stepped out of the parish house into the walled-in yard that surrounded it. The Responsible was right at my heels. The yard was supposed to be a garden. Sadly, it was as barren as the church—a patch of weeds. Once again the Responsible was beginning to dictate who I would see, and I knew this was the moment.

"I think I will visit Habib today," I remarked casually, looking up at Habib's home which could be seen beyond the garden wall.

"No. You will *not* see him!" the Responsible snapped.

I tossed up my hands. "All right. I'm not going to argue with you."

Surely he thought I was surrendering. A self-satisfied grin played at the corners of his mouth. I pressed my advantage.

"Will you wait here for me? Just for a moment?" I asked innocently. "I have something to take care of before I go with you. And I know this won't interest you at all."

Appeased and off guard, he agreed.

I stepped out of the garden into the street alone. Once the gate slammed shut, I hurried along beside the wall, turning in at the outside stairway that led up to Habib's second-floor apartment. As I mounted the steps, I could see down into the church garden—and I could *be seen* as well. The Responsible spotted me immediately, and even from a distance, I saw the color rising in his face.

Before he could shout at me, I called out pleasantly: "I knew you would feel uncomfortable visiting here. So I didn't force you to come with me. You can relax and wait if you like. I won't be long."

As it turned out, that was untrue. Habib and I found such a ready kinship of spirit that I quickly lost track of time. I was charmed by his knowledge of agriculture, his love for the soil and growing things which reminded me of Father. And besides his knowledge about trees and grapevines, Habib knew the New Testament thoroughly. It distressed me that such a person had been shunned and badly treated by the Church. I promised myself—and Habib—that this was just the first of many visits and, of course, I invited him to the church. Understandably, he did not accept the invitation at once, but I knew we would be fast friends.

As he saw me out the door, I glanced at my watch and started. *Two hours* had passed, and I had promised the Responsible I would return in a few minutes. Uneasily, I walked down the stairs from Habib's apartment, scanning the empty churchyard.

Thankfully, the Responsible had given up and gone home. Nor did he confront me when next I saw him. I would continue to see Habib, quietly so it would not become an issue. Yet I knew by the Responsible's bitter silence that it was only a matter of time.

Some weeks passed, and again I drove to Nazareth. The sooner I had help from the Christian sisters, the faster I could reach out to all the families of Ibillin. I had even begun to tramp the streets each Sunday morning for two hours before the church service began, knocking on doors and reminding the believers that our church was not *the* Church without them. It was tiring, ceaseless work, and I was desperate for some support. Eagerly, I bounded into Mother Josephate's office to keep our appointment.

One look at her face, and I knew that all was not right. Seated behind her desk, she folded her hands carefully, cleared her throat and picked a cautious path with her words.

"You know the difficult position I am in. I've always supported my superior's authority. After all, he has been placed over me by the Church." Here she stopped, pursing her lips before delivering the hard words. "I asked his permission to let two sisters work with you in Ibillin—and he denied my request."

My heart felt empty as she relayed their conversation. Her superior had asked if any families in Ibillin were Roman Catholic. When Mother Josephate said no, he asked if any might convert. Patiently, she told him that conversion was not the point. "In that case," he said peremptorily, "you cannot send two sisters there."

I supposed that was the end of the matter. With a heavy sigh, I was about to thank Mother Josephate and leave. As I started to rise, she motioned for me to sit.

"I told you I am in a difficult situation. That's true. But I have to answer to a higher authority than my superior or the Church. I have to answer to God, and I can't blame my superior if I fail to do what is right." And now I saw the familiar glimmer in her eyes again, a mischievous compassionate smile. "I was forbidden to send 'two' sisters—and so I am going to send *three*."

I was thrilled. Even more, I was moved with the deepest gratitude. Mother Josephate had struggled with this decision, I knew. She would never flippantly defy her superiors but was acting on a heart-set conviction. I squeezed her hand, thanking her over and over. We were like two sparks, I thought—not quite enough to set Ibillin afire, but there was the faint promise of brightness in my work now.

And the promise proved to be faint enough, indeed.

The very next Sunday, I drove to Nazareth again to pick up the three sisters Mother Josephate had recruited. When I arrived at their residence I was prepared to meet my three eager, enthusiastic workers.

At the door, Mother Josephate greeted me, introducing the volunteers. Mère Macaire, the eldest, seemed the strong, politely commanding type. However, a cough that shook her whole frame told me she was in poor health. Ghislaine was a short, cheerfully plump woman with graying hair and wistful, pale eyes. She looked like the universal grandmother. The third, Nazarena, was younger and darker. Her skin was a smooth, rich olive tone, and she was thin almost to the point of frailty. What these three had in common, besides the gray outfits of their community, was the wary-eyed, sullen way they stared at me. One look told me they were far less than enthusiastic.

We marched out to the car together and as I opened the door for them, Mère Macaire demanded, "You *are* going to return us here right after your service—is that right?"

I was dismayed. It was not my intent to ferry them back and forth from Nazareth to Ibillin just to have warm bodies sitting in church. I was about to close the car door and think up some polite way to get out of this arrangement. I was busy enough in Ibillin without taking on extra driving. But there was Mother Josephate, smiling at me from the doorway. I could not refuse her graciousness, and so, hardly flinching, I replied, "Yes. I'll return you immediately."

To my sheer amazement, when I deposited them back at the convent that afternoon, Mère Macaire insisted that I come for them the following Sunday. The next Sunday it was the same and the week after that. It was quite confusing to me since they showed little outward interest in the people of Ibillin, but kept to themselves all during the service. And afterwards, they marched straight out to the car, waiting with tight-lipped faces for me to say goodbye to the two dozen villagers who were now reluctantly coming to the church. I fully expected each Sunday to be their last—and sometimes I secretly hoped it would be. When I hinted that they might stay and talk to the village women, they were silent. Still, they came faithfully each week as winter settled about us.

The reason for their strange persistence—and their seeming indifference—became clear to me one day several months into their "volunteer work." Mother Josephate cornered me one afternoon, asking if all was going well with the sisters. I tried to answer politely without lying outright. She saw through my words at once.

"Don't give up on them," she said wistfully. "They have a 'convent mentality.' It happens for some. Everything is regulated by the clock. There is a time to eat, to pray, to sleep—a time to close the door and turn people away. They will change though. Be patient. They have good hearts or they would never go with you."

I learned in that conversation, too, that many in the Church considered the villages of the Galilee tough places to work. They were poor, the populations were mixed with Christians, Moslems, and also many Druze whose faith blended together Christianity, Islam and Judaism. And though Christ Himself traveled and taught and performed miracles of love in these villages, many Church people preferred to huddle safely and comfortably around the holy shrines.

The week following our conversation, I decided to help the sisters change a little faster. After church I simply refused to take them back to the convent immediately. Instead, I had a modest lunch prepared—the best I could do. I had also told some village women that the sisters would be staying and that they had minor skills in nursing. Since colds and viruses attacked their children savagely during these bitter, rainy months, the women were elated.

Before we could set the table for lunch there was a knock at the parish house door. I ran to answer it, for an icy drizzle was spattering the streets. When I opened the door, a young mother stepped timidly inside, cradling a blanketed bundle in her arms. Her face was tense, fearful. She lifted the folds of the blanket and inside was a very small boy about two years old. His curly, dark hair was damp, not from rain, but from fever.

"His name is Ibrahim," said the mother. "You know, like Father Abraham."

To my delight the sisters did not hesitate a moment, but swarmed around the woman comforting her, clucking over the child. Nazarena, who knew the most about nursing, took the listless child on her lap, gently rocking him as she stroked his hot, moist forehead. Ghislaine hurried to the stove to make some hot tea. Mère Macaire fussed over the young woman, asking questions about the boy's illness. I watched the mother, swaddled in such sudden care and affection, as every trace of fear drained from her face.

Standing quietly aside, I could not help but think that this poor child had been sent by God. It was one thing for the sisters to meet unfamiliar men and women in church. It was quite another matter to sit a sick child on their laps. Each time Ibrahim looked up into Nazarena's face, his dark eyes glassy and pain-filled, I sensed that the powerful, wordless bond between woman and child was forming. In that rare way that women have, all three sisters became Ibrahim's mother that day.

The sisters were alight with plans for the next week's trip as I drove them home. They would bring cold medicines and aspirins in case others were sick. I smiled and drove on silently.

Though the sisters tacitly refused to go into the homes, their new contact with the people of Ibillin brought an unexpected benefit. Since my arrival the previous summer, an occasional batch of flatbread would be delivered to the doorstep, a few pieces of fruit, or a basket of vegetables. After the sisters began dispensing their nursing care, food began arriving every day of the week. Increasingly, I received gifts of cheese, milk, eggs, oranges, meats, cakes, bread, olives, honey, coffee—all from the grateful hearts of Ibillin.

Somewhere during this time, I realized my own growing love for this village. My one-month trial period had gone on for almost six months and I could not think of leaving. I was still sleeping on a hard bench. The village and even the church were still rife with hatred. But I was seeing past the hardships and divisions. Perhaps it was the joyful eyes of the mothers bringing their babies for the sisters to doctor and for me to bless. Or the bands of older boys—young men, really—who milled about restlessly on the street corners. Or the shy, sweet faces of girls who demurely served coffee when I visited their fathers at home. Beneath the surface of Ibillin—a surface cracked by religious, social and political tensions, toughened by poor conditions—were tender, timidly opening hearts. Hearts of common people who did not want division, but peace. Men who once passed me on the streets with hostile indifference would pump my hand, grateful for some small ministration that the sisters had performed for a son or daughter. Gradually, I sensed that something was happening here. If so, it was not like the instant, powerful signs performed by Jesus—it would be a tough miracle.

Beneath this surface, too, opposition to my presence in Ibillin was building.

While I was busy with my afternoon and Sunday morning rounds, the Responsible had been gathering support for his cause also. Winter and spring passed, and as the summer of 1966 approached, I could sense that the many factions in the divided church were lining up on two sides—the Responsible's and mine. Others in the village were taking sides, too. I was horrified when this occurred to me and more than a little uneasy that the odds were in his favor. What chance did a young man of twenty-six—an outsider—stand against a lifetime village resident, and a powerful one at that? A head-to-head collision, the very thing I dreaded, seemed unavoidable.

The confrontation came on an early fall morning more than eighteen months after my arrival.

I answered an impatient pounding at my door to find the Responsible and half a dozen other men staring at me sullenly. "Come with us," the Responsible demanded without explanation. Dutifully, I stepped outside and followed.

They marched me around back to the parish house garden where the Responsible pointed accusingly at a young vine that was twining around some posts. "What is this?" he asked belligerently.

"It's a grapevine," I replied.

"Who planted it here?"

I had a sinking feeling. "My neighbor, Habib," I responded. The past spring, after I had reminisced to Habib about my childhood hideout in the vine-laced tree in Biram, he had surprised me with this gift of a hybrid grapevine. It promised to dress up the brown, barren garden.

"If Habib planted it, then it must go," the Responsible raved. "He has no right here, and I don't want him to have any excuse to come onto this property. Tear out the vine!"

I thrust my chin out stubbornly. Anger and exasperation boiled up inside. My thoughts blistered with accusations of *stupidity, small-mindedness*. And at the same moment, amazingly, a small, almost unheard voice somewhere inside prayed, *Father, let me speak with your tongue, not my own*.

Almost before I knew what I was saying, I replied evenly, "Bring me a bucket of water."

Triumphantly, the Responsible sent one of his men hunting for a bucket, supposing I meant to loosen the soil so the vine could be uprooted. When the man returned, lugging water from the outdoor spigot, I had only just determined what to do with it.

He thrust it into my hands, and I stooped, spilling water over the leaves in slow, ritual fashion. Setting the empty bucket aside, I raised my right hand over the vine. In as serious an intonation as I could manage, I said, "I baptize you in the name of the Father, and of the Son, and of the Holy Spirit. Amen."

The men stared at me as if I were dangerously insane. "There," I addressed them warmly, "now this is a Christian vine. You cannot uproot your own brother. So he stays."

Indignantly, they turned on their heels and stomped away.

For the moment we were stalemated. I knew, however, that the bitter hostilities within the church and in Ibillin could not be resolved by mere cleverness. I realized, as I plodded through the days ahead, that the skill of a surgeon was needed to cut away the sick thing that was destroying this village—not suspecting that I would be the first to come under the surgeon's knife.

Early in 1967, the sisters surprised me with an announcement.

"We would like to come and live in Ibillin," Mère Macaire declared one Sunday as we drove out of Nazareth. Ghislaine and Nazarena nodded. "That is," Mère Macaire added, "if you will have us."

I could have kissed them. More appropriately I responded, not wanting to sound over-eager, "Certainly. When?"

I don't know how Mother Josephate convinced her superior, but the three sisters moved to Ibillin the very next week. I knew it would be tough on them, since Mère Macaire was old and had health problems and Nazarena, too, was a bit frail. Besides which, there was a problem with living arrangements. We were able to find three metal-framed beds for the sisters, but we could not all share the parish house. Since no other quarters were offered, I was forced to sleep in the car. In a letter to Lony and Franz, I jokingly thanked them for giving me my "bedroom-on-wheels."

Despite the bitter, cramping cold, I was glad that the sisters willingly received visitors all week now. Cheerily, I stepped up my own pace, visiting in the homes of Christian and Moslem families alike. It was during this time that my painful surgery of the spirit took place.

Late one night toward the end of winter, a message came that a certain woman in the church was dying. She was quite old and had been very ill, so I was not surprised. However, two things disturbed me deeply. First, I had never before attended someone at the door of death. Second, this woman was the mother of the four feuding brothers and it was to the home of the oldest—the village policeman, whose name was Abu Mouhib—that I was called.

Nervously, I hurried out into the moonless night. I groped my way blindly through the dark village, fearful that I would not get to the woman before she died. Or perhaps I feared that I would.

When I finally reached the home of Abu Mouhib, where the woman had been residing, I was shaking visibly. He hesitated a moment before allowing me to enter. He disliked me, I knew, though he did come to church on rare occasions. This was not the time to express personal dislikes, however, and he showed me to his mother's sickroom.

Far into the dark morning hours I sat with the dying woman, whispering a few timid words of comfort. Those years in seminary had failed to prepare me for this. In my sweating palm lay her tremorous, blue-veined hand. It was cold and curled up like an alabaster leaf. Her breathing came in rasps for an hour or so—and then it ceased. With icy fingers, I closed her eyes.

My legs were rubber when I told Abu Mouhib that his mother was dead. Trying the best I could to comfort, I offered to go and tell his three brothers. "They would like to come and see her, I'm sure."

Abu Mouhib's grieving features stiffened into a scowl. "No!" he shouted. "My brothers do not set foot in my house. If they dare to come here you will have five funerals on your hands, because we will kill each other."

A chill shook me. Even the death of their mother would not draw these brothers together. As I helped wrap the woman's frail body, I grieved for her—for her sons, and for the whole village.

A gray, faint light lit the streets as I made my way back home. A deadening exhaustion stooped my shoulders. I wanted only to crawl into my Volkswagen and sleep for hours and hours. As I squeezed myself into the back seat, however, I felt a real ache of grief in my chest—grief and anger. Sleep would not come.

I lay there wrestling against the whole world of conflict that sprawled around me. In my head, I lunged at the four brothers in an angry conversation, telling them how disgusted I was at their behavior. Couldn't they forgive each other now when they needed to honor their own mother?

And they were not the only ones I attacked. The image of the Responsible smirked at me in the half-light, and I flung hard words in his face. I railed at the priest who had stolen from the church; at fellow seminarians who had slandered all Palestinians, calling us "terrorists;" at seminary professors; at the principal who had punished me at the school in Nazareth.

Another image appeared vividly . . . a military policeman

towering over a small boy, whipping him with a stick . . . I heard cries . . . my own voice . . . I was picking up a stick, beating, smashing the man's head until he fell unconscious . . . bleeding . . . There were tanks on the hills of Biram . . . explosions . . . our homes stood fast while the tanks blew apart . . . and the agonized bodies of soldiers. . . .

Then I knew.

Silent, still, I lay there, aware for the first time that I was capable of vicious, killing hatred. Aware that all men everywhere—despite the thin, polite veneer of society—are capable of hideous violence against other men. Not just the Nazis, or the Zionists or the Palestinian commandos—but me. I had covered my hurts with Christian responses, but inside the anger had gnawed. With this sudden, startling view of myself, a familiar inner voice spoke firmly, without compromise: *If you hate your brother you are guilty of murder.* Now I understood.

I was aware of other words being spoken. A Man was dying a hideous death at the hands of His captors—a Man of Peace, who suffered unjustly—hung on a cross. *Father forgive them,* I repeated. *And forgive me, too.*

In that moment, forgiveness closed the long-open gap of anger and bitterness inside me. From the time I had been beaten as a small boy, I had denied the violence inside me. Now . . . the taming hand that had taught me compassion on the border of West Germany had finally stilled me enough to see the deep hatred in my own soul.

Physically and emotionally spent, I fell asleep. Later that morning, I woke with a new, clean feeling of calmness. The change that had begun on my visit to the Mount of Beatitudes was complete. I knew what I must do in Ibillin.

My year-and-a-half of home visits and the sisters' months of ministrations had made a dent—a small dent—in reuniting the believers of Ibillin. Few attended the church regularly and walls of hostile silence remained firm. However, most of them would not think of missing services during the Christmas and Easter seasons, coming to be comforted by familiar customs, not out of desire for true spiritual renewal. True to the pattern, attendance increased markedly on the first Sunday of Lent, growing each week as Easter approached.

On Palm Sunday, every bench was packed. Nearly the entire congregation had come, plus a few other villagers whom I had invited. The weather that morning was balmy, with a warm, light wind straying through the streets, so I left the doors wide open, hoping that passers-by might be attracted by our singing. When I stood up, raising my hands to signal the start of the service, I was jolted by stark, staring faces.

Looks of open hostility greeted me. The Responsible's faction was clustered on one side of the church, almost challenging me with their icy glares. Indifferently, those whom the Responsible had ostracized sat on the opposite side. I was amazed to see Abu Mouhib, the policeman, perched in the very front row with his wife and children. In each of the other three quadrants of the church, as distant from one another as possible, were his three brothers. The sisters, I could tell, felt the tension, too, for their faces were blanched. I rose and began the first hymn, certain that no one would be attracted by our pathetically dismal singing. I thought, with sadness, of the battle lines that were drawn across the aisles of that sanctuary. And nervously, I hoped that no one would notice the odd lump in the pocket beneath my vestment.

What followed was undoubtedly the stiffest service, the most unimpassioned sermon of my life. The congregation endured me indifferently, fulfilling their holiday obligation to warm the benches. But then, they did not suspect what was coming. At the close of the liturgy, everyone rose for the benediction. I lifted my hand, my stomach fluttering, and paused. It was now or never.

Swiftly, I dropped my hand and strode toward the open doors at the back of the church. Every eye followed me with curiosity. I drew shut the huge double doors which workmen had rehung for me. From my pocket I pulled a thick chain, laced it through the handles and fastened it firmly with a padlock.

Returning to the front, I could almost feel the temperature rising. Or was it just me? Turning to face the congregation, I took a deep breath.

"Sitting in this building does not make you a Christian," I began awkwardly. My voice seemed to echo too loudly in the shocked silence. The sisters' eyes were shut, their lips moving furiously in prayer.

"You are a people divided. You argue and hate each other—gossip and spread malicious lies. What would the Moslems, what would the Jews, and others, think of you? Surely that your religion is false. If you can't love your brother that you see, how can you say you love God who is invisible? You have allowed the body of Christ to be disgraced."

Now the shock had turned to anger. The Responsible trembled and seemed as though he was about to choke. Abu Mouhib tapped his foot angrily and turned red around the collar. In his eyes, though, I thought I detected something besides anger.

Plunging ahead, my voice rose. "For many months, I've tried to unite you. I've failed, because I'm only a man. But there is someone else who can bring you together in true unity. His name is Jesus Christ. He is the one who gives you power to forgive. So now I will be quiet and allow Him to give you that power. If you *will not* forgive, we will stay locked in here. You can kill each other and I'll provide your funerals gratis."

Silence hung. Tight-lipped, fists clenched, everyone glared at me as if carved from stone. I waited. With agonizing slowness, the minutes passed. Three minutes . . . five . . . ten . . . I could hear, outside, a boy coaxing his donkey up the street and the slow *clop-clop* of its hooves. Still no one flinched. My breathing had become shallow and I swallowed hard. *Surely I've finished everything,* I chastised myself, *undone all these months of hard work with my*—Then a sudden movement caught my eye.

Someone was standing. Abu Mouhib rose and faced the congregation, his head bowed, remorse shining in his eyes. With his first words, I could scarcely believe that this was the same hard-bitten policeman who had treated me so brusquely.

"I am sorry," he faltered. All eyes were on him. "I am the worst one of all. I've hated my own brothers. Hated them so much I wanted to kill them. More than any of you I need forgiveness."

And then he turned to me. "Can you forgive me, too, Abuna?"

I was amazed! *Abuna* means "our father," a term of affection and respect. I had been called other things since arriving in Ibillin, but nothing so warm.

"Come here," I replied, motioning him to my side. He came, and we greeted each other with the kiss of peace. "Of course I forgive you," I said. "Now go and greet your brothers."

Before he was halfway down the aisle, his three brothers had rushed to him. They held each other in a long embrace, each one asking forgiveness of the others.

In an instant the church was a chaos of embracing and repentance. Cousins who had not spoken to each other in years, wept together openly. Women asked forgiveness for malicious gossip. Men confessed to passing damaging lies about each other. People who had ignored the sisters and myself in the streets now begged us to come to their homes. Only the Responsible stood quietly apart, accepting only stiffly my embrace. This second church service—a liturgy of love and reconciliation—went on for nearly a full hour.

In the midst of these joyful reunions, I recalled Father's words when he had told us why we must receive the Jews from Europe into our home. And loudly, I announced: "We're not going to wait until next week to celebrate the Resurrection. Let's celebrate it now. We were dead to each other. Now we are alive again."

I began to sing. This time our voices joined as one, the words binding us together in a song of triumph: "Christ is risen from the dead. By His death He has trampled death and given life to those in the tomb."

Even then it did not end. The momentum carried us out of the church and into the streets where true Christianity belongs. For the rest of the day and far into the evening, I joined groups of believers as they went from house to house throughout Ibillin. At every door, someone had to ask forgiveness for a certain wrong. Never was forgiveness withheld. Now I knew that inner peace could be passed from man to man and woman to woman.

As I watched, I recalled, too, an image that had come to me as a young boy in Haifa. Before my eyes, I was seeing a ruined church rebuilt at last—not with mortar and rock, but with living stones.

11

Bridges or Walls?

Truly the church in Ibillin resembled a lifeless body returning from the dead. In the jubilant singing and prayers on Easter, I felt the eager breath of new life. In the streaming tears, I saw, as in the story of Lazarus, brothers and sisters rushing to each other's embrace. Gifts of food arrived daily and, amazingly, we never purchased groceries from then on, for the generosity of these humble people was to prove bottomless. Immediately after the holiday, some in the congregation decided that the church building itself needed total rejuvenation and the sanctuary was soon bustling with workmen busy at repairs.

Mornings, I laced my way through the maze of ladders and drop-cloths inside the church, directing the renovations. Carpenters patched the crumbling plaster; painters recoated the walls and woodwork; electricians ferreted through the walls to fix frayed wiring. Plans were being made to enlarge the parish house so that I could have a small apartment, which pleased me greatly.

These signs, I realized, were only cosmetic. I knew that for a body to live, it would take nurturing. Afternoons, I kept up a busy schedule of home visits, breaking the bread of friendship to strengthen those delicate, new ties. And I knew that another step was vital if Ibillin was to become a village reconciled with itself.

One evening, several weeks after Easter, the sisters and I were seated at the table in our small, makeshift kitchen. Mère Macaire set a steaming plate of hot bread, eggs, potatoes and mint before me. In the eighteen months since they had come to Ibillin, these three women had become mother-like in caring for me. As was our custom, we paused for prayer before eating and the sisters bowed their heads.

"Sisters," I began startling them out of their routine, "I have a question for you. If Jesus Christ Himself was somewhere out in the streets of Ibillin needing our help, what would you do?

They stared at me. The answer was obvious: They would hurry to find Him.

"Well, I have great news for you ladies," I beamed. "Jesus Himself is *not* in Ibillin—but He has sent others and He wants to see if we will help them instead. Whatever we do to the *least* of men, we do for Him. And the person He sends may not be Christian, but Moslem. Jesus does not ask us just to preach to Moslems, but first to show His love. Will you go to them, too?

"We can't wait for people to see things our way—to believe and talk and act like us. Isn't it more important to demonstrate the *spirit* of the gospel, rather than battering people with the words? If we are going to represent our God to the Moslems, we have to choose. Do we build bridges . . . or walls?"

Even as I lectured them, I was soon to be confronted with a similar choice—building bridges or walls—and it would not be as easy as I was making it sound.

The sisters, for their part, needed no further prodding. They began the very next day to visit Moslem women at

home. They were wonderfully received, and, in the end, it
was the mutual love for children that bridged the gap between our religions. Soon the sisters were teaching the young
women sewing, tailoring and baking, and they invited these
girls to Bible classes they held for our church young people.
In a short time, they asked my approval to start a kindergarten in the parish house—a school for their "babies."

News about the sisters' tender concern for Moslem and
Christian alike spread immediately through the hill country.
Almost overnight, other villages began contacting me, asking that I send Christian women to live with them, to work
and teach. I had not expected this. Moreover, I was amazed
that so tiny a spark of love could shine like a beacon. Before I
could begin to make arrangements, however, I was brought
up short. In May, I was summoned by the Bishop.

With a broad, friendly grin, he floored me with this unwelcome announcement: "You, Elias, are going to study at
the Hebrew University in Jerusalem. I made some contacts,
and you are to be the very first Palestinian priest they have
ever accepted. An honor—a true honor. All the arrangements are made. You leave in two weeks."

"To study? Why?" I nearly shouted. "I have my work in
Ibillin—where you sent me. Good things are happening."

"Elias," he said, bristling. "do you know how embarrassing it is for me when I talk to rabbis? I'm amazed at their
knowledge of the New Testament—and we don't know half
as much about the Old Testament. I'm sending you because
you were a top student in seminary. Besides you already
know Hebrew and Aramaic."

I bridled inwardly. The church had changed so much in the
few months since our Palm Sunday renewal. The services
were growing weekly, with young and old uniting in prayers
and hymns. It would take time for some people, like Habib
who had been so badly slandered, to feel comfortable visit-

ing the church again. Only a few, like the Responsible refused to come back.

"So. It's all set. You will go," he concluded, ushering me out of his office.

As I returned to Ibillin, I was upset. I had just seen the first breakthrough toward reconciling people in this divided land. The believers were starting to trust the Church heirarchy again. And now I was being sent away.

Not to mention another important development among the villages of Galilee. In recent months a small group of young men from Biram had banded together to rebuild our ruined Church of Notre Dame as a symbol of hope for Palestinian people. Young men came from all the villages where we had been scattered, giving time and muscle power. I had gone with them, laboring, too.

Now all these things—the church in Ibillin, the other needy villages and the reconstruction efforts—would have to wait. I only had time for a few hasty preparations, setting up a church council to govern in my absence and helping the sisters to establish their kindergarten—all with a measure of discouragement and uneasiness.

Neither the Bishop nor I could foresee the incredible, far-reaching impact of my years at the Hebrew University.

Spring 1967 could not have been a better time—or a worse one—to plan a move to Jerusalem, the "city of peace." It was a pivotal moment in the history of modern Israel.

Economically, Israel was in rapid decline. So much money was needed for defense alone that inflation was growing cancerously and soon would top one hundred percent annually. Socially, the hope of a reunited brotherhood of the Jewish people was crumbling. The dark-skinned Jews from Africa and Asia found themselves confined to ghetto-like government housing that was little better than our Palestinian villages and relegated to the poorest-paying jobs. Their anger was beginning to strain Israel to its political limits. And on religious issues, the Orthodox, the Reformed and the secularized Jews viciously attacked each other. The conservatives believed that the country's mounting woes were God's judgment against violence; the moderates and liberals accused the religious of "backwardness." Sadly, the country that was once hailed as Messianic could not heal its root problems.

And at the moment of my arrival, another more volatile issue was about to explode, making my presence in Jerusalem unwise if not outright dangerous. The long-straining tension between Israel and its Arab neighbors was about to rupture.

For nearly twenty years, Palestinian refugees had been trapped in teeming, poverty-burdened camps in Egypt, Lebanon, Syria and Jordan. Untrained in anything but agriculture, they were resented, viewed as a scab that had never healed into the complexion of their new societies. Such frustration had birthed the poorly-trained commando groups, whose night strikes across the borders brought only violent reprisals from the Israeli military.

The United Nations strenuously urged Israel to assume its responsibility for the plight of the refugees. Israel should offer a choice: allow the refugees to return to their villages and homes or pay them for the land that was seized. Similarly, West Germany had paid Israel millions in reparations fees since World War II, so the request seemed fair. Though the Israeli Premier, Levi Eshkol, wanted reconciliation, his opponents inside Israel—including the aging Ben Gurion—ranted furiously at his talk of a peace agreement with Arab nations. Negotiations dragged on fruitlessly throughout the spring of 1967. Threats grew harsh.

Suddenly, on May 22, Egypt blockaded the Gulf of Aqaba,

Israel's only water route for receiving oil shipments from the Persian Gulf. Gunships and mines halted tankers headed for Israeli ports, like a tourniquet cutting off Israel's vital energy supply. The roads from Jerusalem, Tel Aviv, Haifa and Tiberias were flooded with young men and women in khakis, with automatic weapons at their sides, all hitchhiking to join their reserve units. A strange fever—the loathing and the eagerness for war—was in the air.

The war, when it exploded, was actually won in a single day. Early on June 5, air raid sirens wailed through the city. Hours before, Israeli fighter planes had knifed through the skies of Egypt, Jordan, Syria and Iraq in a surprise attack, destroying nearly four hundred Arab jets as they sat wing-to-wing on their runways. The Sinai campaign and fighting in the Golan Heights lasted just a few more days, then it was over, leaving the world stunned in the wake of a "Six-Day War." For weeks Israel rode the crest of excitement, proclaiming a national holiday.

On the morning of celebration, I was still settling into my room in Jerusalem. The day before, I had given blood in a local hospital to aid Israeli soldiers wounded in the fighting. I was still feeling a little weak, but the sound of cheering drew me into the streets. Crowds swept me along the sidewalks to the Jaffa Road—to a sight that numbed me. Columns of soldiers, tanks, cannons and mortars were parading from the far suburb of Ramallah into Old City Jerusalem which had been captured from the Jordanians in bloody combat. Scanning the crowds, my breath caught painfully in my throat.

Hundreds of Christian ministers, priests and nuns cheered on the parade. One trio waved a banner that read: "Blessed is he that comes in the name of the Lord." Another banner said: "Prophecy is fulfilled." All were smiling, applauding—hailing the machinery of war just as religious people had once cast palms before the Prince of Peace.

The scene blurred. Hot tears streaked my cheeks, and I struggled to push free of the crowd. I fled through the narrow streets of Old Jerusalem, searching for a quiet refuge. Instinctively, I found my way past the cluttered shops and slipped inside the massive doors of the Holy Sepulchre.

In the dim, looming church, I sank down on a bench. I felt betrayed. Alone. My difficult work at reconciling the Christians of Ibillin seemed so puny, so worthless in light of what I had just seen. I could understand the love of Christians for Jews—as my brothers I loved them too. But instead of demanding a true resolution to our conflict, my Christian brothers and sisters were applauding destructive might. And if Israel was so squarely in the center of prophecy and God's will, why was the nation coming unglued from within? The question of the suffering refugees was forgotten totally.

Numbly, I stared at the ornate sepulchre at the heart of the huge sanctuary. Surrounded by golden censers and candelabra, it was like a marble jewelbox. I thought of the words Jesus had spoken at His resurrection. Three times He said to His followers: "Peace be with you." And this risen Lord, who proclaimed the reconciliation of God and man, had also told them: "As my father sent me, I am sending you."

Was it more important to preserve these holy stones or to preserve peace between men, and human dignity? To insist and plead and struggle for it if need be? Who was going to become a beggar for peace if Christians did not?

After perhaps an hour, I rose to leave, with the penetrating sense that all my efforts were futile—my hopes and dreams dead. Dismally the thought crossed my mind that in two days I was supposed to face Jewish students and professors at the Hebrew University. I wanted to hide—to lose myself back in Ibillin. For a moment, I thought of fleeing the country entirely. Perhaps the Jesus of my boyhood was not powerful enough to bridge the bitterest hostilities of men's hearts after all. Perhaps His idea of peace only extended to those who came to sit, quiet and contemplative, on a church bench.

As I walked from the church, heading for the dazzling summer sunlight outside, I noticed the words carved deeply in marble overhead. "He is not here. He is risen." Later, I would think back and realize that these words, etched in my memory, were strangely prophetic.

My reception at the university disarmed me totally.

On my first morning, I jostled my way nervously through the crowded corridors with my class registration papers in hand. At the first office a young, Jewish secretary took my forms, studied them, then looked at me questioningly.

"You are Elias Chacour?"

"Yes."

"You are Palestinian?"

At once I was wary. I could not escape the memory of interrogation at the port in Haifa two years before. If she asked me to step aside into a closed room, I was ready to dash down the hall and leave Jerusalem. "Yes," I said, "Palestinian."

She glanced down at my papers again, wrote several lines and handed them back. "Welcome," she said with a warm smile.

During my first semester I was continuously amazed at the graciousness of professors and scholars in each of my classes. I was welcomed and encouraged to express my viewpoint. These, I discovered, were men and women of intellectual integrity, moral and sincere. I had to admit that I was utterly surprised and I hoped it was more than superficial politeness.

One man who became an immediate close colleague was a Professor David Flusser. As it happened I was his only student one semester in a course on Greek Patrology. Flusser had a brilliant knowledge of this field, conversant in all the teachings and writings of the ancient Church fathers. More than anyone I was to meet, he seemed blind to the fact that I was Palestinian, probably because the wisdom of the ages had given him a pastoral sort of love for all people.

It was this love that drew us together into discussions that ranged far beyond course material. Since there were just two of us, our "class" usually convened in his modest apartment where archaeology, religion and politics were stirred together with endless cups of coffee. Slowly, gingerly, the Palestinian issue emerged, until one day toward the end of the semester, he thumped the table, startling me.

"God intended for the land of Israel to be a blessing for all nations—all people. Not just a few."

Delicately, I probed. "So you mean that? Really? For Palestinians, too?"

"Everyone," he insisted. "History dictates it. Not just our past, but our need for a peaceful future as well."

Walking home after our session, Flusser's words stuck with me. In a practical way, Israel's economy could not hold up for long with the tremendous expense that went for arms alone. And his comment about history stirred up memories of my research in Paris. I had concluded then that all Jewish people did not hate Palestinians. Many had been infuriated at the tough-minded government. This fact had seemed an important key, and now I knew it was true from my friendship with Flusser and others like him. I thought, *If only the whole nation of Israel—and the whole world—could understand that Jews and Palestinians can get along when they begin to treat each other with dignity.*

Though I was unaware, that prayer was already being answered in an unusual way. Since I was an oddity—a Palestinian scholar—I was soon invited to receptions and parties in some rarefied circles that included religious and government leaders from Europe, Asia and America. Here I was introduced to ambassadors, diplomats, influential ministers, priests. I also met many leading rabbis from Jerusalem and abroad who received me with apparent warmth. And I was delighted that these powerful men wanted to discuss the Palestinian crisis. As I talked, however, I could not help but wonder whether their interest was purely superficial. They seemed sympathetic, compassionate. Yet, it would be some time before I felt the full impact of these frank discussions.

Not to say that everyone in Jerusalem politely accepted my presence. Just when I felt that the thread of peace was beginning to unite me with Jewish brothers such as Professor Flusser, that thread would stretch to the breaking point again.

In 1968, as my second year of studies progressed, Flusser organized a special symposium for the scholars, in the Bible Department, comparing the concept of love as expressed in Judaism, Islam and Christianity. His real goal, he confided to me, was to promote understanding between these groups whose religious claims to the land of Israel kept them at each other's throats like packs of dogs. And it was Flusser's opening remarks at the symposium that exposed some harbored feelings.

Standing before his audience, Flusser began by saying, "The Judaic concept of love is expressed in the conquest of Jericho. Joshua destroyed the people of Jericho in the name of God, because he loved his own people."

He commented briefly about Islam, then surprised us all with the following statement: "Christian love is the seemingly impossible love. Something amazing to behold. It is the love of the crucified who says, 'Father, forgive them for they know not what they do.'"

At once a young scholar named Greenberg was on his feet.

"You Flusser," he shouted, "you are a perverted Jew. You give the impression that Christianity is better than Jewry!"

There was a gulf of embarrassed silence. Flusser replied gently: "Not at all, Moshe. I'm just trying to tell you what I understand from my readings."

Greenberg persisted. "For me the love of Joshua is the only real love, because he dealt out retribution."

A chaos of voices arose, murmurs and angry shouts. I felt my face grow hot, and I gripped the arms of my chair.

In the din, another scholar rose. "Moshe," he said in a pleading voice, "it seems that your thinking would always lead to violence. You would always crush the opponent. With that kind of logic, what would you do with our Israeli Arabs?"

With an icy glance, Greenberg looked at him—then at me. "I would act accordingly." Around the hall, a dozen others murmured in agreement.

It was more than I could take. I fled from the hall with one of the deans at my heels. "Don't leave, Elias—please," he said, taking my arm. "We will change our discussion."

"I don't care about the discussion," I flared. "I want you to change the mentality!" I tried to pull my arm from him, but his grip tightened.

"Elias," his voice was commanding. "We *can* change the mentality. Are you giving up on us so quickly?"

Later, the dean's words needled me. I was not one to give up. I had expressed my views as openly as I dared, had worked hard among my own people. And I prayed daily for the reconciliation of Palestinians and Jews. What more was there?

As the fall semester of 1968 ground on, I grew fearful over Palestinian-Jewish tensions. After the 1967 war, the *fedayeen* groups that had been striking at Israel for some years were banding together under the name, Palestinian Liberation Organization. One man would arise to try to lead them—Yasser Arafat.

I grieved. Why had no Christian leader arisen to speak for my people?

And then I met Joseph Raya.

In October, I was summoned to meet the newly-elected Bishop of all Galilee. Several months earlier, our Patriarch had passed away and my Bishop had been elected to fill the vacant seat. I was more than mildly disappointed that this Raya, an American Lebanese from somewhere in the Southern U.S., had been chosen as my new Bishop.

When I was shown into his office, I began to bow in the greeting many bishops expected. But he stopped me. "I'm not here for that," he smiled. "Please sit down and tell me about all the people of Galilee."

And indeed he meant *all* the people—not just Melkite Christians. I began, of course, telling about my work in Ibillin. He paced the room as I spoke, watching me. The coiled vitality in his smallest movements made him seem much younger than his graying hair and middle-aged features indicated. If I paused, he would urge me on with probing questions: What about my relationship with the Jewish people? What was happening among the Moslems? The Druze? Was our Church helping the jobless? What were the conditions in Palestinian villages?

When I'd given everything I knew, I was out of breath. Bishop Raya was still pacing vigorously. "And what do you think is the greatest need of all?"

"Hope," I replied. "Palestinians need the hope of a future. Hope that one day we can reconcile with the Jews and live in dignity again."

He pondered this thought. It was then that I happened to

mention briefly the story of Biram and Ikrit and our efforts to rebuild the village church.

"That's it exactly," he sparked. "We'll stage a demonstration of our goodwill. "We'll rebuild the whole village of Biram."

I cringed at his naiveté. Politely, I explained that the only reason we had been allowed to touch the church was because of a government policy allowing the restoration of any religious site. I shook my head. "They won't let us lift a stone to rebuild the homes, I'm afraid."

His response nearly knocked me over. "They won't stop us," he said glowingly, "if we rebuild with living stones."

If I had thought Bishop Raya naive, I was far in the wrong. Before our conversation ended I learned the true story of this gentle firebrand of a man. His first assignment had taken him to Birmingham, Alabama, in 1950. Conditions among black Americans there had hardly changed since the days of slavery. There were still secret lynchings and open hatred. Despite threats and cold water hoses, a young, black minister named Martin Luther King, Jr., began to preach about his dream of equality and justice. Raya became one of King's fast friends, praying and marching at his side from Birmingham to Selma to Washington, D.C.

Now that same zeal, that sacrificial love for the outcast, was transplanted in Galilean soil. I was elated. My hopes, which had withered, caught his fire like dry kindling. Shortly after our meeting, we hit upon a plan: We would assemble fifteen hundred people for a peace gathering in Biram, representing the population of the village at the time of its destruction. Our goal was simply to show the government of Israel that Palestinians wanted only to return to their homes to live in peace. Bishop Raya began spreading the word through priests and village officials. And I, between finishing my last year-and-a-half of studies in Jerusalem, contacted uncles, cousins and other former villagers of Biram.

By the time I had completed my work in Jerusalem in 1970, we had refined our plan further: We would begin in August, staging a six-month camp-in on the ruins of Biram. I had moved back to Ibillin, resuming my pastoral duties, and was caught up in the final whirlwind arrangements for the camp-in. Many young people had begged to join our fifteen hundred enthusiastic supporters. So along with arranging for food and water, medical supplies and tents, I had to assure that a number of teachers would join us, since the demonstration would continue into the school year.

By August, I felt spent. Months of planning, meetings, phone calls and letter writing had drained me. For weeks, I had gotten by on three or four hours of sleep each night, despite the sisters' fussing that I needed to rest. Yet as I rode with a busload of volunteers from Ibillin to Biram, a certain electric tingle of excitement ran through me.

Bishop Raya had arrived in Biram before us, and was directing the first carloads of volunteers from the open square. When I stepped from the bus, I must have looked to him like the Apostle John just waking from his heavenly revelations. "Elias," he chuckled heartily, "come back down to earth. Your feet aren't even touching the ground."

He was right. I felt unearthly, as if I were living in a vision. The hot summer morning stretched into a cool evening, and I rushed about, helping volunteers to settle amid the fallen stones and timbers. The sky darkened, and still a vibrance drove me: voices mixed with laughter; women cooked over blazing wood fires; boys and girls played beneath the olive trees again. And still more busloads arrived, hundreds of Palestinian people coming, wave upon wave . . . and memory stirred me. . . .

. . . I was a young boy again, alone at the edge of the

Mediterranean with salt-spray dampening my face and waves crashing at my feet. Then, in a vivid waking dream, I had seen Biram come to life again—flooded with waves of people. . . .

And now, as a thin moon edged above the dark, eastern hills, I watched as my dream became a waking reality.

For six months, as fall slowly chilled the hill country, we worshipped, played, ate and slept in the open. The brisk rains drenched us, followed by cold winds that moaned through the cedars. From the very beginning, the news media sent photographers and reporters, keeping all Israel buzzing with news about our demonstration.

Though I never imagined it at the time, certain eyes had begun to watch us in secret—waiting for us to make one wrong step.

One frosty morning during the camp-in, Bishop Raya pulled me aside. Rubbing his hands before the glow of a fire, he said, "Elias, since God created us we've been kneeling to pray. For so long we've thought of prayer as hiding ourselves away to talk with God in private about our problems. But there's a time for setting aside our spiritual words and going out to our brother who has something against us. This is prayer, too—real intercession. It requires forgiveness and the strong love of God."

I knew there was some plan behind his words. Suspiciously, I asked, "What are you getting at?"

"It's good that we've rallied these people," he said, gesturing toward all the surrounding demonstrators. "It's a first step of hope for them. But the Jewish people need the hope of peace, too. It's time to march in Jerusalem and give our Jewish brothers the chance to walk at our side and show the world together that we are all against violence. That we all want human dignity."

Something caused me to recoil at his words. Was he mad?

Certainly his office had been deluged with hundreds of letters, phone calls and telegrams from Jewish rabbis and other Israeli citizens. We'd been told that more sacks of mail arrived each day, beleaguring the secretaries, and that the vast majority were in favor of a peaceful settlement between Jews and Palestinians. It appeared that the hearts of many Jews were indeed with us. But I could not believe that Jews would openly support us in a peace march.

He must have read my thoughts—or at least read the look on my face. Staring into the guttering flames, he said, "I'm not going to lie to you. This kind of intercession always involves a risk."

I took a deep breath of cold air and expelled a frosty sigh. "All right. We'll march together. You lead and I'll follow. At least they'll have two of us to arrest," I replied lightly.

"Oh no," said Raya with a sudden laugh. "You've missed the idea. I didn't say I would lead. I'll help organize and I'll march. But," he patted my shoulder, "a Palestinian must lead."

The march took almost eighteen months to organize. When the Biram demonstration ended, I returned to Ibillin and began writing letters to friends at the Hebrew University and to other Jewish acquaintances in Jerusalem. Their return letters were solidly supportive, but still left me with a deep foreboding—like the letter I received from a leading rabbi.

He was terribly dismayed, he said, at Golda Meir's notoriously tough stance toward Palestinians in Israel. With her "land reforms," she was confiscating more and more farmland from our villages. Shortly after coming to power, she had been asked by reporters how she planned to answer the Palestinian cry for justice. Her reply: "What is a Palestinian? Such a thing does not exist."[11]

My rabbi friend then wrote these astonishing words: "We

who seek God are terrified because your story is like that of Naboth and Jezebel. Among the rabbis, many I know are afraid that Golda Meir, like Jezebel, has 'sold herself to do evil' to your people."

My heart skipped. Further on, I read, "When you march, write on your placards: 'Golda Meir is killing justice—she is the modern Jezebel.' However," he hastily penned, "I would be obliged if you did not connect my name with that statement."

With a twinge of uneasiness, I dropped the letter on the stack of mail that covered my desk. All these letters and the gifts of money were wonderful. But what kind of support could we really hope for from our Jewish brothers when it came right down to marching in the streets of Jerusalem?

I had a sinking feeling. Several thousand Palestinian friends had pledged to march with us. Even Mother and Father were planning to come with a busload from Gish. As I thought of my parents—now in their seventies and showing the first tremors of frailty—and the other hopeful marchers, I shuddered, remembering the cold water hoses of Alabama, the police dogs and billyclubs . . . What if Bishop Raya and I were leading our people into a trap?

Early on the morning of August 13, 1972, our fleet of busses ground sluggishly up the steep roads to Jerusalem. Near the outskirts of the city, at a pre-arranged point on the Jaffa Road, we parked. We had chosen for our march the same route over which the victory parade of 1967 had gone. As I stepped off the bus, the sultry summer air engulfed me. The sun was already burning through the haze, but was not the only reason that perspiration streaked my temples.

Other busses pulled in from various regions. Marchers—all Palestinian so far—stepped out to stretch their legs and mix amiably with old friends and relatives from other villages. The jeep and megaphone we arranged for had arrived. But it was already 9:20—just forty minutes until the march would begin. And I was still scanning the road toward Jerusalem for any sign of the Jewish friends who had promised to march with us.

Bishop Raya tapped my shoulder. When I turned, he read my look immediately. "Trust, Elias," he said with a calm smile. "We have risked. Now it's in God's hands."

More minutes passed. As I waited, Mother and Father stepped from one of the late-arriving busses. Father came slowly down the steps, his white hair hidden beneath the familiar *kafiyeh*. Mother followed. Her legs had weakened, but she still had a certain spunk in her step. We embraced, and I wished so deeply that they had stayed safely at home.

"You're worried, Elias," said Father, his clear blue eyes studying mine.

Mother took my arm. "I've been worried for *you*, but only because you work too hard." I tried to ignore her comments—though it was true I had been plagued by fatigue—and she persisted. "You do work too hard. But I didn't come all this way to tell you that."

"Elias," Father continued, "You won't mind if we don't walk, will you? While you are out praying for peace in the streets, we are going to stay here on the bus and talk to someone who is more important than anyone in the government. We will pray here."

I felt such warmth for them in that moment—and I was thankful for their decision. But as they retreated to their bus, I was still plagued with doubt that our friends from Jerusalem would come.

In a few minutes, several cars pulled up, delivering about fifteen to twenty professors from the Hebrew University. With sinking hopes, I was about to greet them when I noticed other cars turning the corner onto Jaffa Road. More were coming—in small groups. In a few more minutes, they were arriving on foot a dozen at a time. Among the growing crowd, more professors appeared, making a total of seventy supporters from the University. And at the same time others were arriving, groups of Moslems and Druze who had heard about the demonstration. And then my heart was racing.

Climbing nervously into the jeep, megaphone in hand, I hurriedly organized the marchers into lines. As I stood up before this sprawling crowd, the sight brought a lump to my throat. Near the jeep stood Bishop Raya, along with several priests and rabbis. Their heads were bowed, praying to the same God. A young Jewish man was handing out placards that read: "Justice for Biram and Ikrit," and "Justice for Palestinians." Further away, the marchers had already intermingled—Christian, Jew, Moslem and Druze. We had become one in this cause, ready to beg together for peace. And I noticed, too, as the driver started the jeep's engine, that a certain calm had come over me. My legs were no longer shaking as we moved slowly out onto Jaffa Road, the crowd surging behind us. Still I wondered—remembering all the volatile issues our presence represented—how we would be received.

As the march rolled block by block toward the heart of Jerusalem, it grew. At 10:00 a.m., the sidewalks were bustling. Though stands of policemen had set protective cordons along our route, more and more people flooded our ranks. By the time we had reached our destination, the *Knesset*. I sensed the feeling of unity that ran like electricity through the marchers—now nearly eight thousand strong. The last shred of worry left, for it seemed that much of the city was behind us.

Surrounded by banks of cameras and friendly reporters, we congregated on the *Knesset's* wide, stone steps. The newsmen seemed amazed, snapping photo after photo of young Jewish men in *yarmulke* and older Palestinian men in *kafiyehs* sitting side by side. Here, Bishop Raya announced that he was requesting a formal meeting with Golda Meir to discuss reconciliation between Israel and the Palestinian people. If she would not see him, we would wait—as many as were able—to fast and pray.

Hundreds of us did wait—for four days as the blistering sun of August glared off the pavement, keeping prayer vigils by night or sleeping on the steps. Many, especially the elderly like Mother and Father, returned to the villages. And while I was deeply moved that we could pray and fast together for the peace of Jerusalem, the *Knesset* continued to present its closed, stone-silent face to us.

Bishop Raya's request to meet with Golda Meir was never answered. Though Jerusalem's police chief was quoted in newspapers as saying that ours was the most amazing demonstration of unity he had ever seen in Israel, the government ignored us. At the end of four days, when we called an end to our fast, I fought down disappointment.

As the crowd broke up, I walked dejectedly toward our bus. A university professor stopped me. "Elias, what's wrong? You're not pleased?" And before I could respond, he pointed back toward the *Knesset*. "Look there."

At the top of the steps was a large group of young men and women. By their varied dress, we could tell they were Christian, Jewish, Moslem and Druze. They stood with their arms around one another.

"You see, Elias," he announced. "Change is here. It's happening in people's hearts. Even if slowly. 'Righteousness and peace have kissed,'" he said, quoting a psalm. "And it was you who brought us together. You are a son of God."

We were nearly back to Ibillin. The rattling of the bus kept me awake as I stared out the window into the dark. Had something been accomplished? It was then that the inner voice—was it only memory?—reminded me of the professor's words. He, a Jew, had called me a "son of God." And that inner voice reminded me of a phrase I knew so well: *"Happy are the peacemakers. . ."*

Walls were coming down.

12

"Work, For the Night is Coming."

I lifted my head, listening, momentarily forgetting the mound of letters on the desk before me. Laughter rang from the next room of the parish house where Ghislaine was teaching a squirming bunch of kindergarten children. It was just a few weeks after the march in Jerusalem and school was well under way. Faintly, through the window beside my desk in the back room, I could also hear Nazarena's choir practicing in the church. Not long before, I had celebrated my thirty-second birthday and the children had eagerly serenaded me. Usually, these sounds made me smile—joyful sounds of what I had come to call "my love affair with Ibillin." But this morning the singing and laughter did not at all match my mood.

I slipped out to the garden, pacing up and down. Habib's grapevine had grown thick and hearty, webbing its greenery over a lattice of wooden poles. I fingered one of the coarse leaves. Mère Macaire could make some savory grape leaf dishes—but she was gone. Age and hard work and our tough living conditions had eroded her already poor health. She had given six good years to Ibillin and, only weeks before, had passed away from us.

Her death, however, was not the only thing that stirred me as I strode between the new banks of flowers. A feeling of urgency tugged at me following our march for peace. A deskful of supportive letters from both Jews and Palestinians told me that a first bridge of reconciliation had been laid.

Yet I felt as though the stones had been set in place without mortar. Thousands and thousands of Palestinians were still struggling with basic survival—with poor housing and health care, no education, low-paying jobs or no jobs at all. Not surprisingly, they resented their position as the laboring class with no hope of raising themselves from the bottom of our society. If things did not begin to change for them, talk about reconciliation was wasted. How could I begin to get them across the bridge with me?

Several weeks later, when I visited Bishop Raya on some Church matters, he, too, seemed unsettled. He paced the office with his usual vitality, like a graying lion, but some underlying feeling clouded his face.

"Is something wrong?" I asked.

He looked directly at me, paused, and released a deep sigh. "Yes. Unfortunately, I had an angry visitor—from Rome."

Our march, it seemed, had gained international attention through the media. Immediately, one of our most powerful cardinals who lived in Rome had flown to Israel, descending upon Bishop Raya without warning.

"The Cardinal was angry—nearly raving," he said incredulously. "He demanded that I stay out of the streets and stick to Church affairs. What was worse, he said to me, 'What do you care about these damn Palestinians?'"

Bishop Raya, however, dismissed the affront with a wave of his hand. "It doesn't change a thing. I'm still here—and I'm not about to live in comfort, or like a mouse, while people are suffering.

"And," he shifted abruptly, "I shouldn't lay my burdens on you when something is obviously on your mind. You've been frowning since you walked in, Elias. What's the trouble?"

I shrugged. "The march is over. We had some good, brotherly feelings. What do we do now?"

He pursed his lips thoughtfully. "You once told me that Palestinians need hope. You've seen how many Jews are for you. There's hope in that. But you've got to continue to build up the Palestinians. They're like sheep without a shepherd."

"I know. And they need someone to unite them. They need to work for common goals. Our young people need the hope of a future. They must learn that they are worthwhile and productive citizens. If they don't gain self-respect they will always resent the Jews."

Bishop Raya nodded. "Exactly. When you build dignity, you begin to destroy prejudice."

"That would be easy," I grumbled, "if our communities were already united. Or if we had good schools. But our children study in broken down buildings with outdated books."

"Elias," he said, with his innocent smile, "sometimes you must work and sweat if you are going to be a peacemaker. Not just talk and shout about it. *You* build the communities. *You* build the schools."

Driving back to Ibillin I was rankled. What was he suggesting—that I magically produce buildings, books and teachers out of thin air? With all the work on my hands, I firmly dismissed the notion.

It would be a full two years before the thought crossed my mind again. Besides my work in Ibillin, which had blossomed in my seven years there, I had thrown myself into another project shortly after my return from Jerusalem.

Other villages throughout Galilee had continued to ask that I send Christian women to live and work with them.

Finally, I had chosen seven of the poorest villages and promised to see what I could do. With Bishop Raya's eager permission, I had arranged with Mother Josephate to send twenty-one young women from her community—three to each village—on short "Apostolic Holidays." They would teach hygiene, homemaking and use their minor skills in nursing, and they would teach the young people Scripture. With the enthusiasm Ghislaine and Nazarena had spread on their occasional returns to Nazareth, we had no trouble finding volunteers.

The love and goodwill these young women carried with them was contagious in the villages, too. Early in 1973, in fact, the village of My'ilia invited me to a gala celebration to honor the three sisters whom the villagers had quickly come to cherish. A small, makeshift platform stood at the center of the town, and crowds of men, boys and women with babies had already clustered around it when I arrived.

I sat beside the sisters and an array of local dignitaries, ready for the usual niceties and over-long speeches. Not to disappoint me, a stout little man, his suit vest nearly bursting its buttons as it stretched across his middle, rose and launched a rambling tribute. The young women at my side pinked with humility.

"Until the sisters came we had no one to care for us. Now we do not want them to leave. And so," he beamed at me, "we have collected a large sum of money as a gift for Abuna Chacour and the sisters—if they will stay."

The other dignitaries were nodding, but a warning sounded inside me. Allowing the sisters to stay would be no problem. From our conversations I knew their hearts had found a home here. But the money—it was like a scorpion I could not touch. Like other villagers, these people had long felt that the Church was too much in love with money. Yet, refusing a gift would violate our customs; it would be an insult.

The speaker was thrusting an envelope thick with money into my hands. Instead I jumped up and stepped to the podium.

"My friends, you are gracious—" I began delicately, "—too gracious. We cannot accept your money."

The crowd murmured uneasily. At once the little man beside me objected harshly: "It's a gift, Abuna. You cannot refuse—"

"But I do," I pressed. Something crucial was at stake here—the self-respect of this village. "Bread and olives are enough for these young women. They have come here as servants. They see God in your faces.

"And this," I said emphatically, snatching the envelope and waving it in the air, "does not repay them. Giving money to the Church cannot fulfill your obligation of love. You must give more than that. You must be willing to serve, too."

Even as I spoke, Bishop Raya's thoughts on building came back to me, igniting a plan in my head. I rushed on.

"The gift we *will* accept is a commitment of service. You, too must give your hands and your backs to work—not for us, but for your children. This money will be used to start a library where your children will sharpen their minds. And there is more."

I could see by the dawning smiles that the crowd was suddenly with me. "We are going to build a community center—a place of learning and friendship for the whole village. Will you help? Will you give your time, your hands and back? I am willing to give mine, but I cannot build alone."

The challenge caught like fire, and the crowd burst into applause.

Immediately, the whole band of dignitaries rose and embraced me, their honor intact. "We will give our hands *and* our money," my little friend announced proudly.

The sisters happily remained. The front room of their small home was soon stacked from floor to ceiling with shelves of new and used library books.

And over the next two years, men, women and young people gladly sacrificed hours of free time to build their community center. Three or four times a week, I would return to My'ilia to help and supervise. And with each layer of blocks, I could feel the dignity of the village strengthening.

One disturbing event marred the excitement. Late on a summer night, some men were returning home through the dark streets when they heard loud crashes coming from the nearly completed building. They sprinted up to the open doorway in time to see two or three figures slip away through the blackness, down the street and out of My'ilia—and they found windows shattered, buckets of paint dumped.

We never did catch the vandals, but the question nagged: Who were they? To prevent further incidents, we stationed night watchmen in the center. And construction went on.

For me, the *real* work was still ahead. In these centers, I planned to have lecture series and films to promote village unity. More than physical buildings, I wanted to construct a bridge of understanding about our Jewish brothers.

Before I could pursue these further plans still another challenge opened before me.

Evidently, some of the Church leaders I had met at the Hebrew University had carried back to their home countries reports of a certain Palestinian Christian whose words had some spark. While the building in My'ilia rose slowly, I received several invitations from churches in Holland and Germany that wanted to hear my ideas about peace. Still I puzzled as I drove to the airport: What could I, an unknown priest from the poor parishes of Galilee, have to say to sophisticated Europeans?

At the bustling airport in Germany, Lony and Franz threw their arms around me. In the nine years since I had last seen them, Wolfgang had grown into a tall fourteen-year-old who gripped my hand tightly, and two lovely daughters had been born, Rita Maria and Michelene.

After exchanging pleasantries, Wolfgang surprised me. With a look that seemed too intense and searching for an adolescent, he asked, "Have you heard about the nuclear arms race?"

Franz, who was loading my bag into the car, shook his head. "Who is going to bring the world back to sanity, Elias?" And as we drove away from the airport toward home, he told me about the contagion of fear, like a plague from the Dark Ages, that was over-shadowing Europe: It's name was *nuclear holocaust*.

I knew, of course, that the United States and allied powers were locating nuclear-tipped missiles throughout Europe, weapons of death that were aimed at Russia. The Russians made no secret of the fact that their own missiles were aimed both at the U.S. and the European bases as well. Lony and Franz now informed me of the strangling despair among the young people of Europe. "Many of them feel there is no answer—no hope."

As I kept my engagements, with these words in my head, I knew I was addressing sophisticated men, women and young people who were jaded by political rhetoric, opportunism and broken promises. Yet, standing before each crowd, I could only begin with the words that had long captivated me: "Blessed are the peacemakers. . . ."

Not that I was simplistic; nor was I easy on them. I told them the way of a peacemaker was difficult—it required deep forgiveness, risking the friendship of your enemies, begging for peace on your knees and in the streets. My audiences seemed rivetted when I talked about the schools and community centers I hoped to build throughout Galilee in an attempt to restore the dignity of my people.

The response surpassed my most far-flung expectations. Church leaders, for their part, amazed me with pledges of financial support for construction. The young people astounded me more: On the spot, many of them volunteered their time and labor to help the Galilean villagers. I was grateful beyond words. And before I left Germany, churches were planning to organize and send out these volunteers as soon as possible.

And in Holland, the response was even more overwhelming. Wherever I traveled throughout the green, canal-veined countryside, I met a simple, plain-spoken people who were also hungry for words of peace. And they were eager for a true report about the Palestinian people.

Through a friend, I was introduced to Cardinal Alfrink, a leader in the growing, international peace movement called *Pax Christi*. The Cardinal, in turn, surprised me by arranging a meeting with Princess Beatrix, soon to be Queen of Holland, in her stately and flower-trimmed residence in The Hague. At this stunning reception, I was moved to tears when the Prime Minister presented me with a huge bouquet of roses—one for each year of the Palestinians' exile.

As I returned to Ibillin, I rode on a cloud of excitement. The German churches had promised finances and young workers; the Dutch churches had promised volunteers also. The Reformed Church of Holland and the powerful Inter-Church Coordinating Committee had pledged their strong financial support. A television producer had even cornered me to plan a documentary—"One Day of My Life in Galilee"—for Dutch national television.

However, when Nazarena and Ghislaine greeted me, frowning with worry over my travel-weary appearance, I realized that my excitement was for something else: A tremendous and growing group of people were becoming true intercessors for peace—not just for the preservation of their own countries, but for the future of the whole world. I was not alone.

The trip to Europe was a bright spot amid the growing tension in and around Israel. For several years the Middle East suffered many swift blows against any peace efforts. The most horrible were the murders of eleven Israeli athletes by a radical group of *fedayeen* at the Munich Olympics, and the 1973 Yom Kippur war—the third major Middle East war in twenty-five years. The PLO, which had been driven from Jordan by King Hussein, had settled in peaceful Lebanon from which it masterminded raids and the hijacking of airliners. The Israeli government, still fighting the symptoms without doctoring the real disease, quietly launched an aggressive plan in reprisal: first, to crush the PLO out of Lebanon at all costs; and second, to tighten its hold on Palestinians within Israel.

However, I tried to ignore the government sanctions against us—the land "reforms" that took away more and more arable land from Palestinian villages, the unwarranted week-long curfews particularly in the West Bank and Gaza at crucial times in the planting or harvesting of crops. In a time of private meditation, another of Jesus' sayings gripped me with force: *Work . . . for the night is coming. . . .* And I would work.

In the summer of 1974, I threw my energies into building another community center in the village of Fassutah. Some of the first young Europeans had arrived for a summer of volunteer work, and with them the promised finances, so we began construction at once.

I had driven to Fassutah one morning to deliver letters from Europe to several of the volunteers when a bank of village boys swarmed my car. "We talked to your friends last night, Abuna," one of them shouted, leaning inside the car window. "There were two of them and they asked a lot of questions—all about you and the center. They wanted to know what it was going to be used for. . . ."

He jabbered on, and I felt an uneasy curiosity about these men who called themselves "friends." The only description the boys could give me was so vague it could have been almost any two men in the country.

Since these phantom friends did not return, I brushed the incident aside. What captured my total attention was the amazing transformation in the people of Fassutah—just as it had occurred in My'ilia. As the center rose, the leaders were already planning bigger things: a library and eventually a school. Bishop Raya's instincts had been correct. With a little help and a common goal, the bent backs of these people were straightening. By working together they were building more than walls and windows, they were restoring the dignity that was a first step toward becoming first-class citizens again.

The following year began with the same running excitement that had carried me since my trip to Europe. With my work intensifying, and with more volunteers soon to arrive, I was fortunate that several men had become stalwarts in the church in Ibillin. Abu Mouhib, for one, was no longer the crusty policeman who used to swagger the streets, but a trusted brother. And though I was still leading services and was involved in community decisions, I had to trust to their wise judgment on some matters while I was busy in other villages. For in 1975, the cry came from Gish.

Gish was so remote that, unlike the more southerly villages which had some limited school facilities, it had few if any teachers to call upon and nothing but the most delapidated textbooks. They desperately needed a school. Since

Mother and Father had been living in Gish for the full twenty-eight years of our exile from Biram, acting as loving grand-parents to many of the children, I expected great support and an easy time.

But not so. The first problem began when Bishop Raya telephoned to say that he urgently needed to see me. When I arrived in his office, his face was ashen.

"I'll tell you straight, Elias. The Church has reassigned me. I'll be leaving for Canada very shortly."

I felt wounded. Reassignment is not uncommon for clergy in many churches. But in Bishop Raya's case I felt that the reasons were all wrong. Recently, he had sold a few of the Church's many land holdings to poor farmers at a very, very low cost. It seemed obvious to me that the hierarchy was distraught at the loss of their *terra sancta*, as well as Bishop Raya's outspokenness. And so they were removing him.

"Don't be upset," he said, his expression lightening. "It's not the Lord you're losing. And others are behind you—others who see our goals."

In a few weeks he was gone. Despite his assurances, things began to sour.

The new Bishop, it appeared, was bothered about projects and building plans over which he had no control. And some-how a dispute arose over the fact that Moslems were helping with the construction of the school in Gish and that Moslem children would be allowed to attend. Though I was disturbed, I offered to step out of the project entirely, trusting the people of Gish to make the right decisions. I certainly needed a rest. The people would not hear of it though, and it was also at their insistence that the Bishop finally gave his blessing.

What shook me most was a near-fatal "accident."

That summer, seven German boys had come to Gish to work on St. Chrysostom Academy, for that was what we had christened this, our first new school. Construction was moving rapidly—and then our phantom "friends" made their presence felt again.

Since Gish was so far from Ibillin, I made fewer excursions to the site each week. Early one morning in August, however, an urgent phone call summoned me—something about trouble at the school. I hung up impatiently, for I had pressing matters in Ibillin that day, and sped off—a little too recklessly—toward the upper Galilee.

A group of young men, German and Palestinian, were gathered outside the shell of the school when I sped into Gish. In their paint-spattered work clothes and boots, they nearly dragged me from the car.

"Abuna," said one German boy, "we had prowlers last night. We heard some noises, but when we got here we saw no one. Then this morning we found these." He pointed to the ground.

It had rained during the night, and the churned muddy earth was pocked with fresh footprints all around the building, leading inside.

"We haven't checked to see if anything was stolen or destroyed, but we decided to call you—"

I was not listening. I was angry. Angry about similar annoying incidents at the previous building sites. All seemed calculated to induce fear. What did these prowlers want? Were they, in fact, the same men who seemed to be stalking me from village to village? *Who* were they? And I was angry at myself for forgetting to post a watchman.

Like a charging bull, I stomped through the mud to inspect for damage. Gripping the main support of a huge scaffold, I swung myself underneath to get inside the building.

"Abuna! *No!*"

I jerked around to look at the boys who had seen—too late—that the support had been forced out of its mooring. And in that second, huge planks loaded with bricks and mortar pails thundered down at me. A sickening *crack* stung my head, and I was pitched down into the mud—away from the collapsing scaffold.

In a haze of pain I lay gasping for air. The boys were around me—distantly—shouting my name. As my eyes cleared, I reached up with dirt-covered fingers and gingerly touched my throbbing head. My hand came down soaked with red, and suddenly my eyes were stinging. I felt faint.

The boys lifted me to my feet. Once I had steadied, I refused their offer to go for medical help. Instead, pressing a cloth to my wound with one hand, I drove myself to a doctor nearby, where it took more than two dozen stitches to close the gash. I felt foolish at my own charging carelessness and angry at the men, whoever they were, who were trying to scare me. However, I would not give up.

Perhaps I might have recognized in all this the taming hand that seemed to be trying to slow me. I would do it my own way though, with dogged determination. And I hardly noticed that the inner quality that gave me stability—the very quality I was trying to teach my people—was dangerously strained. Even the completion of a comfortable apartment for me above the old parish house did not induce me to relax. Nazarena would peer at me with her dark, caring eyes, and Ghislaine would shake her head in a grandmotherly way, for they could see that I was becoming a brusque, snappish, driven man.

By the time the school in Gish was finished two years later, I was deeply engrossed in three major activities.

The first was the construction of a Peace Center in Ibillin.

In 1977, as we laid its foundations, the world was thrilling at the possibility for peace in the Middle East as Egypt's President Anwar Sadat made his famous pilgrimage to Jerusalem. Throngs of Israelis greeted him, cheering, weeping, hungry for peace after years of fighting. But peace was a long way off. Before Sadat's arrival, Prime Minister Begin told the press that Sadat would ask for a solution to the Palestinian problem and that anything but the present arrangement was impossible. Two years later, when the two leaders would sign the much-applauded Camp David peace treaty, their "solution" for Palestinians was so ambiguous it would prove useless.

As Jerusalem prepared to raise Egyptian flags to welcome Sadat, I knew that political agreements could not change hearts. My work in the community centers was all the more urgent if reconciliation was ever to come. In fact, I inaugurated each center by showing the film, *The Diary of Anne Frank,* so that Palestinian young people could understand the horrors Jews had suffered under the Nazis and forgive. And it was a warning against turning to violence. Always there were tears, for the story could well have been that of many Palestinian girls as well.

The second project was a youth camp. Since my years in Paris, I had often winced at the deprivation of Palestinian youngsters. For the boys there was only the endless game of soccer. And for girls, who were obliged to help in the home, there were few opportunities for recreation. So I had invited young people in several villages to camp beneath the olive trees of Ibillin for three weeks of sports activities, trips to the Mediterranean and teachings in the Scriptures. To my great joy, the five hundred young people we expected turned into a swarm of eleven hundred boys and girls. Each one was, to me, another living stone in the great bridge of understanding I wanted to build.

And thirdly, since my first speaking engagements in Europe, invitations had continued to come. I saw each one as a crucial opportunity to teach the Beatitudes, to proclaim the message of peace and to tell the outside world about our life in Galilee. I made several trips, first throughout continental

Europe where the Dutch television special and a few magazine articles about my work had drawn much favorable attention. In several countries there, and later in Ireland, I
marched with groups for the *Pax Christi* movement, raising
my voice with theirs against the threat of nuclear destruction
and militarism. On another occasion I was invited to India
where I read the words of Jesus, not only to Christians, but to
several thousand Hindus.

My travels would eventually take me to America and
Canada. Though I would have the privilege of speaking at
Harvard University, to me, the greatest support in these
countries came from many rabbis who invited me to speak to
their congregations. In Washington, D.C., for example, I
was a guest in the home of Rabbi Eugene Lipman of the
Temple Sinai, and in Chicago, I spoke to a large group at the
K.A.M. Isaiah Israel Congregation led by Rabbi Arnold
Jacob Wolf. I was pleased and grateful when many of these
rabbis sent me off, not only with their prayers but with gifts
of money for my work.

Like a parched man squeezing drops from a waterskin, I
drew encouragement from this outside support. Throughout
the Middle East, the political situation was swaying, and I
had begun to feel that I was teetering between hope and fear.

Real trouble was brooding just across the border in Lebanon. In 1978, in the wake of a two-year civil war, Lebanon's
so-called Christian Militia was still struggling against the
Moslems. The PLO had taken opportunity during the turmoil to entrench itself further, and now the Syrians were
intervening against the PLO. I sensed a deeper trouble, too,
for Israel was planning to send in "peacekeeping forces,"
which alarmed me. It alarmed large numbers of Jewish Israelis, too, for peace seemed so close, and popular anti-war

groups like Peace Now, Courage and Peace and others were protesting military involvement.

As the world watched our teetering scales of peace and war, the direction of my life tipped drastically.

In January 1980, I was again planning a special project for our young people. In three years the summer camps had burgeoned to include nearly four thousand from Akko on the coast to far Gish. My greatest hopes were pinned on these boys and girls, for from them I received the greatest rewards. One group of Moslem children, for instance, had presented me at the end of one camp with an inscribed tray. It said: "Thank you, Abuna. You have taught us how to love Christ."

But summer was still months away, and I had another exciting plan.

Whenever I worked with our young people, they prodded me—with an endless fascination—to tell about Biram and Ikrit which had become legendary. As I described our past, Father's prayers, Mother's stories, the rhythm of an easier time, I longed—deeply longed—for a place of quiet and rest, for my life had become such a whirlwind. To my delight my young friends listened, their faces intent with a wistful longing for such a place, too. I saw in these yearnings, a chance to usher them across the bridge of reconciliation with me.

On a crisp morning one month later, I was marching up the steep road to Biram. It was February 23, a special day for planting trees in Israel. Pacing along behind me were nearly four hundred Palestinian boys and girls, each excitedly bearing an olive sapling. We were going to plant our trees amid the ruins as a sign of peace to the government. I had sent special invitations to members of the *Knesset,* and I hoped that at least a few of them would come.

We climbed the sloping road, between groves of trees,

with white and gray clouds scudding across a cold blue sky, and my spirit quickened. I was going to show these young friends *my* Biram. The church, now fully restored, had been painted the previous summer by several of the German boys, and I had brought in a new bell to hang in its tower. I would ring the bell after . . . then my heart skipped.

Rounding a sharp bend, I saw in the road ahead a barricade of barbed-wire and a dozen jeeps. Behind the wire, their guns braced across their chests, were soldiers.

Behind me, the marching footsteps stopped uncertainly, but I did not look back. I kept on marching, my small olive tree held out in the open, right up to the barricade.

"Let us through. We have come with olive branches, not guns."

From behind his barricade, the commanding officer replied stiffly, "Go away. We have orders not to let you pass."

"Why?" I demanded.

"Those are the orders. You don't need any other reason."

Farther up the hill, where the road wound past Biram and on toward Lebanon, I could hear the growl of truck motors. What were they doing?

"We have come for peace," I said as calmly as I could. "What have *you* come here for?"

His eyes were unwavering. "I'm afraid that's not your business. Now leave."

When I turned, hundreds of other eyes met me. A moment before, they had been bright with hope. Now the light had gone out.

Later that night, I sat alone in my apartment. In front of me was a copy of the letter I had sent to the Speaker of the *Knesset*, Yitzhak Shamir, along with a surprise gift of almost four hundred olive trees. And in my mind's eye were the unforgettable faces of the young marchers. I had led them to a bridge and we could not get across. Could we ever?

And what does it matter? The thought surprised me. I knew it had been creeping around the edges of my conscious mind for months. I tried to fight it, listing the accomplishments—schools, libraries, community centers, the caring friends around the world. Somehow it was not enough.

I was forty years old, and feeling every bit of it just then. I had prayed and worked for something for more than thirty years. I was exhausted—and suddenly willing to be finished with it all. The sense that my moves were being watched had become too much.

Wearily, I rose from my chair, switched off the light and went to bed. It would take a good deal of time, perhaps, but I could begin a new life for myself.

Chapter 13

One Link

The morning sun was already blistering and I had a headache. It was July 1981. I was again walking on a hillside near Biram. This time I had come bearing, not an olive tree, but a casket.

Mother was dead. She had slipped from us peacefully in her sleep.

Age had eventually forced Mother and Father to move from Gish to Haifa to be near my sister and brothers. Mother's last wish was to be buried in Biram. It grieved me that she had died so far from the home she had longed for until the end. Atallah, Musah, Rudah and I set her casket beside the tomb, then took our place beside Father, Wardi and a hundred tearful relatives and friends.

Inadvertently, my hand slipped into my pocket and found the precious memento Mother had given me. Had she known death was so near when she parted with this small treasure? I fingered the familiar shapes—the doves and fish of her beloved necklace. One day she had surprised me by slipping it off and placing it in my hand. "Be strong, Elias," she had said. "What you do matters. Especially for the young ones."

"Grant her rest, O Lord . . . ."

Rest. I stared off over the heads of the mourners as the priest intoned, stared at the rising mountains and beyond them to Lebanon. When I had last come to this place more than a year before, I had concluded that there was no rest for us in this life. It was not just the aborted march with the olive trees that had convinced me. I was remembering a recent incident far more terrifying. . . .

I had been summoned by the Patriarch on Church business, and was traveling through Lebanon. Unknown to me, as I displayed my papers at the border, some unseen watcher was making a phone call.

Hurriedly, I caught a taxi and headed north toward Beirut. The driver launched a monologue that rambled on about recent skirmishes and the hardships his family was suffering in Lebanon's political turmoil. I listened politely, and in a while the jagged skyline of Beirut rose in the distance.

Just at the outskirts of the city, we stopped at a red light. I leaned forward to give the driver further directions—when suddenly the rear door next to me jerked open.

"Get out!" A man in dark clothing was shouting, pointing an automatic rifle just inches from my face. "Quickly. Or I'll shoot."

Another gunman stood at the driver's window, a weapon trained on the poor man. "You say nothing," he growled. "If you report this, we'll find you. We have your license number."

Reflexively, I grabbed my suitcase, and the two men shoved me into the back seat of an old car that had stopped beside us at the light. The men slid in on either side of me and the driver slammed down on the accelerator, squealing tires on pavement.

"Who are you?" I demanded. I wanted desperately to sound brave, but my voice quavered. "Where are you taking me?"

"Shut up," growled the man who had dragged me from the taxi.

"Just tell me what you want with me. I'm no criminal. I'm here on Church business—"

"*Shut up!*" he roared, his unshaven face red with anger. He cursed me furiously, and I dared not speak again.

For nearly an hour we drove around the outskirts of the city. If they were trying to confuse me as to my whereabouts, there was no need. I was too shaken to notice anything but the guns still cocked and ready.

Near West Beirut, they turned abruptly onto a rubble-strewn street amid decaying buildings. Men and women sat idly on steps as we sped by. And suddenly I realized that this place—more decrepit than any big city ghetto I had ever seen—was one of the refugee camps. Why were they taking me there?

We stopped before a two-story building on a deserted street and they dragged me from the car. "You won't be needing this," grunted one of the men, wrenching my suitcase from me.

Up a flight of stairs we marched, a gun muzzle stuck uncomfortably in my back. In a panic, I thought, *They're going to murder me and no one will ever know.*

Instead, they shoved me into a room that was no more than a cement cubicle. They did not enter, but slammed the door behind me. In the middle of the room was a table with one chair on either side. Trembling, I sat down, resting my forehead on the table.

In a moment, I tried to pray, and the only words that came to mind were from Psalm 33: *The eye of the Lord is upon them that fear him, upon them that hope in his mercy—to deliver their soul from death.* . . . I repeated these words of comfort as the minutes passed. I had no certainty that my kidnappers would not murder me and fling my body in some vacant building. But a quietness of spirit came over me.

After nearly half an hour, the door burst open. I looked up to see a short, handsome young man swagger in with the two gunmen following. On the young man's hip I spotted a pistol. He sauntered over and sat in the chair opposite me, staring with fathomless eyes.

He kept staring and finally asked with a cold directness. "What's your business in Lebanon?"

"I'm a Melkite," I responded. "I was on my way to see the Patriarch when your men—"

"The *truth!*" he shouted, startling me. "I want the truth. You call yourself Chacour, but who are you really?"

That he knew my name surprised and scared me. I realized then that this bantam of a man was not an ordinary thug, but part of an organization. He had power.

For the next forty-five minutes he alternately coaxed and bullied me, sometimes impatient to the point of fury. I could not understand why he was asking me questions on military matters, and said so. The gunmen at the door were getting restless. Strangely, the calm did not leave me. In fact, I got bold enough to challenge him.

"Look," I faced him squarely. "I am Elias Chacour. I have cousins in a camp near here. We were driven out of northern Galilee. My family lived in Biram where—"

"From Biram?" he asked, suspiciously. "If that's so, tell me about it. Who did you know there?"

Gladly, I named the village *mukhtars* and a dozen families. I described the coming of the soldiers. When I began to tell about my current work in the villages, the schools and community centers he stopped me.

"That's enough," he said quietly. "I believe you." He motioned to the men to put down their guns. "Please accept our apologies, Abuna, for scaring you. If you want to come and sit in my chair, I'll answer any of your questions."

Without hesitation I fired, "Who are you?"

With a respect as great as his former belligerence, he replied, "I'm a commander in the PLO, and you must understand that we are very much afraid for our women and children."

"Is that why you kidnap?"

"Please, Abuna. Let me finish," he pursued. "Our intelligence had learned that some three hundred infiltrators have been coming into Lebanon. They have orders to burn churches and mosques so that Christians and Moslems will turn against each other. But we know there is another purpose. Once Lebanon is in turmoil, they will sweep through and kill us—and not us only, but our wives and our babies, too."

I listened, still too rattled to comprehend this supposed plot he was revealing to me.

"And so we followed you from the moment you entered the country. I had to have my men pick you up for questioning."

"And if I had not mentioned Biram, what then? Who would have known that you brought me here—or what you did with me?"

"No one," he replied levelly. "No one at all."

Suddenly I was too eager to be free of that desolate room—away from these desperate-sounding men—to ask more questions. I asked if I might leave, and they politely ushered me outside to the car. The commander asked, "Where can we take you, Abuna?"

"Just leave me outside this camp," I said, trying not to sound too eager. "I can find my way somehow."

As we drove toward the outskirts of the camp, I noticed a group of small boys playing ball amid the litter. They were laughing and shouting, lost in youthful abandon. Despite their shabby clothing, they might have been the children of any other country in the world.

When at last the car pulled up to a curb at the far end of the street, I hoisted out my suitcase. Even if I had to walk a ways I suspected I could soon catch another taxi.

"By the way," I said, turning to the driver, "what do they call this place?"

"It's called Sabra," he replied.

Mother's funeral was over. Wardi helped Father into a waiting automobile, hurrying him out of the sun's heat, and I climbed in next to him. We wound our way down the hills as I drank in the beauty of the cedar groves, the streams that still cascaded even in the dead of summer. Beside me, Father looked regal even in his loss. I had not told him, nor anyone else, about my decision yet.

Many times the face of my kidnappers had come to me. Then, as now, I had concluded that this "plot" to kill them sounded far-fetched, like the paranoid hauntings of violent men. Still the kidnapping had been a large factor clinching my decision. It had taken some time to disentangle myself enough from work in the villages and the church in Ibillin, but I was ready. I glanced at Father. Wardi and my brothers would take good care of him. And I would visit from time to time. Visit, but not stay.

On previous trips to Europe I had been offered a teaching position at a prestigious, Christian university. My superiors would certainly have approved such a move, but then I had declined. Now, I convinced myself, I deserved a rest. More than that, I could most likely do more good for the Palestinian people by educating others to our situation. And after all, hadn't my travels brought in so much support in prayers and money over the years? And what more could I do here?

I would be leaving Israel.

It was a pleasant morning in September 1982, and I was traveling in West Germany, speaking again in various churches. That day in particular, I would be speaking to a group in Böblingen, a lovely town near Stuttgart. I rushed about the room, rummaging through my suitcase and muttering about all the things I had forgotten. Nazarena and Ghislaine had just nodded somberly when I had told them I would be sending for more of my things when I was settled. Then I would write to the Bishop.

But somehow, I was finding it hard to settle into the new life I so wanted. A few offers had come my way. I had even opened my mouth to accept one—but something inside had stayed me.

Not that my mind had changed. Two months earlier, in July, Israel had invaded Lebanon on a "peacekeeping mission," though many Israeli soldiers had accepted prison sentences rather than fight in what they felt was an unnecessary war.

So I had stubbornly set my face like flint to find my new life in Europe. Perhaps, I thought as I hurriedly drove to the church in Böblingen, I'll find what I'm after on this trip.

At the church, I began my usual talk on the Sermon on the Mount. As I went through the lessons I had learned about being a peacemaker, however, I felt a certain flatness about my words. In the audience, several people yawned and a man in the very front pew kept checking his watch. At the back, I noticed that a friend of mine, a woman I knew from previous visits to West Germany, had slipped in late. But, trying to push on with my faltering message, I did not catch her pained expression.

"And," I insisted, hammering home my points about reconciliation, "it does no good for you to sympathize with me as a Palestinian if it means that you hate the Jewish people as a result. That's not what I'm here for. We, all of us, have to become the preserving salt of the earth. Do you agree?" I asked, leaning into the microphone.

Many were nodding, but my friend in the back surprised me by jumping to her feet. It was then I saw her tears.

"Abuna," she said, her voice cracking, "You have not heard the news?"

"No, what news?"

"In Lebanon, near Beirut, they have massacred hundreds of Palestinian refugees. Men, women, babies. In two camps—called Sabra and Shatila."

I was aware that all eyes were upon me. Inwardly I felt only hazy, roiling emotions through the numbness. I could not go on speaking, but closed with a brief, stumbling prayer. As I hurried out of the church I scarcely heard the words of condolence.

"We are so sorry for your people."

"A tragedy."

One young man was shaking his head, with a look of such utter desolation. "Senseless. It's all senseless."

In my room I sat rivetted to the television as newsmen confirmed the horrifying tragedy in more vivid detail throughout the day. Scenes of buildings blown to rubble flashed on the screen, and splayed bodies. The announcers said that the death toll was climbing. Lebanon's own Christian Militia had swept into the camps, ostensibly to drive out the PLO. They had been allowed into the settlements by Israeli defense forces which had dismissed the multi-national peacekeeping troops, promising to protect the unarmed refugees. Instead the militiamen had machine-gunned everyone in sight—mothers with babies in arms, teenagers, old men and women too feeble to flee—and bulldozed many of the bodies into mass graves.

And, the reports continued, European sources in the Middle East had confirmed that Israeli troops had sealed off the two camps just before the massacre, warding off newsmen with the assurance that they were just "protecting" the camps despite the sounds of gunfire coming from within.

The Israeli government would balk at a worldwide outcry for a complete investigation. Only after Israeli citizens insisted, outraged at the massacre, would Prime Minister Begin concede. And the world would know the truth: Though Israeli soldiers had not actually killed the people of Sabra and Shatila, they had known it was planned and stood guard outside the camps while innocents met their death.

All over the world, reporters interviewed citizens who were shocked and saddened by the tragedy. Most moving were the scenes from Jerusalem where thousands of mourners—Jews and Palestinians together—had gathered in the streets, weeping and bearing candles.

One woman so poignantly expressed the anguish of the crowds amassing outside the *Knesset*. "I was awake all night crying and despairing," she said, her face a mask of pain. "What will become of us? What is happening to us?"

When I could watch no longer, I switched off the set and fell back on the bed. Before me was the face of the young PLO commander who had told me of his desperation. Was he among the dead? I remembered the bank of boys playing ball in the street. Were they buried in the rubble now?

Senseless . . . senseless . . . The words of the young man at the church in Böblingen tormented me. Certainly the killing was senseless, but not the lives that were lost.

Then I was remembering another band of small boys who were playing soccer in a sand lot years before. I was among them. I had found the arm buried in the sand. But I had lived. Was that, too, senseless? An accident? Chance? Or was there some reason that I had been spared?

Then I spotted it, lying in the suitcase I had flung open haphazardly that morning. Mother's necklace. It was the only memento from home I had packed. I rolled over, and the doves and fish jingled brightly as I lifted it.

With the sound, Mother's voice returned to me. *Be strong, Elias. What you do matters. Especially for the young ones.*

Now, suddenly, her words burned within me—burned with consuming force. If I simply allowed time to sift its dust over these latest deaths, I would be like those who had ignored the sufferings of the Jews for centuries, or like those who had turned their backs on my own people. Like those others, I had been trying to find the easy life of blindness to pain.

These thoughts sparked another memory, from the writings of the Apostle Paul to his friends in Colosse: *And now I am happy about my sufferings for you, for by them I am helping to complete what remains of Christ's sufferings on behalf of his body. . . ."* Here was mystery, a deep treasure of the faith that I had not understood before. Now I saw that Paul had given his hands and feet and tongue, his whole body, to carry on the work of Christ after His death—even if it meant the work of suffering.

Was I willing to go back, if it meant more hardship, living in the midst of violence—possibly death? Could I, by continuing the long, slow labor of teaching young people the treasures of the Sermon on the Mount, point them toward true peace? I was not sure, but I could only think of the faces I had just seen on the television—people young and old around the globe, weeping, linked by their yearning for peace.

That inner calm pressed in on me again, as I had not felt it for a long, long time—a calm that seemed to come from a familiar, taming hand.

I looked at Mother's necklace curled neatly in my palm. Each link was beaten and hand-fitted by some skilled craftsman. I had not fully known about peace before. It was not at all like a slim thread, as I had thought. Peace was like a chain. And every link was important in its rightful place.

Before me stood my two commitments—one to God and one to my people. They were inextricably bound together. And suddenly, I knew I would rather be on God's side which is stronger than human might.

Then I knew where I should be—not living in comfort, but back in the place where villages and churches were being reunited, where schools and community centers and spirits were being built up, where, amid the terrible noise of violence I could hear the whispers of the Man of Galilee, saying, *Behold, I make all things new.*

Standing, I walked briskly from the room, the old necklace clasped warmly in my hand. I had to find the nearest phone and book a morning flight.

Nazarena and Ghislaine would be surprised to see me.

———————————

Elias Chacour continues his work of reconciliation in the strained atmosphere of Israel, hoping to "change hearts, not simply institutions." His ventures are bold, often risky: Palestinian students visit *kibbutzim*; Jewish students live for short periods in Palestinian villages; Jewish and Palestinian educators face each other for head-to-head dialogue. Too, Chacour keeps a grueling schedule lecturing worldwide, always relying on the simple and urgent message of the Beatitudes. And though he is welcomed by friends on all continents, his home address is unchanged:

Fr. Elias Chacour
Ibillin
Galilee
Israel

References

1. Jonathan Dimbleby, *The Palestinians*, Quartet Books, New York, 1979, p. 86.
2. Jacques de Reynier, *A Jerusalem un Drapeau Flottait sur la Ligne de Feu*, Editions de la Baconniere, Neuchatel, 1950, pp. 71-76. Cited in Walid al Khalidi (Ed.) *From Haven To Conquest*, The Institute of Palestine Studies, Beirut, 1971, pp. 353-356.
3. Dimbleby, p. 35.
4. *Ibid*.
5. Chaim Weizmann, *Trial and Error*, London, 1950, p. 115.
6. Yehoshua Porath, *The Emergence of the Palestine-Arab National Movement 1918-1929*, Frank Cass, London, 1974, pp. 56-57.
7. Walter Laqueur, *A History of Zionism*, Schocken Books, New York, 1976, pp. 215-217.
8. Morris Ernst, *So Far So Good*, Harper & Bros., New York, 1948, pp. 170-177.
9. William A. Eddy, *F.D.R. Meets Ibn Saud*, American Friends of the Middle East, New York, 1954, pp. 36-37.
10. Elmer Berger, *Who Knows Better Must Say So*, The Institute of Palestine Studies, Beirut, p. 64. Cited in David Hirst, *The Gun and the Olive Branch: The Roots of Violence in the Middle East*, Harcourt, Brace, Jovanovich, New York, 1977, pp. 162-163.
11. Reported in the *Sunday Times*, London, June 15, 1969. Cited in Dimbleby, p. 10.

For Further Reading

The Arab-Israeli Conflict, Edited by John Norton Moore, Princeton University Press, 1974.

The Arab-Israeli Dilemma, by Fred J. Khouri, Syracuse University Press, 1968.

The Cairo Documents, by Mohamed Heikal, Doubleday, 1973.

The Gun and the Olive Branch: The Roots of Violence in the Middle East, by David Hirst, Harcourt, Brace, Jovanovich, 1977.

History of Palestine, by Jacob De Haas, McMillan, 1934.

A History of Zionism, by Walter Lacqueur, Shocken Books, 1976.

The Middle East, Yesterday and Today, Edited by David W. Miller and Clark D. Moore, Praeger, 1970.

The Non-Violent Alternative, by Thomas Merton, Farrar, Straus, Giroux, revised edition 1980.

The Palestinians, by Jonathan Dimbleby, Quartet Books, 1979.

The Politics of Jesus, by John Howard Yoder, Eerdmans, 1972.

The Thirteenth Tribe, by Arthur Koestler, Random House, 1976.

Whose Promised Land? by Colin Chapman, Lion Publishing, 1983.

STREETWISE

Streetwise

JOHN GOODFELLOW

WITH ANDY BUTCHER

KINGSWAY PUBLICATIONS
EASTBOURNE

To Floyd and Sally McClung

– for your love, friendship and humble walk with God

Contents

Acknowledgements

This book wouldn't have been written without the prayers, practical help and support of some very dear people.

First, I want to thank my wife, Terry, for helping me find the time to work on the manuscript, and providing the fine detail my memory missed. I'm grateful, too, for Mandy Butcher's patience in freeing her husband, Andy, to spend so many evenings at the typewriter putting our conversations together. Andy took this on despite his already heavy work load as Editor of Christian Family magazine at that time.

My sister, Trish, brother-in-law, Jamie, and Mum provided timely encouragement and comment as the project developed. Sister Joan helped in this way, too, as well as typing some of the manuscript along with Myrtle Thompson.

Finally, I'm indebted to Floyd McClung for his initial spur to put pen to paper, in the hope and belief that telling this story may be a way that God will touch and change other people's lives in the way he has mine.

I have changed the actual names of a few of the people and places where it seemed appropriate to do so. But most are identified, and all the incidents and experiences are recounted just as I remember they happened.

John Goodfellow

Introduction

Owning Up

I pulled the cast-iron gate closed behind me, and as it snapped shut I paused for a moment with my hand resting on the cold metal. 'It could well be bars of a different kind by tonight, John,' I thought to myself as I flicked the gate rods, taking a last look up at the house. Would I be coming back?

The prospect of this being a one-way journey brought my senses alive as I strolled up the quiet street in the cool, spring morning air. I looked around at the other houses – tall, well-decorated semis – as I passed by. How welcoming and warm they looked, with their bright front doors and stylish curtains. What a pleasant area this was to live in ... how could its calm, peaceful pleasantness have escaped me for so long?

Up round the corner I crossed the main road, busy with traffic heading for the city centre and another week's commuting and cursing the queues. My first appointment was over on the other side, a couple of hundred yards away. The muscles in my stomach started to tighten, and as the building loomed closer my steps slowed slightly.

Pictures of just what I could well be letting myself in for flashed across my mind, chased hard by the idea that I could simply crumple up the list I was fingering in my pocket, throw it away and forget all about this crazy business.

No one would ever know, after all. I could drop the screwed-up paper into the gutter, and it would soon be swept up with all the empty cigarette packets and fish-and-chip wrappers. Out of sight, out of mind. Just another scrap of litter on the municipal dump. Maybe a seagull would even carry it off somewhere remote.

But I knew that it wasn't really that easy. The refuse collectors may cart off the words I had scribbled there, but nothing could remove what they stood for. I had to complete the task on which I had set out. Straightening my tie again nervously, I took one last deep breath and pushed open the door. This was it.

It was just a few minutes after opening, so I didn't have to wait long before I was greeted by one of the clerks at the enquiries counter. She flashed me one of her best Monday morning smiles.

'Hello, sir, can I help you?'

'Good morning. Yes, please. I'd like to see the manager if that's at all possible.'

'Certainly. Could you tell me what it is in connection with, please?'

That threw me for a moment. I had a vague idea of what I intended to say, but I'd not expected to start quite yet. I hesitated. 'Well, it's very confidential and important. It needn't take very long. . . .'

She looked at me quizzically for a moment or two. Despite my best efforts, it was all too obvious that I wasn't used to living in a suit and collar. With my long hair and beard I hardly fitted the bill of the average businessman, and she seemed to notice that the tie felt as though it was tightening like a noose round the growing lump in my throat. She slipped away to an office at the rear.

The seconds stretched into long minutes, and I had to fight the urge that was rising in me to turn round and walk quickly out. It still wasn't too late to forget this crazy business! And then she was back, and with another smile she was opening the security door and leading me through into the manager's office, beyond the brass plaque and solid oak door.

Half-rising from behind his broad, dark wooden desk, he greets me with a smile that is checked by his obvious uncertainty as to quite what I want an appointment for. But he recovers his executive composure swiftly, and with a sweep of his right hand invites me to take the seat in front of him, set slightly at an angle.

The moment is here, the thing I've known has to be done. And despite the confidence I have that it is right, apprehension grips me. Only the anchor of my breakfast prevents my stomach from doing a double flip and leaping out of my mouth. Galvanised by anxiety, I don't even wait until he's seated again.

I stretch out my right hand to shake his, and launch into my half-rehearsed speech.

'Good morning' – accompanied by my best effort at a confident smile. 'Thank you for agreeing to see me. My name is John Goodfellow . . .' and as the words start to flow it's like a button has been pressed deep inside. A warm sense of security seems to flood my body. This is right, it's OK – everything is going to work out.

'. . . and I don't know if you remember me or not, but I was a customer of yours for several years.'

He looks at me encouragingly but without recognition. Fingers stroke the side of his blotting pad – green, clean and just changed for the coming week, no doubt – as he waits for me to continue.

'And, well, I want you to know that I have recently become a Christian, and I feel that God has told me to come to you today and to confess to the fact that I owe you a lot of money.'

His face registers confusion for a moment, and I press on to spare him having to try to respond.

'When I had an account here, I cashed many cheques with no way of meeting them from my balance, and then ignored all your letters demanding repayment. I did it intentionally and deliberately, with no thought of repaying you. I stole it all, in effect. I'm very sorry about that now, and I would like to ask your forgiveness for doing it, sir.'

He nods slowly and silently, with a continuing look of puzzlement, as I go on. 'And I would like to pay back all the money that I owe you. I hope to be starting work very soon, and will be able to post the first instalment to you in a fortnight or so, if that is all right?'

By now he seems more nervous than I was when I entered the bank a few minutes earlier. He laces his fingers together on the desktop and responds as though we have simply just completed an ordinary business transaction.

'Well, thank you,' as he takes my name and address, 'that all seems to be in order. Fine. We appreciate your having come in like this, and I look forward to receiving your first payment before the end of the month. Thank you.'

And within minutes I'm out on the street again, sucking in the fresh air with relief and gratitude. With rising confidence I step out across the road and on to the next address on the list.

By the end of the day I'd walked and talked myself bone tired. The feelings of nervousness before each appointment hadn't entirely gone, but they had decreased with each visit. It was a tremendous feeling to push open the front gate again – I patted it 'hello' as I came through – and walk up the path.

Since leaving home that morning, I'd visited half a dozen locations around the town and admitted that I had been a thief, a common criminal. I had explained how I had taken their money and property – in some cases without them ever having discovered the loss. I told them that I was sorry, and that I wanted to pay back every penny.

And I gave them the opportunity to call the police, if that was what they wanted to do – even though I was already due to appear in court to face another criminal charge, and knew that the reporting of any further offences would almost certainly ensure that I went to prison for a long time.

I'd been prepared to go down. The idea frightened me a little – my mouth had gone dry a couple of times as I explained the purpose of my unannounced visit, and waited to see if their hand would reach for the telephone. It had been a distinct possibility when I set out that morning. Back home, I was thrilled to have made my peace and been spared what could have been the harsh consequences.

But what burned even more brightly within me was the excitement of having been able to explain to a couple of those I had visited just what had made me set out on such an apparently risky and unnecessary venture.

It was the story of someone desperately trying to put together the pieces of a broken life. But for him it was like trying to complete an abstract jigsaw puzzle with no master pattern to follow. And as each piece in turn failed to fit, there grew an increasing sense of anger, frustration and despair.

Sex, drink, drugs, violence, crime, occultism; they had all tumbled together in a meaningless jumble. Until just when it seemed too late, just when there seemed to be no hope of making any sense of it all, he'd found the way to put the pieces in their right place.

He was me, and I had met Jesus Christ.

That list of addresses in my jacket pocket symbolised the first half of a life that had contained no hope and little meaning. With the new purpose I possessed, I was excited at what could be written on a clean sheet.

1

Street Fighting Man

The beer was free, and you didn't need to pay more than a half-hearted compliment to get one of the young holidaymaking girls to spend the night with you.

Working in a bar on Spain's tourist coast was everything I'd been promised and hoped for; an endless round of drink and free sex that somehow only made you thirst for more. And if the pace of fast living ever got a bit too much, there was always a plentiful supply of drugs to charge you up for another night of partying.

By daylight you would probably have just dismissed the Crazy Horse Saloon as a shabby, hastily-constructed set of a second-rate cowboy film. Thrown together in rough cheap wood, with a large verandah facing the dusty street, it seemed a little out of place only a couple of hundred yards from the beach at Santa Suzanna, a small seaside town just outside Lorette del Mar.

But by night it took on an altogether brighter image, putting on its best face for the public. It turned into one of the top nightspots for the young sunseekers who were flooding into Spain with the package holiday boom. Nightly, scores of young people from England, Holland and Germany crowded into the cavernous bar, where they would drink noisily and dance until 2 am – and later.

For a small-time crook with a drink problem and a growing dislike for the hard graft of bricklaying in the wet, cold British Midlands, it was like paradise. I had been delighted when two friends who had been contracted to run the place for the summer season asked me to join the bar staff. The fact that our drinks were on the house, for as long as we could stand on our feet, was an added bonus.

For some strange reason, the visiting girls were impressed by our macho image. They had come from their boring nine-to-five jobs in anonymous offices in grey cities, looking for a holiday romance. We were as close as they got. At the end of each night there would always be a group of them waiting behind – giggling, and slightly the worse for wear – for us to choose from. We'd pair off dispassionately and decide which couples would get to go back to the staff quarters – a cramped, dirty bunkhouse at the rear of the bar – and who would go back to the girls' hotels, where we would give the nightwatchmen a knowing leer as we crept past.

Most mornings I would wake up wondering first where I was, then who I was with, and finally where I could find a drink to get rid of the awful throb in my head. If we never even exchanged names, then it was all right by me; I didn't particularly want to see her again, and some of her friends would probably be in line the next night. Once the night's passion was spent, I couldn't wait for them to get their clothes on and go.

Then I'd stumble out of bed about mid-day, and meet up with the other lads for a large cooked breakfast, washed down by a few pints of beer to get the circulation going again. We'd swap stories and comments about the girls, comparing notes like buyers at a cattle market. Then it would be time to catch up on some sleep in the sun for an hour or so before heading off on our daily 'propaganda patrol'. We'd strut along the beach like we owned the place, handing out leaflets and urging all the sunbathers to come along to the Crazy Horse Saloon that evening.

Not that we worked hard for the sake of it. The more customers that were there, the more opportunity there was to rip them off or get them into bed – or both. It was as simple as that. We would be keen to see everyone spend as much as possible, so we'd whip up the party atmosphere, joining in the dancing and larking with the customers, generally behaving as though we were having a great time. But there would always be one eye out for the chance to carve an unwary girl away from her circle of friends, or to steal.

One of the simplest ways we found to make money on the side was to shortchange someone. As it started to get late, people drank more and the place became even more sweaty and crowded, so it was easy to delay returning with someone's change for a while. I'd keep half an eye on them and if they persisted I'd go and make a vague excuse about having been kept busy and then try to shortchange them, hoping they didn't notice. More often than not they didn't, and the secret pocket I'd made in my uniform would be bulging with stolen notes by closing time.

In an atmosphere charged with alcohol and sex, violence was never far away. We welcomed it with open arms and clenched fists as the only thing missing to make our job satisfaction complete. Partly we recognised that if we could win a reputation as the toughest team of bouncers on the coast, then we would have less trouble to cope with; and partly because we knew how it impressed some of the girls, and a little bit because we simply revelled in a good fight. So we dealt with any problems ruthlessly and efficiently.

If someone started to create a scene – maybe over a girl, a spilled drink or an unguarded remark – they would be bundled outside unceremoniously and given a swift beating, before being advised to get on their way. As far as we were concerned, the cardinal sin a customer could commit was to hit a fellow waiter. It happened from time to time if one of us was a little too slow in sorting out a situation, or if we were caught trying to get away with someone's change. But within seconds the assailant would be felled by two or three other bouncers.

Outside he'd be held down and kicked and stamped on viciously. We broke arms, legs and ribs – and laughed as the victims crawled away. As long as we didn't disturb the locals, the Spanish police didn't really care too much what happened to some unfortunate holidaymaker who'd had a bit too much to drink and maybe fallen on their way home.

We weren't too keen on allowing Spanish visitors into the saloon because they weren't as freespending as the well-heeled holidaymakers, and simply blocked the bar space, slowing down trade. We also had some complaints that the Spanish men were pestering the girls; claims that brought out a muddled sort of patriotic gallantry. So we tried generally to discourage them from staying too long – until one night.

It was getting on for closing, and most people had already drifted away. The floor was awash with spilled beer, empty glasses and cigarette packets, as usual. The air was thick with tobacco and the smell of cheap perfume. We were trying to clear up so that we could get away to meet the latest groups of girls, but a small group of local men insisted on being served with one last drink. They wouldn't take no for an answer, and then one of them reached out and swung an ashtray round, crashing it over Dave's head.

That was it. The place exploded in a flurry of kicks, punches and oaths. They were outnumbered, but the leader was a big bull of a man – he looked as though he had escaped from one of the local arenas. It took four of us to subdue him as his friends fled. Finally we battered him to the ground, and dragged him outside where we laid into him with our fists and boots. We left him in the dust, moaning quietly. When he fell silent, I thought that we might have killed him.

Satisfied that he was still alive, we spat on him and turned back inside. The thrill of combat led to more celebratory drinks all round, and inflated our view of ourselves as the meanest, toughest crew around. We enjoyed our notoriety, and were greatly pleased at the way customers held us in awe as the story of the fight was subsequently embellished and retold.

A couple of weeks later word filtered back through the grapevine that our victim had been badly hurt. He was a popular figure in the area, and had ended up in hospital with severe internal injuries, a broken arm, fractured leg and cracked ribs. The rumour was that a revenge attack was planned.

We took this threat seriously. In our off-duty moments we fashioned ourselves a brutal armoury to repel any would-be attackers. There were iron bars, wooden clubs with nails driven through or wrapped with barbed wire, bottles and bricks. I selected a three-foot long wooden stave and painstakingly carved jagged teeth into the end. When we had all finished, we posed for a photograph, trying to outboast each other as to what we'd do if called on to use our weapons. Wearing building site hardhats and clutching our batons and bars, we lined up for the photographer with big grins, in a crude parody of a victorious football team.

For a week or so we were especially careful to be on our guard, and meticulous about checking every visitor to the Crazy Horse Saloon. But then the free drink and rich pickings must have made us careless. One night I was grabbed by the arm by one of the other waiters as I passed from the bar with a trayful of orders.

'Johnny, look over there in the corner,' he shouted in my ear, above the drumming disco beat.

'Where?' I turned and looked where he was pointing. Over in the corner, in one of the darker parts of the room, away from the dancefloor, were a couple of faces that seemed familiar from that earlier night. We both scanned the room more closely, and to our horror spotted two or three other young men who had been involved in the fight.

A hurried council of war was held at the bar, and we decided that we had better close early. Some excuse was offered by the DJ, and we managed to usher everyone out apologetically. Then we locked and bolted the doors, and gathered together at the shuttered windows. A small group of men could be seen standing just at the end of the street. Wolf cries and shouts carried as we reached behind the bar for our weapons.

All went quiet for a few minutes, and then they were at the door. They must have been using a log or a bench as a battering ram, because they pounded their way in through the heavy doors. As soon as they burst through we set upon them, and a bloody brawl ensued in the darkened bar. Chairs were thrown and sticks swung. We managed to beat them back and then, suddenly, they bolted.

Inflamed by the fighting, we whooped and ran out after them into the street. As we turned the corner in pursuit we realised what a dreadful mistake we had made. There were another fifteen or so heavily-armed men – batons, bricks and bars – making more than thirty in all. The others stepped in behind, blocking our escape. The twelve of us had run straight into a trap.

Fear and hatred swirl together to fuel my arms as I swing them wildly around my head, lashing out with my stave in all directions. Everywhere around me in the grey moonlight is a blur of bodies, a fog of violence. Screams of pain and shouts of fury mix with the sickening thud of wood and metal on flesh and bone. Grunts and sighs follow the impact.

The sheer weight of numbers presses us back, and in a moment of rational thought plucked somehow from the storm of the fighting I realise: 'If one of us goes down, we'll never get up again. They aim to kill us!' My blood runs cold.

A thick-set, curly-haired man with an iron bar lunges forward, trying to smash it across my head. I manage to jerk to one side, ducking his blow, and swing my heavy rod savagely, clenching my teeth to throw every ounce of aggression into the movement. It connects, shattering his cheekbone, and jarring my hands painfully. I give out a satisfied yell before stepping forward, pulling my stave back ready for another strike. 'Come on, which one of you is next!'

The fear has gone. In its place is an ordered, calm appreciation of how pleasing it is to inflict serious injury. I face the next man stepping into my path and try to decide where to hit him for the maximum damage, with grim enjoyment.

It's still and quiet all of a sudden, but for the gasping for breath and raw terror all around. We face the other gang, a few yards away, and are sharing a common thought – the fighting seems to have transformed us into a machine of violence. 'It's no use us trying to run for it: we'll never make it. . . .'

By now the smell of violence has intoxicated me so much that it seems to have triggered off my last safety valve. 'OK, then, let's go and get the dirty . . .' and with a roar I spring forward, leading a charge at the surprised enemy.

Pain bursts across my face in a rainbow of sensations, and there's something warm on my cheek. Blood. A hurled brick splits open the skin, down to the bone, as broken bottles, chains, bars and other weapons are wielded again.

Triumph fills me as I see them start to break and run. It takes a few moments to realise that it's not us they're fleeing from. Residents terrified by the vicious battle boiling over in the street below their windows have called the police. La Garda has arrived in force.

I drop my stick to the ground and touch the wound on the side of my face gently. The fighting is over, and all I can think is how I wish I'd had the chance to smash someone else real good before it ended.

Not surprisingly, we weren't exactly popular with the Spanish authorities. But the locals with whom we had been tangling hadn't wanted to hang around to explain what was going on, so we poured out a story of how we had been defending ourselves from an attempted armed robbery.

I don't think they really believed us for one moment, but there were no other witnesses to the fighting's early moments. So they had no choice but to believe our tale and leave the matter there.

Pretty soon any vague memories of having been scared or horrified by the brutality had been washed away in a few rounds of celebratory drinks, and our reputation grew. For the next few weeks we were even granted a police guard to make sure that there were no further 'attempted robberies'.

Thankfully, the policemen who were keeping a protective eye on us didn't step inside, though. Had they done so, what little tolerance they had left for us would have evaporated instantly. The Spanish authorities were ruthless in opposing the spread of drugs – there were harsh penalties for people found possessing or pushing. But that didn't stop us from risking arrest.

Even just a few weeks of living with my foot hard down on the accelerator had swept away any last grains of self-control or restraint that I may have possessed within me. I soon found myself using drugs heavily, despite having sworn to myself that I would never touch them again after a frightening first-time experience.

It had happened the previous year – again in Spain, on my first working trip for the summer season. It had turned out to be fairly unsuccessful, because by the time I arrived all the good jobs in the bars and discos had already gone. I managed to find temporary work in a small drinking place in Lorette del Mar, but it was well off the beaten track and I soon got bored. It had none of the action I'd been promised. To pass the time after closing, one night, I went along to the disco-bar popular with all the other English seasonal workers.

There, over a couple of beers, I was offered a tab of

LSD – 'acid' – and being a little curious, and a lot concerned that I shouldn't seem chicken, I'd swallowed it down. But as the psychedelic drug bubbled through my bloodstream, I was pitched into a frightening trip.

Sitting at a corner table, trying to keep a grip on my rebelling senses, I glanced around and had to rub my eyes hard. It was no good; they were still there. As I gazed around, all the other people – dancing, drinking, talking, laughing – had pigs' heads. It was like something out of a bizarre, comic opera and I laughed aloud to myself, oblivious to the way people looked at me with concern. This was amazing! But it was like being on a rollercoaster, where after every plunge you were slowly and surely winched up for what you knew would be another shock. Yet there was no way to stop it all happening. You just had to sit there and hope that, somehow, you would come through.

The walls started to blister and ripple, seeming to expand and contract in time with my breathing. Colours began to dance in front of my eyes; beautiful globules of rich reds, yellows, blues and greens, twisting and melting into one another in front of me like a giant paint palette. Then I saw that some of the people around me were surrounded with some sort of a strange glow that pulsated in time to the beat of the music. It was like watching colours breathe, with the shades rising and falling in time with my own inhaling and exhaling. As the night wore on, my mind and imagination continued to turn loops and spirals, and I was thankful when the sensations of sight, sound and smell began to recede; so I could finally collapse into bed.

Next morning those experiences seemed frustratingly close at hand, yet impossible to reach. But while I had emerged unscathed, I was too scared or too cautious to risk another 'trip'. The story my friends had told of their group experience – when they had been horrified to see each other apparently with their heads chopped off, blood gushing from the severed arteries – had been enough to convince me of the hazards of dabbling any more.

Besides, I argued, plenty of drink and the chance of 'pulling' a girl were all that I needed.

That's how it had been until the Crazy Horse Saloon. But by the height of the season, my body was already crying out. An endless round of heavy drinking, not enough sleep, poor diet and promiscuous sex was taking its toll. So one night when we were introduced to 'boogaloo' we thought that it was the answer to all our needs.

Amphetamine, speed, uppers — it had a variety of names, but the same effect. After an hour or so, the first four or five tablets would start to make me buzz. It was as though someone had started up a generator deep inside that began throbbing away, pouring more energy into my system. I felt wildly alive, and would talk away nineteen to the dozen, my words accompanied by rapid action and body movements. The rush of the drug kept me constantly fidgety; on the move. It was uncomfortable to stand still for even a moment without hopping from one leg to the other, and we'd serve and carry drinks at a furious pace.

By about midnight it would be time to drop some more, and these would send us scorching through until 3 am or later, when the final late-drinkers were either guided or carried out. But by then we would most likely be too wide awake and full of energy to consider sleep, so we would go into town and meet up with some other English lads for further drinks sessions. With so much 'boogaloo' inside me I felt like King Kong. It pumped me full of all the confidence I lacked in my sober times, and I thought that I'd found what I required to make my life complete.

Sometimes we would push even our stretched bodies and minds to the absolute limit. We would be so switched on that we didn't stop for two or three days at a stretch — partying, working, more partying and more working.

And even then, finally, it was a question of little more than collapsing on the sand for a couple of hours' sleep during the afternoon before getting up, washing another handful of tablets down with a beer or two, and getting ready for another night at the Crazy Horse Saloon.

By and by, though, the numbers started to trail off, and the temperatures began to cool. It was getting towards the end of the season, and after a final, drunken celebration, the cowboy bar pulled down its shutters for the last time that summer.

In a matter of just a few short months, the paradise I thought I had discovered, had exacted a huge toll. My weight had dropped to just over eight stone. My teeth and gums were sore and yellowing. My hair was lank and falling out, and I was addicted to consuming huge quantities of alcohol and drugs.

The party was over, the girls had gone. And as I packed my bags and returned to Nottingham with no job lined up, and the few pounds I had managed not to squander out of the hundreds I had earned and stolen – I wondered just for a moment if it had all been worth it.

For all the girls I'd been with, all the good times my friends and I had drunk to, I arrived home feeling just as empty as I could always remember.

2

Distant Relatives

I'd known from an early age how it was possible to be in the middle of something and yet feel on the outside. That's what home had always been like. Our house was always the centre of a lot of noise, laughter and high party spirits — yet even as a small child I seemed to be isolated from it all. Everything always seemed to be going on just beyond my grasp, and this inability to reach out was like a clamp that squeezed me tight inside, keeping me squashed and distant.

As first-generation settlers in England, my parents were keen to remember their Irish roots, and most weekends the house would almost hum with the music and dancing. Crowds of friends would be invited back from the local pubs for more drinking, dancing and remembering 'the old days'. Many tears were shed as the whisky and beer added a rosey hue to the memories of what were, in reality, more often than not hard times. And then the blows would follow as the spirits quickened fiery temperaments.

Dad had arrived in England as a young man back in 1930. He was a Roman Catholic from Tempo, a small farming community north of the border, not far from Enniskillen, where even then the seeds of sectarian enmity were being sown. Despite his willingness to work hard and a capacity for tough labour, he was unable to find regular work. So, like so many of his friends before him, he looked 'across the water' to where opportunities for hard physical work were plentiful and, by comparison, well rewarded.

He soon found work digging roads with a pipe-laying company in Kent. Tall, broad and with a talent for playing the fiddle, he quickly became a popular figure among the expatriate groups that would meet most nights of the week to drink to and sing of the beloved homeland they had left behind. It was through one of these Irish nights that Harry Goodfellow, or Paddy as he was more commonly known, came to meet a young lass by the name of Bina.

She was from Macroom, near Cork, south of the border. Also a Catholic, she had shown her strength of character and independence at the tender age of fifteen by running away from home to seek employment in England. As one of eight children, she had experienced a happy childhood, but had decided that she wanted still more out of life. By making contact with an older sister who had already made the crossing, she was able to find work as a private maid in Sevenoaks.

By the time they married, Dad had secured a better job, working for Fremlins brewery in the same town. Settling into their first home – rented rooms – my older brother, Tony, was born within the first year of their new life together.

Joan arrived seven years later and I weighed in at just under seven pounds, three years after that. By that time the Goodfellows had moved on again, to the Midland town of Nottingham. The industrial heartland of Britain was growing healthily, and Dad had decided to relocate the family after being invited to go into business with relatives. They operated a haulage company that transported open-cast coal around the region. It suited his temperament down to the ground, combining hard work with a personal pride in giving value for money and good, reliable service. The business prospered, and soon our home was a comfortable, well-appointed house with its own garden – a far cry from my parents' early days.

Dad was well liked and respected by customers, colleagues and friends alike. He was uncompromising, but also scrupulously fair by his own standards of behaviour. He also prided himself in caring for his family – but his love for a drink with the boys would sometimes leave good intentions unfulfilled. On countless occasions I would hear my mother and father rowing late into the night about the money he wasted on drink and friends. What was a man if he couldn't look after his own mates, he would counter, and they would scream back and forth at each other. Sometimes they would throw more than accusations and insults, and I would hear crockery and ornaments crashing against the wall. I remember kneeling against the bannisters at the top of the stairs, my eyes squeezed tight and my jaw clenched hard in the forlorn hope that I could make it all go away.

When they really set to with each other, their rage seemed to know no limits. Dad was always doing home improvements around the place: he spent many hours putting new panelling in around the stairs. Not long afterwards there was another homecoming row after the pubs had shut, and in uncontrolled anger he systematically put his fist through every piece of board that he had only just finished fitting.

I would lie in bed at night – sometimes awake for what seemed like hours – with dread in my heart. What if she really left him, as I'd heard her threaten? I wished so much that they would stop fighting, but their violent disagreements just seemed to fuel their relationship, and act as a strange kind of cement for the love they had for each other, but just couldn't seem to express more tenderly.

Although Dad endeavoured to care for us all well in practical ways, we never seemed to spend much time together as a family. He would either be working long, hard hours, or he would be drinking with his friends down at one of the local Irish pubs.

So I used to relish the times when he would arrive home in time for a big, cooked tea before slipping his jacket on to stroll off for a few beers. Together with Tony and Joan, I'd clamber up onto the sofa with him and beg him to tell us one of his war stories.

He had been one of the first into the services when war had been declared in September 1939. As a bombardier in the Royal Horse Artillery, he had landed in France with the British Expeditionary Force and shared the belief that Germany's military arrogance would be sorted out very quickly.

Dad would hold us all spellbound as he told how he had been in the thick of the fighting in those early days. The British infantry had been forced back under heavy artillery fire, and soon the crack Panzer tank divisions were pushing through. Dad's unit was ordered to blow up their own guns to prevent them being taken and turned on the British army. Then they were to fall back, after delaying the German advance to allow the others to make their way to the French shores.

During their flight, Dad and his group found themselves caught in a bombardment that had them pinned down in a wood for three nights. They joked about sending one of their number over to a nearby vineyard to bring back some bottles to help pass the time. And when they drew straws in a jokey poll, Dad pulled out the short one. True to character, he then took the bet as a serious pledge – and snaked his way over to the building, despite the risk from shells landing all around. Once there he had to lie low for five hours while another barrage screamed overhead, before returning, grinning with his grape trophies.

'And, you know,' he would always say, pausing in the tale as we looked at each other with wide eyes, ' I believe that the hand of God was on me then. . . .'

This conviction was born out of what he said happened next. Arriving finally at Dunkirk, Dad and his friends found a scene of carnage and chaos. Heavy casualties were being inflicted on the British forces as they were plucked from the beaches by an armada of small boats. Dad and his mates dug themselves into foxholes in the sand as they waited their turn to find a spare seat on one of the craft bobbing up and down as close to shore as they dare come. At last they were given the order to run for one of the boats, and they set off at a dash across the sand.

As they charged into the water, two of his friends made for the nearest boat, shouting for him to follow. There were spaces for eight or nine men on board, and they were first in line. But something deep inside told Dad not to head that way. 'No, not that one lads,' he screamed, grabbing them by the arms and pulling them back. Instead they waded across to their right and another, smaller craft in the distance – and as they did so, a direct hit shattered the other boat and the men on board.

Arriving back in Ramsgate on a small liner called The Daffodil, Dad was allowed home leave like many of the other fortunate Dunkirk survivors. And when he returned for further service, he had another experience that convinced him that there was some divine intervention in his military service.

He was due to be posted overseas to Burma when, shortly before, a bout of food poisoning – ironically on his home visit – had him hospitalised for weeks. In fact it was so serious that his stomach was affected for the rest of his life. By the time he was well enough to be discharged from hospital – and the services – his unit had already gone ... and later suffered massive losses in the Battle of Irawodi against the Japanese.

These experiences had obviously made a great impact on him, for he told these stories with a mixture of wonder and curiosity. And while the whisky may have raised passions and added lustre to other yarns, these wartime memories never altered whether he was sober or not.

After listening to Dad recall those days, I would jump down from his knee and play soldiers with the rifle he had carried back from Dunkirk – a long, heavy weapon handed to him by a Belgian cavalryman during their flight. I'd shoot imaginary enemies, and puzzle over why God, whoever he was, would be interested in my father.

It never occurred to me that this was one and the same person about whom so much fuss was made each week. If Saturday nights meant a party without fail, then Sundays meant church with a fuss. Coming down for breakfast, the rooms would be stale with the smell of beer, whisky and cigarettes.

Mum would be struggling to get us all dressed, smart and ready for morning Mass, while also organising breakfast and making sure that the Sunday lunch was ready to go. All the while she was busying herself she would be grumbling about last night's party and complaining to Dad, who would be nursing a hangover that screamed for relief, or another drink.

Somehow, though, we would all manage to squeeze into our best clothes in the nick of time, and march off solemnly down the road together to St Patrick's, the big, square redbrick church on the corner.

It's dark, cold and confusing. All the adults sandwiched in around me, solemn-faced and weary-looking, are standing and sitting at regular intervals like some sort of a party game. They are talking, flat-voiced and disinterested, in a language I don't understand. I know it's so terribly important to be here – it must be, judging by the arguments we have making sure we arrive in good time – but I can't seem to work out why, because no one seems to be enjoying it.

I'm certainly not; nor, as I squirm to look round, are any of the adults, as far as I can see. Their faces seem grey and set, their minds on something other than what's happening here. Dad's fingers reach out to pinch me, to stop me from fidgeting, but it only makes me feel even more uncomfortable. How many hours is it since we slid in here, nodding our heads at the altar on the way?

Dad's in an even worse mood than most Sundays because we were a little late setting off. That means we haven't managed to find a space in one of the hard, wooden form rows. In one way I'm glad, because they make me want to wriggle about even more, but that only makes Dad even more annoyed with me. On the other hand, no seat means that we've got to stand up at the back here, hemmed in by all the other latecomers. There is an almost overwhelming aroma of fetid breath and suited bodies, and I feel as though I'm drowning in a sea of tailor's dummies. I'm not tall enough to see what's happening up in the front, and the back-and-forth responses drone on over my head. I crane my head forward as Father Saul approaches and leans towards us; it's worth catching a smell of the pungent incense to stifle some of the other less sweet odours.

At the back of the church on the way out, I look again at that picture of Jesus, similar to the one we've got hanging in all the bedrooms at home. He's looking out in a mournful, wistful sort of way, with two large wounds on the palms of his hands. There seems to be a lot of blood about, and I'm told that he died for me. I don't know how or why, though, and I find the idea rather disturbing. Sometimes I think that he's looking out at me accusingly.

Although it's horribly boring in here, at least it's quiet for a while and there are no rows. It's almost enjoyable for that reason alone. But I know that they'll be falling out again only too soon. In a few minutes — though it seems like days, it's all going to be over again for a week, thank goodness — all the waiting and standing and sitting and looking serious. Then there is going to be a mad rush out of the doors, when all the men disappear in a cloud of cigarette smoke as they light up in unison.

Then Dad and his friends will smile for the first time in the last couple of hours and saunter off down to the pub, while the children will head back home for lunch with Mum. Later there will be more arguments, shouts and confrontations when he rolls home too drunk and too late to eat. She will throw it at him, or the wall perhaps, and there will be screams and scuffles. Then he'll fall asleep until teatime, and as I climb into bed I will look over at that strange picture to see if the blood's stopped flowing yet by any chance. It never has.

The only time I can ever remember church without a fight was at my first communion. Dressed in white robes and sighed over by relatives and family friends, I was chosen to carry the banner in the parade of children receiving the sacraments for the first time, which made Mum very proud. Afterwards there was a party with tea and cakes and soft drinks laid out on trestle tables in the yard behind the church.

There was one bright spot on Sundays, though. After Dad had eaten his lunch – if it was still edible – and slept off most of his lunchtime drinking, he would often take us down to the local cinema, at the bottom of the street. It was a fairly tatty old picture house, but I remember it with great affection because it was one of the few times that we ever did anything together as a family. True we didn't speak to each other and it was dark, but as I sat there in the flickering atmosphere watching the cartoons and features, I used to drink in the sense of closeness, contentment and well-being. I used to wish that I could catch hold of it and take it home with me, but when the final credits had rolled we would head back to the house and reality.

Somehow all the good times seemed to get spoiled. We would make a great effort at Christmas, on St Patrick's

Day and birthdays to enjoy our family celebrations, but something would always go wrong. I'd invariably end the day feeling desperately unhappy because what had begun with such high hopes had ended in arguments and bitterness again.

Even without visitors and guests – of which there was an endless stream – ours was a busy house. Yet I still felt alone and left out. I shared a bedroom with Tony, but with his being ten years older he didn't have a lot of time for a baby brother. Sometimes at night I'd be terrified by the thought that there was a monster lurking under my bed, just waiting for the right moment to snake out a tentacle or a scaly hand and drag me under. I'd call out, and plead with Tony to check that I was safe, but he'd only jeer and tell me not to be so stupid. At times the fear was so heavy that I'd pull the sheets high up over my head and whisper: 'Please, God, don't let them get me, don't let them get me.' I didn't know who God was, whether he could hear me, or if he'd have any interest in helping me should he be listening. But I felt that I had nowhere else to turn, and my terror made me clutch at any straw.

I felt closer to my friends than I did my family. Although my sisters were nearer to my age than Tony, we never seemed to get on – there were always fights and rows over what belonged to who, and whether we were allowed to use it. My best friends were the boys I played with out on the streets near our home. By the time I started secondary school, we'd lost the nice, comfortable house with the garden. Dad's business involvement had turned sour, and he'd lost everything. As he tried to get another business going, a corner café, we moved into tatty rented rooms at the top of a private house on the London Road. This was one of the worst slum areas of Nottingham, directly across the road from the county football ground. We always knew when one of the teams had scored from the roar that went up and sailed through the windows.

Our family squeezed into the three upstairs rooms, and we shared the bathroom and kitchen with the owner and her son Keith. He was one of my closest mates, and we ran and played together in the street most days. We were careful never to venture too far, though. The crowded, back-to-back houses and alleyways were a maze of small communities, and there were only a few streets within sprinting distance of our front door where it was safe to walk. Go too far afield, and we would get set upon by the local gang for daring to venture onto their territory.

For all the hardships, there was a strong sense of community in the predominantly Irish neighbourhood. This sense of national spirit was important to my parents, whose lives seemed to centre on the weekly gatherings to reminisce and sing the songs they had grown up with. So much so, that when the opportunity came to better ourselves and move on out, it didn't last long.

With conditions being so cramped for our growing family, Dad was one of the first to be offered corporation housing in the Woollaton district, a new suburb being created on the other side of Nottingham. When we moved into our new house, the estate on which it was situated still hadn't been completed. To reach our front door we had to clamber across planks, over the unmade main road.

Although it was the best-equipped and maintained home they had ever lived in, my parents just couldn't seem to settle. They missed the local pubs and the bustling sense of neighbourliness, the nosiness and the squabbles. After just a few months they moved out, and packed us all back to the slumland area – this time into the very heart of the notorious Meadows district. By now Dad's fortunes had improved slightly, and he had managed to get a job as a steel erector on the new power station sites springing up around the region.

The sites were dangerous and demanding places to work. But they suited my father down to the ground. He was made foreman, which meant that he had to keep the hard-drinking, wild migrant workers in check. It was a job that demanded quick thinking, a quick tongue and quick fists. He had all three.

Once he found out that a scaffolder's shoddy work had put an entire team at risk as they worked high up; so he had him sacked. The angry worker – a big, broad Cockney – came down to the Meadows looking for Dad. He found him in one of his favourite locals, and went in to challenge him to a fight. Dad went outside with the man, and laid him cold, flat out on the pavement. When he came round, he took the man back into the pub and bought him a beer. They became good friends.

The good money Dad earned meant that we were able to rent a large, rambling house in Wilford Grove, a tree-lined street from the centre of which you could see the top of Nottingham Castle, cresting the highest point of the hill a couple of miles away. Dad renovated the house from top to bottom, and in addition to throwing the doors open at weekends for parties, we began to take in Irish lodgers who were working in the sites and roads up and down the Midlands.

Among the tenants in our double-fronted home was a cousin who came home drunk one night and got into a violent argument with Mum. It ended with him attacking her and then Tony, who tried to go to her assistance. When Dad came home, he beat the man up savagely and threw him out of the house.

We thought that was the end of it until later that night. With screams and oaths, the man burst through the front door brandishing a wicked-looking butcher's knife. 'I'm going to kill you all,' he screamed in a drunken rage. Dad bundled us all into the front room, and held the door closed as the cousin ranted and swore on the other side. Then he began to attack the door, and I watched in horror as the blade started to break through the thin panelling.

Thankfully, neighbours must have realised that the

commotion was more than the usual and called the police. They arrived just in time to disarm him and bundle him away.

After that, Dad redoubled his efforts to teach me to fight. He'd show me how to punch and guard myself, and insist I repeated the manoeuvres until I'd got them right. He'd also train me repeatedly so that I knew just how to knock someone to the floor with a swift kick of the legs.

'The best way to settle an argument, Johnny,' he would tell me earnestly, 'is to get the first punch in. Worry about the talking afterwards.'

3
Letting Go

Dad's bruising philosophy became the hallmark of my young life. And it was in the second year of school that it exploded in a fashion that was to be repeated – with increasing ferocity – in the years to come.

My first day at school had been fun. Everyone at St Patrick's, the small primary school attached to the local church, made a special effort to make us feel welcome, and I really enjoyed it ... for the last time in my whole school life. I soon discovered that this was not a bright new world opening up in front of me. It quickly became apparent that I was not suited to the academic life.

These days it might even be given a special name and put down to some sort of learning difficulty. Then I was just written off, at an early age, as one of those who wasn't going to go very far. They never actually said so, but I picked it up from the teachers. They took more time and care with some of the brighter kids in the class, while my efforts were hurriedly looked over, if at all.

The feeling of being on the outside of things extended from the classroom into the playground. Although I'd had regular 'lessons' from Dad, I wasn't too confident about getting into a tumble. Photographs of me at the time show that I was smaller than average; and they also capture a pinched expression on my face that I couldn't hide. It was a combination of alienation and fear. The playground scared me; its openness and seeming free-for-all in the rough and tumbles. To make matters worse, the school bully – ginger-haired Mick, who was about two years older – seemed to have antennae that picked up my uncertainty. He regularly singled me out, goading me and making fun of me. I longed to lash out and hurt him, but fear of retaliation kept the anger locked inside, where it brewed quietly.

Then, one day, the pressure became too great – and the lid came off. I'd spent ages in a craft lesson modelling a clay submarine. Not being a scholarly success, I'd been pleased to find something I was fairly good at, and was keen to finish some handiwork that I could take home to show off to Mum. Praise for my schoolwork was rare; this would be a real treat.

The piece had been lovingly finished, and then fired, and I was carrying it carefully home along the streets after school when I turned a corner and came face to face with Mick. He was idling along with some friends in tow. They saw me and came over.

'What have you got there, Goodfellow?'

'Nothing ... I'm just on my way home.'

'You're lying. Come on, let's have a look,' and they forced me to reveal my gingerly-held treasure. As I lifted it up for them to see, Mick whipped a hand forward and shoved, pushing the model out of my hand. It fell onto the pavement and shattered into a dozen pieces. He laughed harshly, as his friends smirked and giggled.

All the bottled-up frustration, loneliness, insecurity and resentment must have escaped in a single, fizzing rush of emotion. I'd never normally have considered taking him on, but I screamed at him: 'You rotten swine, I'm going to kill you for that!'

He looked at me contemptuously and sneered. But his expression turned to bewilderment and then alarm as I balled up my fists and started screaming and lashing out wildly. He jumped back, turned and stumbled away, and even as it all happened in a flash, I sensed a rush of excitement at the realisation that my unguarded rage had scared him, and given me the upper hand.

My hands were empty when I got home from school that day, but I felt as though I'd found something special. If I just let go and gave my feelings free rein to express themselves through my fists and feet, then even the biggest, toughest opponent could be made to listen. Suddenly I realised that I didn't need to feel intimidated by anyone else if I was prepared to make sure they had more reason to fear me.

This lesson made me feel more physically secure in the playground and on the streets around my home, but it didn't take away the tension inside. Arguments and scuffles at home, emptiness and confusion at church, inferiority and loneliness at school, all combined to leave me coiled up like a spring.

I can only recall a couple of occasions when that inner tightness was unwound and replaced by a calm and peace. They were the summers when my mother took us over to Ireland to spend some time with her relatives. We visited members of the family living in and around Cork, staying with them in little thatched cottages and running freely in the fields and country lanes. So much space, fresh air and beautiful countryside was in marked contrast to the dirty brick streets of the Midlands. We'd spend hours with our distant cousins, learning how to trap rabbits, and helping to carry huge baskets containing packed lunches down to the grown-ups working in the fields where they were bringing in the harvest.

But then, all too soon, it was back to the big, old house in Wilford Grove, the weekend parties and the battles in the home and playground.

Being that much older, big brother Tony had never really had much to do with the other children in the family, especially me. If relations with my two sisters were anything to go by, we probably wouldn't have got on anyway. Joan was a few years older than me, and I only ever saw her as competition. She was the one I was in a contest with over everything: being first to read the weekly comic, getting the best chair in the room, winning the second helping at the dinner table, and most importantly earning the affection of our parents. If family closeness was in short supply to start with, I hated having to share it with anyone else. I wanted to hug it all to myself and savour every last ounce.

So we were always looking for ways to outdo each other, and when Mum and Dad weren't looking, our spiteful teasing and tormenting would quickly give way to full-blooded slaps and punches. As she got older, Joan would tease me in front of her friends when they came round, pushing me about and trying to humiliate me. I responded by making sure that my punches went home hard and hurtfully when we tangled.

I'd already started school by the time Trish arrived, and to begin with she was the much-loved baby of the family. We all helped care for her; I even took my turn feeding her and changing the occasional nappy. I wasn't very good at it, but it made me feel very adult to be trusted with such a responsible job.

Perhaps she took her cues from the examples of her older brother and sister, but as Trish got older she too joined the fighting for first place. As time went on, we began to clash more and more fiercely – worse than I had done with Joan. When Mum and Dad were out, we would dive at each other, fists and feet flying, having driven each other to breaking point. By now I was learning to let the tripwire on my temper go almost at will. The results could be alarming. I had no qualms about striking either of my sisters as hard as I would a schoolground opponent. It didn't make any difference to me that they were girls; they got what they deserved. But on a couple of occasions I frightened even myself when I laid Trish out cold by throwing her against a thick panelled door. I dragged her into the bedroom, opened the window, and with the help of the fresh air managed to bring her round before our parents got back.

By the time I became aware of my emerging sexuality, my attitude towards women – as exemplified by my treatment of Joan and Trish – was already so confused that even a course in human relations would have been hard-pressed to correct my flawed character; much less the crude playground education I received.

A delicious sense of disgust charges through my body, making me tingle, as we head off down the street. I've told my parents that we are going round to a friend's house for a while. It's not a lie, really; only it's not the full story, either.

She's not actually a friend, I suppose. Because if the truth's told we're not really very interested in her as a person at all. We are going for her body, which she seems to get a kick out of feeding to our fascination. I sometimes think that she's using us more than we are using her.

I wonder, too, about what her parents would think if they knew what their daughter was up to in their bedroom while they're out – though we are always careful to cover our tracks. But mostly I don't care. All thoughts seem to get locked away, frozen out, when we are faced with the reality of our schoolboy fantasies.

This is even more unbelievable, exciting and hypnotising than all the stories we've swapped in the bike sheds, or the men's magazines we've leered over. Since falling into this weekly ritual, my three friends and I have felt strangely older than the other boys in our second-year secondary school group. But there are other emotions, too, spinning away inside.

Even as we arrive at her door, trying to look relaxed in case the neighbours are watching, I know that the sensory overload of the next couple of hours is going to be followed by a flood of shame, guilt and horror; even self-loathing.

Part of me wants to run away from it all – I don't think I'm big enough to cope with all the emotional demands

it makes on me – but the rest just pulls me back
magnetically. I just hope that later I can get in and up to
bed, calling a 'goodnight' from the stairs, without having
to talk to Mum face to face. I don't think I'll be able to
look at her because I'm convinced that she'll know
simply by looking into my eyes all the dreadful things
that have been happening.

I'm also slightly in awe of this thing that seems so
easily capable of dominating my life with a kind of
arrogant ease. Already I'm finding my days and nights
are being swamped by thoughts of sexual activity; there's
scarcely a day goes by when my mind's not running riot.
Just sometimes it's as though I've opened the door of a
lion's cage, and out has roared a beast that's going to
devour me.

But now we have arrived, and I'm lost again in a blur
of anticipated senses. I'll forget about how hollow I'm
going to feel because of the fullness of the moment.

Those early sexual experiences not only scarred me for
future relationships, but they also saw the severing of
the last threads that had held me – albeit tenuously – to
church.

For two years I had served as one of the altar boys at
St Patrick's. My understanding of God – or, rather, lack
of it – hadn't changed in the slightest: he still seemed to
me to be no more than a vague and guilty idea in a few
people's minds. But my serving at the altar thrilled my
parents – it was a note of social standing to have your
youngster hold such an office – and it had also helped
the ordeal of Sunday morning pass more quickly. If I
had to go to church, I figured, I might as well have
something to do to help the minutes along.

So, each Sunday morning, I'd join the other lads with
their close-cropped, slicked-down hair. We'd fight over
who got to wear the cleanest, newest robes – the white
linen shirt and the long, black cassock over the top. We
would put on our most angelic-looking, innocent faces

as we stood solemnly at the front of the church, assisting Father Saul with the mass.

But within a few weeks of starting to experiment with sex, I began to dread having to serve at church. Once the girl with whom my friends and I were meeting came down to our part of the Meadows looking for me. I heard that she was coming and ran inside, closing the door. I didn't come out again until she'd given up the search and gone home. I didn't want anyone to know that I'd been associating with her.

In the same way I dreaded being caught out at church. I sometimes wondered whether Father Saul could read my mind when he looked at me with his gentle, caring eyes. I was horrified at the prospect – the thought that he might know I'd let him down. Having to attend Saturday evening confession with Dad was an awful trial. Waiting to enter the small, screened box, which always smelled strongly of a cocktail of whisky and perfume, my hands would start to sweat profusely and I'd wipe them repeatedly on the sides of my trousers.

Once inside I felt compelled to confess all that I'd done, and my cheeks would burn with shame as I recounted the moments. I hated having to admit the things that my uncontrolled desire had made me do. It left me feeling horribly exposed, and I wondered whether the priest would recognise my voice despite my best efforts to disguise it or, worse, tell my family all I had said.

My experimentation wasn't limited to sex, either. Eager to grow up and leave behind the schoolboy mould into which we felt squeezed, my friends and I also began to dabble in other activities that we reckoned were a sign of maturity beyond our years. With a few pennies each it was possible to scrape together enough money to buy between us a packet of five Woodbines. They were plain, rough cigarettes that roared against the backs of our throats and made our eyes sting as we inhaled. The first few times I tried it, it was all I could do to prevent myself from retching on the spot. Somehow I managed to effect a seasoned sigh of satisfaction as I exhaled between pursed lips.

After a while the level of disagreeability began to drop, and I found myself looking forward to the next smoke snatched – if we were in a brave mood – in a quiet corner of the school, or near to one of the private alleys round our homes. Very soon my liking for nicotine had developed into a craving, and I was finding most of my money going towards the cost of the next packet.

The rest was soon spent on drink. There had always been alcohol around in our home, of course, where it flowed as naturally as tea. My parents had never objected to us having a sip from their glass if we were staying up for one of the weekly parties, but this was different. My friends and I started to smuggle bottles of beer away from our parents' supplies, and then drank them together secretly. I'd already acquired the stomach for alcohol; the taste followed very quickly.

All this rebellious activity fuelled my hatred of authority, which I came to see as personified by anyone connected with school. I loathed every moment of my time at secondary school – a passionate dislike that would not change over the years, even if the reasons for it did.

At first it had been resentment. There had been a good deal of arguing back and forth about whether I should be allowed to attend Trent Bridge Boys' School in the first place. Tucked away at the edge of the Meadows, neighbouring an industrial works and just a few hundred yards from the River Trent, it was a Protestant establishment and so viewed with considerable suspicion.

However, all my closest friends were going there, so I wanted to as well. Finally Mum and Dad gave in and let me go – and from the first day I discovered just why it had a reputation as being one of the toughest schools in the town.

Although I'd learned to take care of myself at primary

school through sheer rage, here I found myself once more at the lower end of the pecking order. The boys in the upper forms were bigger, broader and beefier by far – and determined to make sure that we new pupils knew just what the score was. The first few weeks were a real time of trial for us all. Before and after school, the bigger lads would pick us off and with a brisk roughing over make certain that we knew our place. Favourite tortures were to bend our arms behind our backs and stretch them agonisingly over the metal school railings, or for two more to hold us still while a fourth burned the side of our necks with a lighted cigarette.

I hated the feeling of helplessness before these bullies, and despised them for making me aware of my insecurity. Then, when we were away at a school camp, the chief architect of the fourth formers' reign of terror singled me out for special attention. He began by taunting me and swearing at me, and then started to push me away from the small group that had gathered to watch my humiliation.

'Go on, Goodfellow, get lost, before I beat you up good and proper,' he hissed, pushing me away by the shoulder.

Somewhere inside the trigger went, and I exploded again. I tore into him, grabbed his arms and threw him over my hip as Dad had taught me to do in countless sitting room 'lessons' at home. As he landed on the ground, I dropped on top of him, straddling him with my knees, pinning his arms at his side. And then, methodically and with cool satisfaction, I began to pound his face – right, left – with my fists. He couldn't wriggle free because my weight was pinning him down, and I continued my onslaught with delight until I was finally dragged away by two or three other boys.

It turned out to be the worst possible thing to have done. All the older boys felt slighted that a younger pupil had got the better of one of their classmates. They seemed to think that they each had to take me on to prove their own toughness, and after that I was constantly trying to avoid unnecessary confrontations. One particular time I wasn't quick enough on my feet, and I was cornered and 'branded' by a group of them.

It wasn't so much the pain that enraged me; though it took some time for my singed flesh to heal. More it was the shame and humiliation that seemed to tear a hole deep inside me. I couldn't disguise the blistered record of the attack, no matter how I tried, and I seethed against those who had left me with the visible marks of having been beaten.

Dad didn't seem to worry about all the scrapes I got into at school; many's the time I would return home with skinned knuckles or a bruised cheek. He was more interested in getting a blow-by-blow account of what had happened. Just sometimes I wished he would express some concern or tenderness for me. Instead he quizzed me on how I'd handled myself, and offered tips on what to do the next time it happened.

My standing in the staffroom wasn't too good, either. My inability to absorb information was still there, although a love for reading had somehow kept me in the so-called A stream of school life – by the skin of my teeth. But most of the teachers had little time for me. Their general opinion was that I would never amount to much, and I sensed that I'd been written off as far as they were concerned. 'You'll probably end up in prison, Goodfellow,' one of them told me flatly.

This lack of interest, coupled with their positions of authority, made them prime targets for my fierce hatred. I used to daydream about how I'd like to get my own back on them, particularly when I'd been punished for some misdemeanour or other. Each teacher had his own preferred method, and there were leather straps, bamboo canes and rulers. One teacher in particular used to insist that we held our hand out, palm up, while he administered stinging strokes from a strap. If we pulled our hand away – which was the immediate painful reaction – then he simply doubled the dosage. We all loathed him.

My clash with authority came to a head in the metalwork class in my last year. The teacher was called Marcisniak; he was a squat, muscular Pole who had come to Britain during the war and stayed on afterwards. Generally he just ignored me during his lessons, but on this particular day he came over to see how I was getting on. I'd been trying to make a brass bowl, and hadn't done a very good job of beating out the shape, although I had tried hard. At least I didn't have to struggle with paper and pen.

Marcisniak ripped into me with criticism. He told me that I was doing it all wrong, and had to start again and do it the right way. 'Concentrate this time. Don't be an idiot all your life, boy!' he snapped.

Being picked out for failing to do the work properly – despite my best efforts – was bad enough in front of a workroom full of my friends. But to be ridiculed like that was too much.

'Don't you call me an idiot!' I shot back.

The teacher reached over and slapped me hard over the top of the head for answering him back – and the next thing I knew we were fighting over a bench in the middle of the class. He screamed and kicked as I tried to land one really good punch in his face, but he was too powerful for me and he finally managed to subdue me with the help of another member of staff who had rushed in to find out what all the commotion was.

They hauled me off to the headmaster's study, where I was given a dressing down and threatened with immediate expulsion. I didn't really care if they did throw me out, but I argued that Marcisniak had started it all because he'd struck me, and that there was a classroom of witnesses – my friends – who had seen what had happened.

The episode seemed to blow over in the days that followed, but it made me only more keen to leave school

as soon as I possibly could – and for the authorities to
see the back of me.

On our last day, we departing fifteen-year-olds were
gathered together by the headmaster and given a fatherly
pep-talk about going out into the big, wide world and
making our way as young men with the future before us.
I remember looking over at him as he droned on and
thinking with delight that I'd never have to see his smug
face again as long as I lived. Walking out of the gates
that afternoon, for the last time, was like being released
from prison. I felt strangely, euphorically free.

'This is it,' I thought, as I walked home along the
streets. 'I've finally made it. No more yes sir, no sir. No
more people stopping me from doing what I want to.
From now on, people had just better make sure they
don't get in my way!'

4
Squaring Up

Three left jabs with my fist smashed into his face almost before he knew what was happening. Another series of blows followed, as inwardly I hoped that someone would step in pretty soon to break up the fight: if they didn't, I was in for trouble.

I was in my late teens, and months working on building sites had toughened me up physically so that my body was as hard as my heart. But Dave was more than a match. He towered over me by about four inches, and must have carried three or four stone more than I onto the scales. I knew that picking a fight with him was asking for problems, but the risk of physical injury was less worrying to me than the danger of losing face. I'd prefer to have mine re-arranged, instead.

The problem was that carpenters thought they were better than those of us who laid bricks, as though their skills were somehow more artistic. It was an unspoken snobbery that occasionally spilled over into words and violence – such as the morning I tangled with Dave.

We had been working well enough together up until then. I was helping him with his heavy tools bag on a first-floor level at a city-centre building site, when he had to climb down to get some more materials leaving me to wait for his return. Even my toughened arms couldn't hold onto the weight indefinitely, and my grip slackened. Some of his tools slipped out of the side of

51

the bag and tumbled down to the ground, where they crashed against a pile of bricks.

Dave saw the accident and shouted angrily: 'Can't you do anything right, you weakling? I only asked you to hold my bag for a couple of minutes. What a pathetic excuse for a brickie you are.'

His taunt was like a red rag to a bull, and I snapped back: 'Who do you think you're talking to, then, you fat slob?' Peering down at him from above it seemed relatively safe – but the gathering of a small group of lads who had overheard our altercation forced me to climb down, where the scale of my confrontation became more evident. And so without waiting to complete the usual round of oaths, taunts and accusations that would pre-cede a fight, I tore into him with my knuckles.

It took him completely by surprise, and thankfully my gamble paid off. Before Dave could gather his senses enough to come back at me, some of the onlookers had stepped in and pulled me away, while another couple went to Dave to calm him down and defuse the situation.

I was prepared to face the prospect of being hurt because I was determined not to lose the sense of identity I had discovered, for the first time, since start-ing work on the building sites. People recognised my abilities, and respected my character, and I was almost prepared to kill to make sure I didn't lose that standing; that sense of personal value and worth. It didn't allow for people – of any size – attempting to belittle or taunt me in front of others.

It was hard work on the sites, but I felt that I belonged; that I fitted in. It was something I hadn't experienced before – at home, at church, or at school – and I valued the feelings of purpose and position. Particularly as early experience on leaving school had shattered my initial dreams of working life as an adult.

Despite my academic failings, I'd somehow managed to secure a job as a trainee inspector at a small, grey engineering factory on the other side of town, a twenty-minute bus ride away. It soon became apparent to me that I was once again a small, inconsequential fish in a big pool. I hated being the butt of the older men's jokes and taunts, and singled out as 'the new lad'.

My supervisors quickly realised, too, that I wasn't really capable of grasping all the things an inspector apparently needed to know in a factory that turned out brass rings by the thousand. After a few weeks I was unceremoniously downgraded, and put to work on a capstan lathe. I was embarrassed and humiliated, sure that everyone in the place knew I wasn't up to the job I had been given originally – unaware that most of them probably didn't even know my name, and cared about that fact even less. Somehow even the sequences of lathe operation were too much for me, though. Next I found myself handed a plain brown overcoat and a brush. I was at the bottom of the pile, reduced to mundane labouring jobs – sweeping the floors, moving heavy loads of metal from one end of the factory floor to the other, and brewing tea.

This rapid slide confirmed all my worst fears. I felt stupid, worthless and despised. To make matters worse there was no one I could turn to, because I couldn't bring myself to tell my parents. They still thought I was a trainee inspector, and I'd pass over their occasional questions about how things were going with a deliberately vague answer, or attempt to change the topic of conversation. I couldn't bring myself to admit that I had failed, and I feared my father's scorn for not making the grade.

So for a year or so I simply had to endure it quietly, spending my time daydreaming about sex, or how I'd like to get my own back on all the people who seemed to be squashing me down. I wove violent fantasies of revenge and lust that somehow only managed to make the mundane reality around me seem even more infuriating.

Eventually I handed my notice in and managed to

convince Mum and Dad that I'd left because there weren't enough prospects for me at such a small firm. If only they knew!

For a couple of months I kicked my heels trying to find new work. While I was still at school I'd toyed with the idea of following my brother, Tony, down the pit. I knew that life underground could be dangerous – he'd been off work the best part of a year at one stage, recovering from a cave-in that had damaged his back. But I still fancied the idea of becoming a miner – until we went down a pit on a school visit. The heat, dirt and darkness hundreds of feet below were alarming, and I left my romantic thoughts of attacking the black seams behind me when we returned to the surface.

Then, one day, I decided to try my hand at brick-laying – and found myself a new identity. I was apprenticed to a local firm, Costain and Sons, who were contracted to build on the big city-centre development sites in Nottingham. I soon discovered that here, at last, I'd found something I was good at. In a strange way I felt free for the first time that I could recall.

A cold, crisp morning and my steamy breath rolls away in a cloud as I blow on my hands. There's an art to laying bricks well. It's all to do with touch and feel, so gloves are out. After a few weeks your fingers become toughened up, though, and you get used to the cold. Sometimes the temperature drops so low that we have to spend the first minutes of the day chipping the ice off the bricks that have been left out overnight.

Up on the higher levels you get a fine view of the city. It's really warming to walk out to the edge of the building, way up high, and look down on the crowds of people scurrying to a day in the office. This is a man's world, rough and tough. It's good to be accepted as one of the blokes, and to share a coarse joke or guffaw as a young girl blushes and hurries away from one of our rooftop wolf-whistles.

I also enjoy the sense of achievement and satisfaction – something I could never find in all the days I struggled with books and pens. I appreciate the adept way I have learned to 'roll the board' – cutting off a fresh slab of cement, and slapping it down on top of a row of bricks so that it spreads along a couple of feet. Then I smear it out flat so that the next row of bricks lie level as they are placed carefully and firmly on top. Next comes 'buttering the edge' – running a spread of cement up the side of each brick to be laid, so that they are mortared to the next one in line.

They say that a good brickie can lay a thousand bricks a day, and I'm just topping that total. I know that I'm appreciated because I'm always given the best jobs, and I push myself hard to make sure that no one else manages to knock me off my top spot. Sometimes, standing above everyone else on a high work point, that's just how I think of myself, and I love the sense of importance, of being someone!

The long hours of climbing, stretching and carrying have wound a steely thread into my body, and I relish the sense of power and strength. I'm fitter and stronger than I can ever remember, and this awareness heightens my readiness to let go with a punch or two. I'm not someone to tangle with lightly.

The guys on the site are also a good bunch of people to work with – family, in a strange way. We swear and fight and try to outdo each other, but there is most of the time a feeling that we're all in it together. I like being a part of something. It's new.

My employers soon spotted that I had a natural talent for the job, and teamed me up with one of their most experienced men. The old-timers in turn, responded warmly to my efforts and took me under their wing, in a way.

My apprenticeship involved a four-year course with day training sessions at a local college. I was working towards my City and Guilds certificate in bricklaying, but the freedom and achievement I'd found on the site only compounded the sense of inadequacy I experienced back in the classroom. The college kicked me out after eighteen months, for being too rebellious and argumentative – which included a study room brawl with another young apprentice who had dared to criticise my practical work on one occasion.

Because my abilities won me the respect of the older men, I was spared some of the treatment handed out to newcomers. There was a definite pecking order on a site, and everyone held their place with threats and abuse and – when it was needed – violence. Many of the guys on the crews were fresh out of prison, too, and they brought an extra sense of aggression and anger to the arguments that would take place. 'You learn inside never to back down to anyone,' one of them told me one day.

My good standing on site brought my dad's admiration for the first time – but he showed it in a strange way. Maybe it was because of the way he had to keep the young men in his construction gangs in line; anyway, he turned to fighting.

There had been many scuffles and tussles in the past, and the prospect of a real battle had bubbled for a long time. After I'd been at work for a few months, I decided that Mum and Dad couldn't make me go with them to church on Sunday mornings any more. So when Dad's voice came roaring up the stairs telling me to get up and get dressed, I ignored him, rolled over and went back to sleep.

A few minutes later he thundered up, crashed through the door and barked at me: 'Johnny, I just told you to get up. It's almost time for church, and we are not going to be late, by God . . .'

I rolled over and peeked over the top of the sheets. 'I'm not going any more, Dad,' I told him flatly.

'You what!' he exploded. 'Don't you think you can

tell me what you are and aren't going to do ... just get yourself downstairs straight away!' And with that he stormed out and stomped downstairs again. I continued to lie there, tensing myself for another confrontation, and a few minutes later heard the front door slam as Mum and Dad and the girls set off for St Patrick's.

Dad and I never talked about that confrontation again, but he would always glare at me at lunchtime when I'd finally surface after a good, long lie-in. As well as welcoming the escape from the insufferable boredom and choking guilt that used to swamp the hours I spent at church, I was secretly thrilled because I'd stood up to Dad and he had not been able to face me down. I sensed that it was the beginning of the end of his domination of me.

He must have been aware of this shift in our relationship, too, because after I started bricklaying he began to try to provoke me into a full-scale fight ... especially on nights when he'd had a few too many drinks down at one of the locals. He would come home and try to spur me into a brawl: 'Come on Johnny, my lad, let's see what you're made of,' he would say, inviting me forward with a wave of his left hand – his right held up to his chin in a boxer's stance.

Usually I would walk out of the room or wave him away and say: 'Oh, come on, I don't want to fight you, Dad. That's stupid ...'

One night he continued to bait me. 'Are you frightened of me, or something?' he asked as we stood close by, near the door. I didn't even get round to answering. The next thing I knew my head had exploded in a galaxy of bright stars, and I was lying spread backwards across the kitchen table. Dad had sent me sprawling with a right hook to the chin.

The inner safety catch went again, and with a scream I came to my feet. In a burst of raw anger I grabbed him by the lapels and slammed him backwards against the wall, almost lifting him off his feet. Then I threw him down into a chair, bent his head back and snarled into his face: 'If you ever do that again ... I will kill you.'

I truly meant it – and he knew. All the anger, hurt and bitterness I felt I'd stored up over the previous years came out in that simple threat. For a brief moment there was a flicker of uncertainty, perhaps even fear, in his eyes.

It was a sweet moment of bitterness.

5
Easy Money

The stale, foul smell stole into my nostrils and slid down to the back of my throat where it seemed to curl into a ball and threatened to make me gag. I wished that I didn't recognise it.

Gingerly I opened one eye a fraction to investigate, careful not to allow too much harsh light to spill through into my head. It felt as though it had been put through a blender, and too much brightness would have sent me retching.

Looking across from where I lay, I could make out a plain, grey wall, and as I looked up ... the source of my nausea. Smeared across from left to right as far as I could see was dark human excrement. I groaned and clenched my teeth to try to stop my stomach from rebelling against this revolting start to the day.

My sluggish efforts to piece together just where I was and what I was doing there were abruptly halted as the light seemed to fade. A large shape thrust into my face, and I could gradually make out the form of a square human head. Rancid breath blew into my face as this unshaven, sweaty countenance peered at me.

'What have they got you in for then?' the voice demanded in a flat tone.

The question brought bits and pieces of information tumbling into place. This man was sharing the cell into which I had been pitched the night before after my abortive attempt to escape from the police. The realisation only added to the feeling of sickness deep inside.

'Err, theft ... they caught me breaking into a jeweller's shop in the town centre ... how about you?'

'Rape.'

Shocked, I sat up and backed against the wall at the side of the bunk, trying not to show that I was alarmed. Far better if he thought that I was a police cell regular, rough and tough and used to looking after myself behind bars.

Fortunately I was saved from having to try to make any further conversation by a rattling at the heavy iron door set in the far wall. It swung open slowly, and a short-sleeved policeman stepped through holding a mug of tea that he set down at a small, scratched table before giving me a disinterested look and disappearing again. The thick door swung to and closed with an air of finality. I sipped the warm, weak tea and ran my fingers through my untidy hair.

My previously smart blue suit was crumpled and creased; my mouth felt as though a crowd of maggots had been sleeping in it; and my stomach pitched and turned like a cork on a wave. An awful aroma clung to my clothes and hair. So this was how my high-living Friday night out had ended.

It had started like so many others, full of hopes for a few hours of wild excitement. Besides earning an identity and feeling of worth for myself working on the sites, I'd also found out what it meant to have plenty of money to throw around. Working hard to pump down my thousand bricks a day, I was soon bringing home top money. The small brown envelope that was slapped down into my waiting palm every Thursday was always satisfyingly full. At least, for a while.

Alcohol was by now second nature, and I naturally responded to the hard-drinking habits of the older men around, whose consumption I was easily able to match. There would be a pint or two at lunchtime and a few more each night down at the local, but it was at the weekend when the serious socialising would begin.

Hurrying down a big cooked tea, I'd be washed and changed and out of the house early on Friday evening. A stroll down the road and I'd sink a couple of pints with the neighbours before straightening my tie and sauntering on into town to one of the busy bars near the city centre. The Flying Horse was a favourite; always seeming to be packed with more people and noise than the room could comfortably take. There would be a swirl of laughs and drinks and tall stories and more drinks.

The lads would gather there and swap stories about the week, or discuss the prospects of female company in store at the dance hall later on. Later in the evening we would drift on to Yates' Wine Lodge, a place for some serious drinking. With its sawdust covered flooring, large mirrored walls and cast-iron ceiling poles, it looked like the deck of a ship stripped bare and tied down in prospect of a storm. That wasn't far from the truth, in some ways, because as the alcohol loosened tongues, ties and fists, fights would break out as the night wore on. We'd ignore the old Irishmen sitting in the corners with their wives, swapping even older stories about the homeland, and stand in a circle in the centre of the room, downing drink after drink and daring anyone even to consider pushing through us on the way to the bar.

Finally it would be on to the Locarno or one of the other big dance halls, great big aircraft hangars of places with wall-to-wall bars and large dance floors where the girls shuffled around together in time to the strains of the resident band, waiting to be chatted up by one of the leery men standing around at the side eyeing up the talent.

Not surprisingly, this kind of living soon saw off even my healthy wage packet. The fact that I'd gamble over three-card brag during my weeknight pub nights down in the Meadows, coupled with my drinking and dancing appetite, meant that my money never lasted the whole week – sometimes not more than a few days.

So it had been last night. I'd slipped out of the club a little after 2 am, and with only a handful of small change had no option but to start the five-mile walk home. The music and drink were still humming round my veins as I strolled drunkenly down the main shopping area, looking at all the window displays and feeling sorry for myself that I never seemed to have enough money. I couldn't even afford a coat, I bemoaned, as I pulled my thin jacket closer around me in an effort to keep out the early morning cool air.

I'd already turned to crime to finance my lifestyle, with no sense of guilt or wrongdoing. One of the easiest scenes to be made was at the dance hall. A friend and I would choose a couple of girls and get talking. When they slipped off to dance – they always went in pairs, giggling – we'd rifle their handbags and take out the purses. Then we'd slip off to the gents, take out any money, dump the purses in the water cistern, and disappear into another part of the club. We reckoned that if we weren't going to get a girl into bed, we might as well at least get her money.

It seemed to me generally that other people had more than they needed, and I didn't have enough. It was as simple as that – and I also savoured the notion of getting something for nothing. It was as though I was getting my own back on the world that seemed to be against me.

When stealing and violence can be combined, it's even more satisfying. Bob and I are down to our last half pint in a scruffy Meadows pub, with pay day a lot of drinking time away, when I suggest that we simply just empty our glasses and go out and find ourselves the cost of the next round – at someone else's expense.

It's dark as we shuffle back into the shadows of an alleyway a few streets away, within shouting distance of my home. All we can hear is our own shallow breathing as we wait, straining to catch the sound of an approaching step. Someone's coming ... a cough and a shuffle; it sounds like a man, maybe on his way home from a quiet drink down the local with his friends. Or perhaps he's heading home after working overtime. Either way, his pockets should have a few pounds in them.

Half-nervous and half-thrilled at the audacity of what we're going to do we wait until the last moment – and then spring. 'You, give us your money or there's going to be trouble.' Menacing tones and threatening glares that can be clearly understood despite the dark. But this target isn't easy. Crack! He's caught Bob with a blow to the face and it's all starting to go wrong. With the desperation of fear at being identified we redouble our efforts. The man crumples into the ash of the pathway under our combined attack.

He's screaming and shouting for help, and the hairs on the back of my neck are standing on end as I expect half the neighbourhood to turn out of their houses at any moment. 'Shut up, man!' I snarl, kicking him in the face with the toe-end of my boot. This silences him and he curls into a ball, holding his battered face.

We jerk him over onto his side, and rifle his pockets angrily. There doesn't seem to be much, but there's no time to hang around. Only after we've sprinted a couple of roads away do we stop to count our pickings. Two pounds. Just enough for a few drinks each. There's the faint sound of an ambulance siren as we saunter back into the pub we left about half an hour ago.

It's great to share a private joke as we lean over the bar and ask for two pints of best bitter, please. This violent draught tastes great, and we savour it and the excitement of the last few minutes. 'What do you mean, is everything all right?' I ask one of the old chaps who has wandered over to see us again. Why is he asking?

I follow his gaze and look down. Fresh splotches of spilled blood are still clearly visible down the front of my trousers.

'Oh that, it's nothing. We just ran into a little bit of trouble down the road a way, didn't we, Bob?'

'Oh, that, yeah, that's right. Just a little bit of trouble. But we sorted it out all right. Isn't that right, Johnny?'

'Yeah. Cheers!'

And we giggle through the foamy head of the ale.

My mental gears started to whirr again as I weaved my way past the large-fronted jeweller's shop on the corner. A galaxy of rings, brooches and watches twinkled out at me from the brightly-lit display boards. Almost before I knew what I was doing, I had run over to the roadworks just in front of the shop, picked up a heavy red road lamp in which flickered a candle, and began to pound the metal case against the thick glass frontage.

I swung with all my might two, three times. Then, with my fourth attempt, the glass shattered and fell in. Quickly I threw the lamp to one side and, stepping up, jumped into the display space at the front of the shop. I ignored the shrill alarm that had begun shrieking as soon as the glass gave way, and started stuffing my pockets full of everything I could lay my hands on.

Rings, tie-pins, watches, ear-rings, bracelets, brooches, necklaces – they all were scooped up frantically as I tore items off display trays and scattered others aside to grab what I wanted. It was a thrill to snatch these valiable items up and know that they were mine for the taking.

With my two jacket pockets bulging, chains trailing out the top, I grabbed a handful of other display cards to my chest and jumped down from the window, turning to my right up a side street. As I ran away up the pavement, trinkets dropping to the ground all around, a roaring laugh of pleasure broke from my throat. This was marvellous. My previous crimes seemed tame and timid in comparison! I was already planning my next break-in.

But the moment was shortlived. I hadn't got more than a couple of hundred yards up the road when I heard the unmistakable bee-bah of a police patrol van behind my shoulder, pulling up outside the shop. Panic! For all my careful observations before I'd attacked the shop, I must have missed a late-night walker somewhere nearby who had seen my crime.

'He went up that way ... there he is!' The cry pumped adrenalin into my heart, and I picked up my legs and tore off up to the top of the street. At the end I ran round a low wall and into the wide churchyard of St Nicholas, one of the oldest churches in the city. My elation had given way to cold fear, and I crouched down behind a large black tombstone with my heart beating wildly inside my chest. It had all happened too quickly. How had the police managed to arrive at the scene so fast? They'd ruined my moment!

As my breath came in great sobs, I threw the display cards away across the tombstones, where they scattered and rolled, tinkling.

In a half-crouched position, I peered round the side of the gravestone. Thankfully there were no street lights close by, so I was still in some shadow. I could just see the police van pulling up to a halt at the side of the road, and the officer in the passenger seat staring out through the side window with intense concentration.

Careful to keep low so as not to be spotted, I scurried away behind the tombstones and monuments to another wall at the rear of the churchyard. I'd just made my way to the top of a steep drop of steps that would lead me down to a street forty feet or so below – and probable safety – when I heard dogs barking, and a cry.

'There he is! Hey, you, stop. This is the police.'

The shout startled me, and as I turned I lost my footing and tumbled down the steps, cracking my head and ripping my clothes as I went. But the fear was an anaesthetic, and at the bottom I picked myself up without even stopping to think about the bruises, and lunged off through an alleyway and out into another main street.

At first I thought I'd managed to lose them, but then a couple of hundred yards up the street I heard another shout from behind.

'Oi, you, stop – or we'll let the dogs go.'

I slowed to a halt, my chest heaving from the chase. I knew it was pointless trying to outrun the police dogs, so I turned to face my pursuers in the grip of fear, frustration and anger. The last few minutes' physical exertion seemed to have washed some of the alcohol from my brain and I was already thinking fairly clearly again. What had I done? What had I let myself in for? I'd never been caught before. What would my parents say? How could I face it if people found out?

The two policemen didn't appreciate their chase, clearly. The one in front came over and pushed me hard in the chest, backing me up against the wall of an office complex. 'You stupid kid, what the hell do you think you've been doing, eh? You've really gone and landed yourself in it for this, I'm telling you.'

He spun me round and pushed my face up against the rough brick, while he pulled my arms behind me and clicked the handcuffs into place. 'You didn't really think you were going to get away with it, did you? You've just gone and made things worse for yourself, that's all.'

Still swearing angrily at me, they dragged me to their van and threw me in the back, where I was separated from the dogs by only a wire partition. The Alsatians barked and snarled at me through the wire throughout the bumpy journey back to the police cells, and fear of the dogs and anger at myself and the police drove me to smash my fists repeatedly against the inner wall behind the driver's head.

'Let me out of here, you pigs!' I screamed. 'I hate you coppers, I hate you!'

I was bundled out of the van fairly roughly, and manhandled through the booking-in procedure and down into one of the filthy cells beneath Nottingham's guild hall. With a parting warning that they'd remember my face and I'd better watch my back in the future, the policemen slammed the door shut and left me in the dark.

Trapped and in a rage, I pounded the wall a couple of times with my hands before throwing myself full-length onto the bunk, covered only with a thin, old blanket, and falling into a heavy, despairing sleep.

I had just finished replaying these events in my befuddled mind the following morning when another policeman opened up the cell door and stuck his head round.

'Goodfellow, come on out. Your old man's here for you upstairs.'

I followed him uncertainly. I was dirty, uncomfortable and hungry. I hoped that he'd sorted things out and come to take me home. I found out the reason for his visit as soon as I stepped into the small interview room at the top of the stairs.

He lunged across at me from the other side of the room, throwing one punch after another. 'What on earth do you think you've been up to, boy?' he demanded. 'I never brought you up to become a little thief, did I? Is that all you can think of to repay your poor mother after all these years?'

Dad continued to shout and rant as three police officers pulled him away and sat him down in a chair, urging him to be calm and to collect his thoughts. Everything was going to work out. He looked up at me with anger and shame in his eyes – and then crumpled. Falling forwards and dropping his head into his hands he began to weep. 'Oh son, oh son,' he cried.

I just stood there over by the opposite wall, looking down at the ground and squirming inside. I didn't feel sorry for him – but I was horribly embarrassed. I didn't know which was worse – that my dad should try to beat me up instead of wanting to take me home, or that he'd burst into tears.

It was to be another three days before the police finally let me out on bail – time in which I grew accustomed to the stench and dirtiness of the place. But I never could come to terms with the sense of grievance

I felt. It didn't really occur to me that I'd got the just deserts for my criminal actions. I just felt sick that the police had caught me.

Going home was dreadful. Dad shouted and swore again, and Mum burst into tears and wrung her hands. They were scenes to be repeated when my fine, costs and two-year suspended prison sentence were handed down at the magistrates court a few weeks later — and reported for all the neighbours to see in the local paper.

For a while this encounter with the law brought me to my senses. I restricted myself to one or two trips a week down to the locals, where I'd play cards or dominoes with the old men. But pretty soon I slipped back into my old ways, and once again I was finding that the money I could earn legitimately wasn't enough. I decided, though, that I'd stick to crimes that were less likely to get me caught.

I returned to cars, which were one of my favourite targets. It was easy, walking along the road late at night, to casually try the handles of a few of the vehicles parked along the way. And it was amazing how many motorists didn't seem to check the locks properly before leaving. Often I found one of the doors open, and was able to dart in and rush away with a coat, a cassette player, or some tools. I'd sell them to friends for a couple of pounds, and that would finance the next round or two.

One late night I went spying on all the cars left in a temporary car park on a derelict site round the back of the town centre. In the rear of one I saw a whole pile of brand new jeans. I guessed that the driver must be a travelling salesman, and these his samples. None of the doors were open, but with a handy brick I'd soon shattered the rear window and carried the jeans off in a suitcase conveniently left behind, too.

By this time it was about 3 am, and as I walked down towards the station with my booty, I came across a policeman strolling along the pavement. Thinking quickly to avoid suspicion, I went over to him and enquired when the next train left for Derby. My forwardness must have disarmed him, even if it was strange for a young man in a smart blue suit to be carrying a bulging suitcase round the empty streets in the early hours of the morning.

'Oh, it goes out at about six,' he told me brightly.

'Thanks, officer. I'll go in and wait,' I replied.

And I did. After a couple of hours' sleep I caught the train to Derby, the nearest Midland industrial town of any size, and once there headed for the building sites. Even at a pound a pair for top quality jeans, I knew that there would be no questions asked. Within a couple of hours I'd sold my entire 'stock', and the case into the bargain. I returned to Nottingham with empty hands and a bulging wallet, and a private sense of pride at what I'd been able to get away with.

I looked around at the other people in the carriage – a young mother, a schoolboy, a solicitor type, and a couple of shop assistants – and wanted to laugh at them for their safe, respectable suburban lives. If only they knew what I was up to.

6

On the Edge

I had returned from my first visit to Spain. A friend and I had left our bricklaying jobs in the middle of the summer holiday season and travelled over to the continent to investigate the claims we had heard about life on the Costa Brava. We'd left it rather too late to get fixed up with good posts, though, and after just a couple of weeks we returned to England. My time in Spain had been enough to open my eyes to the possibilities, however, and going back to laying more rows of bricks seemed horribly tame.

I enjoyed my drinking, and a fight was the perfect way to finish an evening, but I'd never have considered that I was in danger of losing control. It just seemed to me that I needed more excitement, more stimulation than the average guy in his boring, nine-to-five world. So when an old site friend called me one day and asked whether I fancied joining the steeplejack trade, I jumped at the chance.

Basically, you got paid a lot more for doing the same job as a bricklayer – only higher up. The firm I joined had contracts for repairs and maintenance on industrial chimneys all over the Midlands – big, redbrick fingers that poked anywhere between 80 and 200 feet into the sky.

I thought it was fantastic. Here was the excitement I'd been craving, the thrill that could keep me charged up through the day until it was evening and time to go down the pubs again. I was apprenticed to one of the most experienced jacks, Ted, and he soon had me shinning up and down the sides of these chimneys as though I'd been doing it all my life. It was my job to run up and down bringing Ted's tools, and the ten-foot lengths of laddering he needed to lay a climbing route up the side of the chimney. When he'd climbed halfway up the highest section, he'd turn and balance with his back against the rungs. Then he'd reach his arms down to take the next section as I passed it up to him, swing his arms up over his head and hook the next section up. It took ice-cool nerves and catlike balance, but he made it all seem as easy as hanging out the washing. I loved his casual style, and relished getting to the top.

Our job at the top of the chimney would invariably be to replace worn and damaged brickwork. That would involve fixing up a hanging platform that we'd sit on beside the top of the chimney. Then we'd knock away the bricks before reaching the most crucial part; removing the wire band that held the chimney in. Even the most experienced jacks would take a deep breath before this part of the job, because you were never sure how much tension would be released when the metal sheet was cut through: it could potentially jump back and pitch you off your small seat.

During the months I worked with Ted – travelling all over the country, staying in bed-and-breakfast accommodation and enjoying the drama of the work high above the skylines – there were a number of incidents involving other men in the company. One jack was hurt when he slipped because a ladder section hadn't been properly hammered home, and another actually died when he toppled from the highest point of a factory chimney.

These reports didn't put me off, though. They just emphasised the danger of what I was doing, and I'd mention these incidents to my friends down the pub as though they endorsed my bravery and devil-may-care attitude. Until one day.

We'd been working on an eighty footer at a hospital site, and reached the top. The chimney was still in use, and we could see the warm air shimmering over the hole as we got level with it; a sign every jack hated. Because of the width of the hole at the top, we could only manage to secure the bosun's chair – which could hang from chains stretched across the aperture – by inching round the narrow lip to the other side.

Sitting astride the lip, I began to scoot my way carefully round to the other side. I was halfway there when my sense of confidence and security suddenly drained away just as though someone had pulled a plug out of the bottom of my foot. The ground to my right seemed to leap up at me, and the deep black hole to my left felt as though it was sucking me down. I became aware of the heat rising up and rippling over my leg and side, and shook my head as pictures of me tumbling down, head over toe, raced around in my mind. I froze, gripping the brick wall as tightly as I had ever held anything. I closed my eyes and tried to wish myself down to the ground and safety.

My stillness was shattered by shouts and angry cries from down below. Ted was furious, and thought I was larking around, delaying him. Anger at his lack of concern together with fury that he'd witnessed my failure rose and sparked me into moving. I reached round, tore the chains and fittings from their place and hurled them down to the ground. Then, without looking back, I swung a leg backwards over the ladder and climbed down to earth. Ted was waiting at the bottom, hands on his hips and a sharp word on his tongue. I ignored him.

'That's it, I've had enough. I'm leaving. Today. *Now*,' I told him, turning and walking away from the chimney. I didn't care if I never saw another ladder in my life.

I decided that thrills were better if they were found at other people's expense, and turned my attention back to the pubs and the closing-time pavements, for I knew that I only had a couple of months or so to go until I'd be able to head out to Spain once again, only this time with a full-season job lined up.

The Crazy Horse Saloon gave me everything I was looking for. As much drinking, fighting and sex as I could consume, with no costs and no one to answer to. And while all this was going on, I was quietly hiding away as much money as I could. I sometimes used to wonder if I could possibly stash away any more money under the grubby mattress of my bunk without anyone getting too suspicious. So I just trusted that the other guys were, like myself, generally too tired, too drunk, or too stoned to have much time for observation tests.

That summer was a turning point. While previously I'd been able to run wild and yet still manage to rein myself in enough to complete a good day's work, I returned to Nottingham completely blown away. My summer of excess had ruined me for what now seemed to be very ordinary, everyday life.

To start with, I resented having to pay for my drinks! Having enjoyed a summer when the beer and Bacardi had been free and plentiful, I'd not realised how dramatically my consumption had rocketed – nor what demands that would make on my pocket. I quickly found the savings I had returned with being poured over the counter in the pubs and clubs.

Physically I was in bad shape, too. Heavy drinking and poor diet had taken their toll, and I'd lost the wiry condition site work had got me into. I was exhausted after just a couple of hours of bending and straightening and carrying bricks. I had a hangover until lunchtime, and getting up to be at work by 8 am was like a dreadful punishment.

At lunchtime I would go down to the nearest pub for a few pints to try to keep me going. As often as not, though, it would turn into an afternoon's binge, and I would simply not go back to work. My reputation among the foremen wasn't good, and such absences meant that my pay packet would be slimmer at the end of the week.

It all seemed to be a downward spiral, and one that I readily ascribed to some organised discrimination against me. What I didn't admit to myself was that in addition to being an alcoholic, I was by now a full-blown drug addict too. Such huge quantities of speed and hash had been consumed during the months in Spain that my body seemed to burn without it. I managed to find a few contacts in some of the scruffier bars in Nottingham, but it never seemed to be as readily available as at the Crazy Horse Saloon.

When I couldn't get hold of the drugs I desperately wanted to help me recapture the buzz I'd known, I would find myself going into dark, deep depressions. Never being particularly sociable at the best of times, I would sink into myself. At times like this it seemed as though the most ordinary attempt at making conversation was a physical attack. I'd avoid talking to people, remaining at the bar with my solo drink, or disappearing to my room at home. Family relationships had hit an all-time low on my return. My family were visibly shocked and concerned about my condition, but I'd closed down any efforts to talk with them about what had happened. I simply used their home like a hotel; somewhere to lay my head before stumbling out in search of another drink or another blast of dope.

The offer of work in Switzerland seemed like a lifeline to a drowning man. It came completely out of the blue that autumn – a letter from some friends who had been working at the Crazy Horse Saloon and who knew someone opening a new hotel in the fashionable ski resort of Hoyt Nandes, near Sion. Would I join them as a waiter?

The Bluesy Hotel turned out to be nothing like the Crazy Horse Saloon. Well built, tastefully appointed and well decorated, it was intended to be a haunt for the wealthy and particular. Soon after arrival I found myself starting French lessons so that my serving style would match my sharp uniform. It was a far cry from what I was used to, but I enjoyed this new world in a strange way, and threw myself into learning how to enquire after Monsieur's choice of wine, and how best to serve a dish to Madame.

In addition to waiting on tables in the small restaurant, I was put in charge of the coffee shop and bar. Such responsibilities suited me down to the ground. I may have been enjoying the new job I had, but that didn't stop me from trying to rob my employer blind. With him so trusting, it was an easy thing to take over a bottle of the best red for a client, take his money and then somehow forget to ring it up at the bar. Fairly soon I had another small mountain of money piling up in my room.

My plan was to amass as much as I could in a fairly short time, and then simply to disappear. But before I could pull all the loose ends together, a beat-up old camper van pulled into the car park one night and out hopped two American travellers who were passing through the area.

Harvey and his friend were students, taking some time out from their studies to see Europe. Money was running low, so they were looking for work that would help tide them over. By now I was also running the disco and the restaurant because my two friends had found the quietness of the hotel scene too much and left. I took Harvey and his mate on.

That night as we chatted in my room, Harvey reached into his travel bag. The words dried up on my lips and my mouth dropped open, as he pulled out one well-wrapped parcel after another. It was the biggest haul of hash I had ever seen — enough to keep a dealer in the lap of luxury for years back in England. Just seeing the drug seemed to set my juices flowing, and I licked my lips as he peeled the plastic covering off the greeny-brown substance and smiled: 'Ever tried this, then, Johnny?'

Then he broke off a big chunk, crumbled it, and we

rolled it into a few cigarettes. The rest of the night passed in a delightful haze of warm, cotton-wool feelings as the drug flowed through my bloodstream like a welcome old friend.

The pattern was set. Pretty soon we were smoking for breakfast, lunch, tea and supper, and the days seemed to disappear in a blur of late nights—talking, laughing and smoking. We raced through the dull days of serving the dinners so that we could get to the next hash time. For in addition to the physical pleasure, I sensed that I was on the edge of something else.

The blue-grey smoke of our latest joint curls away lazily up to the ceiling, like a corkscrew. I watch it rather dreamily, and think how the hash is unplugging the cork in me, and that bottled up inside there's something rich and rare, a vintage! Over the past few days I feel that I've suddenly been let in on what may be one of the biggest and best-kept secrets in the world. There's more to life!

I inhale slowly and deeply, sucking the hash right down to my toes. Mellow is the right word for this stuff. I feel warm and relaxed and comfortable, rather like an old slipper. And it makes me feel free and creative as the notes of music from my cassette player ring crystal clear.

'You see, man ...' and a long, studied silence. 'It's all about finding yourself. You've got to find yourself – where you've come from, where it's all at. D'you know what I mean?' he squints at me, with one eye closed, through the smoke.

'Yeah, Harvey,' I nod. 'I think I do. Tell me some more.' I'm not actually sure that I do know what he's talking about, but the way he says it and the earnestness with which he talks convinces me it must be right. It sounds good; like there's something around, maybe just beyond my view at the moment, to which I can belong, where I won't be left out. Something I can find and be part of. The prospect excites me in a way that drinking, fighting and sleeping around never have. It's a curious sensation, and one that I want to last.

And then the mood washes away, changing, and we're giggling fit to bust over a nonsense incident from the day. The dope seems to bring all my emotions to the surface in a way I've never really known before; all the feelings other than anger, resentment, jealousy, rage and aggression. It's like someone's plugged up the sink and left the tap running. The water rises and rises, and then suddenly it splashes over the sides, flowing down.

Other times it would be my taste buds that seemed to be exploding in scale, and I developed a sudden, ravenous appetite. So we would tiptoe down to the hotel larder, sneak away with ten or a dozen bars of chocolate and gorge ourselves on them, revelling in the sticky sweetness of it all. Only the next morning I'd have a bit of a headache and feel slightly nauseous, unsure whether it was because of the food or the drugs. I preferred to think it was the sweets, as I didn't want to believe that anything which could make me feel so wonderfully relaxed, calm and at peace with myself could possibly dump me on the ground so hard.

With such a ready source available, our appetite for hash grew out of all proportion, and pretty soon we were stoned almost round the clock. It was all I could do to manage to hold my head together on everyday matters, like serving behind the bar and giving people the right change – if I knew there wasn't a chance I could rip them off. It transpired that Harvey and his travelling companion – who had moved on in search of more adventures after just a short time at the Bluesy – had been trying to peddle their slabs along the way, but with little success. Switzerland didn't take kindly to drugs, hard or soft, so they'd not been able to make many inroads.

After a few weeks, we decided to move on. I handed in my notice, hung up my working clothes for the last time, and joined Harvey for an overland trek through Europe. With all the money I'd earned and stolen during my time at the hotel we were well provided for, and passed an enjoyable couple of months staying at youth hostels, eating and drinking well, smoking dope – and all the time talking about this increasingly urgent need to 'find yourself'.

We went to Athens, Corfu and finally Crete, where we rented some rooms and moved in with a couple of girls we met at one of the harbour bars. With the money I'd amassed we bought in crates of beer every day. Life was one long party. Finally May arrived, though, and the starting date for my second summer season at the Crazy Horse Saloon. Harvey and I had our last drinks together and waved each other a cheery goodbye – each to continue our own search for something we weren't quite sure of. I sometimes wonder whether he's still looking.

Back at Santa Suzanna it was more of the same from the previous year. All-night partying in the bar, musical beds with the girls hanging around after closing time, and late mornings spent trying to recover from the previous night's activities.

Yet somehow I seemed to be losing my taste for it all. It was like a bottle of lemonade that had gone flat because the top had been left off. All the ingredients were still there, but it had no fizz. I actually found myself on occasions dreading the prospect of having to go through the motions of passion with another sun-burned, vodka-fuelled 'holiday fling' seeker. Even the fighting spirit in me was ebbing away. Partly this was because of my increasingly heavy drug use, which slowed my emotions down, but it also reflected this growing sense I had that I was missing out on something more meaningful, somewhere. Now and then I'd try to talk about it with the other lads at the bar, but they'd laugh it off.

'Say, do you ever wonder what it's all about – life, I mean?' I'd ask casually over a breakfast beer, perhaps.

'What d'ya mean, Johnny? It's women and drinking, isn't it? What more could you want, eh?'

Or someone else would chip in: 'Not thinking of becoming a monk, are you Johnny? Just because you didn't score last night!' And my questions would be drowned in a sea of guffaws, giggles and empty ale-can missiles.

But I couldn't shake my inner restlessness. I worried away at it even while I was at my busiest taking orders, running round with trays full of drinks, and strong-arming those revellers who had had one too many out of the door. I'd watch the young holidaymakers come in, dressed up in their evening best. They'd drink more than they should, stagger away in the early hours laughing and hooting. It all seemed more and more empty to me. 'Surely there's got to be more to life than working in some dead-end job fifty weeks of a year so that you can come and get a hangover in the sun?' I'd ask myself.

Eventually I became so unsettled that I knew I had to do something. One day I hurriedly quit my job to see if I could find some answers to the questions Harvey had prompted me to start asking.

Finding my way to Marrakesh, a hot and dusty city in Morocco, I booked into a cheap hotel and began to hang around in the bars and hostels where young intense travellers from all over Europe seemed to gather to share their drugs and their hunger for reality. Some days I'd consume more than even my hash-saturated system could take, and I'd be unable to do more than lie on my bed staring up at the cracked ceiling, listening to the flies buzzing around and the shouts from the street below, half hoping that someone would arrive at my door to tell me what on earth was going on.

Then I began to get hit by deep troughs of depression. Great, black clouds of gloom would overwhelm me. I'd feel pressed to the spot by foreboding of some un-certain but huge catastrophe. Eating and washing seemed

completely unimportant. I became suspicious of the
other travellers, thinking that they were out to steal my
money or my dope. Everywhere I went I'd be constantly
turning my head to see if someone was trying to sneak
up behind me.

Such paranoia finally spurred me to leave Morocco,
and I found my way to Gibraltar. Funds were low by
now, so I managed to find a few days' work bricklaying
at a new hotel complex. I also went into an expensive
shop and bought a couple of cameras and a cassette
player on HP. I left the country a couple of days later.

Soon I was back at the Crazy Horse Saloon, anxious to
tell the other guys about my travels and experiences. I
stayed on for a couple of weeks, but the job no longer
held any appeal. From there I moved on to Lorette,
where I shared an apartment with Fanta, whom I had
met through the saloon. He shared my appetite for
hash, and we began to push it in the town as well as
taking huge quantities ourselves.

When the season ended and it was time to head back
to Nottingham once more, I was little more than skin
and bone, withdrawn and suspicious of everyone around
me. Large, raw ulcers in my mouth meant that on the
few occasions I felt like eating, I couldn't because it was
too painful. My lips were sore and cracked, and I was
plagued by stomach cramps.

Somehow I managed to stumble back to my parents'
house, where the full extent of my physical slump hit
me. When Mum opened the door, she didn't recognise
me.

By now I was beyond holding a job down. I made one
or two attempts to resume bricklaying, but the demands
of timekeeping and the physical hardship were too
much for me. More often than not I'd simply lie in late
in the mornings, and then manage to shuffle down to
the local pub to drink away the afternoons.

I managed to make enough contacts to feed my drug
craving, but didn't feel free to smoke at home. So I

moved out, into a dirty one-room flat a couple of streets away. There was a bed with a few dirty covers, a tatty old wardrobe, a broken-down chair and a sink. As well as making me more docile, the drugs reduced my sex drive. And I then found that on the nights I did go out looking for some female company, my unkempt, un-shaven, unwashed appearance kept them away.

So it was one morning that I hung over the sink in my damp attic room, and looked up at the mirror. As I examined my face – old before its time – I remembered that time hovering over the industrial chimney, the dark drop in front of me, and thought how similar the situation was now.

'You're falling apart, Johnny,' I told myself. 'You're really on the edge, you know, youth. If you aren't careful, you're going to fall into the flames.'

What worried me most was that the face I was gazing into didn't seem to care.

7
The Silent Scream

I was flying off to start a brand new life – so I got drunk to celebrate. Together with a gang of other bricklayers, I'd boarded the plane taking off from London's Heathrow, looking forward to the prospect of a bright new future in Canada.

The realisation that I was literally wasting away had hit me hard that day in my shabby flat. I'd not been able to shake the sense of alarm it had provoked, which had remained with me as things went from bad to worse. With every spare penny going on drink and drugs I'd fallen well behind on rent payments. When I knew the landlord was coming – I could hear the barking of his two fierce dogs well down the street – I'd turn off the stereo and the lights and lie quietly on my bed, waiting for him to give up knocking and go away. I'd hear him curse and kick the wall as he stamped off.

One day he'd caught me leaving, though, and told me bluntly: 'I want you out, Goodfellow. You owe me money and you're nothing but trouble. You've got to get out.'

My parents had let me move back into my old room. If they were worried for me, they were not prepared to say anything. But moving home again prompted me to try working again, so I found myself back on the building sites for a short time. During one lunchtime break in the snack cabin, I casually picked up a lunchtime edition of the evening paper that had been tossed aside by one of the other men. He'd seen that there were no fanciable runners on the afternoon's race card and decided there were no bets worth placing.

I flipped the pages idly, until I came to the advertisement section. As I looked down the columns, one entry seemed to leap out at me. 'Canada. Top rates for bricklayers. Free flights, good money. Apply now for further information.' I read on, drinking in the details about the money that was waiting to be earned working in the beautiful Canadian countryside. It sounded wonderful – and a welcome relief from the cold, wet monotony of the Midlands.

Perhaps this was what I needed, I thought. A new place. New friends. New prospects. A chance to break with the past and build a new future. I'd been able to discipline myself to work hard in the past, and here was an opportunity to do so once more. I could do it. I could pull myself together if I really tried, and save myself from complete collapse. All it needed was a bit of determination, effort and willpower. I read the advert aloud to the men sitting around and one or two expressed mild curiosity. I then carefully tore it out of the page and slipped it into my pocket.

Within ten days I was in Canada. I'd telephoned the number listed in the advertisement and had been invited down to Birmingham for an interview. After being accepted there I'd simply had to wait for all my paperwork to be processed before I joined the other brickies – including two of my Nottingham workmates – at Heathrow. Three times the salary of Britain, good fresh air and fine living – we toasted each other's good fortune from take-off to touchdown. I saw this airborne party as a sort of suitable farewell to my old life. I was determined to make a go of things in the days to come.

And I did. We had been contracted to work on a major apartment complex in St John, New Brunswick, on Canada's eastern seaboard. Local labourers didn't like the harsh winters and managed to make enough money during the summer months – hence the appeal for British hands to keep the bricks being laid. For the first week we were accommodated at a comfortable hotel in the town, after which we were expected to find our own accommodation. I got myself a smart bedsitting room in a lodging house not far from the site. It was clean, cosy and convenient, and I soon felt as though I'd found myself a new home.

The work was hard, but with my determination to make a new start I responded willingly. We would find that it was so cold on some mornings that big heater fans would be set blowing on each level of the building to keep the freshly-mixed mortar from freezing and cracking before we could use it. Some days it was twenty-five degrees below freezing. But though it was colder than Nottingham, it was cleaner, too, and I enjoyed breathing in the crisp morning air.

I resolved from the word go to keep my head down and work hard. I wanted to make as much money as soon as possible. I was looking for a home, a wife and a family – and I figured that by pulling myself together and really trying, I'd be able to make it all happen. So I disciplined myself hard. No drugs, no crazy nights, no heavy drinking.

At the end of the day I was normally fairly tired because my body was still getting back into the swing of hard labour. I'd go back to my room, weary but satisfied, wash and change and then head down the street to a nearby bar. There I would enjoy a leisurely meal of medium steak and plenty of vegetables, followed by no more than four or five quiet pints with a few of the other regulars (just a sip compared to my former intake). Then I'd stroll back to my lodgings and climb into bed for a contented night's sleep, satisfied with my efforts of the day and the prospects of tomorrow.

This ordered pattern continued for a week or so, until one Friday night. As I was heading along the corridor to my room, I accidentally collided with someone walking in the opposite direction. He was a tall, broad, bearded French Canadian who had moved into the adjoining room. As we stepped away from each other and looked up, I mumbled an apology.

He looked at me for a moment and then asked matter-of-factly: 'Do you smoke dope?'

'Sure I do,' I answered quickly and eagerly, as a part of me seemed to stand back and look on in horror as all my resolutions and plans seemed to be swept away in an instant. Even as we turned to head back to his room I was appalled at the way in which all my efforts seemed about to crumble to nothing. But this feeling was swamped by an overwhelming desire to feel the wonderful rush of floating freedom that hit me as I sucked in the joint. As we closed the door, I hoped it was good stuff.

It was, and abstinence seemed to add to the pleasure. Frankie and I sat down and swapped hash stories as he took his from its hiding place, burned it over some silver paper, and then rolled it into two large joints. The familiar, pungent sweetness made me wrinkle my nose as I drew heavily on my smoke.

We spent several hours getting thoroughly stoned before we went out on the town. In a series of bars and discos I managed to spend most of the money I'd earned during my brief time in Canada. We returned to our rooms with empty pockets, but each with a woman on our arm. They stayed the night, and we alternately slept and smoked through till dawn. The next day was a Saturday, but with us working a six- or seven-day week we were due in on site.

I didn't go. Instead the four of us stayed in our rooms, smoking and drinking through the weekend. I woke on Tuesday morning feeling hung over, heavy-headed ... and defeated. All the pleasure of the past few days seemed to drain away as I realised that my best efforts had come to nothing. I was back where I had started, and there didn't seem to be anything I could do about it.

So began an ongoing struggle, as I'd try to make sure I arrived in time for work every morning and continued to enjoy the wild living at night again. Some nights we would be out dancing and drinking until 3 am, returning for a couple of hours of unrefreshing sleep before getting up again at 6.30 am. Soon I was skipping more than the odd day again, and I was turning up only two or three mornings a week – putting in just enough hours to cover the costs of accommodation, drink and drugs.

I couldn't bring myself to tell any of this to my family back home. My first letters on arrival had been enthusiastic and cheerful. I'd told them how exciting Canada was, and how well things were going. As I slipped back into my old ways, I began to make my notes briefer and less frequent, until eventually I stopped writing at all. Except for one note – to tell them I was getting married.

I'd met Corinne in a disco one night, and I'd been attracted to her immediately. She was a beautiful French Canadian with an oval face, dark brown eyes and long, dark hair. I got talking to her over a drink and so began a relationship that blossomed in the days that followed.

Although fairly quiet by nature, she enjoyed the excitement of nightlife, too, and after an evening's drinking in bars and clubs we would head off back to my apartment with a bottle of whisky and some hash. Within a few weeks I had proposed and she had accepted. We intended to get married in a matter of months and set up home together. Corinne made me happy and lessened the disappointment I'd felt over failing to make a clean break. Here was someone who shared my love for the buzz of drugs and drinking, and simply helped me keep it all under some sort of control. Maybe it was possible to tread a middle line, after all.

I told myself that Corinne made me feel different from the way all the other girls had made me feel. There had been plenty of other women, but they had been objects, not people. I'd never felt comfortable talking to them, thinking of them as people with needs and feelings and hurts. I'd just been interested in whether or not they'd go to bed with me, and how I could drop them afterwards without a scene. It was partly a horrible sense of awkwardness and also a deep insecurity. I'd never got used to that awful moment when you had to go up and ask a girl if she wanted to dance. I dreaded the moment when she may say 'no', and the feelings of rejection and ridicule you'd experience in front of your mates. So I'd kept them at arm's length, except in bed, and continued to be baffled by the way I desperately wanted to pursue them, but didn't seem able to get close once I'd caught them. The threat of true intimacy frightened me.

It had seemed otherwise for a time with Sharon. At eighteen I'd met her in a Nottingham club, a slim, blonde-haired secretary from a respectable, middle-class home. It was before I'd really started to go wild, and we began a courtship that seemed stable and contented. One day she looked ashen as we met after work, and she blurted out: 'Johnny, you'll never believe it: I'm pregnant!'

The shock threw us together. We were terrified at what our parents would say, but there seemed to be no way out. We faced two sets of silent, saddened parents as we told them what had happened, and began to plan for the future. Initially we intended to get married, but as the plans became more serious I began to panic. With little thought for Sharon and our baby, all I could see was my freedom being taken away; a young man with all his future ahead of him stuck at home with a wife, a child and too many responsibilities. The prospect alarmed me, and in an emotional scene I had told her it was all off; then I'd turned around, walked out of her life and concentrated on my own. If I remember rightly, the first thing I did was to go and have a few drinks.

Memories of this failed relationship began to come back to me as Corinne and I found that we weren't going to be following a smooth path to the altar. Although

at first being with her had curbed my excessive appetite
for drugs, gradually her presence began to act as less of
a brake. I would get heavily stoned, or drink myself
almost to a standstill, and we would fall out about it. The
way I pushed the limits of what I could handle seemed
to frighten her, despite her own love of getting high.

Things came to a head one night when we swayed
back to my new room. Erratic work schedules had
slimmed my pay packets down drastically, and as a result
I'd had to move from the comfortable lodgings I'd had
previously to less tasteful accommodation in a poorer
part of the town.

I collapse back on the bed and stare up at the bare
electric bulb swinging from the ceiling. The light burns
into the back of my eyes, but the sharp stabbing pain it
causes is a welcome attack on the spreading numbness I
feel across my chest and stomach.

I can hear Corinne's footsteps fading down the corridor as she leaves. I know that I'm never going to see
her again, that the cottage with the roses round the door
and the smiling kids aren't going to be. She's just
slammed the door shut and walked out in despair, and
I'm not sure what to feel. It's a bit like being awake
under anaesthetic. I'm conscious of my body and the
reality of what's just happened, but I seem to be beyond
feeling anything. The last flicker of hope I had about
this quest for a new life has been snuffed out and I seem
to be beyond reacting.

Water drips maddeningly into the cracked, brown-
stained washbasin in the corner of the room, and
around my ankles I can sense the drift of cool air
that whispers in between the cracks in the uncovered,
wooden floorboards. Unmoving, I look at the ceiling
and run my tongue, thick with alcohol, over my lips. A
thought crosses my mind, definite and direct.

I've completely lost control of my life.

At first it's just a fact, unavoidable and inarguable. But

then it seems to become a lockgate that opens, allowing floods of emotion to come crashing through. A wave of cold, sharp fear surges through me as I try to look into the future and realise that there is nothing there to see, not the faintest straw of a hope to clutch at. I feel like I'm drowning in the sea of my own failure.

Each new realisation beats down upon me like another wave crashing against a harbour wall. No one knows that I'm lying in this filthy room all alone. I have no friends to whom I can turn for help. My drinking is out of any control. I can't seem to get enough drugs to satisfy my cravings. It's beyond me to show care and concern for someone I love dearly. Tomorrow seems like a big, black hole. It's like being on the chimneytop again.

I've heard about dying men who are supposed to see a film of their life flash before their eyes. Well, my time must be near, because I'm staring at a private screening of John Goodfellow's life – a series of explosive, empty adventures. I'm appalled, overwhelmed and terrified. I can't move from the top of this broken-down old brass bed.

Suddenly I jerk forward from the waist as, in an agonising wrench, a huge silent scream bursts from my lips. No sound comes out, but my teeth are bared and my mouth pulled wide as I shriek inwardly in horror. It's like vomiting despair.

Falling back onto the bedspread again, I close my eyes to try to stop the stinging sensation in my eyes. As I drift into a welcome alcoholic sleep I half hope that I won't wake up in the morning because I don't think I'll be able to face the thought of another day in my pointless, hopeless life.

Cold, cramped and hung over, I came round the next morning with the awareness that something strange and frightening had happened a few hours earlier. It wasn't just the drugs and drink, there had been something else clawing at my heart. But I was in no mood for working it out. I simply knew that I had to get out of that room and to leave Canada as soon as I could.

The final reason for staying there had fallen through, together with my hopes for a new, self-made start. And with Corinne out of my life, the possibilities of my staying in Canada had gone whether I wanted to remain or not. A couple of months earlier there had been an early morning visit to the building site by a couple of officials from the Canadian government.

They turned out to be men from the immigration department, and their investigations had revealed that a number of British bricklayers – including me – had made false declarations to get the necessary papers to allow them into the country. What I'd done was fail to admit to my criminal conviction for the jeweller's shop break-in. Now they'd found out and wanted me out of Canada. My engagement to Corrine had worked a rescue, though, because anyone marrying a Canadian citizen automatically won the relevant authorisation to stay. Now with my ring off her finger, my papers would soon come to the top of the immigration department's in-tray again.

If I'd felt threatened like this only a few weeks before, I would have responded with a flash of the violent Johnny of old. It had happened once, despite my best intentions to keep a tight rein on my temper and fists, one night after I'd been out for a few drinks with Frankie. We were strolling home with a couple of girls when we passed two other guys in the street. One of them, a tall, long-haired man in a lumber jacket, brushed my shoulder awkwardly. Instinctively I swore a warning at him to be more careful in future.

Provoked, he turned back and we were soon trading blows in the middle of the street. I was beginning to work him over well when his buddy stepped back from struggling with Frankie and reached into his inside pocket, pulling out a wicked-looking bowie knife and brandishing it at us with a grin.

Our rooms weren't far away, so I turned and ran inside. Grabbing a knife from the kitchen, I charged back into the street to confront them, screaming and yelling like a maniac.

For a few moments we stood off from each other. I was just waiting for them to make a move, and I'd dive at them with my blade. But after flashing us a last look of anger, they turned and walked away.

But now all the fight seemed to have gone out of me. It wasn't that I was peaceful and controlled inside. I was just beaten; whipped like a dog. I felt as though I'd been attacked by a gang and left for dead at the side of the road. I just wanted to crawl into a quiet place where I could wait for the end.

The morning after Corinne's departure, I knew I had to leave. I booked a ticket back to England with the little money I had saved, and the next day boarded a flight home. Stepping down onto the tarmac at Heathrow I didn't dare look further than getting through customs. If there was any point or hope, then all I knew was that it was beyond me. I shuffled in line to the exit that seemed to mock my despair: 'Nothing to Declare'.

8

Beyond Reality

No one ever asked me what had happened to the plans for a bright new life. They didn't have to: one look at me told the whole story of failure. I was thin and sickly, and any shred of confidence I may have once possessed had been stripped away by my experiences in Canada. I was cowed and quiet, and tried to avoid talking with people at all times because I just couldn't cope with attempting to communicate.

Being at home was dreadful, so I'd slope off down to one of the pubs, where I'd buy a pint and sit, withdrawn, in a corner or up against the bar. I'd sip my beer, look around at all the people laughing and joking, and all the feelings of being separated – like I was stuck on the other side of a one-way mirror – would come back at me, magnified. Life was just a mechanical round of finally dragging myself out of bed, shuffling through the day until the bars were open, drinking silently until it was time to go home, falling into bed and waiting for the whole meaningless routine to start again.

Then, one night, I bumped into Alan. I was nursing a drink in a corner of the Flying Horse. I was watching the chatter and drinking going on around me in a detached sort of way when I spotted someone I thought I recognised from school days. We got talking as he waited to be served, and it turned out to be Alan, whom I used to know. But he'd changed.

Back at school, when I'd been recognised as one of the

leading lights – because of my temper and talent for fighting – he'd been quiet. Tall, thin and spotty, he'd been just another one of the boys. Now here was I, introspective and unsure of myself and everything else, and Alan seemed to have made an opposite transformation.

Wearing a smart leather jacket he seemed confident and self-assured. Buying me a pint with a gesture of casual generosity, he mentioned that he had a sports car parked just outside. I got the impression that he was really doing well for himself, although he was faintly vague about what he did for a living. Whatever it was, it certainly seemed to be successful enough. Somehow we struck up an immediate friendship, recalling the old days and wondering what had happened to some of the other boys we had known. By the end of the evening we'd agreed to meet up again the following night to go and score some dope together.

Over the next few weeks, Alan and I became close friends. We'd drink until closing time and then go back to his flat in another part of the town, where we'd smoke dope until we nodded off in the small hours. Early on I discovered that Alan's successful appearance was only that. He was out of work and the TR7 was on hire purchase, with a few payments outstanding. I sensed that, in his own way, Alan felt as empty inside as I did.

One evening as we sat drowsily in his cheap flat, drawing on a joint and talking with the lazy sort of contentment that only dope can give, Alan broke the conversation and asked me unexpectedly: 'Do you ever think about spiritual things, then, Johnny?'

I squinted at him through the smoke, furrowing my eyebrows in a question. 'Eh? Spiritual things? I don't know what you mean.'

'Well, you know, life. Don't you ever wonder what life's all about, like – why we are here and all? You know, the future and death and everything?'

My heart had started to race as he began to talk, but

somehow I didn't dare admit to having shared such thoughts. I was frightened about opening up, about exposing what was really inside me – the horrible feeling of emptiness, loneliness and uncertainty. So I responded in a non-committal way: 'No, I can't say I've thought about that sort of stuff in years.' But I didn't want him to stop talking, so I added: 'Why d'you ask, Alan?'

He got up quickly and walked over to a wall cupboard. Rummaging about in the back, he pulled out a large, black book and walked back. Sitting down next to me on the sofa, he dropped the book onto the coffee table in front of us.

'Well, I was wondering whether you were interested in any of this,' he said, pointing to the book. I looked down at the cover.

Hidden and Forbidden Knowledge it proclaimed in large gold letters.

I picked the book up to have a flip through it, as I could sense that Alan was trying to share his excitement with me about something. Skipping through the thick volume, I saw photographs and articles about all sorts of occult phenomena and experiences. There were features and studies on tarot cards, astrology, astral projection, clairvoyance, clairaudience and black magic. There were guidelines for magic rites and drawing pentagrams and other symbols.

The book seemed to grow heavier in my hands. Here was what I'd been looking for! Maybe there were answers to some of the questions I'd been asking myself, after all! I pored over the pages, thrilled by this whole new world that was being unveiled before my eyes, with all its possibilities for meaning and purpose. Maybe this was the missing piece that I'd been searching for, I thought excitedly.

When I finally left Alan's flat later that night, I had *Hidden and Forbidden Knowledge* tucked under my arm.

For the next fortnight I spent almost every waking moment with my nose stuck in its pages, drawn to reading, rereading and studying it with a strange compulsion. I didn't understand all that was said, but I sensed, reading between the lines, that it was hugely important. My whole life was at stake, and this could be the answer.

From then on Alan and I talked about nothing else. We'd read sections of the book together and discuss what various aspects meant and how they might be applied to our lives. We became particularly drawn to astrology and the idea that our lives might in some way be influenced by the alignment of the planets and the stars.

This possibility both attracted and repelled me. I was filled with hope by the idea that all those times I'd spun out of control – violence, drugs and sex – may have been beyond my governing. But I was also consumed by dread at the prospect that what happened in the heavens was charting my future. There may be worse things ahead.

Every day I'd read what the newspaper astrologers had to say for Aquarius, but I soon began to dismiss these columns as trivial. Through visiting occult bookshops and buying up more literature, Alan and I began to realise that there was a far deeper side to this whole new world that we had discovered than most people were aware of.

Alan's pretty blonde girlfriend, Sarah, shared a flat with another girl, Jenny, and the four of us would spend long evenings talking about the things we were reading. Alan and I began to try to make objects move by psychokinesis, and there were occasions when I really believed that the mug on the table in front of me was shimmering and vibrating because of the power we were releasing from within.

We also became fascinated by what we read of astral projection. These were mystical out-of-the-body experiences that people apparently had after going into a trance. Their inner being, or spirit, would be freed from their physical body and they would be able to travel to different places and dimensions, and learn new and secret truths about life. Despite fuelling our efforts with larger and larger quantities of dope, Alan and I were frustrated by our failure to travel on these incredible journeys.

The girls were more successful, though — and it frightened them. One evening Sarah told us how the previous night she had found herself leaving her body as she was drawn into the astral plane. Suddenly she found herself in front of the bathroom mirror — but there was a different face staring out at her. Then she turned and looked back into the bedroom ... and saw her own body lying in bed. The experience had shocked her deeply, and she never tried to go 'visiting' again in this way. Alan and I were excited by her account, though, and it only added to our sense of annoyance that we had not managed to achieve similar things.

We felt that we were very close to something; quite what we didn't really know, but it was a matter of life or death.

It's like we've been let in on a secret that's too big for the rest of the world. We watch all the people heading off for work in the morning with their briefcases, sandwich boxes and umbrellas, and they look at us as though we're ordinary, just like them. But they don't know. We're on the edge of something so important that only a few people can be trusted with it.

All the things you see around you — houses, cars, children playing in the park — are what most people think are 'real'. If only they knew! We're being shown that in a crazy way everything around us is unreal and that there is a greater reality just a hair's breadth away. It's so tantalisingly close, but it's also just out of reach.

There are keys, you see. Keys to understanding and power that will unlock the universe. They are so important that they are not to be made known to ordinary people – only those with a hunger for more.

Alan and I are part of a small calling who have been chosen to have these truths revealed to us. Some of the others have formed groups that contain secret messages in the music they weave. To us the likes of Hawkwind, Pink Floyd and Jethro Tull are musical prophets, speaking of deep things. We spend hours searching every phrase and tone, looking for the coded words.

It's thrilling and terrifying, both at the same time. I feel as though I could either fall off this planet and go spinning helplessly into deepest space, never to return, or find myself being crowned as a king of the entire universe. Life and death; they dance together inside me, spinning faster and faster. The music is going to stop soon, and one of the partners is going to have to bow to the other. I wonder which one it's going to be.

Our search became so obsessive that we never spoke about anything else. While we felt that we had been chosen especially to learn about these hidden landscapes of life, we also felt a responsibility to share some of this teaching with others.

We tried to explain to drinking partners in the pubs and clubs how the world was on the brink of a series of cataclysmic events, and that people had to find the keys that would unlock the past, the present and the future. We weren't put off by their looks of blank incomprehension, nor the nickname we quickly earned as 'The Prophets of Doom'. We knew, deep inside, that our quest was too important to be put off by people's lack of understanding.

Alan suggested that one way we could be helped in our search would be to seek guidance from the country's top astrologer. We had read all his bestselling books on the subject. Perhaps if we showed him our commitment to finding the truth, he would be able to help. We discovered that he organised a weekly meeting in London to discuss astrological issues, and we excitedly travelled down one Wednesday to the lodge where the group met.

It was a crushing disappointment. We'd been expecting to find a man of hypnotic attraction, a leader. Instead he turned out to be a rather nondescript, quiet little man who couldn't even look us in the eyes when we introduced ourselves. And the other members of the group – who we'd anticipated would be like an inner circle of wise devotees – seemed to us just a group of middle-aged, middle-class surburbanites with a passing fancy for astrology.

We stayed for the meeting, and an elderly man with big, bushy eyebrows babbled on about some obscure aspect of astrology. We left in despair. Our high hopes had been dashed. We felt cheated and yet at the same time agreed that while they had only been playing at it, our exploration of the meaning of life was deadly serious.

In some ways the disappointment only sharpened our desire to find the truth, and we spent more and more time locked in study, trying to fall into trances and searching acid rock music for messages and guidance.

Our search consumed our nights and days. We'd sit up until the early hours, when a restless kind of sleep finally overtook us. By now I was working as a self-employed bricklayer, so if I didn't feel like going in the next morning, I wouldn't. The money I earned as a subcontractor when I was working made up for the days I missed. When I stayed at home, Alan and I would meet over lunch to talk about our thoughts and studies, then go down the pub and drink and talk until afternoon closing time. From there we would head back either to Alan's place or mine (I'd moved out of home again, to my family's combined relief and concern, and found a shabby room to let in the building where Sarah and

Jenny shared) and smoke some more dope. That would keep us going until evening, when there would be another round of drinking and dope and talk about 'the keys'.

We were joined in our erratic work arrangement by a group of other self-employed brickies, who included Mac. Big, broad, with sharp features, Mac loved to drink and womanise, and was always in the thick of the fun. (I'd known him from my time in Spain and Canada.) Yet when he heard Alan and me talking about our search, he didn't just laugh it off and disappear for another drink. He began to ask questions about what we were doing, and gradually joined our nightly sessions of study, drink and dope. With him came Gary, whom we also knew from the local drinking scene.

Shorter than Mac, with a mass of thick curly black hair, he had been married, but was separated from his wife. He always seemed to have plenty of money, but no one was ever quite sure where it all came from. And it was best not to ask.

Between us, we four had sampled just about everything life had to offer a young man. And yet as we sat together, drinking and talking and smoking and talking, we all agreed that for every slice of action we'd known, there was still an emptiness inside. We were only in our early and mid-twenties, yet in some ways we felt like old men with nothing to look forward to. Only this prospect of there being something else, something outside ourselves, held any hope or sense.

One night we were all squeezed into my dirty room, finishing off a couple of joints, when I suddenly felt as though the clouds in my head had parted, and I could see the way ahead clearly.

'You know, lads, we've got to find God.'

They looked over at me and waited for me to continue.

'Look, we all know that there's more to life than what people see out there' – and I pointed to the street below – 'right? Well, then, there must be some kind of supreme

power or being who's in control of the universe, right?
And if we can find him, then he – or it, or whatever –
will be able to help us understand ourselves; show us all
the mysteries we're searching for.'

Alan agreed: 'Yeah ... that's right, Johnny. We all
believe that there is some supreme being out there. So it
must be able to be found – and when we do, we'll find
the answers.'

We all started to grin and nod to each other. There
was a thrill of excitement as we felt that we'd really hit
on something important. We all crammed into Alan's
car and drove down into the town, where we went to
Frodo's, a noisy cellar wine bar, to celebrate.

We got well and truly drunk that night, and when
people around asked what the toasts were about, we
grinned and told them: 'We're going to go and find
God!'

The sense of euphoria carried us over the next few
days, and we began to discuss how we might start to
search for God. We talked about it and agreed that we
should begin by seeking help from holy men who might
be able to put us on the right track. The church never
entered our thinking at this stage. We'd all had similar
experiences of a sterile faith that mouthed love and
mocked sincerity, and we dismissed Christianity as being
as empty as the collection plates that we'd all passed
along the pew in our younger days.

Up to now the people in our drinking circles had
humoured our talk about the supernatural world, but
with our pubtime planning sessions for the search for
God, some began to get more concerned.

'Don't you think you're all taking this a bit too far,
lads, eh?' they would ask from time to time. A few even
dared to catch one of the others when they were alone
and cautiously suggest that maybe Johnny really needed
to see a doctor.

When I read in a library book about a band of mystics
who lived in the remote mountains of Iran, deeply

spiritual nomads who performed ancient rites in their communion with the gods, I knew that I had found the route we needed to follow. I filled the others in about these horse-riding gurus, and said: 'These are the men. These are the ones who can help us find God. We've got to go and find them.'

It quickly became clear, on pooling our limited assets, that we didn't have the money we needed to fund such a trip. My fear of the future spurred me into action. I had to explore this hazy world of spiritual things, yet I was frightened to do so alone. By enthusing the others, I could persuade them to join me. With my desperate passion for meaning driving me, I took on the role of ringleader, and began to scheme of ways to get us on the road to the Middle East. After a few late nights, I had it, and I called a council of war to lay the plan before the others.

I told them that we needed some initial money, so we all had to pull a fraud to get some easy cash. I'd carried out a couple of similar rip-offs in the past and knew that it was relatively quick and easy to get money this way; there would be no problem. With the money we made, we would then have to buy a van and travel overland. If we ran short along the way, it would be easy enough for the four of us to find a victim of some sorts to provide some more money.

Alan, Mac and Gary nodded in agreement. 'Sounds good, Johnny. But where do we get all this together?'

I didn't hesitate in replying, although I don't think I knew what was going to tumble out of my lips as I opened my mouth.

'Amsterdam. We're going to go to Amsterdam and start from there.'

As I said it, I knew that it was right – but I didn't know why. I'd only been to Amsterdam once before, and it had been an experience I had been glad to leave behind as quickly as possible.

It had been during my weeks travelling in search of

'the scene' that Harvey had introduced me to. I'd heard
so much about Amsterdam. It was like the fountainhead
of the drug trail that wound its way from Europe down
through into the Middle East and beyond. All kinds of
drugs were sold openly on the streets. Some cafes even
had little marijuana leaf signs on the windows, and you
were able to buy a couple of sticks over the counter, or
baked into a cake. You just had to go to experience it, I
was told; it was so free and easy, so laid back, so
beautiful.

When I arrived at the city's Central Station, my
pockets were still bulging from the proceeds of my time
at the Crazy Horse Saloon. Yet a crippling sense of fear
gripped me almost as soon as I stepped out of the
cavernous railway station. There were smiling, dope-
hazed faces all around me; young jean-clad groups
clustered around guitars on street corners; and graffiti
urging 'love not war' everywhere – but I felt completely
ill at ease.

I completed a quick walking tour of the city, and then
headed off down into one of the large parks that ring
the centre. Although I was carrying enough to pay for a
suite of rooms at any of Amsterdam's plushest hotels, I
was too scared to set foot inside. Instead, I spent a
nervous night sleeping curled up on a park bench, and
the next morning I took the first train out.

Memories of this unsettling visit came back to me, but
I still knew for some inexplicable reason that Amsterdam
was the place from which we should set off in our search
for God.

There was an awkward kind of farewell at home when
I went round to my parents and sisters to explain,
vaguely, that I and a group of friends were 'going off
travelling for a while'. I'd told them a little about my
fascination with supernatural things, but they'd shown
no interest, and I didn't want to have to try explaining
now. As I left, Trish said to Mum in a matter-of-fact
voice: 'I don't think I'm going to see Johnny again.'

In a curious way, she was right.

When I met up with Alan, Mac and Gary at East Midlands Airport, and we boarded the plane, we were charged up at the thought of starting our pilgrimage. 'Amsterdam, here we come,' I thought, as we were sucked back into our seats by the take-off thrust.

I didn't realise what a crossroads it would turn out to be.

9

Caught at the Crossroads

The Shelter was like a cross between an army barracks and a hospital. There was an air of cleanliness, orderliness and drilled routine about the three-storey building tucked away in one of the side streets in the rougher quarter of Amsterdam's city centre. The crisp well-run friendliness of the place both attracted us and repelled us as we set our bags down at the side of our bunk beds.

We'd been guided here by the people we'd asked on the streets about the best place to stay. 'The Shelter – cleanest and cheapest in the city,' they'd all said. So we'd wound our way through the narrow, cobbled streets; across arched bridges over the tree-lined canals, until we'd found the place, where a small sign at the side of the door announced that it was a 'Christian youth hostel'.

This short walk from the Central Station, where we'd been dropped by the airport bus, had taken us into the very heart of Amsterdam's street scene. On the way we'd passed crowds of young people milling around like a flowing stream of colour with their bright clothes and bags. But we'd also noticed those at the side of the roadways who, by comparison, seemed to have been washed up like so much floating rubbish. Heroin addiction screamed from their dark, grey-ringed eyes, emaciated bodies and unkempt clothing.

In all my desperate days I had never touched heroin because the prospect of what it could do had terrified me. Yet as I passed so many wasted youngsters, lying or crouching every few yards it seemed, I felt as though I was being warned about just where I was headed if this pilgrimage didn't work out. The thought scared me, and I took a tighter grip on my suitcase, increased my pace, and urged the other three to get a move on.

From the crowds and pushers and users we passed into the centre of the city's red light district, famed the world over for its easy-going and permissive nature. Anything and everything went in Amsterdam, they said. Whatever your sexual inclinations, there would be someone prepared to indulge you if you could pay the price, or somewhere you could watch others if that was your thing. We walked down the canal-side streets where the prostitutes sat in small, red-lit windows, wearing little or nothing and urging the passing men to step inside, draw the curtains and hand over the notes.

In days gone by this broad-minded, bold display of liberation would have been heady stuff. I'd have responded like a little boy let loose in a sweet shop. But by now my only thought was our goal; we had to find God! So I scarcely did more than turn my head to one side occasionally to cast a faintly-curious eye over the surroundings as we tramped along the directions we'd been given to The Shelter.

Up on the first floor of The Shelter we were ushered into a large dormitory which was filled with two rows of bunks, enough to accommodate about forty people. Picking our beds, testing the mattresses, we claimed our sleeping pitches, and then transferred our belongings to the lockers at the other end of the room. We then went to explore the rest of the building and found wooden floors and green-tiled walls decorated with posters and paintings proclaiming love and peace. There were a lot of other young travellers like us around, and yet there was an almost unnaturally subdued atmosphere, rather like the reading room of a library.

Next morning, after a good night's sleep, we breakfasted and pulled up stools together in the refectory area downstairs. Huddled forwards with elbows on the tables over mugs of steaming coffee, we ran through the plan again in low voices, casting an eye over our shoulders from time to time to make sure that no one was eavesdropping.

Simplicity was the key. The art of good fraud was keeping it uncluttered; the less fanciful the tale you spun, the less likely people were to quiz you about it. My earlier criminal exploits had already proved that, and I'd successfully completed one swindle back in England. I'd travelled down to London by train and on arriving at Euston pretended that I'd lost all my luggage. Returning to Nottingham – with the 'crime' suitably reported to the Metropolitan Police – I'd claimed on my previously-arranged holiday insurance for the loss of my luggage, clothing and expensive new cassette player. It was a profitable day's outing, really – none of those things had actually existed.

This was the crime we intended to commit to finance our overland trip to the East. We'd all taken out holiday insurances prior to leaving Nottingham, making sure that we used different companies so that we wouldn't arouse any suspicion. From our Amsterdam base, we intended to go four separate ways – Alan to Belgium, Gary to Germany and Mac to France – and report luggage thefts in four different locations. Then we'd meet back in Amsterdam, claim the money and be on our way.

My restlessness spurred me into going first; I also wanted to show the others how easy it was. Driven, too, by a continuing feeling of unease from being in Amsterdam, I decided to launch straight in after breakfast. So, from The Shelter, I wound my way back to the Central Station, where the forecourt was crowded with young people sitting, lying, talking and smoking in groups. Rock music blared from radios and guitars, and the smell of marijuana could be detected in the cool January air.

I found my way into the station building, where a parade of shops ran under the central walkway that linked the platforms. Finding a vacant photo booth, I stepped inside, fed in the relevant coins, and then sat looking impassively at the mirror screen opposite as the machine flashed off my passport portrait.

When they'd been taken, I pulled back the curtain, stepped outside – and held up my hands in fake horror. 'My bags, they've gone. Someone's stolen my bags!' I cried in a loud voice. Looking frantically from side to side I began to run round the station, looking everywhere for my non-existent bags. Travellers stopped and looked at me oddly as I ran round crying: 'Help, please. Someone's stolen my things!'

I must have put on a convincing performance, though. I spotted a policeman and ran up to him with a look of mock despair on my face. 'My bags; they've gone. I put them outside the photo booth while I had my pictures taken, and they've gone!' I exclaimed to him.

He shrugged his shoulders with an air of fatality. 'What d'you expect in Amsterdam?' he said resignedly. I was overjoyed; he'd accepted my story at face value. The officer directed me to the nearest police station, where I poured out my story again, careful to try to present a picture of someone distracted and distressed by the loss of all their worldly possessions.

With the 'crime' duly reported and logged, I headed back to the Central Station. Then I made my call to the Nottingham insurance office, carefully injecting a note of panic into my voice as I told how my trip to Spain had been ruined by this terrible theft. I'd been expecting to be told that a cheque would be sent over straight away – but instead they said there was an overseas office of the company in Amsterdam itself; I should go and report there.

For a moment my resolve wavered; had they rumbled me? But then the compulsion to begin our spiritual search overwhelmed me again, and I set off for the address given to me over the phone. It was an expensive-looking suite in a fashionable old Dutch town house alongside one of the attractive tourist stretches of canal. The moment I stepped in the front door, I sensed that my shiny-worn blue suit, polo-neck sweater, long hair and moustache didn't set quite the right tone.

My fears seemed to be confirmed when, after brazenly running through my script for the third time, the enquiries clerk told me: 'Just wait a few minutes would you, please?' He left me sitting at the reception desk as he disappeared into a back office, and I feared that perhaps he had seen through my lies. Maybe he was fetching the police even as I sat there, wondering what to do?

A few minutes later he returned with another man. I was relieved when I saw that he wasn't in uniform – and then alarmed when he introduced himself as a claims investigator. Still, I was there, I reasoned, so I simply had to stick it out. I went through my story again, slowly and carefully, my brain whirring to try to make sure that I didn't alter the facts and trip myself up in the retelling. For an hour and a quarter they asked me questions and more questions, while I tried to remain as calm and innocent as I could.

Finally they telephoned my mother to verify my story. I could have kissed her! She didn't know enough to do other than confirm what I had told them. Her son was travelling on the Continent and had some friends in Spain that he might be going to see, she told them. The claims investigator put the phone down, and turned to me with a smile.

'Well, Mr Goodfellow, I'm sorry that we've kept you so long. Everything seems in order.' He arranged for the cheque for my claim to be made out, and as he handed it over he said by way of apology: 'You can't be too careful these days, you know.'

I waved a hand away in acceptance of his remarks. 'It's OK. I quite understand – you've got to be sure about these things.'

Outside the door I resisted the impulse to hold the cheque to my lips and kiss it. Instead I tucked it into my inside pocket and headed back to The Shelter to report on the successful completion of the first stage in our four-part swindle.

Next day, encouraged by my fraud, Alan, Gary and Mac spent the day taking trains to their foreign cities, pantomiming thefts, reporting them and then returning to Amsterdam. I waited with growing impatience and discomfort; there was something about Amsterdam that was getting under my skin. Almost an apprehension, a sense of foreboding that something dreadfully important, or importantly dreadful, was going to happen soon.

My frustration increased as it became clear that we weren't going to be able to complete the other three frauds so swiftly. Their insurance companies didn't have overseas offices, and the Nottingham branches weren't happy about sending on cheques for such large amounts without completing some detailed paperwork. It was going to be at least a week before payments would be posted on to Amsterdam.

We resigned ourselves to the wait and spent long hours walking the streets, drinking beer in dark, small 'brown bars' along the canal-way streets, and scoring dope from some of the young travellers we met. Passing the time in this way was turning out to be expensive, and I grew more and more concerned and uptight as I saw the money I had made being frittered away so wastefully.

Then, trooping down the stairs at The Shelter one night, ready to head out to wander round and kill the hours before sleep, my eyes caught a small notice pinned to the wall behind the reception area: 'Free Music at The Ark!'

We decided to go and investigate.

The Ij, the river that divides north and south sectors of Amsterdam and ultimately winds its way out to the

North Sea, slaps up against the harbour front at the rear
of the Central Station. The water even sounds cold as it
slops against the wall beside us as we follow the directions we've been given on this icy, black winter's night.

The Ark turns out to be the two hulking old houseboats lashed together and moored at the end of a line of
floating homes, furthest from the station. They sit squat
and low on the water line, and look rather uninviting.
But as we draw nearer we can hear sounds – warm and
welcoming – drifting towards us.

At the door there's a man with shoulder-length white
hair, parted down the centre, and a huge grin breaking
out from within an equally snowy beard. We reach for
our pockets and make gestures about paying for entrance,
but he just smiles at us even more broadly and waves us
in. 'It's OK; it's free. Welcome to The Ark!'

Ducking our heads, we drop down through the door
into the main room of the longboat. It's a room that
runs back thirty feet or more into the distance, and
that's where most of the noise is coming from: a rock
band pounding out some contemporary rhythms. Sitting around the floor are perhaps forty or so young
traveller types, bunched around low-level tables scattered across the room. Like one of those 'spot the
difference' quizzes I run the scene through my brain
and instantly realise what's missing from a near-normal
scene: there isn't a single beer bottle to be found. And at
the same time I notice that there are only a few spirals of
smoke – and none make my nose wrinkle in the way you
expect dope to. I'm confused: this is a picture I'm used
to, but it's not quite right somehow.

As I lead the four of us into the room, I'm approached
by a slip of a girl. She's no more than five feet four, with
long, blonde hair, a fresh, open face, and a smile to
match the guy at the door. But it's her eyes that unnerve
me. Big and blue, they seem to bore straight into me,
right into my heart, as she looks up at me welcomingly.
It's an uncomfortable feeling, almost as though she can

see right into everything I've ever done, and I find myself unwillingly dropping my gaze to the floor as she says: 'Hi.'

She's small and vulnerable compared to my size and frame, yet I'm the one who feels intimidated, unnerved by the encounter. There's an awkward silence for a moment or two, and all the old feelings of insecurity and fear start to slip back into focus.

She introduces herself as Sherry, and says that she lives here on the boats as part of a Christian community with other people from ten or more different nations. I can hear the words, but somehow they're not really registering; they're flying somewhere over the top of my head.

'Yeah, that's great ... er, where's the beer?'

'Oh, we don't do that kind of thing,' she returns casually. 'We don't need to get drunk any more.'

A glimmer of hope. 'Oh, what about pills, then? What do you take?'

She smiles gently and says: 'No, you don't understand. We're Christians, you see ...' and she begins to explain to me how she and her friends belong to Jesus now.

Suddenly I'm seized by a terrifying, overwhelming sense of suffocation. I don't know what she's going on about, but I know that if I don't get out of this place now, this moment, I'm going to die. I can almost feel thick, strong fingers closing round my throat. I've got to get away from this weird, off-centre place, and this strange, peaceful-yet-powerful young woman.

I turn round, back to the others, who have been hovering a few paces back, looking round the room, as I have this short exchange with Sherry. Thankfully they don't seem to have picked up my alarm, my feelings of fear and vulnerability.

'No dope, lads, no beer either. There's nothing here for us; let's go find somewhere else,' I tell them, and we turn and tumble out up onto the pierside again.

The Paradiso was like a refuge after The Ark. Crammed with people stoned out of their heads, thick with smoke and awash with beer and pills, it pulsed to loud acid rock. We found a table and worked our way steadily into near oblivion, me trying to wash away the uncomfortable feelings I'd had from our brief visit to the houseboats.

Hours later, as we slumped on the floor, letting the music roll over us like breakers on the seashore, I remembered that night in Canada, when I'd seen my life flash before me, and thought again how close to the edge I must be.

The infamous Paradiso—renowned throughout Europe —soothed me for a few hours, but when I woke late the next morning in The Shelter – we'd got back really late, and aroused the ire of the caretaker by calling him from his bed – the sense of impending doom was on me even more strongly than ever.

I couldn't wait around any longer. I told the others that we had to make a move that very day. We'd push the claims along as much as we could on the phone, and then we'd leave Amsterdam for good. Mac knew someone who lived in a small town not far away; we could go and stay there until the money finally came through. Anything was better than staying in that creepy city a moment longer!

I'd just stepped out of one of the phone booths at the station, after arranging the alternative accommodation. We were bending to pick up our bags and head for the bus, when a voice called out: 'Hi, remember me? It's Sherry. We met last night at The Ark. D'you remember?'

I turned and there she was, smiling as broadly as before, and not seeming to be at all uncomfortable or put out by the fact that I'd brought our previous conversation to an abrupt end by turning and walking away from her in mid-sentence. 'Looks like you're leaving the city, eh? What've you guys been doing, then?'

I made some non-committal response, but Sherry didn't seem deterred by my determined indifference. She told us brightly that she'd only bumped into us because she'd left her purse behind, and had been heading back to The Ark to pick it up when she saw us. 'You must at least let me buy you all a hamburger and a coffee before you leave Amsterdam.'

Almost before we knew what had happened, we had shouldered our bags and were following her down to the city's flea market, where the five of us squeezed round a small table in a crowded cafeteria. We didn't speak, but we all seemed to have been similarly knocked back by Sherry's cheerful warmth and openness – and, besides, with money short we weren't about to turn down the offer of a free meal. As I bit into my burger, I couldn't help thinking how self-possessed and confident she was to trust herself to the company of four rough-and-ready customers like us – and I envied her composure.

After telling us a little more of what she was doing in the city, she asked again: 'So what's brought you here?'

We all chewed silently for a few minutes. Finally I decided that I'd tell her straight. I swallowed. 'Well, Sherry, we're travelling through to the East. We've set out on a journey to find God.'

The laughter I'd half anticipated never came. Instead she seemed genuinely excited by what I'd said. I told her more about our experiences and conversations, with the other three chipping in as I progressed. We brought her right up to date: '. . . and so we're on a kind of pilgrimage, if you like, to discover God.'

Sherry was the first person we'd ever spoken to who didn't dismiss us as cranks. Indeed she seemed to identify with what we were saying. Over the course of the next two hours, and further coffees, she told us of her own search for God, for truth, for meaning, and how it had been resolved when she found 'the Lord'.

All the growing excitement I'd been feeling that here

was a kindred spirit evaporated when she began to tell us that she was a Christian, a disciple of Jesus; that he was God and that she loved him. How sad, I thought. She'd fallen for all the fairy stories and the falsehoods that I'd left locked up in St Patrick's.

Several coffees later she told us that she really had to make a move, but if we weren't doing anything in the evening, we could join her for supper at The Ark. It would be fun, she said, to talk some more.

Our eyes followed Sherry as she walked off with a friendly wave, and I think in some ways we'd all fallen in love with her. We began to chatter all at once about this incredible girl: someone who was really interested in us, who recognised the longings we had inside, who didn't laugh at us, who wasn't afraid of us, who accepted us as we were – even if she was sadly misguided about God. What made her like that?

None of us had the answer to that, but we knew two things. We weren't leaving Amsterdam after all. And we had a date at The Ark.

10

Coming Home

The afternoon couldn't pass quickly enough for us. We spent the time trying to decide among ourselves why this sweet, innocent-looking girl should take the time and trouble to befriend us. What was it all about? We decided not to touch any drink or drugs, because we didn't want to disappoint Sherry by turning up with our brains in orbit and exhibiting sky-high smiles.

At the same time, despite the excitement we'd all felt inside as she'd identified with our own inner hunger, I was feeling cautious. Even with the prospect of some sort of answer within my grasp, I didn't feel able to reach out and take hold of it. I feared that such a move would expose me, make me vulnerable and weak in the others' eyes. So when we arrived at The Ark at the appropriate time, I tried to affect an air of casual disregard – about as successfully as a fox might if presented with a trussed chicken. If the guy at the door – the same bearded watchman as the previous night – detected my mask of uninterest, he didn't show it. He just grinned broadly again and welcomed us in.

Sherry was there, smiling and pleased to see us. She guided us through and across to the second houseboat, moored alongside. We stepped over and down into a large kitchen area, where a team of long-haired cooks were bustling round a range stacked with frying pans and pots. It smelled good. From there Sherry led us into the main dining room, where there was a large central table with spaces for about forty people.

'This is the main eating area,' she told us, guiding us to seats. 'We live on this boat – there are dormitories right below, and this is where we invite people to come and spend time with us.' We sat down awkwardly, a little nervous about all the other unfamiliar faces around us. Sherry introduced us to a young man sitting nearby, as people took their places. 'This is Peter Gruschka. He lives on The Ark, too.'

The hubbub of laughter and chatter died away, and I looked up to one end of the table to follow everyone else's gaze. I couldn't quite believe my eyes. Standing up, looking round the room with a broad grin, was just about the tallest guy I had ever seen. He towered about six feet six inches, and the low ceiling of the boat just seemed to accentuate his height. I half thought he might crack his head if he stood up too quickly. Equally striking was his dress – white from head to foot in a baggy, Indian-style shirt and long, baggy trousers. With his long sandy hair, centre-parted and down to his shoulders, his beard, moustache and leather sandals, he reminded me of a larger-than-life version of the Jesus picture that had hung in our home.

'That's Floyd McClung. He leads the community here,' Sherry whispered to me in explanation as the tall guy began to speak. He welcomed everyone to The Ark, and then asked people to introduce their guests. I realised that we four weren't the only strangers, and I cringed with embarrassment as Sherry stood up to tell our names and how she'd come to meet us. I wanted to slip quietly under the table so that no one could see me, but as I looked round they just smiled 'nice to see you' looks at us.

'OK, let's give thanks,' Floyd said, and bowed his head. I looked round and noticed that everyone else had followed suit, so I ducked my head. Then I realised that he was praying over the food. It was the first time I'd ever sat down at a table without diving straight into the meal, and I wondered why we had to wait. Floyd prayed briefly and without fuss, and then sat down as the food was brought out to be served. Soon the air was filled with conversation and chuckles again, and I thought momentarily how people had never seemed as relaxed after prayers when I'd gone to church all those years.

The food was good, and it was free, so we piled in. Concentrating on eating enabled me to avoid more than the briefest word of response to the questions and comments from some of those sitting nearby. As I chewed I felt my old paranoia and insecurity rising quickly. I desperately wished that I'd dropped some speed or sipped a few beers before coming; at least that would have given me some confidence to get through the visit. As it was I felt frightened – like a little boy at a new school – and yet at the same time I sensed how confident and at ease Sherry was alongside me. The contrast hit me hard: the world-weary man who'd seen it all, unable to mumble more than a word or two; and the naive and youthful girl seemingly self-possessed and calm. What did she have that I didn't?

By the time the meal was over I was feeling more and more uncomfortable – and also desperate for a cigarette. It had been a long time since I'd gone more than an hour without lighting up, and I was itching to reach for my packet. But it stayed in my pocket, because as I looked round I couldn't find anybody else smoking, and there was a conspicuous absence of ashtrays. Never mind, I thought, we'll soon be able to get outside.

But then the people sitting round the table started to pass books along. Sherry handed one to me and I turned the brown-covered volume over. 'The New Testament' it said on the front. The tall guy stood up again and began to read from one of the gospels inside. Sherry turned to the page for me. I listened and followed the words on the page curiously; it didn't mean a thing to me. Then he spoke briefly about the passage we'd just looked at, and I wondered how on earth he'd found the things he was talking about in what we'd just

read. Maybe I'd been looking at the wrong page or
something?

Before I knew it, most of the young men and women
sitting around had started singing. They all seemed to
know the words off by heart – something to do with
God's love – and they smiled as they looked around and
sang. I didn't know whether to laugh or hide my face in
embarrassment, so I looked down at the table and
breathed a long, slow sigh of relief when they finished
and the supper party broke up.

Everyone seemed to have a job to do, and no one
seemed to mind. Plates and cups were gathered, tables
and chairs cleared and wiped down, dishes washed and
dried. The clearing up was carried out with a cheerful
air of organisation. Meanwhile Sherry and Peter led me
and the others over to a group of big old armchairs,
where we flopped down and looked at each other. For a
few minutes Sherry and Peter talked to us some more
about 'the Lord', whose name we'd heard repeatedly in
the conversations going on around us at suppertime. We
nodded and made non-committal responses, and were
relieved when a little later came the opportunity for us
to say thanks, but it was really time we were heading
back to our hostel for the night.

Out on the harbour front, drawing heavily on much-
needed tobacco, we buried each other under questions.
What had we made of all of that? Did you see the freaky
tall guy in the white robes? What was all this talk about
Christianity – the only Christians we'd ever met were a
bunch of hypocrites. Was there maybe something in all
their talk of God and his love for the world? How could
anyone really have their act together and yet still believe
in Jesus? Could this be what we were looking for? Our
discussions continued late into the night. Contrary to
our expectations, dope and drink didn't help shed any
further light on things.

For all the awkwardness I'd felt while I was actually
there, I'd come away sensing that there was something

in the atmosphere of The Ark that I couldn't do without. So we quickly accepted their offer to go back again. We returned the following evening – and nightly, over the next week. Each time there were smiling and friendly faces, great rushes of vulnerability and the promise of something fantastic. It was a curious mix of something I couldn't stand to be near, but couldn't bear being away from either.

Eventually I decided that the answer must lie in the fact that they were on something. Maybe the big fellow, the ringleader, had a secret supply of some kind of superdrug stashed away below decks. Peter had always been particularly friendly when we arrived, so I dared to ask him one evening.

'Come on, what are you all taking? What are you on?'

He looked at me and smiled widely. Clapping me on the shoulder with a hearty laugh he replied: 'We're on Jesus, I guess. That's all!'

I wasn't really sure what he meant. But I believed him. I had a gut feeling that he'd been telling me the truth – whatever it was.

During our visits, Sherry and her friends continued to talk with us in broad terms about God and the world, and what we thought life was all about. We looked forward to these conversations because we hoped they might provide some understanding in our search, but even more compelling was the intangible sense of welcome we felt. These people were for real. It was good to feel cared for.

This feeling of identity made us leap at their offer of going to live on board The Ark as part of the community, even more than the prospect of further talks about God. Just being part of a group of people who really cared for each other was attractive. We decided that we'd like to spend some time on The Ark before finally setting out for our gurus in the East.

Before that, though, we had some business to attend to back in Nottingham. The other three had been told that their insurance claims would only be paid out if they applied personally for them back in England, and the final third of my claim was awaiting payment on similar grounds. We decided to risk going home for a few days to complete our swindle.

But we couldn't shake the impression that The Ark folk had made on us. Back in the Midlands we told Sarah and Jenny about these amazing people we'd met, and how they'd asked us to go and live with them. They said they'd like to come, too, but we said we'd better ask to see if it was OK before they set out. We agreed to .call them as soon as we could after we'd returned to Amsterdam.

When I went to claim my outstanding monies, I found myself facing another long interview with a claims investigator. They gave me the cheque for what was still due under my claim, and then asked me to return the following day to complete a few formalities. I sensed that they were on to me, and I reasoned that when I turned up the next morning there would be a policeman or two waiting to arrest me and take me away. In a panic I packed my bags, called the other three, and told them I was flying out to Amsterdam first thing in the morning.

As the plane dropped in to land at Schipol Airport I was seized by a sense of foreboding that forced me back into my seat with rigid fear: I was going to die in this Dutch city! Breaking out in a cold sweat, I tried to pray for the first time since a child, searching in my memory for the words of the 'Our Father'. But I realised that I didn't know what to say, or who to say it to, and as I grappled with a feeling that I was abandoned and lost, the wheels touched down with a gentle bump and we were there.

Back in Amsterdam, my excitement turned to apprehension. What if they'd changed their minds, and they wouldn't let me in? I spent a couple of hours walking round the canals and narrow side streets before I finally plucked up the courage to go and knock on The Ark's big, broad door. It opened to another big smile. 'Hey, it's John Goodfellow, isn't it? Welcome back – and come on in.'

Alan, Gary and Mac arrived a couple of days later with their payments and similar stories of the suspicion that they had been rumbled. But we figured that the police would never be able to trace us to these big old hulks out the back of Amsterdam's Central Station and, besides, pretty soon we'd be off overland in a beat-up van. They would never catch us!

We were welcomed onto The Ark as part of the guest list; there were about a dozen of us outsiders altogether who'd been invited to spend some time living on board. Those who lived there full time explained the routine we were expected to fit into: breakfast communally at 7.30 am, followed by a couple of hours of jobs around the boats – washing, repairing, maintaining, cooking. Then, at mid-morning, we all met together in the main room for what they called their Family Time. Over an hour or so they'd sing a few songs, pray and then Floyd McClung would talk from the Bible about what it meant to live as a Christian.

Gradually I found these times less intimidating and awkward, and while I still didn't really understand what they were all going on about, I was happy to clap along and even try to join in with the occasional song that I picked up from its repetition. The religious talk all seemed a bit remote, but I could put up with it because it was all part of something much wider and deeper – a thrilling, heart-warming, tingling sense of belonging and purpose that seemed to emanate from everyone there. It seemed to me that most of the people around me felt it, and although I didn't, I knew that it existed, and I knew that I wanted it for myself, too! From time to time I would slip away of an evening with the other three to brood over a couple of beers. None of us could put our finger on it, but we all agreed that there was a pulse of real, hard hope beating in us for the first time we could remember.

I'm sitting cross-legged on the floor in a Family Time and relaxing into the familiar flow of a simple song. It's short and expressive, and as I look around I pause to think how the faces seem to shine with its meaning. To me it's just a nice song, but to them there seems somehow to be something more, as though they're not just singing the words – they're telling them *to* someone, or something. The room fills with joyful, enthusiastic voices and the accompaniment of clapping hands and bongo drums.

I snap my head in a shake of disbelief as suddenly a symphony of additional sound breaks into my hearing. It's like thousands of other voices – majestic and proud – have suddenly joined in with our small group. It's so clear and close that I guess someone must have switched on a tape machine or the radio or something, so I twist from side to side. No audio equipment in sight. Everyone else is concentrating on singing; they don't seem to have noticed anything out of the ordinary.

Before I can even start to make sense of this strange sensation, I'm pitched face forwards. The voices of the hidden singers splash into and mix with those of the people around me as I feel myself being doubled over by some kind of wave. And I burst into tears, beginning to sob in gut-wrenching spasms that tear their way out of somewhere deep in the very centre of my being.

It's all happening so suddenly and unexpectedly that I'm almost able to stand back and watch it all – yet at the same time I'm caught up in the very centre. My brain's racing and I'm asking, 'What's happening?' as the tears start to stream down my face, with great gasps of anguish. A detached thought that everyone around me will think that I've cracked up is washed away as the river of emotion continues to burst the banks of my heart. And as the singing gently continues, almost unconcernedly, I feel as though the release of all those pent-up tears have left the real me, deep inside, grounded on firm land. I'm seeing myself as I really am, and it's awful.

Selfish, arrogant, spiteful, vicious, uncaring, proud. The realisation hammers into me. All these years of self-justification, deceit, excuses and avoidance, simply fall away. I see that I've hurt, robbed, cheated, lied, abused and damaged without defence. 'They wouldn't miss the money; she'd been asking for it; he'd hurt me; I needed it.' All these excuses don't matter. It's my life. They're my decisions. There is no one to blame but myself; nowhere to turn with the finger of accusation other than inwards.

From fingertip to toe, head to heel, I'm rotten, filthy and wicked. I'm still weeping uncontrollably, but the initial embarrassment is being replaced by a feeling of relief and welcome. It's all over; I don't have to pretend any more. My tears feel like they're washing away the dirt from my insides.

I look up and over at Floyd sitting on the other side of the room. They're still singing around me, and he reaches into his pocket and passes something to the person alongside. Hand to hand it comes round to me: a big, white handkerchief. As I press my face gratefully into its pure, clean freshness I look over and see him smiling at me with a nod of understanding. It's like he knows what this weird experience is all about, and yet he's saying that he accepts me without question.

Someone puts an arm around me as the sobs subside and whispers: 'It's OK, John, we understand, we understand.'

Which is more than I do. I know this is all about the very essence of my life, but I can't explain it.

The understanding came later. In the days that followed, some of the things that Floyd talked about began to take some sort of shape in my head. And Peter and some of the other Ark community talked to me more directly about their God and his world.

They told me how God had created man in his image, and had intended the world to be a beautiful place of harmony and peace where he and his creation could enjoy each other for ever. But man had rebelled against God's order – he wilfully disobeyed – and that had brought an awful separation between the Creator and his created being.

The Bible explained that everyone had gone wrong, that no one was perfect. So God had sent Jesus into the world to 'pay the price' of our wrongdoing, so that we could be re-united with God. The penalty for all our sin was death, and Jesus, who had lived a sinless life on earth, had been crucified to take the punishment we deserved. But he'd risen from death, defeating the power of sin once and for all, and now everyone who believed in him could be set free from their old life, and begin a new spiritual life that would go on for eternity.

They explained to me that only God's Holy Spirit could bring people to an understanding of these things, and that he had been at work in my life, fracturing the dam of my walled-up emotions during that Family Time. And they said that they'd been praying for this to happen since I'd arrived at The Ark, content to await God's timing to tell me more about him.

This picture was painted for me carefully and gently during the course of long conversations over the next few days. The more I asked, the more they explained, and I felt like a whole new world was opening up in front of me. I was eager to talk about what they believed and what it might mean for my life. But there was one blockage. I accepted all they told me about Jesus – how he was fully God, yet at the same time fully man, and that he'd risen from the grave and now lived for ever – but I just couldn't believe that God had created the world in the first place. It was just too much for me. Until one morning.

Alan, Mac and I were putting our bricklaying expertise to good use by building a small wall round the waste-pipes leading down the back of the boats. We'd dug the hole, laid out the site, and were setting the bricks down in place when it struck me how easily we had made plans and constructed something. With simple logic I then told myself if we – created beings – could design and make something, then a supreme being – God – could surely design and make a world. It felt as though I'd won the pools!

Standing on the top of the half-built wall, I shouted down to Gary who was also below: 'That's it! I understand now. God did make the world! I believe, Gary, I believe!' He looked up at me quizzically as though I'd finally flipped as I grinned hugely. 'That's it! I believe, I believe!' I dropped my trowel and shovel and ran inside, shouting to the others my discovery. 'I know it's true. I believe!'

Later that day I knelt down beside my bunk in the small dormitory room below deck. Despite the heaters it was always cold and slightly damp down there below the waterline, but I didn't notice this time. As the water lapped against the wall a few inches from my head I began to pray for only the second time in my adult life – but this time I knew someone was there.

'O Jesus, I know you're real. I'm so sorry for all the dreadful things I've done in my life . . .' and I slowly and methodically began to list my misdeeds. During one of my conversations with Peter he'd said that becoming a Christian meant you had to confess all your sins – and I didn't want to miss a single one out. By the time I'd admitted everything I could remember, a long time had passed. Then I asked him to come into my life. 'Jesus, I believe that you are the Son of God, and that you died to take away my sins. And I believe that you can forgive me and give me a new life as your child. Please come into my life right now. I've made such a mess of it that I want you to take charge. Please help me. I've hurt so many people in so many ways. Please change my heart, and take away all the anger and the bitterness. Make me a new person, like you promise. I want what you've given all the others.'

I stopped talking, and slumped forward with my head on my bed. Then a ripple of calm, secure peace ran down my body. I was sure that my prayer had been answered.

Somehow I managed to go up to supper disguising the excited smile that wanted to break out on my face. I kept my secret until after the meal. Then I stood up and announced the words I had heard several times before from other visitors to The Ark, but which had always left me mystified: 'I've been born again!'

I was swamped by cheers, shouts of congratulations and slaps on the back. Then everyone started to sing a song of praise to God, and for the first time I was able to join in and feel that I was a part of it.

I had been away for a long, long time, but now it felt like I was coming home.

11

First Steps

It wasn't long before I knew that something truly dramatic had happened. With the warmth of my 'welcome' still surrounding me, I slipped downstairs to my bunk and reached for my jacket pocket. As I pulled out the packet of cigarettes that I always turned to for an after-meal smoke, I realised that things were different this time. My hands had acted out of habit, but I discovered that I didn't want to smoke.

It wasn't that I didn't think I ought to – everything was still so new to me that I hadn't even begun to attempt to think through the implications my new-found faith would have on my lifestyle. All I knew was that for the first time in a dozen years I had absolutely no desire to pull blasts of nicotine into my chest. I turned the packet over in my hand as I looked at it curiously. Then I wandered up on deck, flipped the packet over in my palm a few times, and then flicked it out into the grey water.

I watched it float on the surface for a couple of minutes before it filled with water and sank away. The desire had gone. It was just as though someone had removed it under anaesthetic. I hadn't felt any pain. This previously important part of my life had simply been cut away! Over the next couple of nights it became clear that the same had happened with drink and drugs. This about-turn was perhaps even more remarkable, considering I had been an alcoholic and addict for so many years. But when one of the others would come

over to my bunk at night and whisper that we could slip
into town and score some dope or have a few beers, I
simply didn't want to go.

Yet whatever operation it was that had been performed wasn't so much an amputation as a transplant. I
found that in place of my thirst for smoking, getting
stoned and drinking was the need to drink in the Bible.
All the passages I'd heard read and discussed over the
previous weeks came flooding back into my thoughts,
and I desperately wanted to read them for myself. I
found myself poring over the Bible for a couple of
hours at a stretch, completely absorbed by what I was
reading, and it was making sense for the first time. I felt
as though suddenly I had a personal stake in all that was
written there. While the words had once been distant
and detached, they were now crucially important. My
heart would start racing in excited anticipation every
time I'd turn again to one of the well-thumbed Bibles
lying around The Ark.

I'd spent so much of my life in a fog of confused
thoughts and emotions. Now I knew from the clarity
with which I viewed everything and everyone around
me that a change of momentous proportions had taken
place. And with the help of some of the male workers on
The Ark, I began to explore what it meant. We spent
long hours talking about how becoming a Christian
wasn't just about turning your back on an old life, but
starting a whole new one; and that God had a personal
plan for me that he wanted to unfold.

About three nights after my tea-time admission of
conversion, I was sitting up late talking with two new
friends when they began to explain to me how Jesus was
coming back again soon. It sounded really exciting.
They told me that the Bible taught that Jesus would one
day return to this world, and he would be recognised by
everyone as the sovereign Lord of the universe. No one
would be able to deny his majesty and authority. I began
to thrill to their description, and was waiting to hear

more when it happened again – another 'wave' crashed into me from behind, doubling me forward from the waist.

At the same time I felt a beautiful, sweet warmth ripple over and down and through my body, just as though someone had poured perfumed oil all over me. It was a glorious moment, as I was bathed in this honey of love. The sheer richness of the tenderness I felt all over me reduced me to tears again and I started sobbing – but this time gently and gratefully. Before I'd been a little unsure about my response; this time I simply enjoyed the liberation and freedom of being able to weep unashamedly and thankfully. I felt my own heart melting inside me, responding to the warmth in which I was engulfed; layers of indifference and selfishness were falling away before the presence of God's care and concern.

My head was bowed, but without looking up I sensed that someone was standing above me. Jesus. With hands, wounded and welcoming, open before me. No words were needed, but he spoke clearly, straight into my heart: 'John, you belong to me now. You are mine. I accept you and I love you. John, you are mine.'

In a moment my awareness of this powerful presence was gone, and I continued to weep quietly in wonder and thankfulness. I'd known I needed God's forgiveness for all the evil there had been in my life. Now I knew for a certainty that he had granted it for one simple reason. Because he loved me. I didn't deserve it. I could never repay it. But he loved me, totally and selflessly. It was a wonderful moment, and as I looked up to the two men who had sat by quietly as I bowed to God's love, one of them reached over to hug me. I gripped him firmly in response, with genuine affection, glad to be able to share this moment. Even as I did so I realised what a change had come over me here. For the first time I could recall I felt comfortable sharing emotions with someone else. I thought how great it was to be part of a real family for the first time. God's family.

Somehow I floated down to my bunk later that night, drifting off to sleep finally in a warm haze. I woke early the next morning still intoxicated by the awareness of God's accepting love. Wrapping a thick coat around me I slipped out onto the deck and paced up and down for a couple of hours until other sounds of life stirred below. 'I love you, Jesus. I love you,' I whispered over and over again as I walked up and down. It felt good to say it.

The following days saw no let-up in excitement. Sometimes the inexplicable joy that seemed to well up inside me threatened to make me burst. I revelled in the brightness and freshness I found in everything. Even the ordinary, everyday things like rainstorms and meal-times became a source of fascination and delight as I'd think how God was behind them. They hadn't just come about by accident; they were all a part of God's marvellous plan in shaping this world! It was as though the projector of my life had previously only been able to screen dull black-and-white. Now everything was in glorious Technicolor, and the mundane suddenly became magical.

A couple of weeks later, Gary and I were baptised in a small chapel in an Amsterdam backstreet. Gary had made his own, private peace with God a few days after me. The congregation knew the work of The Ark well and often loaned their pool for the baptism of new converts. We joined with about half a dozen others in giving a short account of our new walk with Jesus, before being lowered under the water and raised up to jubilant singing and clapping.

The newness of everything was so overwhelming for a while that I almost forgot that there was life beyond The Ark. When I finally remembered that we'd arrived on the run from the police, I knew that this was one of the many things I had to sort out now that I had a new life as part of God's family. I went to Floyd one morning and told him rather sheepishly that we'd come to the boats a little under false pretences, and I filled him in with the story. In the short time we'd been there, we'd seen all types coming along – drug addicts, alcoholics, psychotics – but I knew we'd been wrong to mislead them. Floyd didn't seem disturbed by what I told him – he was more interested in what was going to happen next.

He explained that it was up to me. I had decisions to make. But as we talked, he showed me how in the Bible it said that when a thief became a Christian, he should pay back the money he had taken, and live a peaceable life. Later, in my bunk, I flipped through my Bible to find the verse myself, tucked away in Ephesians chapter 4. 'It's pretty clear what you've got to do, John,' I thought to myself as I re-read the sentence. The next morning I sought Floyd out.

'I've decided. I believe that I should go back and confess to all the things I've done wrong, and try to put them right.'

Floyd nodded and smiled. 'I think you're right, John,' he agreed quietly. Later that afternoon, we both borrowed bicycles and pedalled over to the insurance office where I'd made my original false claim. Floyd didn't seem to notice the strange looks given to the cycling, long-haired giant as he strode in and explained briefly on my behalf why we were there.

The man behind the counter eyed me up and down closely, and said that he remembered me. He told me that he knew my claim had been fraudulent, because detectives had been in recently to interview him about it.

'Well, about three weeks ago I became a Christian,' I told him. 'I know what I did was wrong, and I'm planning to go back to England to confess, and I want to pay all the money back.'

He dropped the formal air with which he had been acting, clearly surprised by my openness. After taking a few details down on a scrap of paper he bade us farewell. 'I've never heard anything like this before in my life,' he said, shaking his head with a smile. 'Good luck!'

I knew that it wasn't a decision I could leave to 'luck'.

Before, I'd dreaded having to wake up and get out of bed each morning. But now coursing through my veins was a heady sense of God's love and care for me, which brought me bursting into each new day.

I'd fallen in love, and I wanted to show how much I cared in whatever way I could; putting right some of my mistakes of the past seemed to be the right place to start.

My crimes hadn't only been committed out in the streets, though. I knew that a good many had taken place at home, within the four walls of the Goodfellow household: the bitterness, jealousy, resentment and anger. I wondered quite how I could tackle this history of hurt, but I knew that I wanted my family to know the exciting new life I'd discovered. One night I called home, and over a crackling line told Mum hastily that I'd met some great people. I said that I'd become a Christian, and I was coming home soon to sort a few things out.

She was confused. 'What d'you mean, Johnny? I don't understand. The police have been round here looking for you. What have you been up to? You're not in any trouble are you, son?'

I tried to explain what had happened. 'It's OK, Mum. I've become a Christian. These people here are going to help me. Everything's going to be OK. Honest.'

'What do you mean, you've become a Christian, Johnny? You've always been a Christian, son. Your father and I took you to church for years. What are you talking about?' She sounded anxious and a little baffled.

I didn't know where to begin. It was hopeless trying to express on the phone this revolution in my world. 'I know I went to church for years, Mum, but I never knew Jesus. But I've met him now. He's alive!'

Our conversation ended unsatisfactorily, and I ached to be able to see her face to face and explain. But instead of allowing my frustrations to get the better of me, I punched some more coins into the money slot and dialled the other number on my list. It was the central police station in Nottingham.

It quickly became clear that it wasn't every day someone rang up from overseas admitting they've committed a crime, and trying to arrange to come home to face the music! But eventually I managed to speak to someone in the Criminal Investigation Department who knew of my case, and we arranged details of when I'd be travelling home on the ferry. Officers would be waiting to arrest me as I stepped ashore.

The next few days sped by in a blur of happiness and anticipation. I couldn't express what I felt inside, but it was like all the Christmas Eves of my youth rolled into one: those wonderful hours of expectancy – before arguments shattered the peace – when I lay in bed knowing, hoping that something wonderful was going to begin soon, and wishing it closer. I spent all my waking hours reading the Bible, talking to Ark workers and asking them the million-and-one questions I had about this new life I'd begun. I sat alongside them, too, in the coffee bar in the evenings as they talked about Jesus with visitors. I desperately wanted to join in, but I was too embarrassed at what these streetwise sceptics might make of my naive faith.

I'm standing outside the Central Station, and it's hard to believe how much has happened in just a few short weeks. I can see over to the spot, a few yards away, where the turn-around began; where we were planning to leave the city and start our pilgrimage to the East, when Sherry bumped into us because of a missing purse. It makes me warm inside to think that even then, when I didn't realise it, God was more concerned about finding us than we were about finding him.

But as I pause to consider the different departure I'm planning now, the euphoria evaporates. In a little while I'm due to catch a train to the ferry to go back and give myself up to the police. I know God is with me – I'm sure of it with every fibre in my being – but I'm rather anxious all the same. I sit down on a bench and turn to the Bible that in such a short space of time has already begun to feel so at home, so satisfying, in my hand. I still don't know my way around this fascinating, exciting, confusing, shocking book of books, so it's by no design of mine that I find myself somewhere in Isaiah, and reading a passage that seems to spring off the page at me.

'When you pass through the waters, I will be with you . . . you will not drown. . . . Fear not, for I will be with you . . . I have called you by name.'

A jolt of assurance runs through me as I accept this as a message of support for my ferry trip. 'Thank you, Father God, for giving me this encouragement.'

When the approaching English coastline causes me to waver a few hours later, even just for a moment, I know what to do. I turn to my Bible expectantly, hopefully, and once more find my eyes plucking a passage from an unfamiliar page. It's Isaiah again: 'Don't dwell on the former things . . . I'm making a way in the desert.'

I don't know what is going to happen. I don't know how God is going to work. But I do know that everything is going to be all right. I'm so confident that I'm almost delighted to see the waiting policemen as I come through the terminal building at Harwich. Anyone watching might mistake us for being long-lost relatives!

Having Peter Gruschka sitting alongside me in the police car on the way to the local police station was a wonderfully tangible reminder that I hadn't set off alone.

In the few weeks I'd been on The Ark, he and I had struck up a close friendship. Since that night when I'd knelt beside my bunk and asked Jesus Christ into my life all sorts of things had been happening inside me – it felt like a whole lot of melting, cracking, pounding and dismantling was all going on at the same time. One of the things I knew was that I was finding myself responding to people in a different way – and I had warmed to Peter greatly.

Tall and rangy, with a shock of curly hair, you would probably have counted this easy-going German as one of the visitors rather than staff if you'd peeked into The Ark's crowded coffee bar in the evening. He was still the typical drop-out in many ways, although he'd rejected the drugs-and-sex scene in favour of what he'd found in Jesus.

Before coming to work on The Ark, he'd been a professional actor and singer, touring Europe in the cast of the musical *Hair!* The production was the ultimate statement of the peace and love culture, shocking audiences with its full-frontal nudity, glorification of drugs, and anarchy. During the performance members of the cast would, as well as shedding their clothes, step down off the stage and walk into the auditorium to hand out marijuana to members of the audience.

This was Peter's life – until one night. Finishing a show in Paris, he and a musician friend were leaving the theatre when they met two little old ladies waiting at the rear door, who asked if they could talk for a few minutes. The spinsters began to tell the two long-haired men about how Jesus Christ had come into the world to rescue them from their sins, and to give them a wonderful new life. They didn't leave before handing New Testaments over to the astonished friends.

The encounter made a deep impact on both men, and they later became Christians, and began to share their new faith with other members of the cast. It wasn't long before tracts and New Testaments were being handed round the concert halls instead of dope. Peter was asked to leave – his message wasn't compatible with the show's New Age mysticism. With a burning love for God, and an intimate understanding of others like him he soon found himself working on The Ark.

I loved hearing him tell his life story, and it thrilled me to think that God wanted to perform a similar topsy-turvy act in my life. So when he volunteered to come back to England with me to support me through the various scenes that I would have to face, I was overjoyed. I was also touched that someone would care enough about me to want to put himself to so much trouble. It was another example to me of the selfless love of God I was seeing lived out by people who followed Jesus.

At Harwich police station they viewed us both a little suspiciously to begin with. Finally, though, I was taken into an interview room where I made a full and detailed confession to one of the detectives. He took it all down in longhand as I spoke, and after reading it over and signing it, I was allowed to go free on bail, to await further contact from the police back home in Nottingham.

As Peter and I sat on the train, rattling up the line to the Midlands, my mind kept racing ahead of me. I felt nervous and excited all at the same time. How would my parents respond to the homecoming of the son who had made the family name of Goodfellow a cruel joke for so long?

12

Putting Right the Past

Bursting with excitement, I knocked at the front door. I couldn't wait to see my family – nor for them to see me. In the last few weeks I'd found myself falling in love with them all for the first time properly in my life, and I couldn't wait to look at them with gentleness, in place of that hardness and coldness. And I wanted them to see the difference in me.

I had absolutely no doubt that they would see the change. I was brimming with confidence—not in me, but in the wonderful person I'd discovered: Jesus, who had changed me. I had never known such peace. I was sure that those who had most reason to remember the old me with regret would see the difference. And I was certain that when I explained the how – or, rather, the who – of my transformation, then they would want to invite Jesus into their lives too.

Mum opened the door and I engulfed her in an uncharacteristic hug. She was surprised but pleased, and I went to put my arms round the rest of the family too. It was so good to see them and I realised that the new feelings I had for them were still there. Pretty soon we were all sitting round the table over a noisy tea, and I started to try to tell them all that had happened. From one or two nervous glances I caught out of the corner of my eye, I sensed that it was maybe a bit too soon, so I bit my tongue and instead enjoyed the food. There would be plenty of time afterwards. Chewing and smiling, I had to blink away the tears as I looked round the table at my family.

Their faces were, of course, so familiar. But it was as though I was looking at them through a new pair of eyes. I saw them in a softer light, no longer as people who I felt only wanted to squash me, but as people who had needs and hurts, and wants and pains of their own. There was Dad, tired, proud, self-reliant and lonely. Mum, weary, worried and cheated of the close family she'd longed for. Joan, her young hopes for the glamorous life crumpled, a single parent with old-looking eyes. Trish, in many ways a typical fiery teenager, but also with an angry streak I recognised from my own past.

'Oh, Jesus, I love them so very much,' I whispered silently. 'Thank you for letting me see them more as you do. Please let them see you in me.'

After the meal I hovered in the kitchen to make some small talk with Mum as she fussed and busied herself over the dishes. Finally she made a tray of hot drinks and carried them through to the lounge where Dad and the girls were sitting watching the TV. I sensed that the moment had come.

There was an awkward silence as I asked if they minded if I switched the set off for a few minutes, because there was something very important that I wanted to tell them all. They shuffled and twisted as I pulled up a chair facing them and, breathing a silent prayer for God's help, brought them up to date with all that had happened.

'First of all I want to say that I'm ashamed for so long having been the worst son you could wish for. I've hurt and embarrassed you, and I've dragged the family name through the mud. I know that I have been a disgrace to you all,' I said quietly, watching their faces.

'But I want you to know that three-and-a-half months ago I became a Christian. I began a personal relationship with Jesus Christ. I asked him into my life, and he forgave me for all the wrong I'd done. He lives in my heart right now, and he's completely changing my life. I want to live for him for the rest of my life.'

It had been so important to me to communicate the passion I held that it had all come out in a bit of a rush, and my story was received with an uncomfortable silence. We'd never been a family for sharing our emotions — except for anger maybe — and I'd just opened my heart in a completely new way.

Mum broke the silence. 'Johnny, it's wonderful to have you home again, son, but I don't understand. You've always been a Christian. I'm glad that you've decided to calm down a bit now, but....' Her words trailed away in confusion.

'Mum, it's not a matter of that,' I replied desperately. 'It's really that God's changed my life. Jesus has set me free. He's made me a new person.'

Trish broke the moment by getting up, walking over and turning the television on again, and the strained silence was washed away in the dialogue of another soap opera.

Leaving them to watch, I slipped out of the room and upstairs to my old bedroom. Safely inside, with the door closed, I fell to my knees beside the bed and began to pray for them, individually and by name, pleading with God to reveal himself to them through his Holy Spirit, in the same dramatic way that he had broken into my life. Although I was discouraged, I was sure deep inside that it was only a matter of time.

Peter Gruschka had been given permission to stay in Sarah and Jenny's flat while they were away. It was only a few hundred yards away, so we'd meet up every morning to spend a couple of hours praying together and reading the Bible. These were important times for me, in which I'd draw heavily on his knowledge and guidance, and feel myself growing stronger and stronger in my love for God. Even before I met with Peter I would often have spent an hour or more praying on my own. I'd rise early before there was any other sound in the house, make myself a large mug of coffee, and settle myself down with the Bible. I still couldn't get enough of it. In the afternoons and evenings I'd often wrap up in a heavy coat and slip down to the other end of our road, where there was open land that led down to the edge of the River Trent. I'd walk up and down alone, singing under my breath and praying long and hard for my family, my old friends and for my future. If the occasional cyclist or dog-walker passing by looked strangely at me as I apparently muttered to myself, I didn't care. I was so happy.

I'd determined from the moment I got home that I'd reinforce the change in my character by my attitude. It wouldn't be hard; I'd been such a poor advert for a son previously that any change for the better would be marked. In addition to being up early, I'd be home most evenings if I wasn't meeting Peter or going for a prayer walk. I never went down to the pub as I had in the old days, but would prefer to stay in and read quietly in my room, or watch TV with the rest of the family. And, quietly, privately, I continued to beg God to touch the rest of my family powerfully, personally.

Joan was first. It was the first full Sunday I'd been home, and the rest of the family was out of the house. Joan was at home with her baby son, Sean. A former air hostess, Joan had gone through a number of relationships before getting engaged to be married. Then she'd become pregnant and the plans had fallen through. She had come home to have the baby and was now trying to pick up the pieces of her life. But she was struggling. Tranquillisers and constant cigarettes were the only things that seemed to get her through the day. It hurt me to see the older sister I'd always resented as a tough, self-possessed person, now so vulnerable and needy.

With the house quiet, I sat down with her and began to tell her in a little more detail all that had happened to me. She seemed interested, so I pressed on, telling her how Jesus wanted to transform people's lives if only they would let him. He could forgive them all the wrong things they had done, take away the hurts, and fill them with a peace and a joy and a hope that was almost beyond belief. I knew, because it had happened to me.

As I talked, she suddenly burst out: 'I know it's all true! When you sat us all down the other night and began to speak I just knew that God existed. I don't really know how to explain it, Johnny, but I just knew, deep down, that what you were saying was true. I believe it ... and I know it's what I've been looking for all my life. What should I do?'

I explained to her how she needed to admit all the wrong things she'd done, say she was sorry to God for them, and ask Jesus into her heart as her Lord and Saviour, and that he'd come – no doubt about it. She began to pray, falteringly, along the lines I'd suggested, and as she did she began to weep. She slumped to the floor, crying aloud.

My heart was somersaulting with joy, but I didn't know what to do as she lay on the floor beside me. So I started to pray too, asking God to answer her prayers and give her a new life. I don't know how much time we spent in this way, but eventually Joan's tears dried away. She knelt up with a beautiful smile of peace on her face and began to whisper: 'Thank you, God, thank you. Thank you, Jesus. This is what I've been wanting for so long.'

When she stood up and looked into my eyes, I couldn't believe it. Her face seemed visibly softer already, and it almost appeared to glow. Through the tear-smudged eyes I could see the sparkle of real happiness. We hugged and held each other tight. I buried my head in her shoulder, and murmured: 'Thank you, Father God. Thank you!'

As well as the heaviness that dropped from her features, the anxiety went that afternoon. Joan found out straight away that she no longer needed the tranquillisers or the tobacco to calm her nerves. In the days that followed we began to meet together in my room to read the Bible and pray, and it was wonderful to share my limited knowledge with another young Christian who was as enthusiastic and hungry to learn as I had been. We told the rest of the family what had happened, but they seemed to dismiss it all as a bit of emotional nothingness; everything would be back to normal again after I'd been home a few weeks and things had settled down a bit.

Trish didn't really seem to understand what was going on. As a fashion- and music-conscious young teenager, she thought that her older brother and sister were just going through a religious phase; that it was something they would come out of. I sensed that she was keeping a quiet eye on me, watching secretly to see if I made any mistakes.

A few weeks later, though, she agreed to go to an evangelistic rally at Nottingham's Albert Hall. The speaker was Nicky Cruz, the tough New York gang leader who'd been saved through the remarkable ministry of David Wilkerson. His story had been told in *The Cross and the Switchblade*, and I was keen to hear the man whose life in so many ways seemed to mirror my own.

Joan, Peter and I went along that night, but we somehow got separated from Trish and her young friends. We didn't see her again until much later, on the way home. She was sitting a few seats forward on the top deck of the bus, and when I called her name, she turned round – and flashed me a broad, excited grin. I knew that she, too, had met Jesus. 'Thank you, thank you, thank you,' I softly repeated all the way home.

As the weeks went by and the home Bible study group grew to three strong, my parents seemed to relax a little. They didn't like to talk too much about what was happening in a direct way, but they sensed that it was bringing peace, closeness and happiness to their children, so they were happy enough. Not everyone felt the same. One night Mum came home after seeing relatives, and it was evident that there had been harsh words exchanged about the strange new religion I was bringing into the house — this new kind of faith. What about the Catholic church? Mum was extremely agitated, wringing her hands and chewing her lip. She took her coat off, walked into the room and promptly burst into tears.

'My life's falling apart. I'm losing all my children and we're falling out. What's happening here? I just don't know what's going on, any more. You've got to help me, John,' she said.

I looked up at her, full of pain for her. 'I can't, Mum. Nobody can. Only Jesus.'

'I want to be like you and the girls. How do I get what you've got in your lives?'

'You've got to invite Jesus into your heart, Mum. That's all. Just turn to Jesus.'

Collapsing into the chair she said that she wanted to, straight away. I went over and put my arm around her and led her in a brief prayer, asking Jesus to forgive her for where she had failed and come into her life. As we finished, she jumped up suddenly. 'It's gone, son, it's gone. The burden has gone. All the guilt's gone; I feel lighter!'

Mum stopped drinking straight away. If Dad felt threatened by this latest transformation in his family, he didn't say so. But by now he was an old man, with only a hint of the iron there had once been. Officially retired, he had a part-time job at a local pub, and spent his time pottering about there or in the back garden. I felt so sorry for him. He seemed trapped inside his own past hardness, and I longed to be able to reach inside. He allowed me to start saying a brief prayer for all of us before meals, and we'd work silently but contentedly together when I'd help him turning over his garden. He didn't say very much, but I could feel that he approved of some of the changes he was seeing. Mum, the girls and I continued praying that God would touch his heart.

Another Sunday at home, but so different from many of the old years. We've just finished lunch after morning service at church, and there's a quiet, peaceful sort of contentment about the house. Over the past months, Mum, Joan, Trish and I have grown close in a special way that I still thank God for. It's like he's helping us to make up for all the time we've lost in the past.

The door goes in the kitchen, and I know it's Dad back from his Sunday drinks down at the pub. He's almost timid these days, just a shadow of the man I used to hate and fear in equal measure. Oh, Dad, how can I ever get through to you? The thoughts and feelings tumble together, as I sense God speaking into my heart: 'Go into the kitchen and tell your father the good news about Jesus Christ.'

It may sound strange, but now I've come to trust this inner prompting by God's Spirit. So I walk through to the kitchen where he's sitting on a chair, with his head slumped in his hands. He seems very old and very tired. He looks up at me wearily as I come in, and drops his head again.

'Dad, the Lord has told me to come in and share the gospel with you. And this is the word of God to you. It's the first three verses of Isaiah 61.' And I read: 'The Spirit of the Lord ... has anointed me to preach good news to the poor ... to bind up the broken-hearted, to proclaim freedom for the captives ... .'

I close my Bible and looking straight over at him begin to talk freely and effortlessly. For almost ten minutes I tell him boldly about the good news of Jesus, and the hope he offers. There is a special sense of authority and power, and I'm raising my voice as though I'm addressing a crowd of hundreds. Yet Dad sits, head down, just a few feet away – almost as though he doesn't hear me.

But as I finish, he looks up slowly. There are tears in his eyes and it's the first time I've seen him weep without a bottle in his hand. These are real tears, and something breaks inside me. Dad drops to his knees from the chair, and I rush forward, kneeling down beside him on the lino and putting my arms around him. It feels good.

'Son, what shall I do to be saved?' he croaks.

'Dad, ask Jesus into your heart. Here, like this . . .' and we stumble through a short prayer together and spend a long time just holding on to each other.

Putting my broken family relationships right was something I began work on the moment I arrived back in Nottingham. But there were many other loose ends that needed knotting up so that they didn't entangle me in my new life. In addition to praying for God to work in my family, each morning when Peter and I met together we would ask for help in knowing the way ahead for all the other things that still had to be sorted out.

Within a few days of my return, our old gang was reunited. The other three had all found their way back to Nottingham during the previous weeks when I'd stayed on The Ark, and had, like me, given themselves up to the police with the express intention of putting things straight. With all we had gone through together we were still fairly close, but those crossroads days in Amsterdam had driven something of a wedge between us. Gary had also committed his life to Christ, and was following his own plan for sorting his life out. Mac told me shortly before he left The Ark that he believed all that the people there said about God, but he just didn't want to know. Alan had left in a hurry one night, after failing to persuade me to go with him.

Back in Nottingham we continued to meet together for the first few weeks after my return, and we'd study the Bible with Peter, in effect picking up on the searching, discussing and exploring that had been a feature of

The Ark's life. I was distressed by Alan's apparent continued scepticism; after all, he and I had been closest in the gang. He had been the one who had ultimately focused my search for meaning in life to the spiritual realm, through which I had finally found what I was looking for. Now I was anxious that he should make the same discovery, and yet for all the hours we reasoned and talked, he didn't seem to be getting any closer.

Not long after getting back, he found work as a lorry driver, and as I hadn't sorted out a job in the early days I would often accompany him in the cab to continue our discussions. One day, driving back to Nottingham from Leicester, I became so frustrated with his apparent inability or unwillingness to accept what was clearly staring him in the face that I found there were, after all, limits to my new-found patience.

I turned to him and told him: 'Alan, we've talked enough now. That's it. Give your heart to Jesus, man. Come on – you know it's all true! Don't be stubborn. Let's just do it. This is too important to waste any more time over!'

It was an outburst of deep concern, but I wasn't sure if maybe I'd pushed him too hard. It was all quiet for a moment, and then he looked over at me and said quietly: 'OK, John, let's do it.'

Alan pulled off the road into a countryside lane, and drove up to the end a hundred yards or so away from where the heavy traffic rolled past. Switching off the engine he bowed his head over the steering wheel, and I led him in a short prayer of confession and invitation to Jesus. Sitting up again, he beamed, jumped down from the cab and began to shout at the top of his voice: 'It's really true, John! I believe it, you know!'

He fell to his knees on the grass as I climbed down to join him. 'Look at the trees!' he shouted happily as the tears started to fall. 'God made them, didn't he? God really made them! Oh, it's fantastic!' His stubbornness and fear had finally been swept away, and in their place was a bubbly joy.

Looming on the horizon was our forthcoming trial. We'd been bailed to appear at Nottingham Crown Court some five months after my return. It gave us strength and encouragement to think that we were all facing this thing together. We'd already been warned that the charge – conspiracy to defraud – was particularly serious. And having previous offences, it was almost certain that we would be sent to prison, despite our willingness to help the police as much as we could.

When I'd been interviewed by detectives on arriving back in England, they hadn't asked me if I had committed any other offences: I would have admitted it if they had. This left a catalogue of outstanding incidents still to be dealt with. One of the Bible passages that made a deep impression on me during this time was when Zacchaeus the tax collector became a disciple of Jesus. He immediately said that he wanted to repay all the debts he had—put right all the wrongs. It was a free expression of his gratitude to God. I felt the same, and Peter and I talked and prayed about the best way of going about it.

Finally, one morning, after we had spent an hour or so in prayer I sat down with pen and paper to make a list of all those I had stolen from. There was the jeweller's shop where I'd made my smash and grab; the bank where I'd run up a large illegal overdraft; the insurance companies I'd conned out of bogus sick pay while self-employed; a fashion shop where I'd obtained clothes on forged credit, the takings I'd pocketed secretly at the Crazy Horse Saloon and the Swiss hotel ... the list went on and on.

Then I turned to all those individuals I'd hurt – physically and emotionally. I tried to remember all the names of the people I'd battered and bruised – that included women. Like the evening a girl in a pub had made a rude remark when I bumped into her, and I'd punched her in the face, giving her a black eye. I jotted down the names, too, of the women I had wronged through my selfish relationships. Sharon's name came first.

My wrist started to ache, but I continued to scribble away. We'd prayed that God would help me to remember every last small matter, and other incidents came to mind. The money that I owed on tax from my self-employed days, the muggings and car thefts.

At last, it was finished. I looked at the lengthy list wondering if I could really go through with all this. How blind I'd been! Remembering had been the easy part ... now I had to *do* something with this catalogue of selfishness.

13

Back on the Streets

I'd returned to Nottingham riding so high on being a Christian that I couldn't wait to get out and tell everyone what had happened, even though I was a bit nervous about how I'd go about it. Much of my prayer time concentrated on asking God to help me share in the right ways the incredible good news I'd discovered. And it turned out that there were a number of different avenues to explore.

Having been a part of Nottingham's low scene, word soon seemed to have got round that 'Johnny's back and he's got religion'. I found that most of the old faces I came across knew that something had happened in Amsterdam, and that I was different, or at least claiming to be. They treated me warily, although whenever I got the chance I made stumbling attempts to tell them some of what had been going on inside me since that tearful night on The Ark. One night I drifted into the Flying Horse looking for Cupe. He was one of the city's most well-known hard men, and a man I had really admired.

The Flying Horse was as smokey and noisy as ever, and squinting through the haze I spotted him in a corner with a crowd of friends. They were laughing and drinking freely, and when I went over to their tables, there were some knowing nods and glances in my direction. Undeterred I sat down next to Cupe and said hello.

'Now then, Johnny, how's it going?' he asked brightly.

'Great, Cupe, great,' I replied. 'Maybe you've heard. I've become a Christian.'

'Yeah, that's right. Word's got round. What's it all about, then, youth?'

As he spoke I thought I detected some genuine interest beneath the brusque, rough-and-ready exterior. I began to tell him, hesitantly, about all that I'd been through, and as I did he turned to his drinking mates with a wave of his hand and snapped: 'Quieten down, will you! We're trying to talk here.' They turned to their drinks and we spent twenty minutes or so together, Cupe seeming to hang with interest on my account. Then I said that I'd got something for him, and reached inside my coat pocket for the spare copy of Nicky Cruz's autobiography *Run Baby Run* that I was carrying. Before I'd gone over to Cupe, I'd scribbled a brief greeting in it – 'To Cupe: we've both travelled a hard road' – and prayed for an opportunity to hand it over.

As he looked at the inscription with curiosity, Cupe's eyes filled with tears. I pressed on: 'I want you to know that coming to know Jesus has transformed my life. It's the most wonderful, beautiful thing you can ever imagine. And he can do the same for you.'

Cupe looked up, embarrassed and vulnerable. 'I know, Johnny, I believe it,' he whispered. Pulling himself together, he turned away with a laugh and snapped back to his former self. 'Well, thanks, Johnny, I'll read this some time,' he said, and went to order another drink.

I was a little disappointed that the moment seemed to have passed, but I was delighted that he'd been so keen to listen. It encouraged me to believe that my old friends would want to hear about God if I persisted in prayer and waited for the right moments to speak out. That encounter with Cupe encouraged me to look for other opportunities to explain what had happened in my life.

They came thick and fast the day I set out on my trail

of restitution. Peter and I had decided that it would be good to complete the journey in one day, if possible. So I got up extra early and spent a couple of hours praying and reading the Bible before heading off for my first appointment at the bank. With that successfully behind me, I was heartened for the calls that followed: at the insurance offices, the guild hall, the jeweller's shop, the tailors. ...

Some of the people I dealt with were businesslike or even a little short with me – although none took up my invitation to call the police. If they had decided to call in the police for a criminal prosecution, my pending Crown Court appearance for conspiracy to defraud would have meant certain jail. And then there were those, like the manager of the local insurance office, who were warmer. He half smiled when I told him about the false sickness benefit claims I'd made while I was self-employed. He'd been unwilling to pay up, and had only done so when I'd become extremely threatening over the phone.

'I never did believe you, you know,' he said. 'So what's all this change of heart about?'

His genuine interest gave me an opportunity to talk longer about my loneliness and insecurity, the desperate hunt for meaning in all the wrong places, and the incredible new life I'd begun since meeting Jesus. I could have gone on for the rest of the day, but he pulled me up short with a laugh. 'I see you've already started trying to convert people, then!' he chuckled.

'That's right,' I answered.

'Well, I think your coming in here and owning up is the most amazing thing that's ever happened to me in all the years that I've been in this business,' he told me with a shake of his head. 'I wish you well!'

When I finally got home that night I added up all the money that I'd promised to repay. It amounted to several thousand pounds, and I didn't have much more than the cost of a bus fare. But I wasn't downhearted. I was sure that God would give me the strength and ability to see it through to the end. I soon found work back on the building sites, and I laboured hard. Each Friday night I'd bring my fat pay packet home, hand some money over to Mum for my keep, and save myself a few coins for travel and the odd cup of coffee. The rest went down to the Post Office with me the following morning and, converted into a series of postal orders, got posted off to meet my debts. Every week's contribution was duly ticked off in a little black book I had bought for the purpose.

I knew that going back onto the sites would be a real test for my new faith, and I was determined to make it clear from day one that I was a Christian. So when lunch break arrived and I headed over to the cabin with my lunch box, I'd already decided what I had to do. We flopped round the table together, and the other guys opened up their flasks and packs of sandwiches. Meanwhile, I purposefully dropped my head to say a silent grace – and stayed in that position slightly longer than usual in case anyone had missed it. Then I looked up again as I opened my lunch box. One of the men opposite, Lenny, was staring at me with a big grin.

'What's all that about then, eh?'

It was just what I'd hoped for. 'I was praying – saying thank you to God for my food.'

'Oh,' Lenny guffawed, 'that's all right, then. I thought you'd slipped into a coma!' I laughed with him, and the ice was broken. They knew where I stood. Over our break he began to ask me further questions about what a Christian was, and I had a great opportunity to tell him about my journey of the past few years. From that time on the men never sneered at me or joked about my faith, as I'd half thought they would. In time, in fact, I found that they'd single me out to have a quiet word with me. They'd want my advice about what they should do about their relationships with women, or to voice their concern about a teenage son going off the rails. A few asked me to pray for them, and I did – along with all those who hadn't asked!

My wish to make exhaustive attempts at paying restitution involved firing off a series of overseas letters to people I'd ripped off on my travels. Not being a great writer I found this particularly difficult, but in due course the replies came back saying there were no hard feelings, and wishing me well. The toughest letter to write was the one I sent locally in Nottingham, however – to Sharon. I figured that it would be wrong of me to seek her out personally. So I told her all that had gone on, as best I could, and asked her to see if she could find her way to forgive me for the dreadful way I'd treated her and ruined her life. I offered to meet up with her if she wanted to, and told her I'd set in motion repayment of all the maintenance that I'd for so long refused to pay.

I never did hear from her, and the silence was painful. But I resolved to pray for her and our daughter – whom I last saw as a six-month-old in a family snapshot – in the hope that one day they may be able to find it in their hearts to forgive me. Not because I deserve it, but because they've found the love and healing and wholeness that Jesus can bring. Perhaps one day.

While I decided it was best not to try to make direct contact with Sharon, I did seek out a number of other women, with whom I'd had fleeting relationships, as I went round my old circle of friends specifically to put right incidents from the past.

I saw one woman in The Flying Horse one night, drinking with a group of friends. I'd had a brief affair with her when her marriage – to a friend of mine – had been breaking up. I went over to her and asked if I could have a private word with her for a moment. She seemed surprised to see me, but stepped out into the hall. It was an awkward moment, and I didn't know where to begin.

'Look, Suzy, you'll probably think I'm crazy,' I said, shifting uncomfortably. 'But I've become a Christian. . . .'

'I know,' she interrupted, looking at me uncertainly. 'I'd heard that you'd gone all religious, like. I hope you're not going to try to lay any of that on me, are you?'

This wasn't going at all as I'd hoped. 'Well, I want to tell you that I'm sorry for having committed adultery with you, and I want to ask you to forgive me if I caused you any hurt.'

She bristled. I'd obviously offended her. Her eyes flashed. 'So what's wrong with a bit of sex on the side?'

'Well, I'm a Christian, and I believe it's wrong to have sex with someone if you're not married.'

'Well I don't,' she almost shouted as she turned on her heels and walked off. 'I'm not sorry, and as far as I'm concerned there's nothing to forgive, so you can just get lost with all your Holy Joe stuff, mister.'

I was glad it was over. Heading home that night I felt wounded and tender, but I knew that I'd tried to do the right thing.

My efforts to tell others about Jesus were limited to conversations with one or two people at a time – usually against the backdrop of a noisy bar – until the day came for us to present ourselves for trial. Mac, Gary, Alan and I had all pleaded guilty to the offence, and had been delighted to find a solicitor who volunteered to take us on. He was from the congregation of the small evangelical church we'd begun to attend.

We arrived at the guild hall, where the Crown Court was sitting, having prayed for the strength to accept God's will that day. I'd already been day-dreaming about how I'd start a prison Bible study if the worst came to the worst and I was jailed. I was determined that whatever the outcome, I'd make it count for God. But we were greeted by an excited solicitor who told us: 'God is already at work – they've dropped the conspiracy charges!'

It was thrilling. This massively reduced the seriousness of the offence in the eyes of the law. When we finally stepped into the dock, we all pleaded 'guilty' and waited as the prosecuting officials told our story. Then our defence representative told how we'd given ourselves up to help the police clear the matter up, and how our experiences on The Ark had changed our lives radically. Within a matter of minutes we were walking free with fines, costs – and an eighteen-month prison sentence suspended for two years! We hugged each other and our families and thanked God for giving us our freedom. And the next day the story of our transformation – which the judge had said was so remarkable that it had prompted him to sentence us as first-time offenders, even though we had previous convictions – was recounted in the city's evening paper for all to see.

The evangelical church through which we'd found our legal help had been marvellous to us. They were a fairly traditional, middle-class congregation, but if they'd been shocked by this small group of enthusiastic, young people who had appeared in their midst, then they had done their very best to disguise it. We felt accepted straight away, and loved to attend all the meetings; the Sunday services, the mid-week prayer and Bible study evenings. As time went by, though, and we continued to make contacts among the old group of friends I'd known – and found a number of them turning to Christ – we began to feel a little uncomfortable. My heart was bursting for people who were as lost as I had been to find Jesus; yet evangelism seemed to have a low priority in the church's life.

Eventually a group of us began meeting in Sarah and Jenny's flat. They'd returned from The Ark turned upside down after their own encounters with God. In time they'd introduced us to Sarah's brother, Jamie, a young tailor, whom we had befriended. He'd become a Christian at the evangelical church, and was soon leading the informal fellowship meetings in the flat, with me.

Before we knew it we were thirty or more young people
there each week; new Christians converted through our
circle of contacts, or others from churches in the area
looking for more dynamism and vibrancy in their walk
with God. Although it was still only a few months since
I'd become a Christian, God seemed to equip me in a
special way and I was able to pass on all the teaching I'd
absorbed during my intensive time of study on The Ark.
Our mid-week meetings were alive with the presence of
God, as the Holy Spirit would move powerfully and yet
at the same time gently among us. There would be tears,
laughter, prayer and praise in an easy-going, open way
that soon made newcomers feel at ease.

After one particularly moving time of praise and
worship, I suggested that we should take this meeting
out into the open air. After all, what would God do if
non-Christians were around to witness it all? The others
agreed, so one Sunday afternoon we headed down into
the centre of Nottingham, to the square in front of the
guild hall.

Nervously we tuned up our guitars, picked up our
maraccas and bongos, and began to sing praises to
God, slipping from one short, happy song to another.
Within a few minutes we'd attracted a sizable crowd of
afternoon strollers who watched and listened. After
about twenty minutes we stopped and tried to engage
some of the onlookers in conversation, but it was a toss-
up as to who was more ill at ease about it all – them or
us. So we made our way home, happy at the way things
had gone, but frustrated that they hadn't been even
better.

We repeated this pattern for a few weekends until at
the end of one singing session I was approached by
Ansell. He was a short, wiry miner, originally from
Jamaica, who usually occupied the square before we did.
Dressed in his smartest suit, he stood on top of a
concrete post and, holding a Bible to his chest, shouted
out how people need God in their lives. I'd seen him in

action a couple of times when we'd arrived early to set up, and I'd been at once impressed by his bravery and intimidated by the negative reaction of some of those listening.

This particular Sunday Ansell stayed on to listen to us sing, and afterwards singled me out. He smiled and thanked us for singing about Jesus so freely. I was pleased. 'But, you know,' he added seriously, 'you've got to preach the gospel. You've got to tell them how Jesus can save them. You won't see anyone converted simply by your singing alone. You've got to tell them the good news!'

Deep down I knew he was right, but I was alarmed at the prospect. What would people think if we did what Ansell did? Would they laugh at us in the same way? Were any of us brave enough? At that week's Tuesday meeting we all talked and prayed about what he had said – and we agreed that he was right. We had to stand up and speak out next Sunday. The only question was, who?

Everyone's eyes turned in my direction.

The last of our songs is ringing round the square, and I realise that the moment has come. I'm terrified and breathe a silent prayer for help as I step up on top of a wooden bench and look out towards the crowd that has gathered to hear us singing and clapping.

I'm not really sure what I'm going to say, but it's too late to back out now, so I raise my hand in a gesture of acknowledgement and open my mouth. As I do I'm aware of a flood of confidence surging through my body, rising up from my feet and welling into my heart – and out through my mouth. My mind's suddenly racing with thoughts and ideas, and the words come out unexpectedly. They're not hesitant or timid, but bold and confident. It doesn't sound like me at all!

'D'you know,' I begin, 'I never used to be up this time

on a Sunday! I used to stagger across this square dead drunk most weekends, and if I'd seen somebody doing what I'm doing now, I'd have thought that he was completely barmy!' I pause and smile, and see some of the crowd turn away. But others smile back and look interested. I continue.

'You see that jeweller's shop just down the road, there? I broke into that one night . . . smash and grab. Got caught by the police a bit further up the street. I used to get into fights in that pub there, too . . .' and I begin to tell my story of drinking and fighting and sex and drugs and violence and lostness. And Jesus. The words spill out almost effortlessly, and the fear has gone completely. In its place is a keen thrill I've never known before.

Finally I've come full circle. 'And so that's why I'm here today with some of my friends. We're going to be staying here for a bit yet, so if you want to know any more, just come and have a chat with us. Thank you.' And I step down, tingling with excitement and satisfaction. Ansell's right – there's power in preaching the gospel. I for one feel as though I've just been plugged into the mains. This is something I'm going to want to do again and again. . . .

Encouraged by the warm response our first public preaching received, other members of the group wanted to try it over the next few weeks. I was keen to give them an opportunity so long as I was able to speak again as well! I found myself looking forward to the Sunday afternoon meetings with great longing. I'd still be nervous when the afternoon finally arrived, but once I stood up and opened my mouth I sensed God filling me with authority, clarity and confidence, and I enjoyed telling the passers-by about Jesus' tremendous love.

If any of those who stopped to listen wanted to talk further, we would sit down with them for the afternoon, or invite them along to our Tuesday night meeting. And soon we found that there were a number of new Christians through our street meetings. Our weekly numbers grew to over forty as God's love was shared with family, friends and acquaintances, and they responded. Wherever possible we tried to encourage newcomers to find their way through to local churches, but many felt that the closeness of God they felt in our Tuesday meetings wasn't there at some of the more formal Sunday services they attended.

As winter drew nearer, the cold weather meant that people were less keen to stand and listen to us – and, indeed, we were less enthusiastic about being there – so we turned more to prayer and Bible study. Within a matter of a few months we had developed a growing fellowship, comprising mostly young and new Christians. I felt confident that God had enabled me to cope with all the demands this made up to now – I certainly knew that I didn't have the resources within myself – but I began to worry about future direction. I didn't think our young leadership could run things for ever this way.

I'd kept in touch with The Ark over the months, advising them of my spiritual growth and all that was happening in a series of lengthy letters. I'd also asked them to pray about our fellowship's situation when, in a reply, Floyd McClung suggested that a couple from The Ark should perhaps come over to England to lend some experienced hands to the scene. We were delighted, and in due course welcomed Paul and Mary Miller, an American couple who had become Christians while following the hippy trail in India, and had been key workers at The Ark for a couple of years.

It was a brave move on their part. They arrived in grey, cold Nottingham knowing little about what they faced, and found themselves a small bedsit. I relinquished formal leadership of the fellowship and handed the responsibility over to Paul, acting as his assistant along with Jamie. Under the Millers' direction and gentle guidance, the fellowship continued to flourish and grow – both in numbers and in the knowledge of God's love and power in our lives.

The days were busy, bursting with an ever-deepening love for God and this wonderful, exciting new life he had given me. I was so happy with our newly-united family; the opportunities to talk about God at work on the sites; the debts being paid off and the new things we were all learning in the fellowship. Life seemed as full as it could possibly be.

There was only one shadow. One day I was laying bricks on a housing scheme down in the old Meadows part of the town – in fact just across the street from where we'd lived and been attacked by the cousin with the knife. It was early morning, and I'd not been going long when my heart spasmed. I went cold inside. 'Home, I've got to get home,' I told myself. I knew it was God prompting me. I threw my tools into my bag, thrust them back into the store shed and leaped over the wall to run off to the bus stop, shouting back over my shoulder that I'd got to go home suddenly.

When I got back, I was met at the door by a distraught Trish. 'It's Dad, John. There's been an accident. . . .'

Poor Dad. He'd been struck by a bus down in the town, and had suffered serious head injuries in the fall. He was in the intensive care unit down at the hospital. Joan, Mum and I fell into each other's arms and prayed for God's help to be strong.

Two days later Dad died without regaining consciousness, and we all wept together. We'd only been close as a family for a few short months. It almost seemed cruel. And yet through our grief of bereavement, we could see a test of our faith. We knew that if we weren't careful we could easily become negative towards God for having allowed this tragedy to happen. But as we wept and mourned and comforted each other, we agreed that we could trust God. Though we didn't understand fully, we knew there was a reason for the way things had turned out. Our tears of grief were mixed with thankfulness for God's goodness to us in allowing us the days we had enjoyed together as a family, in him. Gradually we came to see how different it was to face death with God in our lives. Even in the sadness, there was a real sense of hope for the future.

14
Plenty to Learn

There were three high points to my week; each of them a far cry from the sort of pastimes I'd looked forward to in former days. There were Tuesday evenings, when we'd come together in the girls' small flat to praise God and learn more about him. I often used to smile when I thought back to how, a matter of months earlier, I'd been living in a small bedsit in a room upstairs, frightened of living and scared of dying. Now life and death thrilled and consumed me. Every day was an adventure in living for Jesus, and the prospect of being with him for ever was almost too much to contemplate.

Saturday mornings were special, too. It gave me a great sense of satisfaction to bundle off my small pile of payments in the post. I enjoyed knowing that I'd put in another week's hard work, and that another entry could be made in my account book: a visible record of my determination to put right, with God's help, all that I could of the old days.

But most of all I loved Sunday afternoons, when we'd gather to sing and preach in the town centre. That marvellous buzz of adrenalin and excitement that had charged through me the first time I stood up, never failed to return every time I took my turn talking to the crowds. I knew that this was what I wanted to spend the rest of my life doing, and as soon as I'd paid off my final debts, I would commit myself to full-time evangelism out in the open air. For a short period I actually stopped work and joined Paul in a daily programme of street preaching near to Nottingham's main shopping precinct. We'd spend the morning praying together and the afternoon taking turns to preach and talk with shoppers and passers-by who paused to listen and chat. This 'work experience' time only whetted my appetite further, and I returned to the building sites more determined than ever to work my way through my repayments as swiftly as possible and get into full-time ministry as quickly as I could.

A way of helping things along seemed to pop up when I came across an advertisement for bricklayers wanted in Germany. I'd been working hard and steadily in Nottingham for around two-and-a-half years, and while I'd made a large dent in my debts there was still a frustratingly long way to go. But the firm seeking brickies were offering money well over the odds found in England — perhaps here was the route God was providing for me.

I calculated that if I worked flat out for six weeks or so then I could come home with all the money I needed; as against the year or more it would take me at British rates. So I followed the offer up, got myself an interview and almost before I knew it found myself travelling out to the site, a small German town not far from the Dutch border. I was to be picked up at the station by the guy in charge of the building programme, the English manager of a small firm.

When I arrived I found myself being met along with two or three other British brickies who were making the trip. Memories of my Canadian travels came back to me, but I shook them off.

The last time I'd been trying to master my own destiny — and failed abysmally; this time I knew God was firmly in control. Our first port of call was the nearest pub, where the other men immediately ordered a couple of beers each. My request for a Coke raised their eyebrows, and I was able to spend a few minutes telling them about why I'd turned my back on drinking.

After a while the site manager offered to take me over to the hotel in which I was to be accommodated, to sort out the final few details. On the way, in the car, I asked him about what arrangements had been made to sort out my tax payments.

He laughed and looked over at me.

'What's so funny?'

'You've got to be kidding. We don't pay tax!'

'What do you mean?' I asked. All was not as I had expected, obviously.

'It's cash in hand. No tax, no questions. In fact, nobody really knows that we're over here on the job. We're sub-contracted out by somebody else back home.'

My heart sank. I hadn't even got as far as unpacking my bags, and it seemed like the whole arrangement was falling apart. 'You mean it's black money, then?'

'Well, yeah, if you want to call it that,' he replied, shifting uncomfortably in his seat. 'But everyone does it, you know, it's all accepted.'

'Maybe,' I cut in. 'But not for me. One of the reasons I'm here for the job is to pay off a load of money that I owe the taxman! I can't work on this basis. I'll have to go back home.'

The driver looked at me with a mixture of annoyance and amazement. 'You've got to be kidding! That's good money down the drain. What are you, some kind of weirdo, or something?'

'I'm a Christian,' I explained. 'I've given my life to Jesus, and he wouldn't want me to do this. I'm sorry.'

My driver turned the car around, and we headed back to the station. It was an uncomfortable few minutes' drive, and he spent the time trying to justify his actions by explaining how it was all part of the system; nobody expected you to do differently. Nobody really lost out; the government wouldn't miss a few hundred pounds. I didn't answer.

Standing back outside the station, with my bag over

my shoulder, I sagged. In just a couple of hours my carefully-made plans seemed to have been dashed. I was confused and a bit disappointed. I knew that God had some sense in all of this, somewhere, but right then it was beyond me. I needed some time and space to think and pray it through so that I could see what he was doing. I decided to travel over the border and back to Holland.

My destination was Heidebeek, a picturesque little hamlet about sixty miles to the north of Amsterdam. Since I'd left The Ark, they had become part of Youth With a Mission, an international missionary organisation with operations all over the world. They had also expanded their work in Holland, keeping The Ark going while opening a training base out in the Dutch countryside.

Joan had contacted them some months after my homecoming, and with her toddler son had gone out to Holland. There she'd gone through the new Discipleship Training School in which young Christians were given a thorough grounding in their faith, before going into full-time service of one kind or another. Joan had then stayed on to become part of a ministry house in Epe, near Heidebeek. She and Sean loved the environment – the love of the people and the beauty of the countryside setting made it a real haven of peace. I'd been impressed by what I'd seen in the two previous brief visits that I had made.

So I arrived unexpectedly, but to a warm welcome. And later, over coffee with Floyd McClung – renewing our friendship with smiles and hugs – I told him about my hopes and dreams, and how they all seemed to have collapsed. He looked at me in his thoughtful, 'I've-got-an-idea-coming' way.

'John, why don't you just stay here and go through our Discipleship Training School? We've got one starting next week.'

I knew from the past that Floyd had a knack of

making the most outrageous ideas seem matter-of-fact, but this one seemed too way out – even for me. I had my near-future mapped out, and studying the Bible in the middle of a Dutch forest had no part in it. I had to work because I had to pay my debts. I spluttered a dismissive answer, tailing off with: '... and I've not finished paying restitution, either.'

Floyd didn't seem perturbed by my objections. He smiled. 'Well, why don't you just go away and pray about it, and ask the Lord if this is right or not? If it is, then he'll provide for you, John.'

I was certain that I already knew what the answer was, but my respect for this gentle-spoken, smiling American packed me off praying. And I had to admit that I'd become so determined to do what God wanted me to, that I'd failed to recognise that he wanted to help.

During my prayers my mind was filled with a simple picture. I saw a series of different doors that seemed to represent the ways open to me, avenues I could explore to pay back all the hundreds of pounds that I still owed. And as I gazed at them, one by one they closed. Firmly. At last there was only one door still open, tucked away at the side of my mind's eye, and above it was one word ... Heidebeek. The door was ajar, and flooding through and round the gap was a bright, welcoming light. It seemed like warm sunlight, the sort you just want to go and throw yourself into. That's how I felt, and I realised that God was speaking clearly to me: he did want me to go through the DTS (Discipleship Training School). And if I left to go home again, I'd be acting disobediently.

I didn't understand, but I knew what I had to do. When I found Floyd I told him: 'You're right. I've prayed about it, and I believe that the Lord wants me to stay here.'

It's a bright, sunny morning, and the sun filters through

the trees in a haze of glorious colours. The woods smell fresh and crisp, and the only sound comes from the few farm animals grazing nearby. It's a beautiful morning a world away from my early starts on a Nottingham building site, and I almost pinch myself again to make sure that it's real. Yes, I'm still here!

As I walk over to the main building, where the DTS classes are due to start soon, I wonder again at the turn of events. I realise that I'd made the mistake of narrowing down God's plan for me into a specific pathway. I'd decided that there was only one way to do what he expected of me – and that was working my debts off. Now I'm beginning to understand that there may be other possibilities. I've still got a long way to go to clear my outstanding monies, and I've got nothing to meet the fees of this course – only a few pounds in my pocket. So something beyond my best efforts is needed.

I'm idling these thoughts over in my mind as I check my post. My phone call home had caused excited bewilderment, and I'm anticipating some letters from the rest of the family. Nothing there, though – except one envelope. There's no stamp on it, though, so it's not come through the mail. I slit it open ... and pull out sixty pounds in folded notes. Tucked in the middle is a scrap of paper with just two words on it, 'With love.'

It takes a moment or two to sink in, and then the tears are stinging my eyes. I'm so moved by the quiet, loving kindness of whoever has left this gift. But even more, I'm overwhelmed by the love of the God who has prompted them to do this. For me.

I whoop and speed off down the hallway to tell what's happened. And as I go I realise that I'm learning another deep lesson in my new life. I see how my determination to do the right thing in clearing my debts had almost become a matter of pride. *I* was going to do it. *I* was going to put things right.

Then I see that God's saying: 'No, not that way, John. I've forgiven you. I love you. You don't have to try to

earn that love through your repayments. Thank you for
your commitment to doing what you should – but now I
want to meet you halfway.'

The envelopes were there week by week as the DTS
continued. Sometimes ten pounds, sometimes thirty,
once as much as 200. Always neat and tidy; always
anonymous, but for a note of love or encouragement.
And always enough to enable me to continue my repayments, pay the school fees and leave a little left over to
buy a cup of coffee.

Occasionally I'd feel almost guilty. Why should God
provide the money in this way when I could earn it? And
then I'd remember that it was because he loved me;
because he wanted to; because I could never justify or
deserve that love. So I knew I had to stop worrying and
look to what else he wanted for me.

As well as learning to trust him for my material needs
in a completely new way, I discovered that he wanted me
to be a good student. In the nearly three years since I'd
become a Christian, I felt that my life had been turned
completely upside down. I'd learned a lot in the early
days on The Ark, and continued to grow back in
Nottingham. Seeing my family and friends come to faith
in Jesus too had fuelled my love for him and hunger to
tell others.

And yet there was still a lot of refining in me to be
done. There was a job of smoothing down and polishing
that I only began to see as necessary in the quietness and
tranquillity of Heidebeek. In those months of the DTS I
came to appreciate that there were still secret hurts and
insecurities inside me that had to be dealt with. And
through prayer and times of teaching, counselling and
ministry with the staff and guest speakers, I knew a
deeper, cleansing work of the Holy Spirit in my life.

I still found it quite hard to relate to other people. In
the past I'd have hidden that in a bout of drinking or
drugs. Now I had to face it and work it through.

Although I was still a bit of a loner, avoiding the snack bar at coffee breaks in preference to being on my own, I could feel changes slowly coming about.

I used to get up early in the morning, before the duties of the day, to enjoy uninterrupted time alone with God. Wrapping a thick blanket around my shoulders, I'd stroll out into the pre-dawn woods, and settle down on the ground by a tree with my Bible at my right hand. There I'd spend a precious couple of hours praying, praising God and mulling over the Bible, as the first rays of the day's sun began to percolate through the branches.

At night I'd devour biographies of Christian pioneers like General Booth, the founder of the Salvation Army, and William Carey, the missionary pathfinder. It used to excite me to think what God had achieved through these men, and I'd fall asleep praying that he might one day use me in a similar way.

The more I grew in my relationship with God, the more clearly I saw that my walk with him depended to a large degree on the choices I made. Not that I directed my steps; he did. But I also had to choose to walk that way. I had to accept the things that he wanted to give me. In a sense God's love could only work as far and as deep in my life as I was prepared to let it. This understanding helped me come to terms with the way our old gang of four had dispersed in the days after our Amsterdam turnaround: we'd pretty much drifted apart after our court appearance.

Mac had never made a commitment. He'd told me back in Nottingham that he believed all that he'd heard and seen on The Ark, but he just wasn't interested.

Gary had followed my tearful steps to Jesus a couple of nights later in Amsterdam. He had returned to Nottingham with a similar desire to tell his old friends what had happened. He went after them in the pubs and clubs, spurning the offer of a beer, settling for a soft drink, and sitting them down to tell them all about Jesus.

In fact he was so anxious to go out and tell others that he couldn't be bothered to waste time, as he saw it, meeting with Peter and me to pray and study the Bible. We began to see less of him; and then, the next time I spotted him in a pub, he was nursing a half-pint of beer. On the next occasion it was a pint – and soon he was back in his old ways. An awkward shrug was the only explanation he could offer when we had an opportunity to talk about all that had gone before.

Alan's situation was probably the most difficult for me to understand. We had been through a lot together. He had been the closest of the other three, and I'd been so excited that day he had prayed for Jesus to come into his life. But then the inner struggle began. 'I know that being a Christian means giving up chasing women, and I just don't know if I can do that,' he told me. My attempts to encourage him that God did have a precious plan for a man and woman—but in the proper context of a committed marriage relationship—just seemed to wash straight over him.

He too turned back. Of the four young men who went searching for God, I seemed to be the only one who found who he was looking for.

At Heidebeek I came to know much more about the wonderful God I served and it only made me even more anxious to get out on the streets to tell others about him.

As the school approached an end, I expected to return to Nottingham to start full-time preaching with Paul and other members of the old fellowship. But Floyd had other plans, and when he asked me to stay on as a staff member, to assist with the next DTS, I knew that it was right to accept.

I'd found that being at Heidebeek was helping me work out a new way of relating to women. Since becoming a Christian I'd been freed from the crude, selfish, disposable view I'd had of the opposite sex from my early teens. But although that twisted attitude had been torn out of my life, in its place was awkwardness and uncertainty. I hadn't had a girlfriend in the last three years. I never looked for one. Instead I'd filled my life with a passion for God, and found him to be all I wanted or needed. Or so I thought.

Gradually I found myself easing up in the company of the female staff members and students. I was able to start treating them like my sisters, and I enjoyed the freedom that brought.

But I was still rocked back on my heels when, one morning, I strolled through the grounds on my prayer time and sensed God speaking to me in that gentle, quiet, assured voice of his: 'John, the girl for you will be in the next school.'

It sounded totally absurd. But I was sure that it had been God speaking.

15
Terry

A few weeks later I realised I'd heard right. Her name was Terry Gray, and I fell hopelessly and wonderfully in love with her at about fifty paces. The moment my eyes fell on her as I scanned the group of new arrivals for the next DTS gathering in the main hall, I knew that my life would never be the same again. One glance set off a chain of reactions that had me reeling inside. My heart started to race.

Self-consciously I made to walk away, as though I had an important errand elsewhere. I was sure that everyone could see my cheeks flushing, and I was horribly un-comfortable with the feelings churning around inside me. I was still busy working through what it meant to be a new man in Christ, and I'd committed my life to telling others about him out on the streets. Falling in love with a girl at first sight just didn't fit in with my plans; and it hardly smacked of the spiritual maturity and solid faith I was aching to see grow in my character! Somehow I managed to force down the emotions that were rising within me, and I pulled myself back together again before the newcomers were introduced to the staff.

Our role was to go through the classes with the students, encouraging them to work through and apply to their own lives the biblical teaching on the character of God and discipleship. In addition, we were there to support and befriend them, and generally ensure that their days at DTS were a time of personal growth, while laying foundations for future service. To help pay my way there, I was also in charge of all the maintenance programmes at Heidebeek – everything from changing a light bulb to laying a new foundation for a service road. If it needed repairing or making, it was my job to see that it happened.

Despite my thirst for Bible knowledge, and the rich discoveries I'd made during my time in discipleship training, I found it hard to apply myself this second time around. I struggled to concentrate, like holding a rudder to the right course in a strong wind, but my thoughts kept veering away. They would be followed by my eyes when I'd turn casually to sneak a quick glance at the young woman who had thrown me into a secret turmoil.

Concerned to make sure that no one else picked up the inner confusion I was experiencing, I made a point of avoiding any real contact with her, other than in the odd times when I'd sit and share a coffee in a group. I continued to carve myself away for long hours alone with God, reading the Bible or Christian biographies. But I also ran through my mind the few things I'd managed to glean about her from overhearing the odd conversation.

She was twenty-one, and came from a respectable, middle-class home in the American South. Terry had become a Christian as a teenager, and felt that she was called to missionary service in Europe at sixteen. A French and Bible student, she had gone on a summer ministry trip with Wheaton College in Europe when she'd met Floyd McClung during a brief stop-over on The Ark, and he had told her about a YWAM community to be opened along similar lines in France. Now she was at Heidebeek preparing to join the staff at this new centre.

These details were in addition to all that I had been able to observe. Trim, with long auburn hair parted down the middle, dark brown eyes and a ready smile, her personality was equally attractive. I soon realised that Terry was a popular figure with her open, easy-going nature and warm sense of humour. I'd often hear her bright peal of laughter from a group of students sitting together talking, or playing board games in the evening.

It was paralysing. The few times we did speak I felt tongue-tied and clumsy, and was sure that she had dismissed me as some kind of awkward schoolboy. And secretly I told myself that I was crazy to feel the way I did about someone I hardly knew – particularly in the light of our past. She was a nice American girl from a good background, and had grown from attending church to a powerful, personal walk with God without so much as a hiccup. And here was I; a rough-edged Englishman from the slum area who had tasted most of the forbidden fruits before they had finally turned to ashes in my mouth. Chalk and cheese went together better than we did!

There was another dimension to my struggle, too. One that seemed to call into question everything I'd been aiming for. All I'd dreamed of in serving God seemed close at hand, and now I found it hard to concentrate because I was mooning over an unreachable girl!

I'd been given the go-ahead to try some street evangelism in Amsterdam. The work of The Ark had always been based on what Floyd called 'friendship evangelism'; gentle, caring, low-key and long-term. He had seen too much 'plastic preaching', and believed that many of the young drop-outs with whom he came into contact would be completely turned off by too direct an approach. Instead, The Ark workers set out to win hearts through friendship – and then talk to them about Jesus. And I knew that it worked, because it had drawn me.

But I also knew the powerful urge I had to tell others about Jesus; those who either may not have the opportunity of being befriended over a period of time, or who needed a more direct challenge to their lives. Many travellers were already disillusioned with life – that's why they were on the road. But others didn't think there was anything missing from their lives. They needed to be challenged. We had seen it work time after time in Nottingham, and I had grown in confidence and assurance as the weeks went by. I knew that, eventually, it was what I wanted to do full time.

To this extent, coming to Heidebeek had been like going through withdrawal. Floyd was delighted to hear about our experiences in Britain, but he clearly didn't think them appropriate to Amsterdam or the work there. Occasionally we'd talk more about it, and I'd ask if he might let me at least go and try it. He'd listen, discuss – and say, no, the time wasn't right. It was frustrating, but I respected Floyd's wisdom and experience, so I'd accept his decision. Then I went away, prayed again that God might one day make it possible for me to preach in the streets of Amsterdam, and waited for another good opportunity to talk some more about it with Floyd.

I started to make the occasional visit to Amsterdam with Paul Filler, another DTS staff member with whom I had grown especially close, and who shared my enthusiasm for the idea of going onto the streets. We'd tour the city, talking about what it would be like to start a programme of open-air evangelism, and praying for God's leading.

One day, as we strolled around, I had a strange experience. All the faces of the people we passed – old and cheery, young and angry, foreign and lost – seemed to be caught, frozen on the back of my mind. It was like a private slide-show of the lostness of all the people packed into the city. I felt that God was showing this private screening to say: 'Look, John, in all the crowds there are people. And they need to hear about my Son.'

Then, finally, one day, Floyd agreed. I could take a small team from the school onto the streets!

We began with one-day excursions, when we'd all pile into a van to drive into the city from Heidebeek. We'd

sing some praise songs in one of the squares, and then
I'd preach – just the way we had done in Nottingham.
We were pleased with the way things went, and so was
Floyd, who had joined us out of curiosity. He suggested
we extend the scope of what we were doing. I was
thrilled, and set about planning a summer outreach
programme for the city. It would be a four-week event,
with a small group of us based at one of the campsites on
the edge of the city. We'd set up a base there among all
the drug addicts and travellers, try some open-air evangelism in the city itself, and invite those interested in
learning more to come and spend some time with us at
the camp – rather like The Ark under canvas.

After a morning of prayer and praise with the rest
of the Heidebeek staff and workers – who had some
mixed views on the idea of the outreach – I and my
small team headed off for Amsterdam in two crammed
vans. Among the group was Terry Gray, who had discovered midway through the DTS that the French community she'd been intending to join was not now going
ahead as planned. Instead she proposed to join the
YWAM base out at Lausanne, Switzerland, where French-
speakers were required. But that left a month to kill –
and the Amsterdam outreach seemed like a good idea.

'No sex! No violence! No war!' The words are repeated
over and over, like a litany, cutting through the bubble
of street chatter and music. A few heads turn to see
who's chanting, but many don't. It's not uncommon for
people to do their own thing on the bustling streets of
the city – this is just another guy overloaded on acid, or
maybe speed.

But I sense otherwise. Our first few days working in
the open air have gone well. We've sung some lively
praise songs as a group, I've stepped up to preach
briefly, and we've then split up to try to engage the
listeners in further conversation. There has been great
interest, and already some of the young people have

begun drifting back to our campsite to hear more over coffee or dinner.

I know that this positive start is because of the way the ground has been prepared over the previous weeks. Ever since the go-ahead was given, I've been travelling into the city with a couple of other staff members. We've walked up and down all these streets, past the sex clubs and brothels and cafés selling drugs over the counter and teenagers lying stoned on the pavements, and we've prayed as we walked. We've prayed over all the places to be used as preaching spots, claiming them for God's power and purposes, and in Jesus' name shackling the forces of evil at work there.

So the repetitive cry I hear stirs something within me. This isn't just someone's scrambled gospel; there's more to it. The man is dressed in baggy, flowing clothes, and his eyes have that clouded, faraway look that speaks not of drugs, but of someone whose life is gripped by spirits of evil. Calmly I get him to talk a little more, and he tells us his message comes from his guru. Do we want to go and meet him, too?

Terry decides to come along as well, and the two of us follow eagerly. Only when we're nearly at the top of the stairs, in an old, derelict building a few streets away from the main centre, do I realise that I've misjudged things. Too late, now, though; must just pray for God to protect us.

Stepping into the dusty, dark attic room at the top of the house there's an almost tangible sense of oppressive, heavy evil. Three or four men are lounging around on cushions scattered across the floor, and in the middle is the guru: bare-chested, hard-faced, bearded, suspicious. He views Terry aggressively, speaks to her harshly and fiercely. I sense a wave of hatred, and it all seems to be directed at her. Not waiting to let the situation get out of hand, I smile and tell him what we're doing in the city; how much God loves him, and that he can have a new life in Jesus. A battle is taking place.

Clearly there aren't going to be any takers of an invitation for coffee! I make our excuses, and we back down the stairs, out onto the streets again. It's wonderful to be outside in the clear air again; the weight lifts from us and Terry bursts into tears, burying her head in my shoulder.

I'm annoyed that I hadn't been a bit more discerning before walking into that confrontation. It has obviously shaken her to the roots. The reality of spiritual warfare is new to her; the closeness of the battle between God and his enemy. As I try to comfort her, I'm aware of two things — how I want to make her feel safe for the rest of her life, and how I want to keep fighting the likes of which we've just encountered.

The four weeks were over almost too quickly. We returned to Heidebeek exhausted but happy. We'd made an impact on the streets, quickly learning to adapt what we did and how we did it to the climate of the city and the nature of the laid-back, liberated people who passed through. We'd seen a good number come to Christ through our contacts on the street, or back at the campsite, where at one stage we'd been asked to move on because we were bad for business; the usual drug pedlars who used the place as a base stopped dealing!

My mind was already racing with further possibilities, and how we'd do things bigger and better next time. And I was also wondering what was going to happen with Terry. The last month had only deepened my feelings for her and I couldn't bear the thought of seeing her go off to Switzerland. And yet while I didn't think twice about shouting out in public how I'd become a Christian, I was terrified at the thought of trying to tell her in private what I was thinking.

Finally, after a couple of days skating round each other, it was almost time for her to leave. Just before, she came up to talk about the incident with the demonised man. I explained some more about spiritual warfare, prayer and the supernatural, and we stayed together talking.

There was an awkward silence for a moment, and then Terry said: 'There's something else we need to discuss, isn't there?'

My insides flipped; she knew! Taking a deep breath, and feeling the colour burn my cheeks bright red, I started hesitantly to tell her how I felt. I didn't find it easy, and I stumbled and mumbled my way through. But I managed to say enough, because by the time she did board the bus, Terry and I had agreed to pray about God's leading in our lives.

I was on cloud nine. My thirst for evangelism was being met – Floyd approved of what he'd seen and heard of the outreaches, and was now keen to extend them further – and I'd been able to tell the girl of my dreams that I was in love. Well, at least something along those lines. For the next few weeks I worked in a factory near Heidebeek, raising funds to settle the last of my debts. Those days spent ladling egg powder passed in a happy dream, as I thought about Terry. Even the Scripture memory verse I habitually carried in my shirt pocket couldn't make me concentrate.

I wrote to her two or three times a week; me, the uncommunicative one who'd rarely managed more than a postcard before. I found that I just wanted to sit down with a pen and paper and tell her all about my days: what was happening at Heidebeek; the things God was showing and teaching me; and encouraging her in her walk with him.

The path of true love didn't run smoothly, though. We hit a pothole a few months later when somehow our still-cautious exchanges failed to communicate clearly enough. The upshot was that she spent a day on The Ark when passing through Amsterdam, and took my non-arrival to see her – a visit I didn't realise was expected or possible – as a sign of uninterest. Her letters began to tail off, and mine did in return – my heart sinking at the thought of her not being interested in me any more.

Somehow I managed to bury my disappointment in the business of life at Heidebeek, the prayer walks and plans for further evangelism in Amsterdam. Seven months later I found myself setting off for Venice with a team from Heidebeek. YWAM groups from all over the Continent were to be meeting up at the waterside city for a programme of mass training and outreach. Workers from the Lausanne base were also to be there, Terry among them.

My hands were cold and sweaty and my throat was dry when our coach pulled into the campsite just outside Venice. We were greeted by a welcoming 'orchestra' of other YWAMers, thumping out a symphony of arrival on everything they could lay their hands on: pots, pans, bottles and cans. And there in the middle of the smiling, cheering crowd was Terry. My spirits rose at just seeing her face again, and slumped at the thought of what might have been.

Deliberately I hovered about on the coach while everyone else got off, hoping there would be no need for an awkward encounter. But she was still there, waiting for me, when I finally stepped down. And as I looked at her again, I knew that I was still cartwheelingly in love with her. We exchanged a 'hi' and managed a stiff sort of hug before I had to move on to arrange our accommodation and food. I had plenty to occupy my mind, but other thoughts were in the way. They continued to crowd my thinking over the next few days, even though we didn't see much of each other.

Eventually I plucked up the courage to invite her out for a pizza, and one evening a group of us went into the city. Gingerly we started to explore our feelings again, and my heart soared as I sensed that maybe there was hope to be salvaged here somewhere. In our spare moments we continued to meet, talk, laugh and just enjoy one another's company.

Still being unsure of myself when relating to women, I decided that I needed the wise counsel of an older Christian man. I singled out one I had in mind and poured out my problem. He listened intently, and then advised me: 'John, if you believe that she's the girl for you, then tell her and ask her to pray about it.' It seemed pretty direct to me, but I felt that this man knew what he was talking about; so I did.

Sitting over a cup of coffee in a noisy bar I told Terry: 'You know how things have been going between us. Well, Terry, either you are the girl for me, or you aren't. I've prayed about this; would you, too?'

I'm not sure what kind of reaction I expected, but it certainly wasn't the one I got. Terry burst into tears. 'Well, if it's all or nothing now, it's nothing!' she snapped, picking up her things and storming out of the café leaving me with two cups of coffee and a horrible feeling of failure.

Until the Venice outreach came to an end and smaller teams came together to head off for evangelism programmes all over Europe, I didn't see Terry again except for one brief exchange. I asked her to join the group I was leading on a six-week outreach to Crete. She refused coolly. She was going to Israel, she told me. Fortunately the next month-and-a-half was a busy time of leading a team, preaching and follow-up, and I didn't have much time to dwell on what had gone wrong. My team lived out on the beaches, and by the end of the programme we were all bronzed, fit and happy with the way we had seen God touching the lives of many of the young holiday-makers with whom we had come into contact.

Back in Venice the various teams came together to share stories of their successes, failures and adventures. It was thrilling to hear of some of the things that had happened, and to see how God managed to work through the enthusiasm and open-heartedness of so many students and young people.

Already my mind was taking on some of the demands of the next challenge ahead – I was to be leading our second summer of service, working on the streets of Amsterdam from our base at the campsite.

I shared details of this venture at the Venice gathering and appealed for anyone willing to join in to approach me. I couldn't resist seeking out Terry – suntanned from the outreach in Israel, looking even more lovely than ever – to ask if she wanted to come along, too. Her response was non-committal; she had to think it over.

Minutes before the bus was leaving, on our final day in Venice, Terry came to me. She seemed nervous – something I'd never noticed before.

'I've done a lot of thinking and praying, John,' she told me. 'And I've realised something . . . that I really do love you, and I want to come to Amsterdam with you to see what the Lord has for us.' She would meet us in a few days.

These were the words I'd been dreaming of hearing for so long, and now they didn't seem to go in. I stared at her open-mouthed for a moment, and she smiled at my surprise. Then I smiled back as I boarded the bus. I still can't remember the trip back at all.

16

The Beach-head

We made an unusual orchestra. Dressed in overalls and
shabby work clothes, we played guitars, bongos and
drums as we sang our hearts out along the way. We were
going to take possession of our new base in the red light
district of Amsterdam, and we wanted everyone to know
we were coming! We'd read again how King David had
celebrated and praised as he led the Ark of the Covenant
back to its rightful home, and we had decided that it was
appropriate to make a thankful song and dance about
our new premises too.

Following the success of our second summer outreach, twelve months previously, we had realised that
our 'commuter' programme of evangelism wasn't ideal.

The Ark wasn't far from the bustling city centre, but
there wasn't room to put up a team of twenty or so
without taking away from their work. The campsites
were really too far out. We wanted somewhere close to
the city that could be a base and a coffee bar back-up to
our efforts on the streets. As I talked and prayed about
this with the other leaders, we came across a rundown
hotel in the centre of the red light district. It was dirty
and derelict, and as a result was for sale at a ridiculously
low price.

It was located in the worst part of the city's sex and
drugs artery. There were sex clubs, brothels and porno
cinemas on each side, and pushers and addicts on every
corner. Until now YWAM's work had effectively skirted
round this portion of Amsterdam; it was considered too

big a challenge. But now we felt the time was right. We were spiritually strong enough to go into battle there. So, trusting God to provide the money – which he did – we had agreed to purchase the building. I was to lead in a team of volunteers that would renovate it and then use it as a base for another summer's outreach. It was a thrilling prospect.

Thirty young people had 'signed up' for the clean-up. Among them was Terry Gray. We'd had a year of ups and downs, but we were still trying to work out what our futures might be – together or apart.

Another forty or so volunteers would join us in a few weeks for the actual programme of evangelism. The Ark – the houseboats, that is – had opened their doors to us and given us room to lay our sleeping bags, side to side, while the building was made ready.

It was a great morning when we headed down into the red light district. As we neared the city quarter, famous throughout the world for its vice and drugs, we began to sing worship songs and clap our hands. Noise isn't uncommon in the district – there is music and shouting almost round the clock – but of a far different nature. So our singing began to attract curious stares from the prostitutes, pushers and pimps as we wound our way through the narrow streets.

Finally we arrived at the edge of a canal beside the Old Church, a beautiful gothic building almost six hundred years old. We stood and looked across the water to our new home; a narrow, four-storey building squeezed into one of the most notorious avenues in the whole of the neighbourhood. On either side was a satanist church, a homosexual bar, a twenty-four-hour porno cinema and drug joints. We moved round, over the small bridge and along to the front door. A great cheer went up as I turned the key in the lock and led the way into the old Budget Hotel.

It had been well named, apparently. No one could have spent any money on its upkeep in years. The building, used as a cheap hostel for students and travellers, seemed to have been deserted in an instant — like the ghost ship, the Marie Céleste — when it closed down a couple of years previously. There were plates of half-eaten food left on tables, mouldy packages in the kitchen larder, empty bottles and, more grimly, hypodermic syringes scattered all over the place. Undaunted, we burst into praise and worship. There was a huge job ahead of us, but we felt that by even just taking possession of this seedy old place we had dealt a positive blow for God in this dark area of the city. There would be battles ahead, but we had established a strong beach-head, and we sensed God's pleasure. After a final prayer of thanksgiving, we split into twos and threes to begin the huge clean-up operation.

It started in prayer. The groups headed off all over the building — a rabbit warren of a place with small, odd-shaped rooms dotted all round without any apparent sense of design or layout. In the kitchens, lounges, bathrooms and bedrooms we stopped to pray that God would sweep away any dust of evil that may have settled from the past. We claimed for God the place and the people who would live, work and visit there.

Then we rolled up our sleeves. With the job of project manager, I'd drawn up a rota of three six-hour work-shifts. It was a pattern I'd seen modelled in an Old Testament passage, and one I felt was appropriate to what we were doing. In addition, those teams not working shared a 'prayer patrol' — based in one of the small rear rooms — that ran from the moment work started until tools were finally downed late at night. We had been impressed in reading how Nehemiah had rebuilt the walls of Jerusalem to note how he had arranged for guards to watch over the workers as they laboured. We wanted every hammer blow, every stroke of the paint brush, to spring from God.

It was a filthy job. There were years of dirt and decay to tackle, but no one complained. Indeed the way in which the teams went about their work seemed to characterise all that we were hoping for from the new base. They laughed and joked together as they worked, and good humour seemed to spill from every room. It was a profoundly marked contrast to the rest of the area. Although there were always lots of people around – those peddling drugs and bodies, and those buying – there was a strong absence of warmth or personableness. Early on we found that our new neighbours were intrigued by our friendliness and the evident enjoyment we had in each other's company.

One morning the work crew were stripping paint from the front windows. They were all leaning out over their respective window-frames, hard at work, when someone remarked that it was just like one of those TV game shows. There were nine windows at the front of the building in three rows of three, each with someone leaning out. Just like the quiz programme where the celebrities have to answer nonsense questions. It wasn't long before Terry had a full-blown version of the game going in this Amsterdam sidestreet – and the squeals of laughter gathered a small crowd. Later, as Terry recounted what had happened, she reflected sadly: 'I couldn't work out why people looked so amazed. Then I realised. I guess you don't get much genuine laughter round these parts.'

We'd set ourselves a forty-day time limit – again, there seemed to be a good precedent in the Bible – and we just managed to finish in time before the rest of the team joined us for the start of the actual outreach. Their arrival stretched accommodation to the limit, so I devised a system of three-tier bunkbeds. It meant that people with large noses couldn't sleep on the top one, otherwise they would be brushing the ceiling, but with a little care and good humour we all managed to get in.

Only as we came to a special evening meeting before our first proper outreach did we really see how important the last few dusty and yet fun-filled weeks had been.

As well as preparing the building, God had taken the time to knock us into shape. In the short space of time we had been based in the area, we had begun to sense in a new way the real spiritual oppression that hung over the neighbourhood like a big blanket. You could see it in the eyes of the people who passed by, the way they would flick away to avoid contact.

It was becoming clear to us that one of the keys to our effectiveness would be the degree to which we responded in an opposite manner. In place of furtiveness and secrecy, we wanted to display openness and honesty. And that had to begin among ourselves, in the relationships that existed in the team. We were glad to have had the time to get to know and love each other. We had come through a lot, and were looking forward to what was next.

In addition, the renovation programme had given some of the locals time to get used to our presence. There had been some uncertainty that first day we'd arrived with our songs of praise and worship. We didn't expect the suspicion to disappear overnight. In fact we were sure there would be much outright opposition in the days to come. But at least they could see that we had come to stay. Whatever followed it wasn't just going to be a hit-and-run campaign – we were the new neighbours.

At that end-of-renovation meeting, we also renewed our commitment to prayer and spiritual warfare. The importance of these two aspects of Christian service had been impressed upon me early on during my time on The Ark. In fact, I'd been told after my conversion that three of the team members had secretly been fasting and praying for me for three days before I made my commitment. From that, and my experiences in Nottingham and the early forays into Amsterdam, I knew that much of the spiritual battle took place not on the streets, but in the heavenly realms. It was there that bondages and barriers – sexual, emotional, physical and environmental – were broken down and removed to give an entry point for the good news about Jesus.

So prayer continued to be one of the main thrusts of our new base. We named it The Cleft, symbolising the source of fresh water in a desert, like that which Moses found when he struck out with his staff. We would meet together daily for times of worship and intercession, asking God to move against the wickedness so evident in the area, and to save the people who were so lost. We would sometimes take these gatherings of praise out onto the streets around the area, singing and praying past the brothels and sex shops. We attracted curious gazes, furious stares and some outright hostility. There was even the odd barrage of water or waste food from an upper window! We would also go out in twos, walking round the streets praying for all the premises and people that we passed, asking God to prepare their hearts. We trusted that when we did go out to proclaim the gospel, he would bring along those who were ready to hear and respond.

Because this whole initiative was new territory for the YWAM community in Amsterdam, we were learning the whole time; reassessing and revising the way we tried to reach out to people according to their particular needs. We soon recognised that we needed to do more than just go out, sing a few songs and then expect people to stand and listen to someone talk about Jesus.

With its famous hurdy-gurdy machines and street performers, Amsterdam has long been known for its colourful city life. And with the garish attractions of the red light district drawing crowds of tourists, we needed something a little more visual than standard group singing.

As I thought about this, I went back to the biography I'd read about William Booth. I'd been so impressed with his courage and boldness in starting the mission work in the violent East End of London. It had struck me, too, how clever the early Salvation Army had been in adapting to the times. These days the brass bands are sometimes dismissed as old-fashioned and out-of-date, but they were originally formed to play the popular tunes of the day – to which were added new words that preached the gospel! After talking some of these things through with some of the other team members, we decided to take a leaf out of General Booth's book. So we held a funeral.

Some of the men in the team disappeared into The Cleft's basement and knocked up a giant-sized coffin. This was then led on a silent sorrowful procession around the red light district streets and into the Dam Square, the city's famous focal point right in front of the royal palace. By the time they got there, surprising the tourists who had gathered to feed the pigeons, the funeral party had attracted hundreds of interested men and women. The coffin was set down in the middle of the square, and as the crowd closed in, a man shot up out of the box!

It was Dave Pierce, a young American with a talent for drama and music. Face whitened and wearing dark clothes, he looked just like a corpse. But as he sprang up he began to shout and scream about how Amsterdam's sex, drugs and violence had killed him. It was startling.

All this time I would be on the other side of the square, with some other members. Discreetly mingling with the sightseers, we were the Light Team. As Dave's wails reached a peak, we would start to sing songs of praise and worship to God, and gradually make our way over to the coffin, cutting a path through the crowds. By this time the people watching wouldn't have a clue what was going on – from Dave's horrified reaction to our arrival, they wouldn't imagine we were linked in any way.

Finally as we drew near to the coffin. Dave would start shouting at me. 'Amsterdam ripped me off. There's no hope. There is no meaning to life!'

'But there is hope!' I would shout back – and we

would begin a loud debate about Jesus bringing light into people's dark lives. After a few minutes we would close abruptly and the 'mourners' and 'worshippers' would turn to talk to onlookers about what they'd seen and heard. Those who wanted to talk or hear more would be invited back to the small coffee bar we were running in the main reception area of The Cleft.

Other times we would act out the funeral at night, when we would light the way with burning torches. The procession never failed to draw hundreds of people, and we saw that it was possible to present striking images that would make people want to stop and find out more about what was going on.

We worked on other presentations, too. For what we called The Madman, there would be a regular, sober-faced, sing-for-Jesus meeting in the middle of the Dam. Only a few people would stop to listen, but we didn't expect much else – until I arrived. I'd wait until the square was fairly busy, and then make my entrance from the other side. I'd be dressed in a torn and dirty suit, with my hair dishevelled and dusty, and my arms bound to my sides with ropes. Screaming and shouting and wailing, I'd run across to the other group, stumbling and falling. I'd be shouting that Jesus couldn't help me, really attacking the 'nice little Christians' gathered there. Naturally passers-by would stop to watch the confrontation – and we'd won another audience. Many wouldn't leave the square before they'd prayed with members of the team for Christ to come into their lives.

Another small drama involved a human wall blocking off part of the square, and one of us trying to force our way through. It was a simple symbol of how we can't get into heaven by our own efforts, but it too proved effective in grabbing people's attention.

It wasn't all easy, though. We accepted that you couldn't really preach the gospel without risking people's wrath, or offending the unseen spiritual enemy.

I'm on top of a small table, and there's a good crowd standing back to listen. I scan the faces as I talk, and I can see the familiar reactions; amusement, scorn, intrigue, awkwardness, interest, suspicion, mocking. It never ceases to amaze me that people will stop and watch someone eating fire or swallowing razor blades in the open air without thinking anything of it, but get up and start talking about God and they suddenly become very edgy.

Open-air preaching is a little like performing from a stage. You've got to work your audience well, and I'm constantly darting my eyes over those listening as I talk to them in short bursts. I'm telling them about how my life was turned upside down by a seeming 'chance' encounter just a few hundred yards away and then I pick up some sense of disturbance out of the corner of my eye. Turning, but not breaking my delivery, I spot three young men stepping through the crowd and into the kind of 'no-man's land' of open space that's always left between a street preacher and his audience. It's as though people don't want to come too close in case you reach out and try to snatch them into God's hands. When they break that invisible barrier, I know it means trouble.

A quick prayer as I continue to talk without apparent concern. Complete outward assurance and confidence is one of the absolute keys of open-air preaching, we've learned. Show any sense of not being in control and you've lost your territory and the attention you can command. 'Help me handle this one, please Lord,' I ask behind my spoken words.

The three lads have marched up to the table, and they're trying to drag me off. 'Shut up, or we'll make you!' one snarls. I'm told later that they were heaving and pulling for all they were worth, but all I feel is fluttery touches like birds' wings, so I carry on talking and ignore them. 'What shall I do now, God?' I ask as I sense the concern in the faces of some of the listeners.

Responding to that quiet-but-clear voice inside which I've learned to trust, I squat down until I'm face to face with the lead protagonist. He's thick-necked, crop-haired and clearly looking for a fight.

I lean forward and say to him, as quietly and calmly as I can manage: 'In the name of Jesus I rebuke and bind you violent spirits, and I command you to leave this square. Now!' I straighten up to carry on preaching, heart racing but unafraid deep down.

The light of fight switches off in the faces of the other two immediately – it's a transformation I've often seen in moments of spiritual confrontation. The other hesitates for a moment before turning to the crowd with a sneer. 'D'you know what this bloke's just said to me? He's just told me to go away – in Jesus' name!' The last is uttered with a roar of harsh laughter but, nevertheless, he shrugs his shoulders and leads his two friends off.

Thanking God for helping me through, I finish my story of conversion and reflect again on the commitment I've made. My job is to preach the gospel on the streets, like this, and I can't afford to let anything, or anyone, intimidate me.

We learned that the fear of man was a major stumbling block to effectiveness in streetwork. If someone in the team was worried or anxious about what people might say or do in response, then their efforts were shackled. Usually after a couple of days' experience and plenty of prayer, they found themselves able to let go of all their concerns and trust God for their safety and sense of value.

There were rare moments of threatened physical violence – these were usually resolved by silent spiritual warfare and claiming Jesus' authority over the disruptive spirits trying to stop what we were doing. More common was the emotional aggression we'd face from people offended by the idea that a God of love should have to die for them because of their failure to live according to his standards. Usually this could be channelled into positive times of talking and discussion, particularly when we broke up into ones and twos to mingle with the crowds. On other occasions, though, we'd be left with an earful of abuse.

Many days there would be no apparent results from our efforts, no interest. At these times it was easy to feel discouraged and to question the value of the time and effort we were putting in, but as we prayed together and came to God asking him about it we were renewed again in our determination to keep going and trust God for the rest.

One key spiritual victory involved the cults that flourished in the city. The whirlpool of drugs and liberal philosophies in the city attracted every kind of fringe religion – and they all wanted their opportunity to 'recruit'.

From the start of our streetwork I felt that the Dam Square was crucial. The largest public open space in the city, under the façade of the royal palace, it hosts fairs and performing troupes, and always has a crowd of sightseers. In addition, I sensed that it symbolised 'ownership' of the city and that God wanted it.

We staged regular prayer walks, agreeing together for the Lord's name to be honoured over all others on the Dam. We found that other groups using the area – notably Hare Krishna and Bhagwan devotees – were beginning to stay away. They'd walk up to the edge of the Dam from one of the adjoining streets, stop, then skirt round the edge as though prevented from coming any closer by an invisible force field.

Even with all the excitement of the new base and the new ministry, my thoughts were never far from Terry. We'd managed to find time to be together during those hectic days of renovation and preparation, until I was confident enough about asking her to marry me.

One night at The Ark I took Terry into what had been the captain's quarters. I'd lit a row of candles to create just the right atmosphere for what I hoped was the perfect moment. I took hold of her hand and told her: 'Terry, I love you. I want you to be my wife. Will you marry me?'

She looked wonderful in the soft candlelight. 'I need some time to think,' she responded.

I was taken aback. 'But ... why ... what?'

'I just need time. I have to ask my father,' she explained.

'But that could take ages!' I was frustrated at her idea. It could take a long time for her to go to America and talk it over with her parents. Terry sensed how my thoughts were going.

'No, John. I mean my heavenly Father!' she smiled.

I was still anxious to know, but I reckoned that at least this wouldn't take so long. So I smiled and agreed.

And a couple of nights later we were crossing the Ij on a ferry – just up from The Ark – when Terry told me: 'John, I'm ready to answer you now. Ask me again.' The stars were twinkling, the water rushed past below us as we stood looking over the side, her hair streaming in the wind. Her answer was: 'Yes.' We headed back to The Cleft that night, hand in hand, with a wedding to plan.

17
Firm Foundations

It was a seedy threshold, but we hardly noticed. I swept Terry up into my arms, and carried her into our new home – being careful not to bump her limbs on the narrow walls. It was a tight squeeze. Home was a single small room tucked away at the rear of The Cleft. It wasn't the sort of quiet, clean place you would normally expect to find newlyweds, but we didn't mind. We were happy, we were together – and we knew that God was with us in our marriage.

Ten days earlier we had exchanged vows and rings in the gardens of Heidebeek. A beautifully crisp, clear autumn day, with the fallen leaves from the trees layering the grass in what looked like a carpet of woven gold and amber. The fairytale picture had been completed when the music group struck up the bridal march, and I turned to see Terry as she walked towards me. All my nervousness at having to remember my 'lines' evaporated as I looked at her in wonder. Walking on the arm of her father, wrapped in a gorgeous white dress, she looked like a dream. I stole a look at my best man, Peter Gruschka, and thought again of all that had happened over the previous few years. As Terry looked at me and smiled, I silently thanked God for this wonderful new life he had given me – and this lovely wife: beautiful, fun and with a heart that longed to see others find Jesus.

It was terrific to share this moment with all those who mattered to me. Mum was in the front row, dressed in her best new frock and beaming from ear to ear like the Queen Mother. Joan and Sean were there, as well as Trish and Jamie – a love story from the early days of the Nottingham fellowship – and their baby son. Peter Gruschka was the best man, Paul Miller and Paul Filler were two of the stewards, and standing in front of us to conduct the service was dear Floyd, looking down with a twinkle in his eye and a smile that threatened to split his cheeks.

Friends of Terry's performed a lovely dance to a song of worship and, after more songs of praise, we were eventually pronounced man and wife. We walked hand-in-hand down the grassy aisle, and as soon as we reached the main building we took off, running out of sight.

Safely hidden around the corner, we stood to get our breath back, looked into each other's eyes and laughed aloud with sheer delight.

During the reception, friends from home and The Ark and students at the current Discipleship Training School kept coming up to me to slip their hands into my jacket pocket. I later found wads of notes – all gifts for our honeymoon. Through Floyd, a wealthy Christian businessman had made available his countryside retreat. It was a secluded holiday cottage up in the hills near the Baltic Sea, not far from the Danish border. And it was all ours!

We were thrilled by this surprise provision, and after our wedding night in a small hotel, we drove by borrowed car to our holiday destination ... and had an early lesson in the way our married life would go. It was getting late in the day and we were just outside Bremen, hammering along the autobahn, when the Audi started to judder and slow. 'Quick, pull over!' I shouted to Terry, who was having a spell at driving, and she managed to guide us to the side of the road. An exit was just ahead, and as the car continued to lose power we managed to coast up to the junction roundabout, cross it and finally come to a halt at the side of a small link road.

It was pitch dark by this time, and we were in a fairly remote spot. There was little passing traffic and no sign of help. I tried everything I knew about fixing tired engines, but nothing seemed to work. 'Come on, Terry, let's pray. God has got us this far. He won't let us down now, I know.' We bowed our heads together and asked for help.

We had barely opened our eyes again when a small car appeared out of nowhere and pulled onto the side of the road in front of us. Terry and I looked at each other in surprise – but there was more to follow. The driver got out and walked back towards us; a little man with a round, kindly face and sparkly eyes. I moved to get out to join him, but he just smiled and motioned to me to sit tight. Then he went back to his car, pulled a tow rope out of the boot and connected it to our front bracket. With a smile, the next thing we knew he was back in his driving seat, and we were being pulled off down the road.

With half an eye on the road ahead, I tried to catch another glimpse of the couple in the car in front. The lady in the passenger seat turned and her face was wreathed in a kindly, encouraging smile. She nodded her head gently as if to say 'It's OK' and our follow-the-leader journey continued. After a few minutes we found ourselves rolling into a garage with a connecting hotel. We coasted to a halt on the forecourt and one of the attendants came over to my window.

Distracted for a moment, I didn't turn back until Terry called: 'John, they're going!' Sure enough the couple with the gentle faces had packed the tow rope away and were driving off, with a final backward smile and wave. They hadn't spoken a single word throughout the entire 'rescue', nor waited for us to be able to express our gratitude.

As they pulled away, we turned to each other and said simultaneously: 'Do you think that they...?' and we laughed aloud at the idea that hit us both.

There was no mechanic on duty, so we spent the night at the adjacent hotel. The next morning, after half an hour or so of scratching his head under our bonnet, the mechanic declared that there was nothing wrong – which a flick of the ignition switch proved. It started first time. Even more perplexing!

As we drove on once more, we reminded each other of the previous night's curious happenings, and the strange way we had come to find such a romantic stopover.

This sense of God's intimate concern and care for us was to prove a rock in the months that followed. For things didn't work out as we had anticipated. The plan had been for us to return to Terry's South Carolina hometown. I'd secured a place at a respected Bible College – I felt as though it was important to do some more serious studying before moving on further in Christian service – and we wanted some time in which Terry's parents, friends and home church could come to know me more, and I them. In addition, we believed that it was vital for our new relationship to be given some room in which to grow and blossom, away from the harshness and busyness of work in inner-city Amsterdam.

But the temporary stay we had planned at The Cleft for a week – between the end of our honeymoon and our flight out to the States – turned into six months. And it heralded the start of another new initiative in evangelism.

My criminal record was the problem. Those past convictions created all sorts of concerns for the authorities whose job it was to give me the relevant paperwork allowing me to reside in America. Extra forms and declarations had to be completed and made, and we were advised that it could be several weeks, if not months, before it was all sorted out. It was a frustration we hadn't expected, but we decided to make the most of our time by earning some extra money.

The YWAM community agreed to let us stay on at The Cleft, and I picked up my bricklaying toolbag once more and went back onto the sites. I found work on a huge civic flats complex being constructed on the outskirts of the city. The work schedule meant that I had to be up at 5:30 am to be on site by 7 am. So I found myself going to bed mid-evening to ensure I got enough sleep – just when Terry's 'nightbird' character was coming to life. Accentuated by the cramped quarters, those early weeks created some tensions as we learned to love our way round the practical difficulties that faced our new life together.

As the weeks stretched into months, the waiting became much harder for Terry. Working on the sites, all my energies were absorbed in earning money. So I didn't have much left over for worrying about The Cleft and its work. In fact it was good to have a break from all the responsibilities of leading such a project. I hoped that if and when I returned to such a role, it would be with a freshness and new vigour. But for Terry it was different. She wasn't working, and being in and around the building all day, she was more keenly aware of the struggles that were going on in order for the base we had opened up some months before to find its feet with a permanent role. Some of those who had helped in the renovation and summer evangelism had stayed on as full-time team members, but the future direction of The Cleft was still unclear.

The seeds of something new were sown as Terry talked with me in the evenings. She told me how she and other girls living at The Cleft were concerned about the prostitutes who worked in the area right round the building. The working girls hire windowed rooms in the houses up and down the canal streets where – backlit by a red glow – they sit on view semi-nude, advertising their 'wares' to the passing crowds. When someone wants business, they just step inside and close the curtains.

Several thousand prostitutes work this way in Amsterdam's red light district, and the brazen way they operate attracts guided tours of holiday-makers filing past the city's infamous liberal sex shops and brothels.

'These people are our neighbours, you know, John,' Terry said one night. 'I just don't feel that I can walk past them like I do every day – going to the shops, or the park – and not try to reach out to them ... not without losing my integrity as a Christian. I've got to try. But what can I do?'

I was excited to see her being moved in this way, and we prayed together to ask God to show the next step. A few nights later Terry told me that she and another Cleft girl with whom she regularly prayed – Mientje Brouwer, a part-time nurse – had agreed they should set a date on which they would go out and try to make contact with one of the prostitutes in the neighbourhood.

It was to be the following Tuesday.

It's been another long and tiring day, but I almost run up the steep stairs at The Cleft. My thoughts have returned to Terry and Mientje often during the day, and now I'll get to hear how it went. Up in our room Terry's waiting, looking elated. I make us both a hot drink and sit down facing her to hear the story. Her excitement bubbles over as she recounts their first efforts at reaching out to the prostitutes.

As the clock ticked towards the late-morning starting time they had set themselves, Terry and Mientje met together again for prayer. They asked God to lead them to just the right person. 'And,' Terry says, 'we didn't know what to do, so we asked the Lord to show us. We felt him say that we were to buy some flowers and just walk right on in and shut the door.' She smiles with glee. 'So we did!'

I can tell from her bubbly mood that the story gets better, so I urge her to go on. 'Well, what happened next?'

'We went out and walked round the nearest streets. And d'you know, all the windows were empty. We couldn't believe it! It isn't so busy at that time of the day, of course, but there wasn't a single girl to be seen. We even wondered for a moment if we'd got it wrong. But we decided to keep looking, and finally we found just one window with a girl there – and we decided that this must be the one the Lord was leading us to,' Terry relates.

'We were really nervous, so we just walked in quickly and shut the door behind us hard. Poor girl. I'm sure she didn't know what to think! Anyway, I just said, "Hi, we've moved into the area. We just came to introduce ourselves and chat for a while. Here are some flowers." And we got talking, just like that. We were able to tell her that we are Christians, and what we are all doing here at The Cleft. She was really listening, you know – not anxious to get rid of us or anything. In fact she let us pray for her just before we finally left. Her eyes were watery as she told us that she didn't really want to be here in the red light district, but that she needed the money and she couldn't think of any other way of getting it.'

Terry's elation at their contact is dimmed as she recalls the girl's sad story, and her eyes fill with tears.

'On the way back we prayed that she'd get away from this place and find some other work. Oh John, do you think that God can really do something in the lives of people like that?'

'Sure,' I answer. 'It won't be easy, of course. But the Holy Spirit can touch the hardest of hearts. He did mine, remember?'

We sit down together in our poky little bedroom and pray for the girls in all the scores of other rooms within close proximity of The Cleft, and ask God to help Terry and the others in their efforts at bridge-building.

Most days after that Terry and Mientje, followed by the other staff women, would either go out on prayer walks for the girls they passed in the windows, or make contact with them. They would take a gift of flowers – a Dutch custom – or pack a thermos of coffee into a basket together with some biscuits, and go into the rooms to offer refreshments. Sometimes they met sharp words and stony faces. Other times they found open ears and bruised hearts.

And we discovered in a new way the reality of the unseen battle that was being fought over the red light area. Some evenings I'd return home after a hard day, and almost as soon as I reached for the door handle of our room, I would know that Terry had been out visiting the prostitutes. I could sense a presence of evil, wickedness, in the room – just as though she'd stepped in something that didn't smell too sweet and had brought it back on her heel. We learned to pray hard and bind the enemy from our home and our lives. Terry began to pray for protection before every visit, and then for a special cleansing of the Holy Spirit as she left, so that she wouldn't be 'contaminated' by coming into contact with people so clearly bound by the enemy.

On occasions, though, it would be a struggle. One particular woman she visited was unyielding and inhospitable – yet Terry felt it right to keep going back from time to time, trying to show love and care. 'Every time I go in, it is like walking into a mental fog,' she told me. 'Sometimes I really have to struggle to get the next word out of my mouth. There is a terrible feeling of tightness round my head, just like someone is screwing on a metal band. And I find it hard to get my breath, as though there is a great weight bearing down on me. It's scary at times.'

The more she and the other girls at The Cleft worked with the prostitutes, the better we understood their plight. And it made us desperately sad. We could see how poverty, greed, anger and rejection were often woven into the lives of these women. There were young girls still with childish faces and teenage bodies and older women, some even grandmothers. Some were there because they were illegal immigrants in Holland and couldn't get a regular job. Others had been abused at home or unwanted and had run away. They needed to support themselves. Some were there to support their own or their partner's drug or alcohol habits. Others needed money to help pay for their children's clothes and meals because they couldn't manage as single parents. One respectable young wife was there because she and her husband wanted to open a tennis training centre and needed the capital!

Six months had almost rolled round by the time we were finally given clearance to leave for the States. But we were no longer too frustrated. Looking back we could see the reason for the delay. Terry had been instrumental in beginning a whole new initiative in YWAM's evangelism in the city, and as we left, there were plans to consolidate it with extra workers and prayer support. We were pleased and excited, and felt that in some small way the work had already been 'approved' by God. The young woman Terry and Mientje had visited on that first morning had not been seen in the district since.

From the crowded backstreets of Amsterdam's maze of brothels, porno cinemas and sex shops, suburbia USA was a shock. But we quickly came to love the airiness, lightness and freedom – physically and spiritually – that there was to enjoy.

Terry and I found ourselves a second-floor apartment not far from her parents' spacious home. It was well appointed, with fitted carpets and all utilities, and we revelled in the space after the squeeze of The Cleft. The apartment building had a pool right outside our door where Terry would swim most mornings before breakfast and going to work. It was a time of real refreshment and enjoyment. It was good, too, to grow closer to Terry's parents. They had been very nice to me the only time I'd seen them before the wedding, during a brief

visit to the States. But it had understandably been a little
strained. I'd been nervous at what they would think of
me, and overwhelmed by their large home and standard
of living. The large detached house in its own spacious
grounds was a far cry from my childhood slums.

But during our time in America we grew to know and
love each other. As I learned more about them, I came
deeply to respect their love and care for their family,
and the faithful way they supported their friends and
their local church. If they didn't quite understand the
way we wanted to live, serving God in a foreign country
with no apparent concern for the practicalities of life
and little income, then they didn't show it.

Almost before we knew it, January had rolled round
and it was time for us to return to Amsterdam. We had
kept in touch with Floyd and the others, and heard how
they had acquired another large building in the city. A
former grand hotel and the one-time Salvation Army
headquarters that had been over-run by squatters for
years had finally been vacated, and YWAM had taken it
on. Standing on the edge of the red light district, it
was only a few snaky streets away from The Cleft, and
strategically placed for the city centre.

In addition, the YWAM leaders were looking for us to
help lead a DTS and some new evangelism work in the
city when we got back. Rested, happy, established, we
flew back to Europe keen for a new challenge.

One small problem was that we didn't have much
support. All YWAM workers joined 'in faith'. There
were no wages, and they looked for friends and home
churches to back them in meeting their needs as they
served in missions. Because of the way our paths had
led, Terry and I didn't have many folk who knew what
we were involved in, so we had only a few pounds a week
to live on.

It clearly wasn't enough to find somewhere to rent,
particularly in water-ringed Amsterdam, where building
development is restricted and rooms are at a premium.

But Floyd came to our rescue. 'We're still renovating the Samaritan's Inn, but there's a spare room there, if you are interested at all,' he offered.

He took us round. And at first I thought he'd shown us the broom cupboard by mistake! There wasn't enough room to swing a cat, if it had a long tail. Neither was there a washbasin, and the toilets were on the next floor. With renovation work going on all round, it was like living in the middle of a building site. But it was to be our home for two years.

After some initial tears from Terry and frustrated attempts to find somewhere else, we knuckled down to making the most of what we had, and being thankful for it. I constructed a bed on stilts, so that we had to climb up close to the ceiling to go to sleep, but it meant that there was space underneath for living during the day. We could just about squeeze two chairs in when we had guests, and with some pretty pictures on the walls we did our best to make it home.

As we asked God to help us to be happy with our lot, he answered our prayers. We grew to love our little corner, and if ever we started to murmur again inside we only had to look to what was happening outside – in the streets around – to know that it was no accident that we were there.

For God was at work, and we were excited to be part of the action.

18
Still Burning

We were running a full programme of outreaches on Amsterdam's streets. Music, drama and dance were all being employed to draw a crowd with whom we could share the gospel. It was tiring, thrilling, frustrating, rewarding ... but it still wasn't enough. I felt we needed yet another way of trying to grab people's attention, one that managed to capture their curiosity while at the same time making an unequivocal statement of what we were about.

So we built a large cross. A group of guys went down to the basement again, as they had when the coffin first appeared, and took apart a packing case. With some saw cuts and bolts they constructed a huge wooden cross, standing over eleven feet tall and weighing forty pounds. Just standing in front of it as we heaved it up straight made me realise in a new way what Jesus had done when he died for our sins at Calvary. It made my heart race in thankfulness and gratitude; and I sensed that it would provoke similarly strong feelings out on the streets.

Some were clearly offended by the visual statement. They would stop briefly to shout and curse at us before stamping off. Others stayed to hear what we had to say as we preached from beneath the apex. But the full impact of the cross was only brought home to us when we were visited by someone who knew its power from years of personal experience.

Arthur Blessitt had started walking round the world with his cross twenty years before, and many thousands of miles later he was still going. By the time he arrived in Amsterdam he had experienced extraordinary things in scores of countries – and repeatedly seen the incredible way in which God uses the very symbol of his love to touch people's lives and to transform them. Arthur was used to attracting huge crowds out of which hundreds would kneel on the streets to commit their lives to Christ there and then, weeping before friends and family without a thought for how others would view them.

As he joined our street teams for a couple of weeks, we felt a clear confirmation for our cross plans. We built five others, and had teams carrying them all over the city for meetings and outreaches. In fact, they became such a common sight that a young German girl visiting the city stopped and observed to one of the team members that Amsterdam must be a very Christian city, because everywhere she went there were people carrying crosses. She wouldn't have needed to stay in the city much longer, or ventured much further, to have discovered things to be otherwise!

One morning we had set the cross up on the open ground in front of the Central Station, and I was preaching in front of the cross. As I spoke, an angry-looking man stepped out of the crowd and pulled the microphone from my hand. I let him take it, and he threw it to the ground, cursing and abusing me. I stepped back a pace or two to give him a wide berth, but just carried on talking, raising my voice to make sure that those at the back could still hear. Past experience told me to keep an eye on the intruder, so I kept him in the corner of my sight. Suddenly he lunged forward, fist bunched to strike me in the face. I braced myself for the blow – which never came. Just before his punch landed, I saw the man pitch through the air, landing on the ground with a crash. He lay there unmoving. The meeting was brought to an abrupt halt as we called an ambulance to the scene to take the injured man away to hospital, and I discovered what had happened.

The shouting man had been felled by a huge ox of a
man who was standing nearby. The attacker wasn't a
Christian, but he had spent some time talking with
Arthur Blessitt in a city park a couple of days earlier,
and the encounter had so impressed him that he didn't
want any of Arthur's friends to have any trouble!

Arthur's brief visit confirmed for me that the streets
were my 'pulpit', and that was the way it would stay.
Secretly, I'd sometimes thought in the past that my days
leading that kind of outreach were limited; that in
some way they were an apprenticeship for when I'd be
preaching at big missions and rallies. In Arthur I saw a
man totally committed to doing what God wanted him
to, and ignoring the pressures for anything else. He was
a man walking close to Jesus who knew that success
could not be counted in worldly terms, and as a result
the Holy Spirit was able to work miracles through his
unassuming, everyday life. And I realised that the open
air, the pavements, the shopping malls were what I
knew, and where I was most comfortable.

By now our work in Amsterdam was beginning to
attract interest and attention from around the world –
other YWAM groups, local churches, Bible Colleges and
mission organisations. During the summer we ran large,
short-term projects which drew in young people from
all over the world. Many of them went back to their
home churches enthusiastic about all they had experienced, and we began to get enquiries about taking what
we were doing to new places. And so a new initiative was
born: GO Teams, standing for Global Outreach.

The idea was to bring together a team of men and
women interested in short-term mission work, give them
some basic discipleship training and grounding in all we
had learned about street evangelism, and then to earth
all that in several weeks of 'on the job' training. This
would involve us travelling for up to four months –
across Europe, India, or parts of northern Africa – and
taking part in evangelism alongside local churches in

cities, towns and even remote villages along the way. By being fairly small, mobile and independent, we could aim to take the gospel to even the out-of-the-way places. The people there had as much need to hear about Jesus as anywhere else.

As we planned, it became clear that some of the things we did in Amsterdam were peculiar to that city. We couldn't hope to repeat the funeral procession or the cross march in other parts of Europe and have the same results. So we needed another new way of drawing people together. Talented Dave Pierce came up with the solution once more.

He pointed us to *Toymaker and Son*, a musical parable about creation, the fall of man and salvation through Jesus. Mixing drama and dance, the fifty-minute production had little narration and no dialogue, although its message soon became clear. At the end there would be a clear opportunity to step forward and talk some more about what people had just witnessed.

Working on *Toymaker*, we devised a series of costumes that could clearly depict the different characters and yet at the same time easily 'travel' to different parts and be recognisable. And so it was that I found myself dressed up like an overgrown Pinocchio – complete with knicker-bockers and white knee-socks – for my part as The Toymaker.

Packing all our kit, clothing and possessions into an old Swedish city bus, our small team of eighteen set off for a four-month cross-Europe trek. We would arrive in a village or town about mid-day, and through local pastors who would pre-arrange permits begin to pre-pare for an outreach, having joined with local Christians in prayer. In the early evening we would begin to set out the simple 'staging' and music system in the town square or largest plot of open land available. This would quickly draw a crowd, and by the time we were ready to perform – usually about nine or ten o'clock – word of mouth would have brought a large crowd to see the

visiting players. The piece required a small baby, and by
this time we were able to replace the plastic doll used in
the early *Toymaker* days with our own son, Sandy, who
was fourteen months old.

Once the performing and preaching were over, there
would often be conversations that carried on until well
after midnight. Many times, too, these one-to-one talks
would be followed with prayers in which people asked
Jesus into their lives. The local Christians would translate for us, and would invite them to their churches the
following week. With the twin demands of leading the
team and caring for a toddler in primitive travelling
conditions, Terry and I found it hard work – but the
nightly rewards kept us going. For several summers we
trailed *Toymaker* across Spain, Italy, Portugal, Greece
and England.

It was strange to be back in Nottingham again, especially with my Toymaker costume on. At the end of
the performance I was able to stand up, as I had done so
many times before, and point out the places from my
past: the wine lodge, the jeweller's shop that I had
robbed, the alleys in which I'd fought and thieved.

We were packing everything into the bus when someone tapped me on the shoulder. 'John, it *is* you, isn't it?
Johnny Goodfellow?'

I turned round and saw a friend from the old days.
Short and stocky, Terry had been another hard man. A
boxer of some renown, he'd not been shy of using his
skills outside the ring when the need arose. I was
surprised to find him watching *Toymaker*. We chatted
casually for a few minutes, but I sensed we were skating
round the issue. Finally he managed to find the words. 'I
came down because I saw you on the telly the other
night. D'you remember?'

I did. A reporter for the local TV station had come
down to investigate what we were doing in the town
centre during our week's stay. They had been interested
to learn that I was an 'old boy' of the town, and they had

run a short film report about *Toymaker*, including a brief interview with me as the 'reformed' villain.

'Well, I was dead surprised to see you like that, and to hear what you were saying. So I decided to come down to see for myself what it was all about. I want to know more, John. You really have changed, you know.'

There wasn't time for more right there and then, so I invited him to come over to visit us in Amsterdam a few weeks later. He came, bringing his teenage son with him, telling a story of a lot of pain – including a broken marriage – and thoughts of suicide. When Terry and James flew back to the Midlands the next week, they had both given their lives to Jesus.

Another person touched by *Toymaker* during our English visit was a reporter for one of the local papers. He managed to make contact with me, and we agreed to meet for an interview at a motorway service station. For the first twenty minutes or so his questions were for his article. But for the next ninety minutes they were his own search. The coffees we nursed went cold as he asked me more and more about God.

This time the outcome wasn't as encouraging. When we parted he told me: 'I believe it's all true, you know – everything that you've said about Jesus dying for our sins and all that. I believe it. It's just that ... I can't give what it demands of you. I like women, you see, and I'm just not prepared to make that kind of sacrifice. I don't want to become a monk.' He'd got his story, but he'd not been able to cope with the facts.

In the early days, his rejection would have troubled me. But over the years I had met every kind of response to the gospel. As well as conviction and tears of joy and laughter, there had been venom, scorn, ridicule, un-interest, unbelief and suspicion. I had learned not to worry, but to trust God to work in the lives of those we met, at his pace. Maybe our contact would be the first of several that would eventually lead to Christ. Or perhaps they had already made their choice. It wasn't for me to try to work it all out — just to keep going, talking and praying, trusting that God would prepare the people with whom we would come into contact, and to leave the rest to him.

There were many times when the last thing I wanted to do was to go out onto the streets and preach. I felt tired or discouraged, or maybe the cutting remark overheard from the last outreach was still in my mind; but at these times we learned just to keep going. The closeness we've had in our teams has been a real bonus. And the faith of those who invited us to help them reach their city has helped us through the tough days.

And when the time wasn't right for street work, there were always other possibilities. . . .

Even the rain hasn't driven the hordes of tourists from the streets. They are still milling round the window girls, the sex shops and the pushers, who casually and openly badger you to buy — 'Cocaine, hash . . . I've got the best . . . come on, man' — like they are selling souvenir rosettes outside a football ground. So it's good to step off the streets for a while — into the bars.

This is one of my favourites. A step down and we're in a poky, musty little backstreet place that's about as clean and well decorated as a coal cellar. Its ceiling is tiled with fading beer mats, and there are small lights in each of the drinking booths around the wall. When you look closely at the cracked dirty tables, you're glad that the lighting is dim. It's better not to see too much.

But this place is always busy. The guys come in for a beer and a laugh as they ogle their way round the red light district. And right in the middle of the floor, taking up most of the room, is the pool table. It's such a tight squeeze that when you're taking a shot from the sides you have to hold the cue up in the air at about a forty-five degree angle, otherwise the end gets jammed against the wall. It makes for a more interesting game, though — and as a regular, I'm used to it.

I'd been looking for another way of getting alongside people when it struck me how popular pool is. So I spent some months practising in the lunch-hour, and now I come out two or three evenings a week, drifting round the bars to shoot a few games and see if there is any opportunity for conversation.

The winner stays on the table, taking on the next challenger, so it's useful to know a few shots. And if you can shoot a good game, the other players tend to give you some respect, so it opens up more doors. There's no point beating around the bush, so as we're playing I'll get straight to the point. I ask them where they are from and what they're doing. When they respond and ask me the same, I tell them: 'I'm an evangelist.'

Sometimes they shut up, sometimes they change the subject. But on occasions they want to know more, so we'll talk. It's amazing to think about some of the conversations I've had with guys in one of the booths around this bar, deep in the city's brothel quarter.

One time in particular I remember pulling out all the stops to beat two youngsters. They were from a party of six Englishmen visiting the city for 'a dirty weekend'. As we got talking, I found out that they were all local pool champions for their area. And I beat them all! God must have been helping me play above par for a reason. They invited me over to their table, where they had a crate of beers stacked, and I was able to tell them my testimony during the next hour. There were two of them, especially, that night who wanted to hear more about Jesus.

Tonight it's quiet. I nod at the barman. He recognises me as a regular and presents me with a Coke. Sipping, I slip my guilder over the edge of the table to claim the next game, settle back into a seat in the corner and look around. As I do I pray again: 'Well, Father, if there's someone here tonight that you want me to talk to, then I trust you to bring them to me.'

It's my turn at the table. He breaks, but fails to put

anything away. I slice a stripe into the centre pocket, lining the cue ball up for a second stripe down in the far corner. We're off.

As we make polite chit-chat between shots, I learn he's from Germany. A student, touring the Continent during his vacation, and staying at The Shelter while he's in the city. It makes me smile to myself.

Casually we get there. 'What about you? What do you do for a living?'

'Me? I'm an evangelist.'

'What do you mean?'

'I'm a Christian, and I work with a group of people in the city here. We try to help people by telling them about Jesus. Have you ever thought about God much?'

This could turn out to be a late night. But thankfully the bar stays open almost until the last customer leaves, or falls asleep.

Over the past few years I've preached on the streets hundreds of times. Usually I've shared God's love in the only way I really know how; telling folk about what happened to me when I found myself at the end of my own efforts, and he stepped in. I've told essentially the same story so many times that, in one way, I could almost recite it in my sleep.

But in another way, it's fresh every time. Recalling the days and nights of lostness, loneliness and emptiness when I desperately tried to fill the hollowness up with drugs, or drink, or sex, or occult experiences. And as I retrace my steps, my heart fills with joy at knowing how God hasn't just changed my life. He's literally saved it.

For I'm pretty sure that if that intervention hadn't come near Amsterdam's Central Station, then I'd have been dead by now. My anger, violence and desperation were spinning more and more out of control, and it wouldn't have been long before they would have pitched me into something too far, too wild, too much.

All these thoughts and feelings spill around inside as I

talk to the crowds, and then individually, one-to-one. It's a simple love for Jesus and all that he has done for me, and it's thrilling to be part of something that changes someone's life for all eternity. Just before I start to preach, I remind myself that there are people listening who are going to respond – even there and then – and commit their lives to Christ. And to think they had no idea when they left home that morning!

Just like the man in Rome, who just happened to meet our GO team. He had gone out for an ice cream with his daughter when he was attracted by the noise and crowd. *Toymaker* was in town. Drawn to the drama, he paused to watch for a few moments and found himself gripped. He told us later that he simply couldn't pull himself away.

After the preaching, he and his daughter were among the first to step forward and ask to be prayed with to accept Jesus as their Saviour. The very next evening he returned to the square with his wife and other daughter, and wept with tears of joy as they too chose to become Christians.

Then there was Danny. He was planning a murder when he and his wife strolled past a street team in Amsterdam's pretty Vondel Park. A well-known criminal in the city, he'd been ripped off by an associate, and he was scheming to make the man pay with his life. But he pricked up his ears as he heard me preaching about how I had been a thief and a criminal. They both stopped to listen to what I had to say. When approached by one of the team afterwards, first his wife and then he bowed their heads and prayed for forgiveness for their sins.

Libby wasn't looking for more than a good time when we bumped into her and a friend near the Dam Square one day. They had paused to stare at an open air rally being conducted by another group of Christians. Together with a friend I managed to get chatting to them, and later that night at The Ark she said a simple prayer of commitment. The result was dramatic. When she arrived for work on Monday morning, Libby was surrounded by her friends, all clamouring to know: 'What happened to you over the weekend? You look incredible.' Her face continued to glow as she told them: 'I met Jesus.'

Many more similar stories come to mind: people physically healed by the Lord; people set free from terrible bondages of evil; those released from deep emotional hurts from their past. And all through knowing Jesus.

But I don't want to end this book by telling you another story. Instead I want to close by challenging you to take the opportunity of featuring in your own.

If you have read this far and you're not a Christian, then you need to decide whether you think what I've recounted is fact or fantasy. If you accept that it's true, then I believe you will need to respond by giving your life to Christ. There's a brief prayer to help you in the afterword on the following pages. Please turn to it right now.

If you are a Christian, then I would hope you've finished this book having been encouraged in one of two areas, or maybe both.

First to believe that God can use you to reach the rest of your family if they don't know him. Even if there are big barriers, he can repair relationships so that you are able to share the good news of the gospel, through words and actions. It may take time and some tears, but I'm convinced that after we have been restored to our heavenly Father, he wants to see us restored to our earthly fathers ... and mothers, sisters, brothers, and children.

And I want you to be stirred for evangelism: to see that every day there are countless people who are lost and hurt, who through a 'chance' encounter – because someone's left a purse behind, or they are buying an ice cream – get to hear the fantastic message of salvation.

All they need is for someone along the way to be available to tell them. That's the key: availability. Not ~ersonality or ability. Not everyone is called to street evangelism and open air preaching – although we've found through our short-term mission initiatives that once many try it they wonder why they've waited so long to get involved!

It is simply a question of responding to Jesus' commission in Matthew 28, when he says: 'All authority in heaven and on earth has been given to me. Therefore go and make disciples of all nations.'

Where you have to 'go' may be a foreign city, thousands of miles from home; or your local shopping precinct on a Saturday, with a drama team and singing group; or the mothers-and-toddlers group, where people are looking for friendship; or your school or office, where the name of Jesus is only heard as a swear word.

But don't leave it for someone else to do.

One recent summer I felt the Lord calling me to walk with a cross in Africa. I trained for several weeks by humping a backpack full of bricks round the Amsterdam streets. Then I packed a few spare clothes and flew out to Zambia. For a fortnight I carried a large cross down into the centre of the city each day, prayed and preached. My team comprised just five local people, including a housewife and a teenage girl. Around five hundred people gave their lives to Christ while I was there; it was great to be around as people responded to the gospel so openly.

I expect that there will be other trips like that in the future. I hope so! New initiatives in evangelism continue to develop in Amsterdam where I serve on the YWAM council, and the GO teams are still operating year by year. Other young evangelists and leaders are emerging. It's exciting to see the ways in which God is using and leading them.

After our sons Sandy and Jason grow up, Terry and I do have a little idea tucked away at the back of our minds. We've even started to put a little money by in the event of it developing.

When we retire, eventually, we want to buy one of

those smart little mobile homes and do some touring:
Europe, America ... maybe even Australasia. We could
be free agents, stopping and starting and going where
we wanted; meeting up with other retired folk and old
age pensioners along the way – just befriending them
and sharing our treasure – Jesus!

After all, I hadn't really heard the gospel until I was in
my mid-twenties. But as it was revealed to me, I fell in
love with the simplicity of it all. How Jesus died for me.

I know that there are lots of other people just like
that. They may have heard a little about Jesus, but
they've never really heard the truth. And I figure that
there are lots of older folk who need to be told, too – in a
manner that's appropriate for them.

So when people ask me what I'd like to do when I
finally stop preaching on the streets, I smile and tell
them: 'Buy a camper van.'

If it does work out that way, then I suppose I will
finally get round to making that overland trek I'd
planned once before. But this time I'll already know
where I'm going. And I'll have found what I was looking
for.

Afterword

If you've read this far, then I hope you've understood a little about how Jesus can transform your life – even today, even now.

If you have any questions, then please talk them through with someone. Perhaps a Christian friend gave you this book. Talk with a relative or a work colleague who's a Christian, or go along to a local church this Sunday and ask for someone to talk to afterwards.

You can turn to the Bible, too. As God's timeless word, it tells how we have become separated from him through sin – but also points to the way back, through Jesus. Take some time to read and study it for yourself, maybe starting with John's Gospel. Ask God to help you understand it.

Perhaps you think that you're OK because you've never done anything as wicked as I did. Well, that's not what the Bible says. It states that every one of us has fallen short of God's mark. 'For all have sinned and fall short of the glory of God,' says Romans 3:23. That includes you.

Alternatively, maybe your life has taken you to even darker corners than mine – and you think you've gone too far for God to forgive you. As surely as the Bible says all have sinned, it says all can be forgiven. There's a promise which says: 'If we confess our sins, he is faithful and just and will forgive us.' That covers you, too.

You may want to know that forgiveness in your life. I hope so. Perhaps you want to think it all through a bit more first – or maybe you are ready to receive it right now. You can.

Just pray this short prayer, right now:

'Father God, I believe that you have been speaking to me and showing me that I am separated from you by sin. I believe that Jesus Christ, your only Son, was crucified and rose from the dead, taking my punishment so that I may be forgiven. I ask you to forgive all my sins in his name, and ask Jesus to come into my life and take control. I turn my back on all that has passed, and offer my life to you from this day on. I thank you that you are answering my prayer even now, through the power of the Holy Spirit. In Jesus' name, Amen.'

If you've prayed this short prayer: congratulations! Welcome to the family!

Don't keep it to yourself. Tell some Christians that you know. They will want to encourage and help you in the days to come.

For further information about Youth With a Mission in the United Kingdom, please write to:
Youth With a Mission
13 Highfield Oval,
Ambrose Lane,
Harpenden,
Hertfordshire
AL5 4BX
Tel 0582 65481